The King James Version Defended

EDWARD F. HILLS

CRP

First Edition 1956
Second Edition 1973
Third Edition 1979
Fourth Edition 1984
Reprint 1988
Reprint 1993
Reprint 1996
Reprint 2000

Library of Congress Cataloging in Publication Data

Hills, Edward F. (Edward Freer), 1912-1981
    The King James version defended.

    Includes index.
    1. Bible, N.T. — Criticism, Textual — History. 2. Bible.
English — Versions — Authorized. I. Bible. English.
Authorized. 1984. II. Title.

BS2325.H55 1984   225.5'203   83-73428
ISBN 0-915923-00-9

The Christian Research Press
P.O. Box 13023
Des Moines, Iowa 50310-0023
U.S.A.

EDWARD ROWLAND HILLS
MARY MOORE HILLS
In Memoriam
"I am the God of thy father." **Exodus** 3:6
"Forsake not the law of thy mother." **Proverbs** 1:8

CONTENTS

PREFACE

If, indeed, we are in the midst of "a revival of the almost century-old view of J.W. Burgon" (Eldon Jay Epp, "New Testament Textual Criticism in America: Requiem for a Discipline," *Journal of Biblical Literature* 98 [March 1979]: 94-98.), the question naturally arises: How did such a development come to pass? Our answer in a large measure is to be found at the doorstep of Edward F. Hills (1912-1981), in his comprehensive work *The King James Version Defended: A Christian View of the New Testament Manuscripts* (1956). This publication was, in its day, an indication to the established school of New Testament text criticism that Burgon was not without an advocate from within its own ranks, even if such a position were only to be regarded as an anomaly (v. Bruce M. Metzger, *The Text of the New Testament: Its Transmission, Corruption, and Restoration* [1968], p. 136 n. 1; J. Harold Greenlee, *Introduction to New Testament Textual Criticism* [1964], p. 82 n. 2).

Recently, however, his contribution has brought new entrants into the textual arena who have followed his lead (if not his entire methodology) and thus have opened for fresh debate a forum for the defense of the Byzantine text. Hills lived to see this gratifying development, noting thankfully that his work was finally being seen by some as more than just a "scholarly curiosity" (*a la* Greenlee op. cit.). On the contrary, he will now be regarded as the Father of this 20th century revival of the Majority Text.

It is, nevertheless, ironic that of all who have offered a contribution to the Byzantine text defense, Edward F. Hills is the only bonafide New Testament text critic to do so since the days of Scrivener, Burgon and Hoskier. Why then are his views not playing a larger role in this current stage of the debate? An answer in part is to be found in a sentiment expressed to this author by Gordon Fee when he was asked why Hills had been ignored in the lively exchange that took place in the *Journal of the Evangelical Theological Society* (Vol. 21, nos. 1&2 1978). His response was that Hills' works were "museum pieces." This impression, no doubt, is a result of Hills choosing to publish himself, rather than go through the conventional publishing channels. But, the climate then — in 1956 — was not that of today. It is, therefore, high time to dispel forever any such unrealistic and flippant impressions.

Moreover, the time has now come for this present edition to make its unique contribution felt. Unique in that, while Hills was the only recognized, published New Testament text critic to advocate the primacy of the Byzantine text either in his day or in the present, no one since has been more innovative than he was in attempting to integrate his confessional, theological perspective with the discipline of New Testament text criticism. This is a taboo that even the recent Majority Text advocates have attempted not to transgress, preferring to work from within a purely scientific framework. But Hills' training under J. Gresham Machen, John Murray, R. B. Kuiper and most especially, Cornelius Van Til, would not allow him to rest content with the neutral method to which he had been initiated at the University of Chicago and Harvard. Kuiper recognized the value of this integrational approach to a highly specialized discipline, in which few confessing evangelicals had ever distinguished themselves, in his preface to the first edition of this work:

For more than a decade he [Hills] has taken a special interest in New Testament Textual Criticism. The subject of his dissertation, written in partial fulfillment of the requirements for the Th.D. degree was: *The Caesarean Family of New Testament Manuscripts*. The *Journal of Biblical Literature* has published three articles by him, each bearing directly on the field of his special interest: "Harmonizations in the Caesarean Text of Mark" in 1947, "The Interrelationship of the Caesarean Manuscripts" in 1949, and "A New Approach to the Old Egyptian Text" in 1950. Professor C. S. C. Williams of Oxford University took cognizance of the first of these articles in *Alterations to the Text of the Synoptic Gospels and Acts* (1951), and the second was referred to by G. Zuntz, another Oxford Professor, in *The Text of the Epistles* (1953).

It is evident that Dr. Hills is entitled to a hearing because of his scholarship. I think it no less evident that he deserves a respectful hearing because of his theological convictions. This is not just another book on New Testament Textual Criticism. On the contrary, its approach to that theme is decidedly unique. Dr. Hills founds his criticism of the New Testament text squarely and solidly on the historic doctrines of the divine inspiration and providential preservation of Holy Scripture, and it is his firm conviction that this is the only proper approach. Hence, he not only differs radically with those critics who have a lower evaluation of the Bible, but is also sharply critical of those scholars whose evaluation of the Bible is similar to his but who have, in his estimation, been persuaded that they ought not to stress the orthodox view of Scripture in their study of the New Testament text.

Underlying this position taken by Dr. Hills is a philosophy of truth. God is truth. Because God is one, truth exists as unity. And as God is the author of all diversity, truth also exists as diversity. In a word, there is *the truth*, and there are also *truths*. By reason, which is a precious gift of the common grace of God, the unbeliever can, and actually does, grasp many truths. But for the proper integration of truths and knowledge of the truth, faith in God, as He has revealed Himself in Holy Scriptures, is indispensible. Hence, in every department of learning the conclusions of reason must be governed and controlled by the truth which is revealed in God's Word and is perceived by faith. Any so-called neutral science which seems equally acceptable to the faithful and faithless but sustains no conscious relationship to the Scriptures is by that very token headed in the wrong direction.

Applied to the subject in hand this means that, while willingly granting that believers may well be indebted to unbelieving critics for a number of facts concerning the Scriptures, Dr. Hills insists that the interpretation and correlation of the facts can safely be entrusted only to believing students of the Word. That they too are fallible goes without saying.

Conservative Scholars have long taken that position with reference to the so-called higher criticism. Said James Orr under the head *Criticism of the Bible* in the 1915 edition of the *International Standard Bible Encyclopedia:* "While invaluable as an aid in the domain of Biblical introduction (date, authorship, genuineness, contents, destination, etc.) it manifestly tends to widen out illimitably into regions where exact science cannot follow it, where often, the critic's imagination is his only "law". In the same article he also stated that "textual criticism has a well-defined field in which it is possible to apply exact canons of Judgment". However, the question may well be asked whether unbelieving critics have not in that discipline too at times given broad scope to their imagination. Significantly Orr went on to say: "Higher criticism extends its operations into the textual field, endeavoring to get behind the text of the existing sources, and to show how this 'grew' from simpler beginnings to what now is. Here, also, there is wide opening for arbitrariness". And of the Biblical criticism in general he said: "A chief cause of error in its application to the record of a supernatural revelation is the assumption that nothing supernatural can happen. This is the vitiating element in much of the newer criticism".

The assertion appears to be warranted that the position which was implicit in Dr. Orr's teaching forty years ago has become explicit in this book by Hills.

Recently Hills has received a degree of vindication from John H. Skilton, Professor of New Testament, Emeritus, and former head of the New Testament Department at Westminster Theological Seminary, for the conscious, theological element in his method:

> For men who accept the Bible as the Word of God, inerrant in the original manuscripts, it should be out of the question to engage in the textual criticism of the Scriptures in a "neutral" fashion — as if the Bible were not what it claims to be . . . Whether one realizes it or not, one makes a decision for or against God at the beginning, middle, and end of all one's investigating and thinking. This is a point which Cornelius Van Til has been stressing in his apologetics and which Edward F. Hills has been appropriately making in his writings on textual criticism. All along the line it is necessary to insist, as Hills does, that 'Christian, believing Bible study should and does differ from neutral, unbelieving Bible study.' He is quite correct when he reminds us that 'to ignore...the divine inspiration and providential preservation of the New Testament and to treat its text like the text of any other book is to be guilty of a fundamental error which is bound to lead to erroneous conclusions.' (*The New Testament Student* Vol. 5, 1982 pp. 5-6)

Finally, it must be stated that Hills did not hold to an uncritical, perfectionist view of the TR as some have assumed (*Believing Bible Study* 2d. ed. p. 83); nor did he advocate with absolute certainty the genuineness of the *Johannine Comma (The King James Version Defended* p. 209). What he did argue for, however, was a "canonical" view of the text (*KJV Defended* p. 106), because, in his experience, this was the only way to be assured of "maximum certainty" (*KJV Defended* pp. 224-225) versus the results of a purely naturalistic approach to the text of the New Testament.

Reformation Day 1983   Theodore P. Letis
Philadelphia, Pennsylvania

INTRODUCTION

TEXTUAL CRITICISM AND CHRISTIAN FAITH

Old books have sometimes been likened to little ships which have sailed across the tides of time, bearing within themselves their precious freight of ancient knowledge and culture. None of these books, however, has enjoyed an uninterrupted voyage over the century-stretching seas. The vessels which commenced the journey have perished, and their cargoes have been subject to frequent re-shipment in the course of their perilous passage. The original manuscripts of these ancient works have long since been lost, and they have come down to us only in copies and copies of copies, which were produced by the pens of scribes during the progress of the intervening ages. And just as cargoes of merchandise are likely to incur damage whenever they are transferred from one vessel to another, so the copying and recopying of manuscripts has resulted in some damage to their cargoes of words, which are commonly called their *texts*. Textual criticism, therefore, is the attempt to estimate this damage and, if possible, to repair it.

Has the text of the New Testament, like those of other ancient books, been damaged during its voyage over the seas of time? Ought the same methods of textual criticism to be applied to it that are applied to the texts of other ancient books? These are questions which the following pages will endeavor to answer. An earnest effort will be made to convince the Christian reader that this is a matter to which he *must* attend. For in the realm of New Testament textual criticism as well as in other fields the presuppositions of modern thought are hostile to the historic Christian faith and will destroy it if their fatal operation is not checked. If faithful Christians, therefore, would defend their sacred religion against this danger, they must forsake the foundations of unbelieving thought and build upon their faith, a faith that rests entirely on the solid rock of holy Scripture. And when they do this in the sphere of New Testament textual criticism, they will find themselves led back step by step (perhaps, at first, against their wills) to the text of the Protestant Reformation, namely, that form of New Testament text which underlies the King James Version and the other early Protestant translations.

1. The Importance Of Doctrine

The Christian Church has long confessed that the books of the *New* Testament, as well as those of the *Old,* are divine Scriptures, written under the inspiration of the Holy Spirit. "We have learned from none others the plan of our salvation, than from those through whom the Gospel has come down to us, which they did at one time proclaim in public, and at a later period by the will of God, handed down to us in the Scriptures, to be the ground and pillar of our faith.

1

. . . The Scriptures are perfect, inasmuch as they were uttered by the Word of God and His Spirit." So wrote Irenaeus[1] in the second century, and such has always been the attitude of all branches of the Christian Church toward the New Testament.

Since the doctrine of the *divine inspiration* of the New Testament has in all ages stimulated the copying of these sacred books, it is evident that this doctrine is important for the history of the New Testament text, no matter whether it be a true doctrine or only a belief of the Christian Church. But what if it be a true doctrine? What if the original New Testament manuscripts actually were inspired of God? If the doctrine of the *divine inspiration* of the New Testament is a true doctrine, then New Testament textual criticism is different from the textual criticism of ordinary books.

If the doctrine of the *divine inspiration* of the Old and New Testament Scriptures is a true doctrine, the doctrine of the *providential preservation* of the Scriptures must also be a true doctrine. It must be that down through the centuries God has exercised a special, providential control over the copying of the Scriptures and the preservation and use of the copies, so that trustworthy representatives of the original text have been available to God's people in every age. God must have done this, for if He gave the Scriptures to His Church by inspiration as the perfect and final revelation of His will, then it is obvious that He would not allow this revelation to disappear or undergo any alteration of its fundamental character.

Although this doctrine of the *providential preservation* of the Old and New Testament Scriptures has sometimes been misused, nevertheless, it also has always been held, either implicitly or explicitly, by all branches of the Christian Church as a necessary consequence of the *divine inspiration* of these Scriptures. Thus Origen in the third century was expressing the faith of all when he exclaimed to Africanus, "Are we to suppose that that Providence which in the sacred Scriptures has ministered to the edification of all the churches of Christ, had no thought for those bought with a price, for whom Christ died!"[2]

If, now, the Christian Church has been correct down through the ages in her fundamental attitude toward the Old and New Testaments, if the doctrines of the *divine inspiration* and *providential preservation* of these Scriptures are true doctrines, then the textual criticism of the New Testament is different from that of the uninspired writings of antiquity. The textual criticism of any book must take into account the conditions under which the original manuscripts were written and also those under which the copies of these manuscripts were made and preserved. But if the doctrines of the divine inspiration and providential preservation of the Scriptures are true, then THE ORIGINAL NEW TESTAMENT MANUSCRIPTS WERE WRITTEN UNDER SPECIAL CONDITIONS, UNDER THE INSPIRATION OF GOD, AND THE COPIES WERE MADE AND PRESERVED UNDER SPECIAL CONDITIONS, UNDER THE SINGULAR CARE AND PROVIDENCE OF GOD.

2. Two Methods Of New Testament Textual Criticism

The New Testament textual criticism of the man who believes the doctrines of the divine inspiration and providential preservation of the Scriptures to be true ought to differ from that of the man who does not so believe. The man who regards these doctrines as merely the mistaken beliefs of the Christian Church is consistent if he gives them only a minor place in his treatment of the New Testament text, a place so minor as to leave his New Testament textual criticism essentially the same as that of any other ancient book. But the man who holds these doctrines to be true is inconsistent unless he gives them a prominent place in *his* treatment of the New Testament text, a place so prominent as to make *his* New Testament textual criticism *different* from that of other ancient books, for if these doctrines are true, they demand such a place.

Thus there are two methods of New Testament textual criticism, the *consistently Christian* method and the *naturalistic* method. These two methods deal with the same materials, the same Greek manuscripts, and the same translations and biblical quotations, but they interpret these materials differently. The consistently Christian method interprets the materials of New Testament textual criticism in accordance with the doctrines of the divine inspiration and providential preservation of the Scriptures. The naturalistic method interprets these same materials in accordance with its own doctrine that the New Testament is nothing more than a human book.

Sad to say, modern Bible-believing scholars have taken very little interest in the concept of consistently Christian New Testament textual criticism. For more than a century most of them have been quite content to follow in this area the naturalistic methods of Tischendorf, Tregelles, and Westcott and Hort. And the result of this equivocation has been truly disastrous. Just as in Pharaoh's dream the thin cows ate up the fat cows, so the principles and procedures of naturalistic New Testament textual criticism have spread into every department of Christian thought and produced a spiritual famine. The purpose of this book, therefore, is to show that in the King James (Authorized) Version we still have the bread of life and in demonstrating this to defend the historic Christian faith.

In the world which He has created and in the holy Scriptures which He has given God reveals *Himself,* not merely information about Himself, but HIMSELF. Hence the thinking of a Christian who receives this divine revelation must differ fundamentally from the thinking of naturalistic scholars who ignore or deny it. In this book we shall endeavor to prove that this is so, first in the field of science, second in the realm of philosophy, and third in the sphere of Bible study, and especially in New Testament textual criticism.

CHAPTER ONE

GOD'S THREE-FOLD REVELATION OF HIMSELF

How do we know that there is a God? How do we know that the Bible is God's Word, infallibly inspired and providentially preserved? How do we know that Jesus Christ is God's eternal Son? We know all this because of God's revelation of Himself. In nature, in the Scriptures, and in the Gospel of Christ God reveals *Himself*, not mere evidences of His existence, not mere doctrines concerning Himself, not a mere history of His dealings with men, but HIMSELF. In nature God reveals Himself as the almighty Creator God, in the Scriptures God reveals Himself as the faithful Covenant God, and in the Gospel of Christ, which is the saving message of the Scriptures, God reveals Himself as the triune Saviour God. In this present chapter, therefore, we will discuss God's three-fold revelation of Himself, the foundation of the Christian view of the world and of the Bible and its text.

1. In Nature God Reveals Himself As The Almighty Creator God

Modern ethnologists and anthropologists have discovered that belief in God is general among men. It is found even in savage and uncivilized tribes who have never read the Bible or heard of Christ. "About the existence of some form of monotheism," Paul Radin (1954) tells us, "among practically all primitive peoples there can be little doubt."[1] W. Schmidt (1931) also states that even among the African Pygmies there is "the clear acknowledgement and worship of a Supreme Being."[2] According to Nieuwenhuis (1920), this idea of God was produced "by the impression which the universe made as a whole on reflecting men, as soon as they set about trying to understand the world round about them."[3]

But these discoveries of modern investigators were anticipated long ago by the inspired psalmist, who exclaimed, *O LORD our Lord, how excellent is Thy NAME in all the earth!* (Psalm 8:1). What is God's Name? As many scholars and theologians have pointed out, God's name is His revelation of *Himself*. God's name is excellent *in all the earth*. God the Creator is present everywhere in the world which He has made, actively and objectively revealing *Himself* in all His divine excellence. In the regular motions of the stars and planets He reveals His power and glory (Psalm 19:1; Isa. 40:26). In the immense variety of living things and their harmonious interaction He reveals His wisdom (Psalm 104:24). In the rain, sunshine and harvest He reveals His goodness and His tender mercies (Psalm 145:9; Acts 14:17). In the human conscience He reveals His righteousness, writing on the heart of man His moral law (Rom. 2:15).

4

And in the universal prevalence of death and its attendant sickness and suffering He reveals His wrath and coming judgment (Rom. 5:12).

Because God the Creator is present everywhere revealing Himself in the world which He has made, all men of every tribe and nation may know God if they will and do know Him at least in part. *Because that which may be known of God is manifest in them; for God hath shewed it unto them* (Rom. 1:19). Atheism and agnosticism are inexcusable. *For the invisible things of him from the creation of the world are clearly seen, being understood by the things that are made, even His eternal power and Godhead; so that they are without excuse* (Rom. 1:20). Idolatry and all other false doctrines and observances constitute a departure from this natural knowledge of God, an apostasy which is motivated by human pride and vanity. *Because that, when they knew God, they glorified Him not as God, neither were thankful; but became vain in their imaginations, and their foolish heart was darkened* (Rom. 1:21).

God reveals Himself in the world which He has created. How can we be sure of this ? We can be sure of this upon the authority of the holy Bible. As John Calvin observed long ago,[4] the sacred Scriptures are the God-given eyeglasses or contact lenses (to speak in ultra-modern terms) which correct our spiritual vision and enable our sin-darkened minds to see aright God's revelation of Himself in nature (Psalm 119:130). Therefore the guidance of the Bible is necessary in the study of the natural sciences. In the Bible God has inscribed the basic principles which give unity to scientific thought and provide the answers to ultimate scientific questions. In order to prove this let us consider some of these questions in the light of holy Scripture.

(a) What the Bible Teaches Concerning Astronomy

When we believe in God as the Creator of the universe and receive the revelation which He has made of Himself in nature and the holy Scriptures, then for the first time the mysteries of astronomy become comprehensible, at least in principle. Then for the first time we understand how astronomers with their tiny human minds can know as much as they do know concerning the vastness of the heavens. Then we learn once and for all that the universe is finite and that, however vast it may appear to our human eyes, in the eyes of God it is *a very little thing* (Isa. 40:15). As Thiel (1957) has observed, whether the universe is large or small depends on the way you look at it. According to Thiel, if the nebulae were the size of pinheads, the space between them would be no more than a hand's breadth.[5] And in God's sight the nebulae are mere pinheads. Indeed, the Scriptures teach us that compared with God's infinite greatness the whole universe is *less than nothing and vanity* (Isa. 40:17,22). God created the whole universe according to His wisdom (Psalm 104:24). He understands it completely, and to man He gives the wisdom to understand it partially. And it is from this wisdom which God gives that all that is true in astronomy and every other department of science is derived. *For with Thee is the fountain of life: in Thy light shall we see light* (Psalm 36:9).

In the beginning God created the heaven and the earth (Gen. 1:1). How long ago was that beginning? There are many who say that this must have been ten billion years ago, because light takes this long to reach the earth from the farthest quasi-stellars. But this argument has no cogency for those who believe in the omnipotent Creator. If God created the stars and put them in their places in space, why couldn't He have brought down their light to the earth in an instant of time? There is no need, therefore, to "re-interpret" the first chapter of Genesis and thus to obscure its plain meaning with modern glosses and rationalizations. On the contrary, the more we let this sublime introduction to the written Word of God tell its own story the more reasonable and up-to-date we see it to be.

The first two verses of Genesis 1 tell us how the whole universe was brought into being by the creative act of God, in an unformed state at first, perhaps as mere energy out of which matter was later constituted. The rest of this first Bible chapter describes to us how the Spirit of God, who *moved upon the face of the waters,* brought the whole creation out of its original formless condition into an estate of entire perfection. And it was in reference to the earth that this creative power was first exercised. No mention is made of the sun, moon and stars until after the earth is freed from its layers of water and carpeted with grass and herbs. The sun, moon and stars, on the other hand, are younger than the earth, having been created, or at least brought into their present state, on the fourth day. Next the seas and the dry land were populated with living creatures, and then finally man was created in God's image with a mind attuned to heaven's harmonies and a God-given ability to search out its mysteries.

Although the Bible is entirely true and cannot be in any way affected by the opinions of men, nevertheless it is of interest to note that some of the latest developments in the realm of astronomy agree with what the Bible has always taught concerning the natural world. For example, astronomers for many years believed that the sun was at the center of the universe and ridiculed the Bible for speaking of the sun as moving and the earth as standing still. "The Copernican heliocentric cosmogony," Shapley (1960) observes, "prevailed for more than three centuries and widened its range in that the sun eventually was considered to be not only central in its own planetary family, and in full command through gravitation, but also appeared to be the central object for the whole stellar world." But in 1917 this heliocentric cosmogony was found to have been a mistake. "The sun is no longer thought to be in a central position," Shapley continues, but has now been relegated "to the edge of one ordinary galaxy in an explorable universe of billions of galaxies."[6] Evidently, then, the sun is of little significance in itself. Millions and millions of other stars are larger and more impressive. The sun is important chiefly because its rays nourish the earth and the lives of men who are created in God's image. And this is what the Bible has always taught (Gen. 1:14-18). This is what Jesus teaches (Matt. 5:45).

The earth, then, is more important than the sun because it is the abode of men, God's image bearers. It was on earth that the Son of God was crucified for sinners. It is to earth that He shall return to judge the living and the dead. It is to emphasize this central importance of the earth in the plan of God and in history that the Bible speaks of the earth as being at rest and the sun as moving. And even from a strictly scientific point of view this manner of speaking is not regarded as incorrect. For according to Einstein[7] and most modern scientists,[8] all motion is relative, and one may say with equal justification either that the earth moves and the sun is at rest or that the sun moves and the earth is at rest. Einstein's relativity theory, however, depends on his definition of simultaneity as coincidence in time and space relative to an observer, and this definition is contrary to fact. Observation clearly shows that simultaneous events always occur at the same time but never in exactly the same place. Even simultaneous flashes in a mirror occur at different locations on the mirror.

For this reason and many others scientists will eventually be compelled to lay Einstein's theory aside, and when they do they will probably find that the true view of the universe is that which Tycho Brahe (1546-1601)[9] proposed 400 years ago. He maintained that the earth rotated on its axis and that the sun, moon and planets revolved about the earth. This hypothesis agrees remarkably with the biblical data and is mathematically sound, according to Christian mathematicians such as J. N. Hanson[10] and W. van der Kamp.[11]

(b) What the Bible Teaches Concerning the Fossils

We pass now to geology, the science which deals with the earth and its history. The type of geology which is accepted today by almost everybody is *uniformitarian* geology. Its basic principle is that geologic changes in the past have been effected gradually by the same processes that are at work in the present. The Scriptures, however, do not support this assumption but tell us of a great catastrophe, namely, the Genesis flood, which alone is adequate to account for the observed geologic phenomena. The following therefore is a brief summary of the principal points at issue:

(1) *The warm climates of geologic times.* The evidence of the fossils indicates that warm climates once prevailed in regions which are now covered with arctic ice and snow. Sub-tropical heat, it is said, was experienced in Greenland. Why this tremendous difference between ancient and modern climatic conditions? Uniformitarian geologists are hard put to it to find an answer to this question. A rather recent (1954) symposium of scientists stressed changes in the sun's radiation as the cause of changes of climate here on earth,[12] but astron-

omer F. Hoyle (1955) says that there is no evidence that any such variation in solar radiation took place.[13]

The Bible, however, provides the solution of this problem. The uniformly mild climate which once prevailed everywhere is to be attributed to the invisible vapor canopy which enveloped the earth in the days before the flood, namely, *the waters above the firmament,* which God established in their places on the second creation day (Gen. 1:7). The effect of this canopy would be to distribute the sun's warmth in uniform fashion throughout the earth and to prevent the formation of cold fronts and the occurrence of wind storms. At the onset of the flood *the windows of heaven were opened* (Gen. 7:11), that is to say, the vapor canopy was precipitated on the earth in the form of torrential rains which completely flooded it. The Bible indicates that this was the first time it had ever rained. Before the flood mists watered the ground (Gen. 2:6). After the flood Noah saw a rainbow for the first time (Gen. 9:13).

(2) *Volcanoes and lava flows.* In past geologic ages, we are told, volcanic lava flowed much more plentifully than it does today, both spouting from craters and pushing upward from great cracks in the earth's surface. A stupendous rock formation more than one thousand miles in length along the Canadian and Alaskan shore was formed in this way. The great plateaus of northwestern United States, covering 200,000 square miles, were built by oozing lava, as was also the famous Deccan Plateau in India. Other plateaus of this kind occur in South America and South Africa. Most of the oceanic islands also were produced primarily through volcanic action.[14]

The presence of all this volcanic lava on the earth's surface contradicts the leading principle of uniformitarian geology, namely, that the geologic work of the past was accomplished by the same natural forces that can be observed today. Plainly it was a catastrophe that produced these lava flows, and the Bible indicates what this catastrophe was, to wit, the Noachian deluge. Not only were *the windows of heaven opened,* but *the fountains of the great deep were broken up* (Gen. 7:11), and through the resulting fissures both in the sea floor and also in the land surfaces the vast lava deposits observable today were spewed forth.

(3) *How were the fossils buried?* Uniformitarian geologists have never given a consistent answer to this all important question. Instead they assert a paradox. The fossils, they maintain, were buried quickly, but the rocky strata in which these fossils are buried were laid down very slowly. The reason, Simpson (1960) tells us, why there are so many missing links in the evolutionary fossil chain is that these missing animals were not buried quickly enough. "The possession of readily preservable hard parts is clearly not enough in itself to assure that a given organism will indeed be preserved as a fossil. The overwhelming majority of organisms are quickly destroyed or made unrecognizable, hard parts and all, by predation, by scavenging, by decay, by chemical action, or by attrition in transport. The

few that escape that fate must (with a few exceptions) be buried quickly (within days or at most a few years) in sediments free of organisms of decay or chemicals competent to destroy the hard parts."[15] Howells (1959) says the same thing, observing that it is not easy to become a fossil,[16] and Rhodes (1962) also informs us that the preservation of an organism almost always involves rapid burial.[17]

If the fossils must have been buried quickly in order to become fossils, doesn't it follow that the strata in which the fossils are buried must also have been laid down quickly? Not so, the geologists strangely maintain. In accordance with their uniformitarian dogma, these scientists insist that these strata were laid down by the same slow processes which are in operation today. Zeuner (1952), for example, agrees with Bradley's earlier (1929) estimate that during the Eocene period the mean rate of the deposition of the strata was only one foot in 3,000 years.[18] And according to Dorf (1964), the volcanic sediments in Yellowstone Park were laid down at the rate of three-quarters of an inch a year, and this rate is 100 times faster than that estimated for sand or mud sediments of comparable age in the Gulf Coast region of North America.[19]

The fossils were buried quickly, but the strata in which the fossils are buried were laid down very slowly! Uniformitarian geologists would rather insist on this paradox than admit the reality of the Genesis flood. There is abundant evidence, however, that the strata were laid down and the fossils buried in a great world-wide flood. How otherwise can the frequent occurrence of "fossil graveyards" be explained? The Baltic amber deposits, for example, contain flies from every region of the earth. The Cumberland Bone Cave in Maryland is filled with fossils of both arctic and tropical regions. The La Brea Pits in Los Angeles have yielded thousands of specimens of all kinds of animals both living and extinct. In Sicily hippopotamus beds occur so extensive that they have been mined as a source of commercial charcoal. Frozen mammoths and an immense number of tusks have been discovered in Siberia. At Agate Springs, Nebraska, a vast aggregate of fossil animal bones have been found jumbled together.[20] And according to Macfarlane (1923), there is evidence of sudden destruction of fish life over vast areas.[21]

(4) *The fossil order out of order.* One of the strongest pillars of uniformitarian geology is the alleged invariability of the order of the fossil-bearing strata. The ages of the rock strata are determined by the kind of fossils that are found in them. The strata containing the simpler forms of life are always older. The strata containing the more complex forms of life are always younger. The younger strata are always on top.

This theory, however, often contradicts the facts of nature. Often the younger strata are on the bottom and the older on top. In the Alps such "inverted" arrangements of the fossil-bearing strata occur "on a grand scale" (Geikie). The 19th century geologists explained them by supposing that the strata had been folded together and thus turned upside down. They admitted, however, that there was no physical evidence for this hypothesis. Thus Geikie (4th ed. 1903) acknowledged that "the strata could scarcely be supposed to have been really inverted, save for the evidence as to their true order of succession supplied by their included fossils."[22]

Another hypothesis by which to explain the "inverted" order of fossiliferous strata was that "thrust-faults" had occurred, that is to say, sections of the strata had been raised and pushed up on top of adjacent sections. But B. Willis (1893), U. S. government geologist, had this to say concerning assumed thrust-faults in the southern Appalachians. "These faults of great length, dividing the superficial crust into crowded scales, have provoked the wonder of the most experienced geologists. The mechanical effort is great beyond comprehension, but the effect upon the rocks is inappreciable."[23] Another example of a supposed thrust-fault for which no evidence can be found is the Lewis over-thrust of Montana which measures 135 miles in length and 15 miles in breadth. Here also, according to a recent government survey (1959), the rubble which would naturally be produced by the movement of such a vast quantity of rock is conspicuously absent.[24]

Thus for one hundred years uniformitarian geologists have been putting forth paradoxes. To explain the "inverted" order of the strata they have been assuming tremendous folds and thrust-faults which strangely enough have left no evidence of their occurrence.

But if we acknowledge the reality of the Genesis flood, we no longer need to "explain" the strata but can take them as they come. As Whitcomb and Morris (1960) point out, the bottom-most strata would normally contain the trilobites and brachiopods, because their mobility was least (they would find it hardest to avoid entombment), their specific gravity was greatest (they would sink most easily in the flood waters), and their habitat was lowest (living on the sea bottoms, they would most quickly be affected by the breaking up of the fountains of the great deep). The fish would naturally be found in the middle strata, since in these three respects they occupy an intermediate position. And the reptiles, mammals, and birds would tend to take their places in the higher strata, since their mobility was greatest (they could most easily escape the entrapping sediments), their specific gravity was least (their bodies could float the longest on the surface of the waters), and their habitat was highest (they would be the last to be reached by the advancing flood). These factors would account for the general order to be found in the fossil-bearing strata, an order due not to an ascending evolutionary scale of life but to the circumstances under which the fossils were buried in the deluge sediments. And since these circumstances often varied locally, there were often instances in which the more usual order was reversed.[25]

(5) *Mountains, plateaus, and canyons.* According to Leet and Judson (1954), the formation of every mountain system on the globe has involved the following two-fold process: first, thousands of feet

of sedimentary rocks were accumulated in great marine basins that slowly sank; second, these sedimentary rocks were slowly elevated to form mountains.[26] In other words, the bottoms of certain seas kept sinking down until the streams had washed in a collection of sediment (dirt, sand, etc.) as deep as the mountains are high. Then the bottoms of these seas came up again and lifted all this sediment thousands of feet into the air, and thus the lofty peaks of Tibet were formed, and also the Alps, the Andes, and the Rockies. But why should the bottoms of these seas (marine basins) move down and up, first receiving sedimentary deposits and then pushing them up into the air? Three possible causes have been suggested for this alleged phenomenon, namely, thermal contraction, convection currents, and continental drift.[27] Wilson (1963) believes that the Himalayan mountains could have been thrown up by the collision of India with the Asian land mass.[28] No one of these explanations, however, seems to be generally satisfactory to scientists.

Not only the mountains but the high plateaus that lie next to them are full of problems for the uniformitarian geologist. One such plateau region occupies some 250,000 square miles, extending over most of Arizona and Utah and also large portions of Colorado and New Mexico. It is here that the Grand Canyon is found as well as its smaller but scarcely less spectacular sister canyons. The walls of these canyons are composed of thousands of feet of sedimentary rock strata lying horizontally. According to Leet and Judson, this whole region was pushed up from the bottom of a sea without any disturbance of the horizontal position of the strata. In defense of this hypothesis these authors point to the fact that the rivers which are thought to have hollowed out the canyons flow in curves called *meanders*. These curves, it is maintained, were established before the uplift began, and the uplift was so gentle that it did not disturb them.[29] But according to Whitcomb and Morris, such notions are vulnerable from the standpoint of hydromechanics, A river which is downcutting enough to excavate a canyon will not continue to flow in curves but will straighten itself out due to gravitational pull.[30]

The mountains and canyons of which we have been speaking and also the submarine canyons and the rifts which have recently been discovered in the ocean floor can be satisfactorily explained only in terms of the Genesis flood. These effects indicate the process by which God removed the swollen flood waters from off the land after they had accomplished their work of divine justice and purification. In order to accommodate the water which had fallen from the overhead vapor canopy and would never be returned thither, the oceans were made larger and deeper. And as the seas were widened and deepened, the continents were compelled to rise to make room for the displaced earth crust. As part of this general elevation of the continents, the mountains were lifted up to their present lofty heights. Cracks occurred at various angles in the sediments, and along these cracks torrents of flood water poured down, driven by the force of gravity, to the ample new storage space created by the sinking ocean floors and the rising continents. Thus quickly and efficiently the Grand Canyon was formed and also its sinuous sister canyons. And all this is suggested in Psalm 104:6-9, where the coming and going of the Genesis flood is vividly described.[31]

(6) *The coming of the glaciers.* The Genesis flood narrative also provides the best explanation of the extensive glaciation which took place in past ages, the causes of which are still a matter of debate among uniformitarian geologists. In the words of Whitcomb and Morris, "The combined effect of the uplift of the continents and mountain-chains and the removal of the protective vapor blanket around the earth could hardly have failed to induce great snow and ice accumulations in the mountains and on the land areas near the poles. And these glaciers and ice caps must have continued to accumulate and spread until they reached latitudes and altitudes at which the marginal temperatures caused melting rates in the summers adequate to offset accumulation rates in the winters."[32] Later the earth would be replenished with a new generation of plants and animals. These would fill the air with carbon dioxide, thus warming the atmosphere and causing the glacial ice to recede. Also the carbon dioxide emitted by the volcanoes during the flood would contribute to this warming effect as soon as the volcanic dust had settled.[33]

(7) *Searching for the missing links.* For over a century uniformitarian geologists and paleontologists have been searching for the missing links in the evolutionary fossil chain, but today these links are still missing. "It is a feature," Simpson (1960) tells us, "of the known fossil record that most taxa appear abruptly. They are not, as a rule, led up to by a sequence of almost imperceptibly changing forerunners such as Darwin believed should be usual in evolution."[34] And according to Rhodes (1962), the Cambrian fauna appears with "Melchisedechian" abruptness,[35] without any obvious ancestors, and the same is true of most of the major groups of organisms.

The most interesting fossil specimens, of course, are those which are said to bridge the gap between apes and men. Some of these, however, were evidently merely apes and not men at all. Such were the *Australopithecines*, whose brains were only ape-size. At one time it was said that they walked erect like men, but Zuckerman (1954) denied this,[36] and today R. E. F. Leakey (1971) admits that the *Australopithecines* may have progressed on their knuckles like the extant African apes.[37] Other alleged sub-human specimens were in all probability simply diseased. For example, Sir Arthur Keith suggested that the Rhodesian man might have been the victim of a hyper-active pituitary gland, and Hooton (1946) thought it possible that the Neanderthal men had been suffering from a similar malady.[38]

(8) *Dating the strata and the fossils.* Attempts to date the strata and the fossils by radioactivity methods reveal the unreliability of these procedures. In 1959 *Australopithecus boisei* was considered 600,000 years old.[39] In 1961 his date was pushed back to 1,750,000

years ago by use of the potassium-argon method.[40]   Recently (1970) R. E. F. Leakey has pushed this date still farther back to 2,600,000 years ago.[41]   In 1965 Bryan Patterson of Harvard found an australopithecine arm bone which he dated at 2,500,000 years ago.   In 1967 he found an australopithecine jaw bone.   He then dated the jaw bone at 5,500,000 years ago and pushed the date of the arm bone back to 4,000,000 years ago.[42]

(c) What the Bible Teaches Concerning Space and Time

Isaac Newton (1642-1727), the father of theoretical physics, was a firm believer in the concepts of *absolute space* and *absolute time*.   In his *Principia* (1686) he writes as follows: "Absolute space, in its own nature, without relation to anything external, remains always similar and immovable. . . . Absolute motion is the translation of a body from one absolute place to another."[43]   Thus for Newton space was an existing *thing*, an infinite, immovable tank or framework in which bodies moved and in reference to which their movements could be calculated.   Newton regarded space as co-eternal with God.   In his *Optics* (1704) Newton even went so far as to call space God's *sensorium*.[44] And, similarly, Newton regarded time as a perpetual stream that flowed on and on quite independently of God.   "Absolute, true, and mathematical time, of itself, and from its own nature, flows equably without relation to anything external, and by another name is called duration."[43]

For two hundred years Newton's views regarding absolute space and absolute time were generally adhered to by physicists.   In 1887, however, Michelson and Morley, two American scientists, discovered that the velocity of light is the same in all directions and is not affected by the movement of the earth through space.   This discovery contradicted some of Newton's basic principles, and it was to reconcile this difficulty that Einstein in 1905 published his *special relativity theory,* featuring the following operational definition of time: "Suppose that when an event E happens to me on earth a flash of light is sent out in all directions.   Any event that happens to any body anywhere in the universe after this flash of light reaches it is definitely after the event E.   Any event anywhere in the universe which I could have seen before event E happened to me is definitely before event E.   All other events are simultaneous with event E, since they cannot be demonstrated to be either before or after E and that which is neither before nor after is simultaneous."[45]

On the basis of his operational definition of time Einstein defined motion as progress through a four-dimensional space-time continuum.   And in his *general relativity theory*, published in 1915, Einstein went on to define gravity as the effect of the curvature of this continuum.   There is, however, an inconsistency in Einstein's operational definition of time.   As Reichenbach observes,[46] Einstein made a distinction between the simultaneity of events next to each other and the simultaneity of events far apart from each other. Events next to each other, he maintained, are simultaneous if the observer can know that they are coincident in time and space. Events far apart from each other are simultaneous if the observer cannot know that they are not coincident in time and space. But how can the knowledge or lack of knowledge of a human observer determine the simultaneity of external events? Surely Einstein taught pantheism in the guise of science.

In view of this logical flaw it is not surprising that Einstein's theories are being threatened experimentally. In 1970 Endean and Allen, two British scientists, concluded that electromagnetic fields in the turbulent Crab Nebula are traveling at about 372,000 miles per second, or twice the velocity of light.[47] This is contrary to Einstein's special relativity theory, which makes the velocity of light an absolute that can never be surpassed. Also, as Huffer (1967)[48] and Dixon (1971)[49] remind us, there is evidence that there may be stars which consist entirely of negatively charged anti-matter. This, if true, may endanger Einstein's gravitational theory. At least Burbidge and Hoyle (1958)[50] and Gamow (1961)[51] have expressed such fears.

Newton conceived of time and space as two disconnected absolutes independent of God. In pantheistic fashion Einstein made simultaneity his leading concept but was compelled to operate inconsistently with two discordant definitions of simultaneity. In the Bible, on the other hand, God reveals Himself as the only Absolute. *I am God, and there is none else; I am God, and there is none like Me* (Isa. 46:9). God's eternal plan for all things is the only ultimate continuum. *Declaring the end from the beginning, and from ancient times the things that are not yet done, saying, My counsel shall stand, and I will do all My pleasure* (Isaiah 46:10). God created space and time when He created the world and began to fulfill His plan.

(For further discussion of Newton and Einstein see *Believing Bible Study*, pp. 165-171, 224.)

(d) What the Bible Teaches Concerning Causation and Chance

Scientists for many years have been accustomed to define causation in terms of human prediction. If from a preceding event a following event can be predicted, then the preceding event is considered to be the cause of the following event. Einstein (1934) says that it was Isaac Newton who began to define causation in this way and that this definition is the only one that is completely satisfactory to modern physicists.[52] Similarly, Bridgman (1955) says that the ability to predict is tied up with the ideas of cause and effect.[53]

In the 1920's, however, physicists discovered that the behavior of atomic particles, taken individually, can not be predicted. No matter how hard the physicists strive to make their measurements accurate, a large element of uncertainty will always remain. In 1927 Heisenberg stated this fact scientifically in his famous *uncertainty principle*.[54] According to Jeans (1947), this principle states that it is impossible to determine both the *position* and the *velocity* of an atomic particle with perfect precision. If we *decrease* our uncertainty in regard to the *position* of the particle, by that very action we *increase* our uncertainty in regard to its *velocity* and *vice versa*. The product, moreover, of the two uncertainties can never be reduced below a certain minimum value.[55]

We see now why so many physicists say that there is no causation in the sub-atomic realm and hence no causation at all, since the atomic particles are the basic units out of which the larger world of nature is constructed. They say this because they identify *causation* with *prediction*. Two events are causally connected when the second can be predicted from the first. But there can be no such prediction at the sub-atomic level, because at this level, according to the Heisenberg uncertainty principle, the accurate measurements needed for such prediction are impossible. Hence, since causation and prediction are regarded as synonymous, it is maintained that there is no causation in the sub-atomic realm. According to Heisenberg (1958), classical physics and causality have only a limited range of applicability.[56] According to Bridgman (1955), the law of cause and effect must be given up.[57] And Max Born (1951) tells us that all the laws of nature are really laws of chance in disguise, that is to say, laws of statistical probability.[58]

This statistical probability to which Born refers rests on a principle first discovered in the 18th century when records of births and deaths began to be kept by municipal and national governments. According to this principle, statistics of large groups are regular. That is to say, there is a regularity about large groups of similar events, even when these events seem to occur entirely by accident. For example, it was found that there was a certain regularity about male and female births. Everywhere, year after year, the number of male births was found slightly to exceed the number of female births. In the early 19th century also inspection of government records by the Belgian statistician Quetelet brought to light many other instances of statistical regularity in the seemingly accidental features of life. For example, Quetelet showed (or claimed to show) that year after year the number of suicides bore a fixed ratio to the total number of deaths.[59]

As this statistical regularity began to be discovered, mathematicians began to deal with it mathematically by applying to it the terminology and rules of the probability calculation which had been first formulated in France during the 1650's for the solution of gambling problems. For example, when dealing with birth statistics they began to speak of the *chance* of a boy being born rather than a girl and to calculate it as slightly more than one half. It was in this way, Cramer tells us, that actuarial mathematics was developed and used in the rapidly expanding insurance business. And from insurance the use of statistical probability theory spread into other fields until now its range of applications extends, as Cramer observes, over practically all branches of natural, technical and social science. Automatic computers, for example, make their predictions on the basis of statistical probability.[60]

But if the universe is governed by the laws of chance or statistical probability, what *is* statistical probability, and why does it work the way it does? What is back of statistical probability? According to Born,[61] you are not supposed to ask these questions, and he ridicules those who do ask them. Statistical probability is simply to be accepted as an unanalyzable governing principle of the universe. But is it scientific to reject causation as meaningless and then to put in its place an unanalyzable something which you call statistical probability? Even Einstein[62] and other well known physicists have had their doubts about this. Bridgman (1959), for example, concedes that a world governed by pure chance is completely inconceivable. For then, he goes on to say, he might in the next instant turn into his dog Towser and Towser into his Ford.[63]

Only the Bible has the solution to this problem which baffles top-flight scientists. For the Bible defines causation ultimately not in terms of human prediction but in terms of God's works of creation and providence. The God who created the atomic particles also controls and guides them. He *worketh all things after the counsel of His own will* (Eph. 1:11). Hence causation is still operative in the subatomic realm, even though scientists may never be able to measure or observe its action.

The eternal God is thy refuge, and underneath are the everlasting arms (Deut. 33:27). God rules and reigns even in the seemingly accidental features of life, the flight of an arrow shot at random (1 Kings 22:34), the trampling of a jostling crowd (2 Kings 7:18-20), the casting of lots (Prov. 16:33), the falling of a sparrow from its nest (Matt. 10:29). If we put our trust in Christ, then we know that He so preserves us that not a hair can fall from any of our heads without the will of our heavenly Father; yea, that all things must be subservient to our salvation. *And we know that all things work together for good to them that love God, to them who are the called according to His purpose* (Rom. 8:28). May the good Lord help us to believe this always.

2. In The Scriptures God Reveals Himself As The Faithful Covenant God

The Scriptures are the God-given eyeglasses which correct our faulty spiritual vision and enable us to see aright the revelation which God makes of Himself in the world which He has created. This is the first aspect in which the Bible presents itself. But the Bible also fulfills a second function. The Bible is a record book in which is outlined the history of God's dealings with men from the creation to the final judgment. In the Bible God reveals Himself as a covenant-making, covenant-keeping God. For God's ways with men differ from His ways with plants and animals. God deals with men by way of covenant. He makes His promises and keeps them. All He requires of us on our part is faith and obedience. *All the paths of the LORD are mercy and truth unto such as keep His covenant and His testimonies* (Psalm 25:10).

Hence the Bible is *the Book of the Covenant.* This is the name which was bestowed upon the holy Scriptures when they were first given at Mount Sinai. Here God met with His people and promised that if they would keep His covenant He in turn would be their God (Exodus 19:4-6). Here God called Moses to the mountain top and revealed to him His laws and judgments. And here Moses inscribed these sacred statutes in *the Book of the Covenant,* the first portion of the holy Scriptures to be committed to writing, and then read them in the ears of all the people. *And he took the Book of the Covenant, and read in the audience of the people: and they said, All that the LORD hath said will we do, and be obedient* (Exodus 24:7).

(a) The Covenant of Works

Adam, when God created him, was perfect (Gen. 1:31). He was created in God's image and given dominion over God's creatures (Gen. 1:27-28). Adam obeyed God instinctively, just as dogs bark instinctively and elephants trumpet and lions roar. But God was not satisfied with mere instinctive and automatic obedience on the part of man. From mankind God desires a conscious choice of that which is good, a deliberate dedication of the whole self to the will of God, a devotion which is based on faith in God's promises. For this reason therefore God entered into a *Covenant of Works* with Adam and his descendants, of whom he was the legal head and representative.

This Covenant of Works which God made with Adam and his posterity was negative in form. *Of the tree of the knowledge of good and evil, thou shalt not eat of it: for in the day that thou eatest thereof thou shalt surely die* (Gen. 2:17). But although the form of the commandment was negative, the intention of it was positive. In the Covenant of Works God required of our first parents perfect and entire obedience even in such a seemingly insignificant matter as the eating of the fruit of a tree. If they had complied with this condition, the Bible indicates that they would have been permitted to eat of the tree of life (Gen. 3:22) and together with their descendants would have been confirmed in perpetual holiness. And in this happy state they would have fulfilled to perfection the God-given mandate to *replenish the earth and subdue it* (Gen. 1:28). For it was God's will that Adam and his posterity should erect upon earth a sinless civilization and culture the splendor of which we cannot now have even the faintest conception, a civilization in which every gift of God would be used properly and to the fullest advantage and in which sin, suffering and death would be unknown.

But Adam violated the Covenant of Works, and hence all these pleasant prospects were blasted. By partaking of the forbidden fruit he brought upon himself and all mankind all these miseries which have been mentioned and also the liability to eternal punishment (Rom. 5:12; 1 Cor. 15:21).

(b) The Covenant of Grace

When God created Adam, He gave him dominion over the earth and assigned him the duty of subduing it and of cultivating its resources to his Creator's glory (Gen. 1:28). This divine command, however, has never been fulfilled. Sinful men now exercise dominion in the earth not as the servants of God but as the thralls and minions of Satan, *the god of this world* (2 Cor. 4:4), by whose wiles their first father Adam was seduced into his first transgression.

But the sabotage and subversion of Satan could not thwart the plan and program of God. Even before He created the world God had provided the remedy for Adam's sin. In the eternal *Covenant of Grace* He had appointed Jesus Christ His Son to be the Second Adam who would do what the first Adam failed to do, namely, fulfill the broken Covenant of Works still binding on all mankind. *The first man Adam was made a living soul: the last Adam was made a quickening Spirit. The first man is of the earth, earthy: the second Man is the Lord from heaven* (1 Cor. 15:45, 47).

In the Gospel of John the Lord Jesus Christ frequently testifies that He came down from heaven to accomplish the task assigned to Him by God the Father in the eternal Covenant of Grace. *I came down from heaven,* He tells the unbelieving Jews, *not to do Mine own will, but the will of Him that sent Me* (John 6:38). To accomplish this work of redemption was His delight. It nourished and sustained Him. *My meat is to do the will of Him that sent Me, and to finish His work* (John 4:34). Every moment of His earthly ministry our Saviour labored unremittingly in the performance of this divine duty. *I must work the works of Him that sent Me while it is day: the night cometh when no man can work* (John 9:4). Only when He had finished the work which His Father had given Him to do, was He ready to lay down His life. *I have glorified Thee on the earth: I have finished the work which Thou gavest Me to do* (John 17:4).

What then is that work which Christ, the Second Adam, came down from heaven to do? He came to save His people, to redeem those whom God the Father had given Him before the foundation of the world in the eternal Covenant of Grace. *Father, the hour is come; glorify Thy Son, that Thy Son also may glorify Thee: As Thou hast given Him power over all flesh, that He should give eternal life to as many as Thou hast given Him* (John 17:1-2). Those whom the Father has given to Christ in eternity shall be raised up in glory at the last day. *This is the Father's will which hath sent Me, that of all which He hath given Me I should lose nothing, but should raise it up again at the last day* (John 6:39). They can never be separated from the love of God in Christ. *No man is able to pluck them out of My Father's hand* (John 10:29).

Does this mean that any sinner is excluded? No! Only those that exclude themselves by their own sin and unbelief. In the Gospel Jesus assures us that all those that come unto Him in faith shall be saved. *All that the Father giveth Me shall come to Me; and him that cometh to Me I will in no wise cast out* (John 6:37). It is the will of God the Father that all those that believe on His Son shall receive the gift of everlasting life and have a part in the blessed resurrection. *And this is the will of Him that sent Me, that everyone which seeth the Son; and believeth on Him, may have everlasting life: and I will raise him up at the last day* (John 6:40). If we believe in Christ, then we know that we have been chosen in Him before the foundation of the world and are safe forever in the shelter of His redeeming love. *My sheep hear My voice, and I know them, and they follow Me: And I give unto them eternal life; and they shall never perish, neither shall any man pluck them out of My hand* (John 10:27-28).

As in Adam all die, even so in Christ shall all be made alive (1 Cor. 15:22). Just as Adam represented his descendants in the Garden of Eden, so Christ, the Second Adam, represented His people throughout His whole life on earth and at Gethsemane and on the cross. During the whole course of His earthly ministry Jesus did what Adam didn't do. He perfectly obeyed the will of God. He *became obedient unto death, even the death of the cross* (Phil. 2:8). By His life of perfect obedience and by His sufferings and death Jesus completely fulfilled the requirements of the Covenant of Works and paid the penalty of its violation. Through His obedience Christ earned for His people the gift of righteousness and delivered them from the deadly consequences of Adam's sin. *For as by one man's disobedience many were made sinners, so by the obedience of One shall many be made righteous* (Rom. 5:19). And it was on the grounds of His obedience also that Jesus Christ, the Second Adam, claimed for His people the reward of everlasting life with Him. *Father, I will that they also, whom Thou hast given Me, be with Me where I am; that they may behold My glory, which Thou hast given Me: for Thou lovedst Me before the foundation of the world* (John 17:24).

All God's dealings with men, therefore, from the creation to the final judgment, are summed up and comprehended in these two covenants, the Covenant of Works and the Covenant of Grace. In the Scriptures the Covenant of Works is also called the *Old* Covenant because it was the first to be established in time. The Covenant of Grace, on the other hand, is often called the *New* Covenant because it was disclosed later and was not fully revealed until after the death and resurrection of Christ.

(c) The Old Testament — Emphasis on the Covenant of Works

The Bible, then is the *Book of the Covenant*. This has been its name from the beginning because in it God reveals Himself as a covenant-making, covenant-keeping God. But there is another fact, a very familiar fact, which we must notice concerning the Bible. The Bible is divided into two parts, the *Old Testament* or *Covenant* and the *New Testament or Covenant.* (The Greek word *diatheke* can be translated either *testament* or *covenant.*) This two-fold division goes back to the Apostle Paul, who was the first to apply the name *Old Testament* to the ancient Hebrew Scriptures. The Jews, Paul said, read these Scriptures but did not understand them because of their unbelief. *But their minds were blinded: for until this day remaineth the same vail untaken away in the reading of the Old Testament; which vail is done away in Christ* (2 Cor. 3:14).

But why are the Hebrew Scriptures called the *Old* Testament? Because in them the emphasis is on the Covenant of Works. As we read through the Old Testament from Genesis to Malachi, this fact cannot fail to attract our attention.

According to Genesis 2, the very first dealing which God had with Adam was the establishment of the Covenant of Works. Before God brought the animals to Adam to name and rule and before He created Eve to share in Adam's world-wide dominion, He first of all placed our common father in this solemn, covenantal relationship (Gen. 2:17). The Covenant of Works therefore casts its somber shadow over the books and chapters of the Old Testament, beginning almost with the very first page. The angels barred the guilty pair from Paradise in order that they might be ever mindful of their violation of this law (Gen. 3:24).

This also was God's purpose in giving the Ten Commandments to the children of Israel at Mount Sinai, namely, to remind them once again that they all lay under the shadow of the broken Covenant of Works. *The Law entered,* Paul tells us, *that the offence might abound* (Rom. 5:20). God gave His people His holy Law in order that they might clearly understand that they were sinners and could not save themselves by their own good works. In this sense the Law of Moses was but a restatement and renewal of the original Covenant of Works made with Adam in the Garden of Eden. In this capacity the Law pronounced a curse on all those that violated any of its ordinances. *Cursed be he that confirmeth not all the words of this Law to do them* (Deut. 27:26). And conversely in the Law God offered life only to those who kept all its provisions. *Ye shall therefore keep My statutes, and My judgments: which if a man do, he shall live in them: I am the LORD* (Lev. 18:5).

In the history of Israel also this same emphasis is continued. Repeatedly the children of Israel turned aside from the Covenant which God made with them at Mount Sinai. Repeatedly God visited them with punishment at the hands of their heathen neighbors. *The house of Israel and the house of Judah have broken My Covenant which I made with their fathers. Therefore, thus saith the LORD, Behold, I will bring evil upon them, which they shall not be able to escape;*

and though they shall cry unto Me, I will not hearken unto them (Jer. 11:10-11). Through such chastisements the people of God were again reminded of the broken Covenant of Works.

But even in the Old Testament these dark shadows are penetrated by the light of God's grace. As soon as Adam and Eve had sinned, the provisions of the eternal Covenant of Grace were revealed to them in the *protevangelium*, the first preaching of the Gospel. God announced to Satan in their hearing, *I will put enmity between thee and the woman, and between thy seed and her seed; it shall bruise thy head, and thou shalt bruise his heel* (Gen. 3:15). Jesus Christ, the Second Adam, was to be born of woman and by His active and passive obedience to the will of God was to defeat the stratagems of Satan. *For this purpose the Son of God was manifested, that He might destroy the works of the devil* (1 John 3:8).

Not only so but later God established the eternal Covenant of Grace on earth, in a preliminary way, with Abraham, "the father of the faithful." *I will bless them that bless thee, and curse him that curseth thee: and in thee shall all families of the earth be blessed* (Gen. 12:3). In this way God preached the Gospel beforehand to Abraham and foretold the calling of the gentiles and their justification by faith (Gal. 3:8). *Look now toward heaven, and tell the stars, if thou be able to number them: and He said unto him, So shall thy seed be* (Gen. 15:5).

Still later the Old Testament prophets looked forward to the coming of the Messiah and the complete and final ratification of the eternal Covenant of Grace. *Then the eyes of the blind shall be opened, and the ears of the deaf shall be unstopped. Then shall the lame man leap as an hart, and the tongue of the dumb sing: for in the wilderness shall waters break out, and streams in the desert* (Isa. 35:5-6). Then God's Spirit shall be poured out on all flesh (Joel 2:28). Then *there shall be a fountain opened to the house of David and to the inhabitants of Jerusalem for sin and for uncleanness* (Zech. 13:1). And these expectations were summed up by the prophet Jeremiah when he foretold the coming of the New Covenant. *Behold, the days come, saith the LORD, that I will make a new Covenant with the house of Israel, and with the house of Judah. I will put My law in their inward parts, and write it in their hearts; and will be their God, and they shall be My people* (Jer. 31:31, 33).

(d) The New Testament — Emphasis on the Eternal Covenant of Grace

The Christian Scriptures are called the *New* Testament. Why? Because in them the emphasis is on the New Covenant foretold by Jeremiah and the other ancient Hebrew prophets. The New Covenant is the eternal Covenant of Grace completely and finally established on earth and ratified by the shed blood and death of Jesus Christ, the Second Adam. For this reason the New Covenant is also called the New *Testament*. It is the last will and testament of Jesus Christ which became effective only after His death upon the cross. *For where a testament is, there must also of necessity be the death of the testator. For a testament is of force after men are dead: otherwise it is of no strength at all while the testator liveth* (Heb. 9:16-17).

This cup is the New Testament in My blood, which is shed for you (Luke 22:20). In this manner at the holy Supper the Lord Jesus Christ instructed His Apostles concerning His last will and testament. Its provisions, however, did not become clear to them until after their Lord's death and resurrection. These included the following benefits:

(1) *Deliverance from the Covenant of Works*. It was Christ's will that under the New Covenant His people should be delivered entirely from the shadow of the broken Covenant of Works, and this deliverance He began to accomplish as soon as the Last Supper was finished. *And when they had sung an hymn, they went out into the mount of Olives. And they came to a place called Gethsemane* (Mark 14:26, 32). Here in the Garden of Gethsemane Christ the Second Adam did what the first Adam failed to do in the Garden of Eden. In agony, with supplication, Jesus overcame the temptations of Satan and the power of darkness. Then in His final act of obedience upon the cross our Saviour delivered us completely from the curse of the law of works. *Christ hath redeemed us from the curse of the Law, being made a curse for us: for it is written, Cursed is every one that hangeth on a tree* (Gal. 3:13).

(2) *The Outpouring of the Holy Spirit*. At the last Supper also Jesus announced a second benefit which the New Covenant would bring His people, namely, union with Himself. *I am the vine*, He told His Apostles, *ye are the branches* (John 15:5). This union became effective after His resurrection and ascension into heaven when at Pentecost He poured out the Holy Spirit upon His disciples. *Therefore being by the right hand of God exalted, and having received of the Father the promise of the Holy Ghost, He hath shed forth this, which ye now see and hear* (Acts 2:33). So Peter describes the Holy Spirit's coming. And since Pentecost all true believers are indwelt by the Holy Spirit and are united by Him in deathless bonds to Jesus Christ, the Second Adam. *We, being many, are one body in Christ* (Rom. 12:5). Hence Christians are and should be nothing else than a new race of holy men and women. The early Church was supremely conscious of this fact. "What the soul is in the body Christians are in the world." Diognetus

(3) *The Calling of the Gentiles*. It was Christ's will that the gentiles also should participate in the blessings of the New Covenant. *Other sheep I have which are not of this fold: them also I must bring . . and there shall be one fold, and one shepherd* (John 10:16). The calling of the gentiles was an essential part of Christ's redemptive program. Hence after His resurrection He gave final expression to His divine purpose in the words of the "Great Commission." *Go ye there-*

fore, and teach all nations, baptizing them in the name of the Father, and of the Son, and of the Holy Ghost: Teaching them to observe all things whatsoever I have commanded you: and lo, I am with you alway, even unto the end of the world (Matt. 28:19-20).

At first, however, the disciples were perplexed as to how they should best obey this commandment of their risen and ascended Lord. Was it not through Abraham (Gen. 12:3) that all the families of the earth were to be blessed? Had not God promised to bestow His covenanted blessings upon Abraham and upon his seed? *For all the land which thou seest, to thee will I give it, and to thy seed for ever* (Gen. 13:15). And so would it not be best for the gentiles first to become Jews by being circumcised and then after this to become Christians by believing in Jesus? Would not this Judaizing type of evangelism be most pleasing to God? Would it not be most in line with the teaching of the Old Testament?

It was the Apostle Paul who solved this problem under the inspiration of the Holy Spirit. He pointed out to his fellow Christians that Christ was the seed of Abraham to which God was referring in Gen. 13:15. *Now to Abraham and to his seed were the promises made. He saith not, And to seeds, as of many; but as of one, And to thy seed, which is Christ* (Gal. 3:16). Hence the covenant which God made with Abraham was but an earthly manifestation of the eternal Covenant of Grace which God made with Jesus Christ His Son before the foundation of the world. The gentiles, therefore, need not be circumcised or become Jews in any fleshly way. If they believe in Christ and are united to Him by the Holy Spirit, then they are the spiritual children of Abraham. *If ye be Christ's, then are ye Abraham's seed, and heirs according to the promise* (Gal. 3:29). The unbelieving Jews, on the other hand, who reject Christ are covenant breakers. Like Ishmael and Esau they are children of Abraham after the flesh but not after the Spirit (Rom. 9:8, 12). Both Jews and gentiles must be justified by faith (Rom. 3:29-30). Both Jews and gentiles must be united in one body to Christ (Eph. 2:15).

(e) Future Provisions of the Covenant of Grace

When we come to consider the future provisions of the Covenant of Grace, we enter the region of unfulfilled prophecy, an area in which there is a measure of disagreement among Bible-believing Christians. In this brief summary therefore we shall seek to emphasize the points on which all Christians agree.

(1) *The Evangelization of the World.* Jesus tells us that before He comes again the Gospel must be preached to all nations. *And this Gospel of the Kingdom shall be preached in all the world for a witness unto all nations; and then shall the end come* (Matt. 24:14). Jesus does not say that the whole world must be converted but rather that the whole world must be evangelized. All nations must hear the Gospel. With our modern means of communication,

especially radio and television, the fulfillment of this condition in the near future is a distinct possibility even from a human point of view.

(2) *The Conversion of the Jews.* The evangelization of the world will be followed by the conversion of the Jews. *Blindness in part,* Paul tells us, *is happened to Israel, until the fulness of the Gentiles be come in* (Rom. 11:25). The Jews are like olive branches which have been broken off the olive tree through unbelief. In their place the gentiles, like wild olive branches, have been grafted in (Rom. 11:17). When the Jews are converted to Christ, they will be grafted back into their own olive tree (Rom. 11:24). The return of the Jews to Palestine seems undoubtedly to be the prelude to their promised conversion on a national scale.

(3) *The Advent of the Antichrist.* The last days shall also be marked by the advent of the *antichrist.* This event is predicted by the Apostle Paul. Before Christ comes again, he tells the Thessalonians, there shall first come a falling away in which the *man of sin,* the *son of perdition,* shall be revealed (2 Thess. 2:3). This antichrist shall be the personal and final embodiment of the evil tendencies which have been at work in the Church since the days of the Apostles (2 Thess. 2:7; 1 John 2:18). His power as a world ruler shall be both political and religious. Daniel depicts him from the political side (Dan. 11:41-45), Paul portrays him from the religious point of view (2 Thess. 2:4-10), and John presents both aspects of his abominable career (Rev. 13:1-17). His reign shall bring in the great tribulation, but the period of his ascendancy shall be short (Matt. 24:21-22).

(4) *Christ's Return, the Resurrection and Judgment.* The Lord Jesus Christ shall come again from heaven *with power and great glory* (Matt. 24:30) and destroy the antichrist (2 Thess. 2:8). This second coming of Christ shall be followed by the resurrection and judgment. *For as the Father hath life in Himself, so hath He given to the Son to have life in Himself, and hath given Him authority to execute judgment also because He is the Son of man. Marvel not at this: for the hour is coming, in the which all that are in the graves shall hear His voice and shall come forth; they that have done good, unto the resurrection of life, and they that have done evil, unto the resurrection of damnation* (John 5:26-29). Resurrected believers will be caught up to meet the Lord as He comes, and believers who are living at the time of the Lord's return will be transformed and made partakers in this heavenly rapture (1 Cor. 15:50-55; 1 Thess. 4:16-17). This resurrection and rapture of the believers is the result of their union with Christ, the Second Adam (1 Cor. 15:22).

(5) *The New Heaven and the New Earth.* After the resurrection and judgment Christ's redemptive program shall culminate in the complete renewal of the universe. *And I saw a new heaven and a new earth: for the first heaven and the first earth were passed away; and there was no more sea* (Rev. 21:1). The way to the tree of life shall lie open to all in virtue of Christ's active obedience (Rev. 22:2, 14).

And because of Christ's passive obedience the curse entailed by Adam's first transgression shall be removed (Rev. 22:3). Sorrow, and crying, and pain shall be no more (Rev. 21:4). The people of Christ shall see His face and bear His name and reign with Him for ever and ever (Rev. 22:3-5). Christ's Church, which is His body, shall abide throughout all ages in glorious union with her exalted Head (Eph. 5:23-27).

The Bible, therefore, is the Book of the Covenant. In it God reveals Himself as a covenant-making, covenant-keeping God. The Covenant of Works which He made with Adam in Eden He fulfills in the eternal Covenant of Grace, in Jesus Christ, the Second Adam, in redeemed humanity, the members of Christ's body, and in the restitution of all things (Acts 3:21).

3. In The Gospel God Reveals Himself As The Triune Saviour God

The Bible is the key to the proper understanding of nature and of science. It provides us with the God-given eyeglasses which correct our faulty spiritual vision and enable us to see aright the revelation which God makes of Himself in the world which He has created. And the Bible is also the key to the proper understanding of human history. It is the Book of the Covenant which teaches us God's ways with men. In it God reveals Himself as a covenant-making, covenant-keeping God. But this is not all that must be said concerning the Bible. For the Bible is, above all, the Gospel. The Bible is a message from the spiritual world. The Bible is good news from God. In this Gospel Christ reveals Himself as Prophet, Priest, and King. In this message God reveals Himself in Christ as the triune Saviour God.

(a) In the Gospel Christ Reveals Himself as Prophet

A message requires a messenger to deliver it. Christ is this Messenger. He is the Angel of the Covenant (Mal. 3:1), the Supreme Prophet whose coming was foretold by Moses long before. *The LORD thy God will raise up unto thee a Prophet from the midst of thee, of thy brethren, like unto me; unto Him ye shall hearken* (Deut. 18:15). And as Prophet Jesus invites and warns.

Ho, every one that thirsteth, come ye to the waters (Isa. 55:1). In the Gospel Christ takes up this theme of the ancient prophet, inviting sinners to Himself that they may partake of the water of life freely. *If any man thirst, let him come unto Me and drink* (John 7:37). In His parables He summons them to joy and everlasting gladness. *My oxen and my fatlings are killed, and all things are ready: come unto the marriage* (Matt 22:4). In His witnessing and public preaching He gently calls them to eternal peace and quietude. *Come unto Me, all ye that labour and are heavy laden, and I will give you rest* (Matt. 11:28).

How shall we escape, if we neglect so great salvation (Heb. 2:3)? As a faithful Prophet Jesus warns us that we shall not escape. In severest terms He made this plain to the Pharisees who rejected Him. *Ye serpents, ye generation of vipers, how can ye escape the damnation of hell* (Matt. 23:33)? Those that hate the light and choose darkness must perish in the darkness. *He that believeth not is condemned already, because he hath not believed in the name of the only begotten Son of God. And this is the condemnation, that light is come into the world, and men loved darkness rather than light, because their deeds were evil* (John 3:18-19).

"How doth Christ execute the office of a prophet? Christ executeth the office of a prophet in revealing to us by His word and Spirit the will of God for our salvation." (Shorter Catechism)

(b) In the Gospel Christ Reveals Himself as Priest

At Mount Sinai God ordained Aaron and his sons to the priesthood for the special purpose of offering up sacrifices to atone for the sins of His chosen people Israel. Each of the various priestly sacrifices symbolized some aspect of the atoning death of Christ. For example, the law of Moses provided that before the offerer slew his sacrificial animal he should place his hand upon its head (Lev. 4:29). This was an act of faith by which the offerer indicated that he was presenting the animal as his substitute to bear the punishment which his sin deserved. So also the blood of the passover lamb, which saved them from the angel of death (Exodus 12:3-30), was prophetic of the blood of Christ, which would save them from the just wrath of God. And, above all, the blood of the bullock and the goat, which each year on the day of atonement was sprinkled upon the mercy seat of the ark (Lev. 16:14-15), was typical of the poured-out blood of Jesus, which fully satisfies God's justice and thus provides the basis for His forgiveness.

In the Gospel Christ reveals Himself as the great High Priest who has offered up Himself a sacrifice for believers upon the cross and is now making intercession for them at the throne of God. *Wherefore He is able also to save them to the uttermost that come unto God by Him, seeing He ever liveth to make intercession for them* (Heb. 7:25). As High Priest also He urges sinners to come unto Him. *For we have not an High Priest which cannot be touched with the feeling of our infirmities; but was in all points tempted like as we are yet without sin. Let us therefore come boldly unto the throne of grace, that we may obtain mercy, and find grace to help in time of need* (Heb. 4:15-16). And since Christ is our High Priest, we have no more need of an earthly priesthood. Every believer is a priest unto God through Christ. *Ye are a chosen generation, a royal priesthood, an holy nation, a peculiar people* (1 Peter 2:9). Every believer has access to God through Christ, the great High Priest. *Therefore being justified by faith, we have peace with God through our Lord Jesus*

Christ, by whom also we have access by faith into this grace wherein we stand, and rejoice in hope of the glory of God (Rom. 5:1-2).

"Christ therefore in very deed is a lover of those who are in trouble or anguish, in sin and death, and such a lover as gave Himself for us; who is also our High Priest, that is to say, a Mediator between God and us miserable and wretched sinners. What could be said, I pray you, more sweet and comfortable than this?" (Martin Luther)[64]

(c) In the Gospel Christ Reveals Himself as King

In the Gospel the Lord Jesus Christ reveals Himself not only as a Prophet and a Priest but also as a King. Jesus Christ was born a King. *The book of the generation of Jesus Christ, the Son of David, the son of Abraham* (Matt. 1:1). Such is the beginning of Matthew's Gospel. Jesus was of the kingly line of David, the legal heir to David's messianic throne. He is David's greater Son. At the very outset of His earthly ministry He announced the coming of the Kingdom. *The time is fulfilled, and the kingdom of God is at hand* (Mark 1:15). He was condemned to death as one who claimed royal dignity (Luke 23:2) and on this account was mocked and spat upon (Matt. 27:29-30). And when He was crucified, this superscription was placed above Him, JESUS OF NAZARETH, THE KING OF THE JEWS (John 19:19).

Christ's kingdom is, in the first place, a kingdom of *power.* After He rose from the dead, He entered into full possession of this aspect of His royal dominion. This we know from His parting words to His Apostles. *All power is given unto Me in heaven and in earth* (Matt. 28:18). And this glad assurance is echoed by the Apostle Paul, who speaks as follows of the risen and exalted Christ: *Wherefore God also hath highly exalted Him, and given Him a name which is above every name: That at the name of Jesus every knee should 'bow, of things in heaven, and things in earth, and things under the earth, and that every tongue should confess that Jesus Christ is Lord, to the glory of God the Father* (Phil. 2:9-11). In His kingdom of power, therefore, Christ is reigning as the Second Adam, bruising Satan's head under His heel (Gen. 3:15) and conquering all His foes, including finally even death itself. *For He must reign, till He hath put all enemies under His feet. The last enemy that shall be destroyed is death* (1 Cor. 15:25-26).

In the second place, Christ's kingdom is a kingdom of *grace. The kingdom of heaven,* Jesus says, *is like unto a certain king, which made a marriage for his son, and sent forth his servants to call them that were bidden to the wedding* (Matt. 22:2-3). Three things, Jesus tells us, are required of those who would accept this gracious invitation and enter into the heavenly kingdom. First, they must be born again. *Verily, verily, I say unto thee, Except a man be born of water and of the Spirit, he cannot enter into the kingdom of God* (John 3:5). Second, they must hear the *word of the kingdom* (Matt. 13:19) and understand it. *But he that received seed into the good ground is he that heareth the word and understandeth it; which also beareth fruit, and bringeth forth, some an hundred-fold, some sixty, some thirty* (Matt. 13:23). Third, they must be converted. *Verily I say unto you, Except ye be converted and become as little children, ye shall not enter into the kingdom of heaven* (Matt. 18:3).

Hence the Gospel is often called the Gospel of the kingdom because by it Christ calls His people into His kingdom of grace. This is the Gospel which Jesus Himself preached during the days of His earthly ministry. *Now after that John was put in prison, Jesus came into Galilee, preaching the Gospel of the kingdom of God and saying, The time is fulfilled, and the kingdom of God is at hand: repent ye and believe the Gospel* (Mark 1:14-15). This is the Gospel which was preached by Christ's Apostles. The Samaritans, we are told, were baptized *when they believed Philip, preaching the things concerning the kingdom of God and the name of Jesus Christ* (Acts 8:12). This was the Gospel which was preached by Paul at Rome. *And Paul dwelt two whole years in his own hired house and received all that came in unto him, preaching the kingdom of God and teaching those things which concern the Lord Jesus Christ with all confidence, no man forbidding him* (Acts 28:30-31). And this is the Gospel which shall be preached throughout the whole world before the end of this present age. *And this Gospel of the kingdom shall be preached in all the world for a witness unto all nations; and then shall the end come* (Matt. 24:14).

Christ must reign, Christ must conquer! And with the coming of Christ's final victory God's program for the world shall have been completed. Then Christ shall give back His kingdom of power and of grace to God the Father, since the purpose for which it exists shall have been accomplished. *Then cometh the end, when He shall have delivered up the kingdom to God, even the Father, when He shall have put down all rule and all authority and power. And when all things shall be subdued unto Him, then shall the Son also Himself be subject unto Him that put all things under Him, that God may be all in all* (1 Cor. 15:24, 28). Then when all is finished, Christ's kingdom shall assume its third and final form, namely that of everlasting glory. Jesus Christ the Son of God shall sit down upon His divine throne and with the Father and the Holy Ghost shall reign throughout eternity as the triune Saviour God.

Blessing, and honour, and glory, and power, be unto Him that sitteth upon the throne, and unto the Lamb for ever and ever (Rev. 5:13). Jesus Christ! King of power! King of grace! King of glory! The triune Saviour God!

"O victorious, O royal, O strong, princely soul-Conqueror, ride prosperously upon truth: stretch out Thy sceptre as far as the sun shines, and the moon waxeth! Put on Thy glittering crown, O Thou Maker of kings, and make but one stride, or one step of the whole earth, and travel in the greatness of Thy strength." (Samuel Rutherford)[65]

CHAPTER TWO

A SHORT HISTORY OF UNBELIEF

God reveals Himself in the world which He has made, in the holy Scriptures, and in the Gospel of Jesus Christ His Son. In this three-fold way God reveals not merely information about Himself but HIMSELF. But if God reveals Himself so openly and plainly as this, why are there so few that know Him? Why is His very existence denied and ignored by so many? The Bible gives us the answer to this question. It tells us that this prevailing ignorance concerning God is because of sin and the blinding power of Satan. *If our Gospel be hid, it is hid to them that are lost, in whom the god of this world hath blinded the minds of them which believe not, lest the light of the glorious Gospel of Christ, who is the image of God, should shine unto them* (2 Cor. 4:3-4).

In this present chapter we shall endeavor to give a short history of this satanic blindness of unbelief from earliest times down to the present day and show how it has affected the textual criticism of the Bible.

1. Ancient Forms Of Unbelief

Under ancient forms of unbelief we include heathenism and the various philosophies that developed out of heathenism. These age-old errors may fittingly be called unbelief because they all involve the denial of God the Creator as He reveals Himself in the world which He has made.

(a) False Sacrifices and the Growth of Heathenism

Heathenism (the worship of many gods and idols) began as a satanic perversion of the divine ordinance of animal sacrifice. The Scriptures tell us that not long after the first sin of Adam and Eve Abel, their younger son, began to offer up animal sacrifices unto God. And this he did with God's approval as a sign and pledge of his faith in Christ, the promised Redeemer (Heb. 11:4). But Adam's elder son, Cain, was seduced by the devil (John 8:44) to offer God false, unbloody sacrifices and then, when they were not approved, to slay his brother Abel in a fit of jealous rage. And this sin, the Bible seems to indicate, was the beginning of a false sacrificial system which was continued among the descendants of Cain until the Flood, introduced again after the Flood by Noah's unbelieving son Ham, and then carried to the ends of the earth when the nations were scattered at Babel. At the instigation of the devil (Deut. 32:17; Ps. 106:37) in every land these heathen nations offered sacrifices and worship to the forces of nature, to spirits, to the souls of the dead, and even to birds and beasts and creeping things (Rom. 1:23).

In order to justify their false religious practices these heathen nations rejected God's revelation of Himself in nature and substituted all manner of foolish myths and absurd cosmogonies. The Hindoos, for example, posited a golden egg as the source of this present world.[1] The early Greeks also derived the universe from a similar cosmic egg which was split in two, one half constituting the heavens and the other the earth.[2] And according to the Babylonian creation saga, the god Marduk constructed heaven and earth with the two halves of the monster Tiamet after he had killed her and mutilated her body.[3] It is to absurdities such as these that Paul refers in the passage just mentioned. *Because that when they knew God, they glorified Him not as God, neither were thankful; but became vain in their imaginations, and their foolish heart was darkened* (Rom. 1:21).

But although the heathen had rejected the true God, they could not escape the accusation of their consciences (Rom. 2:15) and the fundamental realities of the spiritual world. Studies in comparative religion indicate that in heathenism there were three areas of major concern. *First,* there was the menace of hostile spiritual powers. Demons were feared the world over, and charms and incantations were devised to ward off their malignant influences. In Babylonia especially these counter-measures were erected into a pseudoscience.[4] *Second,* there was the mystery of the after-life and the problem of providing for its needs. Some of the most characteristic features of Egyptian civilization stem from this interest. The embalming, the mummifying, the pyramids in which the dead kings were buried, all these were part of the care bestowed upon the dead. *Third,* there was anxiety over the judgment after death and the consequences of this great assize. In texts written on the inside of coffins and in inscriptions found in pyramids the Egyptians recorded their conceptions of the rewards and punishments which await men in the next world.[5] Similarly the Greek Orphic literature abounds in descriptions of fearful torments visited upon the wicked after death.[6]

In these heathen thought-ways there was undoubtedly much that was absurd. But, on the whole, the thinking of these ancient heathen was not nearly so foolish as that of modern materialists who derive mind from matter, who deny that there is any essential difference between right and wrong, and who have generated the present tidal crime-wave by their insanely obstinate contention that no one ought to be punished for anything he does but merely "rehabilitated." The heathen were more realistic than these modern unbelievers because they perceived that mind is spirit and that they themselves were spirits as far as their minds were concerned. From this they went on to reason, quite correctly, that there must be other spirits and that some of these spirits must be evil, seeing that there is evil in the world. They saw also that wrong must be avenged and that therefore there must be judgment and penalties after death.

At a much later date these ideas were developed by the Persian thinker Zoroaster (c. 650 B. C.) into an ethical dualism in which two uncreated beings strove together in perpetual conflict. One of these was the good god Ahura Mazda, the other the evil god Angra Mainyu.[7] It is probable, however, that Zoroaster borrowed from the revealed religion of the Israelites and especially from the biblical teaching concerning Satan, "the Adversary." We read in II Kings 17:6 that before the birth of Zoroaster captive Israelites were settled in the territory of the Medes and Persians, and it may be from them that Zoroaster obtained some of his conceptions.

(b) Eastern Philosophy — The Transmigration of Souls, Ancestor Worship

Belief in the transmigration of souls has in all ages been a common feature of heathenism everywhere. This is the theory that after death the soul is reborn into another body, a notion which has dominated the thinking of hundreds of millions of Asiatics ever since it made its appearance in India some time after 1000 B. C. Hindooism and Buddhism are built upon it. Both these religions presuppose that man is caught in an eternally revolving wheel of birth and death, an endless series of reincarnations. How can a man escape this ceaseless cycle of rebirths? Two answers were given to this question.

The Hindoos sought relief through the absorption of the human soul (atman) into the world-soul, which they called "the self-existent Brahman." This Brahman they regarded as the only reality. The material world which can be seen and touched was only an appearance. It was maya (illusion). By spiritual disciplines and ascetic practices it was possible for an earnest seeker to arrive at the insight that his individual soul (atman) was one with the world-soul (Brahman). When this mystic knowledge was attained, the cycle of rebirths came to an end.[8]

Buddha (557-477 B.C.), on the other hand, taught that salvation came only through the extinction of the human soul. Strictly speaking, he even denied that there was such a thing as a soul. He believed only in a succession of rebirths. Each existence depended on a previous existence just as one lamp is lighted from another. To terminate this cycle Buddha offered his famous eight-fold path. Those that followed this program would extinguish their desire for life and enter into Nirvana, a word which means literally, "blowing out the light."[9]

In China the two great molders of thought were Lao-tse (b. 604 B.C.) and Confucius (551-478 B.C.). Lao-tse was the founder of the Taoist system, the only native Chinese philosophy. He emphasized tao, the way of nature. He regarded the operations of nature as effortless and purposeless. The wise man therefore must conform to nature by living an effortless and quiet life.[10] Confucius, on the other hand, was unphilosophic, occupying himself entirely with religious ceremonies and ethics. Filial piety was the essence of his ethical system.

A son who respects and obeys his father will be a kind brother, sincere friend, and loyal subject.[11]   The religion of China, however, antedates these two sages by many centuries and may be defined as a union of nature worship and ancestor worship, a mixture which encouraged the veneration of spirits of every kind.[12]   It is probable that the great bulk of the Chinese people still continue in bondage to spirit worship despite the efforts of the present communist regime to replace this ancient superstition with the materialistic atheism of modern unbelief.

(c) The Greek Philosophy — Materialism and Idealism

In contrast with Eastern thinkers, the early Greek philosophers were chiefly concerned with the external world, and this they interpreted in a materialistic way.   Even God they regarded as in some sense material.   According to Thales (c. 600 B.C.), water was the basic constituent of the universe.   To this underlying cosmic fluid he attributed a certain divinity, declaring that "all things are full of gods."[13] Anaximander (611-545 B.C.) believed that the universal was an infinite (*boundless*) something which was "immortal and indestructible, unbegotten and incorruptible."   This boundless substance controlled the motion of all things, and in this sense Anaximander called it "the deity."[14]   Anaximenes (d. 499 B.C.) regarded air as the basic substance underlying all things, and this air he spoke of as a "god."[15] Heracleitus (540-480 B.C.) assigned the primary place in the universe to fire, which he thought of as the universal reason (*logos*).[16]   And two hundred years later this theory was revived by the Stoics, who also made fire the fundamental element and regarded it as the creative world-reason (*logos spermatikos*).[17]

These materialistic hypotheses led to the conclusion that nothing in the universe was permanent, since water, air, and fire were all subject to change.   This meant, as Protagoras (c. 450 B.C.) and other critics pointed out, that there was no possibility of permanent truth.[18] It was to combat such skepticism as this that the later Greek thinkers developed their idealistic philosophies.   These idealists divided the universe into two worlds, the world of matter which was always changing and the world of ideas which never changed.

There was a difference of opinion, however, as to what these unchangeable ideas were.   The Pythagoreans (c. 450 B.C.) thought of them as mathematical ideas.[19]   Socrates (470-399 B.C.) gave them an ethical connotation.[20]   According to Plato (427-347 B.C.), these ideas were all summed up and included in the *Idea of the Good*, the supreme and immutable purpose of the universe.   Late in life Plato added the concept of the *World-Builder* (*Demiurge*) that molds and shapes the world of matter, using the *Idea of the Good* as a pattern. Because of this many scholars have claimed that Plato believed in a personal God.   But Plato himself warned that he was speaking mythically.   It is probable therefore that Plato's *World-Builder* is merely a personification of his *Idea of the Good*, introduced by him to bridge the gap between the world of ideas and the world of matter and thus to provide a place in his philosophy for the physical sciences.[21]

(d) The Philosophy of Aristotle

Aristotle (384-322 B.C.), Plato's most famous disciple, developed a philosophy which attempted to be neither idealism nor materialism but a fusion of these two tendencies. According to Aristotle, matter is mere *possibility* and ideas are the *forms* that limit and guide this possibility. Matter, he taught, never exists by itself but only in union with these forms that limit and guide it. Perhaps a reference to a children's guessing game may serve to illustrate these basic tenets of Aristotle's philosophic system. One child says, "I am thinking of something." Then the other child tries to determine what it is by a series of questions. "Is it alive? Is it an animal? Is it a vertebrate? Is it a mammal? Is it a meat-eating mammal? Is it a dog? Is it our dog Fido?" The something of which the first child is thinking represents Aristotle's matter. At first it has the possibility of being almost anything, but then it is limited successively by the second child's questions, which represent Aristotle's forms, until finally it takes definite shape as the individual, existing dog Fido. In some such way, according to Aristotle, the forms limit matter, dividing it into classes and sub-classes, until finally individual organisms are arrived at and brought into existence.

Thus Aristotle viewed the world as an eternal process. Always the forms are limiting matter, dividing it into classes, sub-classes, and finally individual organisms. Always matter is moving up through the forms until these individual organisms are brought into existence. Always these organisms are growing to maturity and passing away only to be succeeded by new organisms of the same sort which in their turn are produced by this same union of matter and form. Hence for Aristotle God was not the Creator who brought the universe into being out of nothing at a definite time. Like Plato, Aristotle conceived of God as merely the highest form or idea. According to Aristotle, God moves the world by being "the object of the world's desire." Matter moves *up* toward God through its union with the forms. In this Aristotle differed from Plato, who connected ideas and matter by having the World-Builder (*Demiurge*) come *down* to the world of matter from the world of ideas.[22]

2. Philosophy In The Early And Medieval Church

Beware lest any man spoil you through philosophy and vain deceit, after the tradition of men, after the rudiments of the world and not after Christ (Col. 2:8). Here Paul warns against the ever present danger of corrupting the truth of God with the false philosophies of unbelieving men, and even a brief survey of the impact of Greek philosophy upon the early and medieval Church shows how much this warning was needed.

(a) Philosophy in the Early Church

From the second century B.C. onward the influences of Greek philosophy were at work among the Jews, especially those that dwelt at Alexandria in Egypt. Here the renowned Jewish thinker Philo (20 B.C.-42 A.D.) constructed a philosophic system which attempted to combine the teaching of the Old Testament with the theories of Plato and the *logos* doctrine of Heracleitus and the Stoics. It was in this last direction particularly that he sought a link between Greek philosophy and the sacred Hebrew Scriptures. The ancient Greek version of the Old Testament (the Septuagint) used the term *logos* to translate the Hebrew term *dabar* (word). Philo interpreted these biblical passages in a Greek sense. According to Philo, they refer to *the Logos*, the highest of all divine forces and the means by which God created the world, not out of nothing as the Bible teaches but in Greek fashion out of already existing substance. The *Logos* was employed by God to do this work because, Philo maintained, God Himself was too exalted to bring Himself into contact with defiling matter.[23]

The influences of Greek thought can be seen also in many of the heresies which plagued the Church in the early Christian centuries. One of the earliest of these was *Gnosticism*, which flourished around 150 A.D. Enlarging on the concepts of Plato and Philo, the Gnostics placed between the highest God and the world of matter many Eons or beings, including not only the Demiurge and the Logos but also Christ and Jesus, who were regarded as two separate entities. Other heretical views of the incarnation in the early Church are as follows: *docetism*, the theory that Christ's human nature was not real but merely an appearance; *adoptionism*, the assertion that Jesus was born a mere man and then became the Son of God through the indwelling of the Logos and the descent of the Holy Spirit upon Him at baptism; *Sabellianism*, the teaching of Sabellius (220 A.D.) that the Father, the Son, and the Holy Spirit are merely three ways in which God has revealed Himself. And finally, these false doctrines culminated in the greatest heresy of all, namely, the contention of Arius (318 A.D.) that before the foundation of the world God the Father had created the Son out of nothing.[24]

Amid this welter of heretical teaching there was danger that the orthodox Christian faith would perish, but in the sacred Scriptures and especially in the Gospel of John God had provided the remedy for this perilous situation. Writing under the inspiration of the Holy Spirit, this "beloved disciple" had expounded the true meaning of the Hebrew term *dabar* and the Greek term *logos*. *In the beginning was the Word and the Word was with God, and the Word was God* (John 1:1). The reference is to Christ the eternal Son of God. He is *the Word, the light of men* (John 1:4), who *was made flesh* and revealed His glory (John 1:14). Guided therefore by these teachings of the New Testament Scriptures, the Church was able to formulate at Nicaea (324 A.D.) and at Chalcedon (451 A.D.) the true doctrine of the holy Trinity and of the incarnation of Christ. Three Persons, Father, Son and Holy Ghost, but one God. Two natures, divine and human, but one Person.[25]

(b) Doctrinal Decline — Priestcraft, Image Worship, the Papacy

The triumphs of the Christian faith at Nicaea and Chalcedon were followed by a long period of doctrinal decline in which errors of every sort multiplied and entrenched themselves. The power of the priesthood and the papacy steadily increased as the New Testament doctrine of the universal priesthood of believers was more and more forgotten. Out of veneration for the martyrs and their relics grew the worship of innumerable saints and images. The spread of monasticism induced thousands of misguided souls to renounce the world and in the shelter of cloisters and convents to seek to please God with all manner of ascetic practices and man-made disciplines. The saints who lived in this monastic way were thought to have done more than the law of God required and thus to have laid up extra credits with God. Drawing on these extra credits (the *Treasury of merit*), the popes claimed the power to sell *indulgences* to less perfect Christians, shortening or remitting altogether their punishment in purgatory after death. Thus Christianity, a religion of God's free grace, had been transformed almost entirely into a religion of works.[26]

(c) The Rise and Progress of Mohammedanism

Mohammedanism is the earliest and largest of the cults which have followed in the wake of Christianity. Its founder Mohammed (570-632 A.D.), like many other false teachers, claimed to be the Comforter Whom Jesus had promised His disciples (John 14:26). He made this identification by changing the Greek word *Paracletos* (Comforter) to *Periclytos* (Illustrious) and then equating it with his own name Ahmed, which also meant *Illustrious*.[27] He also claimed that the religion which he preached was not younger but actually older than either Judaism or Christianity, being a restoration of the original religion of Abraham and Ishmael. Mohammed called his religion *Islam* (surrender). Believers were to surrender to the will of God just as Abraham did when he was willing to sacrifice his son Isaac. They were also to renounce all idols and believe in one God just as Abraham (according to tradition) renounced the idols of his father Terah (Azer). Other religious duties were to pray five times a day, to give alms, to fast during the daylight hours in the month Ramadan (in which the Koran had been revealed), and to make at least one pilgrimage to Mecca.

Mohammed proclaimed himself "the messenger of Allah and the seal of the prophets," in other words, the last and greatest of them. Among the prophets whom he claimed to supersede he included most of the outstanding biblical characters, for example, Noah, Abraham, Ishmael, Isaac, Jacob, Moses, Solomon, John the Baptist, and Jesus. He acknowledged the virgin birth of Jesus but denied His deity. "The Messiah, Jesus son of Mary, was only a messenger of Allah. Allah is but one God. Far be it from Him that He should have a son."[28] Instead Mohammed deified his Koran which, he maintained, confirmed and superseded the Law and the Gospel that had been revealed to Moses and Jesus respectively. According to Mohammed, the Koran was a hidden, heavenly book which had been sent down to the earthly plane on a certain night of the month Ramadan. Beginning with that night, Mohammed claimed, the angel Gabriel read to him at intervals out of the Koran, one section at a time. As each portion of the Koran was made known to him, Mohammed would go forth and recite it to the people. They in turn would either write it down or commit it to memory, and from these written and oral sources the present Koran was compiled soon after Mohammed's death by the caliphs Abu Bakr and Othman.[29]

Orthodox Mohammedans (Sonnites) believe that the Koran is eternal and uncreated, subsisting in the very essence of God. According to them, Mohammed himself held this same view and called anyone who denied it an infidel. In spite of this, however, there have been Mohammedan sects that have disputed this doctrine, especially the Motazalites who very rightly pointed out that this deification of the Koran involved the belief in two eternal beings and thus denied the unity of God.[30] This controversy shows us clearly that the Mohammedan doctrine of Scripture is only a crude caricature of the true, trinitarian, Christian doctrine. The Scriptures of the Old and New Testaments are eternal (Psalm 119:89) but not as an uncreated, eternal book. They are eternal in the same sense that God's decrees are eternal. They are the product of God's eternal act. They are the words of eternal life (John 6:68) which God the Father gave to Jesus Christ His Son in the eternal Covenant of Grace for the salvation of sinners. For I have given unto them the words which Thou gavest Me (John 17:8).

For more than one thousand years Mohammedanism was the chief external foe of Christianity. The death of Mohammed was succeeded by a century of conquest in which Syria, Egypt, North Africa and Spain speedily passed into the possession of his followers. Turned back at Tours by Charles Martel in 732, the Mohammedan menace remained quiescent for seven hundred years and then flared up again with renewed intensity after the capture of Constantinople in 1453 by the Turks. Under Suleyman the Magnificent (r. 1520-1566) Turkish power extended deep into central Europe and dominated the Mediterranean. It was not until the Turks were defeated in the great naval battle of Lepanto in 1571 that the tide began to turn against them.

These Mohammedan conquests, tragic though they were, clearly reveal the guiding hand of God's providence. In the first place, they served to isolate and preserve the True New Testament Text until the time came for its transferal to Western Europe. In the second place, by diverting the attention of the Roman Catholic powers during the first critical years of the Reformation they helped to save Protestantism from annihilation. And finally, it is possible that through these conquests the way has been prepared for the fulfillment of biblical prophecy. Perhaps the coming national conversion of the Jews will include their Mohammedan neighbors, these sons of Ishmael who like unbelieving Israel are children of Abraham after the flesh but not after the Spirit. It may be that thus will be brought to pass the saying of Isaiah. *In that day shall Israel be the third with Egypt and with Assyria, even a blessing in the midst of the land. Whom the LORD of hosts shall bless, saying, Blessed be Egypt My people, and Assyria the work of My hands, and Israel Mine inheritance* (Isaiah 19:24-25).

(d) The Scholastic Philosophy — Faith and Reason

During the middle-ages the study of Aristotle's philosophy flourished greatly, at first among the Nestorians in Syria, then among the Mohammedans, then among the Jews,[31] and finally in the educational centers of Western Europe, where it developed into the Scholastic Philosophy. This was the attempt to harmonize the dogmas of the Roman Catholic Church with the teachings of Aristotle, an effort which placed new emphasis on the relation of faith to reason.

The prevailing tendency of scholasticism was to make reason and faith independent of each other, the former ruling in the realm of nature, the latter in the realm of grace. It became customary to say that Aristotle was Christ's forerunner in things pertaining to nature and John the Baptist in things pertaining to grace. The schoolmen differed, however, as to the degree of separation existing between reason and faith. Albertus Magnus (1193-1280) denied that there was any real contradiction between faith and reason. Faith, he insisted, was not contrary to reason but above it. All the dogmas of Roman Catholicism, he maintained, either agreed with the philosophy of Aristotle or at least could not be proved false on Aristotelian grounds. Duns Scotus (d. 1308), on the other hand, admitted that the Roman Catholic dogmas were contrary to the philosophy of Aristotle but held that these dogmas should be believed in anyway on the authority of the Roman Catholic Church. In such cases Duns operated with two levels of truth. What was false on the level of reason was true on the level of faith.[32]

Thomas Aquinas (1225-1274) used Aristotle's philosophy as a foundation for the Roman Catholic religion of works. As has been stated, Aristotle taught that God moves the world by being "the object of the world's desire" and that matter moves up toward God through its union with the forms. Thomas applied this Aristotelian concept to the moral realm. Man strives for the highest end, and the highest end of all is to gain a knowledge or vision of God. Man attains this end through meritorious deeds and through the grace supplied by the sacraments of the Church. Thus not only in a physical sense but also in a spiritual way man moves upward in the scale of being toward God, the object of his soul's desire.[33] This is somewhat similar to the modern theory of theistic evolution, and many Roman Catholics today are attempting to bring Aquinas up to date by substituting evolutionism for Aristotelianism as the philosophic element in his system.

In philosophy and science, therefore, Roman Catholicism has followed its usual procedure of absorbing non-Christian elements rather than rejecting and refuting them. And the same has always been true in the political and ecclesiastical spheres. Today, for example, the Church of Rome is trying hard to draw Greek Catholics, Protestants, socialists, and even communists under its mantle in order that through the addition of these groups its ecumenical organization may become all-powerful. Hence the Roman Catholic conception of faith has always been that of blind obedience, the promise to believe whatever the Roman pontiff at any given moment officially decides must be believed.

In order, then, to understand the relationship of faith to reason we must first of all take a biblical view of our faith. If I really believe in God, then God is real to me, more real to me even than my faith in Him. For if it is the other way round, if my faith in God is more real to me than God Himself, then I am not believing but doubting. Hence in thinking about our faith and in describing it to others we must begin with that which is most real, namely, God. We must confess that God *is*, that He reveals Himself in the world, in the Scriptures, and in the Gospel of Christ, and that our faith in Him and in Jesus Christ His Son is not the product of our sinful, human minds and wills but the gracious gift of His Holy Spirit (Eph. 2:8). In this book, therefore, we are striving to present only this biblical and consistent view of Christian faith. This is why we defend the Traditional New Testament Text, the Textus Receptus, and the King James Version. In them God draws nigh and reveals himself.

After we take a biblical view of faith, we are then able to take a biblical view of reason and of its relationship to faith. Reason is the mental faculty by which we know the facts, the temporal truths which God establishes through His works of creation and providence. Faith is the spiritual faculty by which, through the power of the Holy Spirit, we lay hold on God Himself, the Supreme Truth, as He reveals Himself in and through the facts. Hence faith is not a "super-added" gift, as many of the medieval schoolmen supposed, not reason's cap and crown, but its foundation. We defend the Christian faith by showing that it is the only foundation on which the facts can be arranged and that all the attempts of unbelievers to substitute other foundations result only in confusion and chaos. *For other foundation can no man lay than that is laid, which is Jesus Christ* (1 Cor. 3:11).

Anselm (1033-1109), the "father of scholastic philosophy," was emphatic in his insistence on faith as the foundation of reason and knowledge. "I believe," he declared, "in order that I may understand.[34] But this biblical emphasis on the priority of faith did not long continue. For one thing, Anselm himself lost sight of it in his famous "ontological" argument for the existence of God. Taking a neutral view of his idea of God, he first regarded it as merely a part of his mental experience and then attempted to prove that it was a necessarily true idea. And in Anselm's successors, as we have seen, the Roman Catholic conception of faith as submission to ecclesiastical authority tended inevitably to place faith and reason in separate spheres.

Hence it was not until the Protestant Reformation that the reconciliation of faith and reason became possible. Then it was that believing scholars and theologians began to describe their faith consistently, taking as their starting point that which is most real to every true believer, namely, God, who reveals Himself in the world, in the Scriptures, and in the Gospel of Christ. Such a description opens the way to a better understanding of the intellectual implications of our Christian faith. We see that we are not only justified by faith *but renewed in knowledge* (Col. 3:10). By faith we lay hold on Christ, reason's only true and sure foundation. *And we know that the Son of God is come, and hath given us an understanding, that we may know Him that is true, and we are in Him that is true, even in His Son Jesus Christ. This is the true God, and eternal life* (1 John 5:20).

3. Revelation And The Protestant Reformation

What does God reveal in the world which He has created, in the holy Scriptures, and in the Gospel of Christ? Does He reveal *Himself,* or does He merely reveal information concerning Himself? This is a question of deepest interest to every earnest Christian. For if in nature, in the Scriptures, and in the Gospel of Christ God didn't reveal Himself but only information concerning Himself, our Christian faith would never bring us near to God. We would know certain facts about God, but we would not know God. We would believe in certain doctrines about Christ, but we would not believe in Christ as a Person. But thanks be to God that this is not the case. For the Bible itself teaches us that God's revelation is a revelation of HIMSELF, not of mere information concerning Himself.

(a) The Protestant Reformers and the Living Word of God

God reveals HIMSELF, not mere information concerning Himself. The Protestant Reformers understood this fact. To them the Bible was no mere book of doctrine but the revelation of the living God. In the Bible Christ revealed Himself. Martin Luther emphasized this in the preface of his German New Testament version (1522). "Briefly, St. John's Gospel and his first Epistle, St. Paul's Epistles, especially those to the Romans, Galatians, Ephesians, and St. Peter's

First Epistle: these are the books which shew thee Christ and teach all which it is needful and blessed for thee to know, even if you never see nor hear any other book or any other doctrine."[35]

It is true that Luther in his zeal pushed this principle too far, even to the point of making some unfavorable remarks concerning Hebrews, James, Jude and Revelation, alleging that these New Testament books did not present Christ clearly enough.   But these were mere hasty criticisms which had no permanent effect on the development of Lutheran doctrine.   Under the guidance of the Holy Spirit Lutheran churches soon united in confessing their faith in the canonical Scriptures of the Old and New Testaments "as the only judge, norm, and rule, according to which, as by the only touchstone, all doctrines are to be examined."   (The Formula of Concord, 1576)[36]

John Calvin also regarded God's revelation of Himself as a present reality which ought to guide and govern the whole of human life.   This was the theme of the opening chapters of his *Institutes*, namely, God's revelation of Himself in nature, the clarification and amplification of this revelation in the Scriptures, and the certification and confirmation of this revelation by the testimony of the Holy Spirit in the hearts of believers.   And in the *French Confession* (1559) Calvin and his followers gave a finished statement of their faith in the books of holy Scripture.   "We know these books to be canonical, and the sure rule of our faith, not so much by the common accord and consent of the Church, as by the testimony and inward illumination of the Holy Spirit, which enables us to distinguish them from other ecclesiastical books upon which, however useful, we can not found any articles of faith."[37]

(b) The Thirty Nine Articles and the Westminster Confession

The official position of the Church of England (Episcopal Church), as defined in the *Thirty Nine Articles* (1562), was in agreement with the Protestant Reformers as far as the authority of the Bible was concerned.   "Holy Scripture containeth all things necessary to salvation: so that whatsoever is not read therein, nor may be proved thereby, is not to be required of any man, that it should be believed as an article of the Faith, or be thought requisite or necessary to salvation.   In the name of the Holy Scripture we do understand those canonical Books of the Old and New Testament, of whose authority was never any doubt in the Church."[38]   This Article was included in the *Methodist Articles of Religion*, an abridgement of the *Thirty Nine Articles* prepared by John Wesley and adopted by American Methodists in 1784.[39]

The first chapter of the *Westminster Confession* is generally regarded as containing the fullest exposition of the orthodox Protestant faith concerning the holy Scriptures.   The section on the testimony of the Holy Spirit is especially notable and reads (substantially) as follows: "We may be moved and induced by the testimony of the

Martin Luther (1483-1546)

Church to an high and reverent esteem of the holy Scripture; and the heavenliness of the matter, the efficacy of the doctrine, the majesty of the style, the agreement of all the parts, the purpose of the whole (which is to give all glory to God), the full explanation it makes of the only way of man's salvation, the many other incomparable excellencies, and the entire perfection of it, are arguments by which it abundantly proves itself to be the Word of God. But our full persuasion and assurance of its infallible truth and divine authority is from the inward work of the Holy Spirit, bearing witness by and with the Word in our hearts."[40]

This *Westminster Confession* was adopted not only by Presbyterians (1647) but also by Congregationalists (1658)[41] and by Baptists (1677).[42] Some parts of the Confession were altered to agree with Congregational and Baptist convictions, but in regard to the chapter on the Scriptures all three denominations found themselves in complete accord.

(c) The Decline of Protestantism — Dead Orthodoxy, Pietism, Modernism

By the middle of the 17th century all the great Protestant creeds had been formulated, but instead of going forward in the strength of this achievement Protestantism entered soon after into a long process of decline which has continued unto the present day in spite of intervening periods of revival and missionary effort. One of the factors that brought about this decline was the development of *dead orthodoxy*. Many orthodox Protestants came to regard Christianity as mainly a system of doctrine set forth in a creed and confirmed by proof-texts taken from the Bible. Hence the Gospel was preached and taught in a cold, dead way merely as information concerning God and not as God's revelation of *Himself*. The result of this emphasis was all too often a dead faith, which, because it was centered on a creed and not on God Himself, soon withered away and was replaced by various forms of unbelief and finally by modernism.

The second factor in the decline of Protestantism was *pietism*. The pietists endeavored to combat the evils of dead orthodoxy, but in their protest against the misuse of creeds they went too far in the other direction. Their tendency was to ignore creeds altogether and to emphasize the feelings at the expense of the intellect. "Use your heart and not your head," was their slogan. The result was an unthinking emotionalism which left the door open to many errors and eventually to modernism.

God is truth. But He is also more than truth. He is a living Person. Therefore divine revelation is more than a revelation of the truth concerning God. It is this, but it is also more than this. It is God's revelation of *Himself*. In nature, in the Scriptures, and in the Gospel of Christ God reveals HIMSELF. When once we understand this and commit ourselves to God through Jesus Christ His Son,

John Calvin (1509-1564)

then we cut off all occasion to dead orthodoxy and pietism and arm ourselves to do battle against the modernism which results from these two errors.

4. Modern Philosophy — The Neutral World-View

Modern philosophy made its appearance immediately after the Protestant Reformation. The leaders of this new movement ridiculed both sides in the then current religious controversy. "Once there was a man," they quipped, "who had two sons, one Catholic and one Protestant. And so each brother converted the other, and God had mercy on them both because of their zeal." But in order to escape punishment these early modern philosophers denied that they were antichristian. They were only being impartial, they insisted, and unprejudiced. And from this claim has arisen the modern world-view, which has always pretended to be neutral and unbiased in all religious matters.

Weakened by dead orthodoxy and pietism, conservative Protestants of the late 17th and 18th centuries failed to resist the rising neutral world-view as vigorously as they should have done. Instead of taking their stand upon God's revelation of Himself in holy Scripture and pointing out that the neutral world-view is not really neutral but antichristian and full of contradictions, they began to adopt it themselves, especially in those areas of thought not specifically covered by their Reformation creeds, namely, philosophy and biblical introduction and above all New Testament textual criticism. Soon a serious inconsistency developed in the thinking of orthodox Protestants. At their colleges and theological seminaries especially students and teachers alike were torn between two world-views. In their study of systematic theology they maintained the believing world-view of the Protestant Reformation, but in their study of philosophy, biblical introduction, and New Testament textual criticism they adopted the neutral world-view of Post-Reformation rationalism. Today this illogical state of affairs is still being perpetuated in a few theological schools, but most of them have resolved the tension by becoming completely modernistic. The purpose of this book is to endeavor to reverse this trend by promoting consistently Christian thought especially in the sphere of New Testament textual criticism.

(a) Rationalistic Philosophy — Descartes, Spinoza, Leibniz

The early modern philosophers were rationalists. They made reason (the thinking mind) the starting point of their philosophical systems. And of these rationalistic philosophers the very earliest was Rene Descartes (1596-1650), who is usually considered the founder of modern philosophy. Descartes is famous for his use of doubt as a philosophical method.[43] He began by doubting everything that it was possible for him to doubt. He doubted not only the existence of

God but also the demonstrations of mathematics, the existence of the material world, and even the existence of his own body. Finally, however, Descartes came to something which he could not doubt, namely, the existence of his own mind. Even while he was doubting, he was thinking. Hence he could not doubt that his mind existed. "I think, therefore I am." This, he believed, was the rock-bottom foundation of certainty on which he could build his philosophical system.[44]

After Descartes had established that it was impossible for him to doubt the existence of his own mind, he reversed his reasoning. Discarding doubt as a philosophical method, he endeavored to argue his way back to certainty, using as stepping-stones the very convictions that he had previously doubted. He now asserted that the existence of God was not doubtful after all, because the idea of a perfect God which he had in his mind could not have come from an imperfect, doubting being like himself but must have been created in his mind by a perfect God. Therefore it must be that a perfect God exists and that the material world exists. For surely a perfect God would not deceive him by causing him to think that a material world existed if it did not in fact exist.[45]

But Descartes' attempt to regain his certainty through these arguments is very illogical. For if it is actually possible to doubt the existence of God and the material world and everything else except self-existence, then it is forever impossible to be certain about anything except self-existence. Everything else, having been doubted, must remain uncertain. Hence no Christian ought to adopt Descartes' philosophy since it casts doubt on the existence of God.

Two other famous rationalistic philosophers were Baruch Spinoza (1632-1677) and G. W. Leibniz (1646-1716). They believed that through the use of reason alone it was possible to deduce the fundamental nature of God and the universe. Spinoza was a pantheist. Indeed the term *pantheism* was invented to characterize his philosophy. He believed that there was but one basic substance of which both God and the universe were composed. According to Spinoza, God is nature viewed as active (*natura naturans*), and the universe is nature viewed as passive (*natura naturata*).[46]

Leibniz believed that the universe is composed of simple substances or souls, which he called *monads*. In non-living matter the monads are unconscious, in a stupor, so to speak. In animals the monads are conscious. In human beings the monads are rational. As rational beings we acknowledge God as the *sufficient reason* or cause of our existence. The monads have no communication with each other but cooperate according to a harmony which has been pre-established by God.[47]

(b) Empirical Philosophy — Locke, Berkeley, Hume

The above mentioned rationalistic philosophers (Descartes,

Spinoza and Leibniz) conceived of thought as consisting chiefly of *innate* ideas which were implanted in the human mind at birth and which developed as the human mind developed. The philosophers whom we shall now consider were *empiricists* (from the Greek word *empeiria* meaning experience). They denied the existence of innate ideas and regarded thought as simply a series of mental experiences.

The first of these empirical philosophers was John Locke (1632-1704).[48] In his famous *Essay on Human Understanding* (1690) he sought to demonstrate that the ideas commonly thought to be innate were not really so since they were not found in idiots or children or savages, a contention which modern investigation has not substantiated. At birth, Locke asserted, the human mind is "white paper, void of all characters, without any ideas."[49] He believed that ideas enter the mind only through *sensation* (sense experience, e.g., seeing, touching, hearing, etc.) or through *reflection* ("the notice which the mind takes of its own operations and the manner of them").[50] Hence, in his theory of knowledge, Locke came perilously close to maintaining that the mind can know nothing else than its own ideas. "Since the mind, in all its thoughts and reasonings, hath no other immediate object but its own ideas, which it alone does or can contemplate, it is evident that our knowledge is only conversant about them."[51] Locke, however, was inconsistent and so declined to develop his philosophy to the point of complete skepticism. He allowed the existence of the material world as the source of sense experience and even insisted that we can be certain of our own existence, of causation, and of the existence of God, conclusions which by no means follow from the premises which he laid down.

George Berkeley (1685-1753) and David Hume (1711-1776) carried Locke's principles to their logical conclusion. Berkeley, who later became Anglican Bishop of Cloyne in southern Ireland, used Locke's philosophy as the basis of his famous argument against materialism. He contended that only spirits and ideas exist. Matter does not exist, he maintained, because we do not experience matter but only our idea of matter. Hence matter is God's idea, and the creation described in Genesis was not a creation of matter but only a creation of spirits (angels and men) with whom God could share His idea of matter.[52]

Hume pushed on to other extreme positions. He denied not only the existence of matter but also his own self-existence on the ground that he was not able to experience his self but only his ideas. Likewise, he denied causation, asserting that he could not experience it but only a succession of events in time.[53]

(c) Critical Philosophy — Immanuel Kant

The skepticism of David Hume concerning causation stimulated Immanuel Kant (1724-1804), one of the world's most influential thinkers, to develop his *critical philosophy*, an investigation of the powers and the limitations of the human mind.[54]

In his *Critique of Pure Reason* (1781) and his *Prolegomena* (1783) Kant dealt with the problem of human knowledge.[55] According to Kant, we cannot know things as they are in themselves but only as they appear to us in our human experience. Whenever our minds begin to speculate about things as they are in themselves apart from our human experience of them, we run into *antinomies* (contradictions). We find that there are two sides to each question. Arguments of equal validity can be found to support either the *thesis* (affirmative) or the *antithesis* (negative), so that we cannot determine which side to take. Hence we can know nothing certain concerning things as they are in themselves. Certain knowledge, Kant insisted, is confined to the realm of experience. Space, time and causation are valid concepts because they are facts of our experience.

Such, in brief, was Kant's reply to Hume. But many subsequent philosophers have denied that Kant really refuted Hume, because Kant simply assumed what Hume denied, namely, that the human mind experiences causation. Also many subsequent philosophers have accused Kant of inconsistency. He seems to imply that things in themselves are causes of human experience, and this would make causation not merely a fact of experience but also one of the things in themselves of which we can know nothing certain.

In his *Foundations of the Metaphysics of Morals* (1785) and his *Critique of Practical Reason* (1788) Kant discussed the concepts God, freedom and immortality and their relation to the moral law.[56] According to Kant, it is impossible either to prove or to disprove the existence of God intellectually, but it is helpful to have a rational faith in God as a moral Governor who will reward us in a future life in proportion to our worthiness, our conformity, that is, to the moral law. But we must not think of God as a Law-giver or of the moral law as determined by God's will. Obedience to such a law, Kant maintained, would not be true worthiness. It would be *heteronomy*, obedience to the law of another. In order to be truly free and worthy, Kant insisted, a man must be his own law-giver. He must be *autonomous*. He must obey only the moral law which his own reason supplies, the *categorical imperative* which orders him to behave as he would wish everyone in the whole universe to behave. "Act as though the maxim of your action were by your will to become a universal law of nature." We must obey this *categorical imperative* for duty's sake alone, not from any other motive, not even out of regard for God.

In his *Religion within the Limits of Reason Alone* (1793) Kant attempted "to discover in Scripture that sense which harmonizes with the holiest teaching of reason,"[57] that is, with his own philosophy. According to Kant, Adam's sin is an allegory which symbolizes our failure to obey the *categorical imperative* for duty's sake alone. Regeneration is the resolve to give this imperative the required single-minded obedience. Satan represents the evil principle in human nature. The Son of God is a personification of the good principle. The kingdom of God is "an ethical commonwealth." It will come on earth when the transition is made from an "ecclesiastical faith to the universal religion of reason."

(d) The Philosophy of History — Georg W. F. Hegel

Georg W. F. Hegel (1770-1831) developed his *philosophy of history* as an alternative to the critical philosophy of Immanuel Kant.[58] More clearly than most subsequent thinkers Hegel discerned the basic fallacy in Kant's approach to the knowledge question. Kant's critical philosophy, Hegel observed, was an attempt "to know before we know."[59] In other words, Kant tried to isolate the human mind from the rest of reality and analyze it all by itself. This, Hegel pointed out, is a mistake. We can know nothing certain about the human mind unless we know something certain about the whole of reality, of which the human mind is but a part. We can not know a part until we know the whole.

Instead, however, of receiving by faith God's revelation of Himself in nature, in the Scriptures, and in the Gospel of Christ and finding in this revelation the necessary universal knowledge, Hegel turned his back on the orthodox Christian faith and sought the solution of his problem in a pantheism similar to that of Spinoza. Philosophy, Hegel maintained, must be a system. "Unless it is a system, a philosophy is not a scientific production."[60] At the center of Hegel's philosophic system is the *Idea*. This Idea is the *Absolute*. It is not logically dependent on any other idea, but all other ideas are logically dependent on it. Hence the Idea is the logical ground, or explanation, of the universe.

According to Hegel, philosophy is divided into three parts. "I. Logic: the science of the Idea in and for itself. II. The Philosophy of Nature: the science of the Idea in its otherness. III. The Philosophy of Spirit: the science of the Idea come back to itself out of that otherness."[61] The reason for this three-fold division of philosophy was Hegel's belief that the universe is constantly engaged in a three-fold process which Hegel called *Dialectic* (a Greek philosophical term signifying the discovery of truth through discussion). Logic is continually converting itself into Nature (the material world) and then returning to itself as Spirit. *Thesis* (affirmation) is always transforming itself into *antithesis* (negation) and then coming back as *synthesis* (a combination of the two). Hence, according to Hegel, it is "narrow" and "dogmatic" to assume that of two opposite assertions the one must be true and the other false. We ought rather to recognize, Hegel insisted, that in such cases both propositions contain elements of higher truth.

Hegel regarded human history as the third phase of the universal process (*Dialectic*). Human history is the Idea returning to itself as Spirit. It is Spirit seeking to know itself. According to Hegel, the essence of Spirit is freedom. Hence freedom is the theme of human history.   History, Hegel taught, is divided into three periods.   First, the period of the ancient, oriental nations who were governed by despots and knew only that *one* (the despot) was free. Second, the period of the Greeks and Romans who were free themselves but kept slaves and so knew only that *some* are free.   Finally, there is the period of the Germanic nations, who live under constitutional monarchies and know that *all men* are free.   For Hegel freedom was inseparably connected with the State and reached its most perfect form under a constitutional monarchy.   "The State is the Divine Idea as it exists on earth."[62]

(e) Philosophy Since Hegel — Neo-Kantianism, Existentialism

During the latter part of the nineteenth century there was a trend away from Hegelianism back to the philosophy of Kant and his completely untenable position that it is possible to know something certain about a part of reality without knowing anything certain about reality as a whole.   Various schools of *Neo-Kantians* adopted distinctive attitudes toward this fundamental problem.[63]   At Marburg they attempted to solve it by denying that there is any reality outside of human experience.   At Heidelberg they ignored it, concentrating rather on Kant's doctrine of the will and the categorical imperative. At Goettingen A. Ritschl and his followers pursued a similar course in the theological field.   "Theology without metaphysics," was their slogan.   God is love and only love.   It was in this sense that the Ritschlians called God Father.   Christ they conceived of as the Founder of the Kingdom of God, the ethical commonwealth described by Immanuel Kant.   They regarded Him as God, but not really.   Only in the sense that for them He had "the value" of God.[64]   This Ritschlianism was preached vigorously in the United States by Walter Rauschenbusch (1861-1918) under the title of "the social Gospel" and became the quasi-official theology of the Federal Council of Churches.[65] As such it was a factor in the socialist legislation of the New Deal era.

Existentialism is a philosophical movement begun in Denmark by Soren Kierkegaard (1813-1855).   Kierkegaard's leading thought was that the different possible conceptions of life are so sharply at variance with each other that we must choose between them.   Hence his catchword *either/or*.[66]   Moreover, each particular person must make this choice for himself.   Hence his second catchword *the individual*.   Life is always pressing on and forever leading to new possibilities and new decisions.   Hence we ever stand before the unknown. We cannot be sure that the future will resemble the past.   Hence a logically connected philosophy such as Hegel's is impossible.   Our choices must be made by jerks and leaps.   Only thus, Kierkegaard insisted, will we do justice to our individual existences.[67]

Existentialism was revived after World War I by Jaspers (1883-1969)[68] and Heidegger (born 1889)[69] and popularized after World War II by Sartre (born 1905).[70]   Like Kierkegaard, these philosophers emphasized the individual life situation of each human being and its possibilities, the necessity of choosing between these possibilities, the background of death and nothingness and the accompanying dread and nausea, the choice itself and the freedom obtained by this act of will.   These factors they regarded as the necessary components of authentic existence.   In the theological field the leading existentialist was Karl Barth (1886-1968) who equated the experience of existential choice with the Christian doctrine of revelation.   It is, he maintained, an encounter with the hidden God.[71]

5. The Growth Of Atheism — Materialism, Positivism, The Denial Of Truth

As the modern age progressed, more and more unbelievers threw off the cloak of neutrality in religious matters, openly disclosing the underlying atheism, and this trend has continued until finally it has become dominant everywhere.   This rapid growth of atheism illustrates the impossibility of being neutral toward God's revelation of Himself in nature, in the Scriptures, and in the Gospel of Christ. When men start their thinking from this neutral position, atheism is always the logical consequence.

(a) Materialism — La Mettrie, Holbach, Moleschott, Vogt

Materialism, the view that only matter exists, is one of the most common forms of atheism.   La Mettrie, a French physician, was an atheist of this type.   In 1748 he published a notorious treatise entitled *Man A Machine*[72] in which he denied existence of the soul and ridiculed the natural evidences of the existence of God.   Similarly, in 1770 Holbach published in Paris his *System of Nature,* which has been called "the Bible of materialism."   In it he maintained that belief in God leads to priestcraft and persecution and interferes with natural morality.[73]   And after the French Revolution such materialistic atheism became increasingly common.   For example, Moleschott (1852) taught that thought is produced by phosphorus ("without phosphorus no thought"), and Vogt (1855) asserted that thought stands in the same relation to the brain as gall to the liver or urine to the kidneys.[74]

The principal argument of the materialists against Christianity has always been their demand that the relationship between soul and body be explained in materialistic terms.   But this demand is inconsistent and absurd.   For the soul by definition is spiritual.   Therefore its relationship to the body must be spiritual.   Hence it is illogical to demand that this relationship be explained materialistically.   And materialism also involves many other absurdities.   For example, if thoughts come from matter, then scientific theories about matter must themselves be forms of matter.   And if thoughts are forms of matter, then even fanciful and absurd thoughts, such as golden mountains, round squares, centaurs and winged horses, must all be forms of matter and as such have a real and material existence or subsistence. Then a proposition must be a material substance and truth a physical or bodily state.

(b) The Origin of Life — Pasteur, Darwin, Huxley, Haeckel

During the 19th century the controversy between materialists and orthodox Christians shifted from the question of the relation of soul and body to the question of the origin of life. This change was brought about by the theory of evolution, which logically involves some type of spontaneous generation. At first this was no problem, for from the days of the ancient Greeks until the mid-19th century almost everyone believed that life could be generated spontaneously. For example, the famous Brussels physician Van Helmont (1577-1644) claimed to have generated live mice by placing a dirty shirt in a bowl of wheat germs and keeping it there for three weeks. William Harvey (1578-1657), the discoverer of the circulation of the blood, believed that worms and insects could be spontaneously generated from decayed matter, and Descartes and Isaac Newton held similar views. Even Lamarck mentioned the possibility of the spontaneous generation of mushrooms.[75] But in 1862 Louis Pasteur proved that no known form of life, not even bacteria, could be generated spontaneously, and evolutionists were compelled to adjust their theory to this new discovery.[76]

Some evolutionists made this adjustment by giving God a small part in the evolutionary process. God, they said, created the first germ of life, and then evolution did the rest. This was the view that Darwin had already advanced publicly in his *Origin of Species*.[77] Privately, however, he preferred a materialistic explanation of the origin of life, suggesting that life might have arisen from a protein compound in a warm pool in which ammonia and phosphoric salts, light, heat, electricity and other ingredients were present.[78] Huxley and Haeckel, Darwin's foremost disciples, believed that life had originated in the sea. When some slime was dredged up from the bottom of the ocean, Huxley proclaimed it the simplest form of living matter and named it after Haeckel, but later it proved to be only some inorganic salts.[79]

Present-day followers of Darwin, Huxley and Haeckel look eagerly to space science to confirm their views. In 1959, for example, Urey and Miller expressed their opinion that all the projected space flights and the high costs of such developments would be fully justified if they were able to establish the existence of life on either Mars or Venus.[80] And in the same year M. Calvin named the moon, Venus and Mars as three non-terrestrial environments which might possibly contain life or the traces of life.[81] But subsequent investigations have not encouraged these hopes. Astronauts have walked the moon and found it lifeless. Three American and two Russian spacecraft have sailed past Venus and sent back their reports. According to this new data, Venus is the hottest of all the planets with temperatures reaching 1,000 degrees F, thus rendering the existence of life impossible.[82] As for Mars, in 1976 this planet was canvassed very carefully for signs of life but with negative results. Two space craft were landed on Mars with equipment to test the soil and transmit the results to earth, but the experiments were inconclusive.[83]

What about the possibility of creating life in a scientific laboratory? Some materialists claim that this feat has already been accomplished. Experiments with viruses, for example, have sometimes been so interpreted. Viruses are minute particles which cause certain diseases. When they are not in the cells of an organism which they can infect, viruses seem entirely lifeless, even forming crystals after the manner of inorganic chemicals. But as soon as a virus penetrates a living cell, it reproduces (makes copies of) itself just as if it were alive. Viruses, moreover, consist of two parts, a protein shell and a core of nucleic acid (DNA or RNA).[84] In 1955 at the University of California H. L. Fraenkel-Conrat accomplished the remarkable feat of disassembling two breeds of the tobacco mosaic virus and then successfully combining the protein shells of one breed with the RNA nuclei of the other. But as Fraenkel-Conrat himself observed, this was not a creation of life but an analysis of biologically active structures in terms of chemistry.[85]

Other experiments have proceeded along similar lines. In 1957 A. Kornberg and his associates in St. Louis caused DNA nucleic acid molecules to reproduce themselves by mixing a small "primer" of DNA with a ferment (enzyme) taken from colon bacteria and then adding the proper building materials of nucleic acid (nucleotides).[86] And in 1965 Spiegelman and Haruna of the University of Illinois did the same thing with RNA nucleic acid, using a ferment (enzyme) taken from cells infected by a certain virus, a small amount of RNA as a "primer," magnesium salts, and the proper building-materials.[87] But as Dobzhansky (1964) admits, such experiments, though very impressive, do not really involve the creation of life from non-living constituents, since some of the materials are taken from living cells and, in any case, no living cell is produced.[88]

(c) Positivism — Comte, Russell, The Vienna Circle

Positivism was a type of scientific atheism first advocated by Auguste Comte (1798-1857). His fundamental doctrine was the alleged three stages of human thought. The first stage, according to Comte, was the *theological*. As men passed through this stage, they were first fetish-worshipers, second polytheists, and finally monotheists. The second stage was *metaphysical*. In this stage men no longer referred phenomena to supernatural beings but to unseen causes, to occult powers or forces which can not be detected by the senses. But this stage, Comte believed, had also been outgrown, and thinking men had now entered the third stage of development, to wit, the *positive* stage. Men living in this third stage have come to recognize that there are no spiritual agencies in the universe, no efficient causes, nothing but facts discoverable by the senses, nothing but events which take place according to natural law.   In this positive stage, Comte insisted, it has become evident that theological and metaphysical problems are insoluble and senseless.   All that we ought to attempt is to discover and systematize the laws of nature.[89]

Comte's wide-ranging theories won him friends and adherents in England as well as in France.   John Stuart Mill and the historian Thomas Buckle were numbered among his admirers.   Of the later 19th-century positivists Kirchhoff and Mach, noted physicists, were especially prominent.   And throughout the century there were many other scientists who, though they refused the positivistic label, yet by their contempt for religion and metaphysics showed themselves to be thoroughly imbued with the positivistic spirit.

Early in the 20th century, however, positivists began to discover that they had not really succeeded in eliminating metaphysical problems.   They had only created a new one, namely, the problem of *meaning*.   For if the religious and metaphysical ideas of the past are meaningless, how can positivists be sure that their own ideas have meaning?   What is meaning?   What does "meaning" mean?[90]   The study of this question was given the name *Semantics* (science of meaning).

Semantic studies were carried on first in England by Bertrand Russell in the early 1900's.   A pioneer and outstanding authority in the field of symbolic logic, he applied this technique to the propositions of Kant and other great philosophers of the past in order to discover their meaning or lack of meaning.   This procedure he called *logical analysis*.[91]   Although Russell refused to be called a positivist, he leaned in this direction, and his achievements in symbolic logic had great influence on 20th-century positivism, so much so that it soon became known as logical positivism.

Shortly after World War I a group of logical positivists, usually spoken of as "the Vienna Circle," began to meet together at the University of Vienna under the leadership of Moritz Schlick, a professor of scientific philosophy there.[92]   Ludwig Wittgenstein, who had studied logic under Bertrand Russell, was also influential in the group, although he never actually attended any of its meetings.[93]   In Poland also during this same period similar groups were active.[94] Then during the 1930's interest in logical positivism spread to many lands, especially after the rise of Hitler to power, an event which had a scattering effect upon the whole movement.   Many of its leaders fled to the United States and began to teach logical positivism and semantics in American Universities.   And at the same time Alfred Korzybski, Stuart Chase, and S. I. Hayakawa introduced these subjects to the American public at the popular level. [95]

These semantic studies, however, have not led to any satisfactory conclusion.   Positivists now maintain that meaning is a matter of convention.   Whether you find meaning in a proposition or not depends on the semantic system which you adopt, the linguistic rules which you choose. Positivists say that they prefer to follow a semantic system in which only propositions which can be verified experimentally are meaningful.[96] But this is a purely arbitrary and subjective way to handle the question of meaning. If meaning is anything at all, it must be objective and independent of our wills. The Christian finds this meaning in God, his Creator, and in Jesus Christ, his Redeemer and Saviour.

(d) Cybernetics — The Philosophy of Automation

A new era in the history of materialism seems to have begun in 1948, for this was the year in which Norbert Wiener (1894-1964), professor at Massachusetts Institute of Technology and world famous pioneer in the field of automation, published his well known book *Cybernetics, or Control and Communication in the Animal and the Machine.* The word *cybernetics* was derived from the Greek word *kybernetike,* which means *the art of steering.* Thus the title of the book conveyed Wiener's central thesis that there is no fundamental difference between animals and machines and that even human beings are basically mechanical. The principles, Wiener argued, that are valid in the realms of communication-engineering and automation can be applied also to human life.[97]

Wiener tells us that he was led to these conclusions through his work on anti-aircraft guns during World War II. These guns were aimed by computers which calculated the position of the enemy aircraft on the basis of statistical probability. If the gun failed to score a hit, radar-pulses would be reflected back to the gun both from its own bursting shell and from the enemy aircraft.[98] These radar-pulses would set in operation a correctional process called "feedback," namely an electrical current which was "fed back" into the gun's computer. This "feedback" would then correct the calculations of the computer and thus improve the aim of the gun. Computerized encounters such as these were regarded as contests between two machines, the automatic gun on the one hand and the enemy pilot and his aircraft on the other.

Wiener's work on anti-aircraft guns was soon utilized in the field of communication-engineering (telegraph, telephone, radio, television). In this realm also there is a contest between two opposing forces. The first of these is called *information.* When a message is received over a wire or over the radio waves, the exact content of the message is never absolutely certain. And so out of all the possibilities the most probable is selected by means of mechanical devices which operate on the principle of statistical probability. "Information" is the process by which this selection is made. The second and opposing process is called *entropy,* the scientific name for the electrical disturbances which break up the message and render its reception difficult by making all the possibilities equally probable. The use of Wiener's methods of computing probabilities provided a way to eliminate these electrical disturbances more completely and thus to improve the reception of messages.

Out of these principles of communication-engineering and automation Wiener developed his philosophic system. He regarded the history of the universe as a gigantic struggle in which *entropy* and *information* are pitted against each other. Entropy, he maintained, is the disintegrative force which dissolves the universe by making all the possibilities equally probable and thus doing away with all distinctiveness. Information is the constructive force which uses "feedback" (Wiener's new name for adaptation to environment) to make some possibilities more probable than others and thus to set in motion the process of evolution. Both human beings and machines are products of evolution. Human beings must be used humanly. Since they are high grade machines, they should be assigned tasks involving decision making. Boring drudgery should be reserved for machines of a lower order. But in the last analysis, according to Wiener, all human striving is in vain. Entropy must win the victory over information, and the history of the universe must end in chaos.

Wiener's cybernetic philosophy has been eagerly adopted by evolutionists the world over and now reigns almost supreme in scientific circles, but like all other materialistic thought structures it falls down when handled critically. What is back of the possibility out of which both entropy and information are said to flow? If nothing is back of it, why is there any possibility? Why isn't everything impossible? And what is back of the statistical probability which is said to guide both entropy and information? If nothing is back of it but chance, why isn't there chaos right now? Why don't all the possibilities become equally probable at this very moment? And in what sense can Wiener claim that his materialistic philosophy is true? For if materialism is true, then all ideas, theories and philosophies must be forms of matter or states of matter and as such cannot meaningfully be said to be true.

(e) Truth and Certainty, Probability and Error, Common and Saving Grace

Most modern scientists are convinced of one thing, however much they may differ in regard to other matters, namely, that science has no use for absolute or final truth. Professor Margenau (1963) of Yale is quite passionate, even violent, in his expression of this conviction. Science, he declares, harbors no absolute or final truth. Final truth, he asserts, is stagnant knowledge. Only a fool looks for it. Only a feeble soul insists on truth by revelation.[99] And others have expressed themselves similarly. For example, the eminent scientific philosopher Hans Reichenbach (1938) maintained that human knowledge includes no truth. "All we have," he said, "is an elastic net of probability connections floating in open space."[100]

But can the situation be as these scientists picture it? Can there be probability without truth? Is it possible to abolish truth and leave nothing but probability? Analysis shows that this is not possible. For when a scientist says that his theory is probable, he means that it is *true* that his theory is probably *true*. He does not mean that it is probable that his theory is probably probable, for this would be nonsense. In other words, probability makes no sense unless there is also truth.

It cannot be, therefore, that all propositions are merely probable. Some propositions must be permanently true. Otherwise the probability concept becomes meaningless. What are these permanently true propositions? God gives the answer to this question. The permanently true propositions are those propositions by which God reveals Himself in nature, in the holy Scriptures, and in the Gospel of Christ, which is the saving message of the Scriptures.

God is the God of truth. Through Moses He proclaims Himself as such. *A God of truth and without iniquity, just and right is He* (Deut. 32:4). And Jesus tells His disciples, *I am the way, the truth and the life: no man cometh unto the Father, but by Me* (John 14:6). The significance of these biblical statements and many others like them is explained by the fact that the biblical word for truth is *emunah*, which means *firmness, steadfastness, faithfulness*. God is the Truth, the Supreme Reality on which all other realities depend, the unshakable firmness which supports the universe which He has created, the unchangeable steadfastness, the ultimate faithfulness. Truth is an attribute of God, one of the aspects of His infinite and eternal Being. *His mercy is everlasting; and His truth endureth to all generations* (Psalm 100:5).

If God is truth, what then is probability, and how does probability differ from certainty? In answering these questions we must remember that God is infinite and that therefore not all aspects of His revelation of His truth are equally clear to our finite human minds. Regarding the revelation which God makes of His operations in the kingdom of nature this is obviously so. *Lo these are parts of His ways: but how little a portion is heard of Him? but the thunder of His power who can understand?* (Job. 26:14). And in the realm of spiritual things also, in the study of the Scriptures, our limited human intelligence loses itself in wonder at the depths of the divine knowledge. *O the depth of the riches both of the wisdom and knowledge of God! how unsearchable are His judgments, and His ways past finding out!* (Rom. 11:33).

According to the Bible therefore, the difference between probability and certainty can be defined in the following way: Certainty is our clear perception of God's clearly revealed truth, especially His revelation of Himself in nature, in the holy Scriptures, and in the Gospel of Christ. Probability, on the other hand, is our dimmer perception of God's less clearly revealed truth. In other words, God's clearly revealed truth suggests further truth less clearly revealed, and this suggests yet further truth still less clearly revealed, and so we go forward until at last we stand before the unrevealed truth, namely, the secret things of God (Deut. 29:29). Similarly, statistical probability is the truth suggested, in varying degrees of clarity, by the statistical regularity which God establishes in the world and maintains by His providence.

But what about error and falsehood? Where do they come from? The Bible teaches us that Satan, the father of lies, is the ultimate source of both these great evils (John 8:44). From the very beginning down to the present time Satan has spread his falsehoods far and wide by means of doubt, denial, and deception. By casting clouds of doubt upon God's clearly revealed truth he makes it seem only probable. For example, Satan said to Eve, *Yea, hath God said, Ye shall not eat of every tree of the garden?* (Gen. 3:1). Did God really say anything like this? Then from doubt Satan brings sinners farther to an open denial of God's truth. *Ye shall not surely die,* Satan assured Eve (Gen. 3:4). And having thus prepared the way, Satan completes his work of deception by suggesting a false alternative to take the place of the rejected truth. *For God doth know that in the day ye eat thereof, then your eyes shall be opened, and ye shall be as gods, knowing good and evil* (Gen. 3:5). By such false hypotheses and theories down through the ages Satan has ensnared the lost members of our fallen human race and made them his willing captives (2 Tim. 2:26).

By his deceits and stratagems Satan reigns over the minds and hearts of unbelieving sinners and over their civilization and culture. He is the *god of this world* (2 Cor. 4:4). Yet even here he does not hold undisputed sway. For the Bible teaches that the Holy Spirit exercises a restraining influence over the minds and hearts of sinful men which prevents their wickedness from attaining its full potential and thwarts the evil purposes of the devil. This influence of the Holy Spirit does not save sinners. It merely restrains their wickedness, often making them capable of an outward righteousness (Matt. 5:20). It is called *common grace* because it is bestowed upon all unbelieving sinners in common, both upon those who like Nicodemus later repent and believe (John 19:39) and upon those who like the rich, young ruler persist in unbelief and finally perish (Mark 10:22). To this common grace of the Holy Spirit is to be attributed all the relative truth and goodness that is to be found in unbelieving thought and life. When the Holy Spirit withdraws this restraining influence, public morality sinks to record lows, as in the days before the flood (Gen. 6:3), in the days of the Roman Empire (Rom.1:24), and also, it seems, today.

It is possible, therefore, and useful to make a distinction between Truth and facts. Truth is eternal. It is an attribute of God. Facts, on the other hand, are the temporal truths which God establishes by His works of creation and providence. Facts are revealed by God to men through their thought processes, and in the facts God reveals Himself. Because of common grace unbelievers are able to know many facts. Often their knowledge of the facts is much more extensive than that of most believers. But since unbelievers reject God's revelation of Himself in the facts, their knowledge of the facts is incomplete, and their thinking is full of fallacies and inconsistencies.

When a sinner repents and believes in Christ, he is lifted out of the realm of *common grace* into the realm of *saving grace*. The Holy Spirit no longer merely restrains his sin but progressively eradicates it. The converted sinner becomes a new creature in Christ and acquires a new way of looking at every question (2 Cor. 5:17). He no longer sees the truth as unbelievers do in disconnected flashes but as an organic whole which has its center in God's clear revelation of Himself in nature, in the holy Scriptures, and in the Gospel of Christ. Beginning at this central point, he strives to follow this divine truth out into every sphere of thought and then to communicate this truth to others. *Thou hast given a banner to them that fear Thee; that it may be displayed because of the truth* (Psalm 60:4).

(f) Christian Truth Versus Godless Economic Theory

Currently there is perhaps no area of human thought in which the application of Christian truth is more needed than in the realm of economics and sociology, for it is here that Satan today seems to be making his most deadly impact. It is fitting therefore that we conclude our history of unbelief with a few remarks in this field.

The modern science of economics is generally considered to have originated with the Scottish philosopher Adam Smith, who in 1776 published a book that won him lasting fame, entitled, *An Inquiry into the Nature and Causes of the Wealth of Nations*. In this treatise Smith contended that there are three factors on which the wealth of any nation depends, namely, labor, capital, and the law of supply and demand. The operation of these three factors should be left to the control of private individuals without any government interference or control. "All systems either of preference or of restraint, therefore, being thus completely taken away, the obvious and simple system of natural liberty establishes itself of its own accord. Every man, as long as he does not violate the laws of justice, is left perfectly free to pursue his own interest in his own way, and to bring both his industry and capital into competition with those of any other man, or order of men."[101] This principle of non-interference on the part of government has often been called the *laissez-faire* (hands-off) principle.

Adam Smith's famous book had far-reaching effects. For one thing, it transformed economics from a practical concern into an academic matter. Soon economics was taught in universities and written about in scholarly publications by theorists, many of them with little actual experience in commerce and industry. Then, as the years rolled by, these scholarly "economists" grew more ambitious. No longer content merely to teach and write but desiring to rule, they gravitated more and more toward socialism. Discarding Adam Smith's principle of *laissez-faire*, they founded organizations and political parties to work for state ownership and control of economic resources. One of the best known of these socialistic associations was organized in 1884 by a group of English radicals. Since their strategy was to bring about social changes gradually, they named themselves the Fabian Society after the ancient Roman general Fabius, who won a decisive victory through the policy of delay. Not less sinister, all through the later 19th century there lurked in the background the communist party of Marx, Engels, Bukharin, and Lenin, who developed Adam Smith's emphasis on the importance of labor into a program of world-wide revolution and world-wide governmental ownership and control allegedly for the benefit of the workers.

The catastrophic changes of World War I fanned all these smoldering embers into flames which reached our own country in 1933. Since that date the government of the United States has fallen increasingly under the domination of subversive elements (socialists, Fabians, communists) commonly called the "Liberal-left." With this Liberal-left at the helm, our American ship of state has met with disaster after disaster, especially in the international sphere. Since World War II communists have taken over Eastern Europe, China, Cuba, and parts of other regions such as Indochina, the Near East, Africa, and South America. More than one billion human beings have been enslaved. And when we come to armaments, the situation is still more frightful. In 1962 the United States had $2\frac{1}{2}$ to 10 times as much nuclear firepower as the Soviet Union.[102] In 1972, after the signing of the Salt I armament agreement in Moscow, Dr. Henry Kissinger acknowledged that the Soviets had a 3-to-1 advantage over the United States in explosive tonnage.[103] But the only response of the Liberal-left to this terrible danger has been to cancel the B-1 Bomber, delay production of the neutron bomb, and give away the Panama Canal.

For many years it has been evident that the long-term objective of the Liberal-left leaders is to bring about the surrender of the United States to the Soviet Union. This drastic step, they believe, is necessary in order to establish a World Government. In 1958 the U. S. Senate was thrown into furor by tidings of a book entitled "Strategic Surrender," which had been prepared by the Rand Corporation, the first and greatest of the federal government "think-factories," and distributed to the U. S. Air Force.[104] In 1961 a bulletin was prepared by the State Department proposing surrender of military power to a United Nations Peace Force.[105] This also was discussed in the Senate, but this time there was no furor. Instead the bulletin was defended by a liberal Senator as "the fixed, determined, and approved policy of the Government of the United States of America."[106]

In 1963 a study was made by a group of 60 scientists and engineers headed by Nobel-prize-winning physicist Eugene P. Wigner in the area of civil defense. The group proposed a tunnel grid system which for the price of $38 billion would provide all U. S. cities of over 250,000 population with protection against nuclear attack. Their report was submitted to the Defense Department and placed in storage.[107]   Similarly, on Feb. 9, 1967, the Joint Chiefs of Staff recommended a plan providing a thin anti-missile defense for the entire United States and added protection for the 50 largest cities.[108]   A bill endorsing this plan was passed by the Senate 86 to 2 on Mar. 21, 1967, but Defense Secretary McNamara said it would be too expensive ($4 billion a year for 10 years), and so nothing was done about it.[109] In 1969 appropriations were voted for two anti-missile sites, but only one was constructed, and even this was abandoned in 1975. In contrast, the Russians have a fully operative anti-missile system around Moscow. Most of their new factories are built away from large urban areas, and Russian society is now equipped to go underground at short notice, with immense shares of foodstocks buried. Missile sites also have been hardened to about 15 times the strength of those in the United States.[110]

If the projected "strategic surrender" of the United States to a Russian dominated United Nations actually takes place, Bible-believing Christians everywhere will be facing persecution and death, and the preaching of the Gospel will well nigh cease. Until Jesus comes, therefore, we must do our duty as Christian citizens. We must expose and oppose the evil program of the Liberal-left and work for the re-armament and security of our country. All available resources must be allocated to this end. Wasteful programs must be discontinued.

Does this mean that we are to return to the economic doctrines of Adam Smith? Not quite. For Smith was a skeptic, a friend of David Hume, and because he was a skeptic he failed to appreciate, or even to consider, the most important of all the causes of the wealth of nations, namely, the blessing of God and the influence of Christian Truth. *But seek ye first the kingdom of God and His righteousness; and all these things shall be added unto you* (Matt. 6:33). Even earthly interests prosper best under the sunlight of the Gospel. This is why even unbelievers, even those who reject the Saviour whom the Gospel proclaims, prefer to live in Christian countries rather than non-Christian countries and in Protestant countries rather than in Roman Catholic countries. And the testimony of history is to the same effect. The Near East, for example, was once the richest region in Christendom, but after the Mohammedan conquest it speedily became poverty stricken. At the time of the Reformation Spain and Italy were the most wealthy nations in Europe, while England was poor and Scotland barbarous. Then the Gospel came to Britain, and this relationship was reversed. And in all North and South America the only wealthy nation is our own United States, in which alone (with the exception of the Protestant provinces of Canada) the preaching of the Gospel has had free course.

While defending our country, therefore, we must not forget to defend the Bible, for this is still more basic. Honesty, moral purity, and trust in God are the foundations of national and personal prosperity, and these fundamentals are taught only in the holy Scriptures. *Two things have I required of Thee; deny me them not before I die: Remove far from me vanity and lies: give me neither poverty nor riches; feed me with food convenient for me* (Prov. 30:7-8). *But my God shall supply all your need according to His riches in glory by Christ Jesus* (Phil. 4:19).

(g) Victorious Faith! — The Difference Between Faith and Doubting

Jesus answered and said unto them, Verily I say unto you, If ye have faith and doubt not, ye shall not only do this which is done to the fig tree, but also if ye shall say to this mountain, Be thou removed, and be thou cast into the sea; it shall be done (Matt. 21:21). Here Jesus promises us that if we *have faith* and *doubt not,* even that great mountain of unbelief which now encompasses the earth shall fall before us. But how do we obtain this faith? How do we know whether we have it or not? How can we tell whether we are believing or doubting? What is the difference between faith and doubting? The Bible answers these questions in the eleventh chapter of Hebrews.

He that cometh to God must believe that He is, and that He is a rewarder of them that diligently seek Him (Heb. 11:6b). If I truly believe in God, then God is more real to me than anything else I know, more real even than my faith in Him. For if anything else is more real to me than God Himself, then I am not believing but doubting. I am real, my experiences are real, my faith is real, but God is more real. Otherwise I am not believing but doubting. I cast myself therefore on that which is most real, namely God Himself. I take God and Jesus Christ His Son as the starting point of all my thinking.

This is the victory that overcometh the world, even our faith (1 John 5:4). In the past true believers won great victories for God through their faith. *Who through faith subdued kingdoms, wrought righteousness, obtained promises, stopped the mouths of lions, quenched the violence of fire, escaped the edge of the sword, out of weakness were made strong, waxed valiant in fight, turned to flight the armies of aliens* (Heb. 11:33-34). Today we also can be victorious through faith if we *doubt not,* if we take God and His revelation of Himself in holy Scripture as the starting point of all our thinking. In science, in philosophy, in New Testament textual criticism, and in every other field of intellectual endeavor, our thinking must differ from the thinking of unbelievers. We must begin with God.

(For further discussion consult *Believing Bible Study,* pp. 2-3, 219-222.)

CHAPTER THREE

A SHORT HISTORY OF MODERNISM

There are many scholars today who claim to be orthodox Christians and yet insist that the New Testament text ought not to be studied from the believing point of view but from a neutral point of view.[1] The New Testament text, they maintain, ought to be treated just as the texts of other ancient books are treated. And in this they are followers of Westcott and Hort (1881), who still remain the best known advocates of this neutral principle.

In this present chapter we will endeavor to point out the error of this neutral, naturalistic New Testament textual criticism and to show how it has led to skepticism and modernism.

1. The Skeptical Tendency Of Naturalistic New Testament Textual Criticism

The following short history of New Testament textual criticism will show how the use of the naturalistic method leads inevitably to skepticism regarding the New Testament text.

(a) The Reformation Period — The Theological Approach to the New Testament Text

New Testament textual criticism cannot properly be said to have begun until the New Testament was first placed in print in 1516, one year before the commencement of the Protestant Reformation. Hence the first New Testament textual critics were editors such as Erasmus (1466-1536), printers such as Stephanus (1503-1559), and Reformers such as Calvin (1509-1564) and Beza (1519-1605). A study of Calvin's commentaries and the notes of Erasmus and Beza indicates that these 16th-century scholars had not worked out any clearly defined system of New Testament textual criticism. In this department of biblical study they were unmethodical, and some of their remarks concerning the New Testament canon and text reflect the humanistic culture in which they had been reared. But in their actual editing and printing of the New Testament they were guided by the common faith in the Received Text. For in their appeal to the New Testament against the errors of the papacy and the Roman Catholic doctrinal system these Reformers were not introducing a novelty but were falling back on a principle which long before the Reformation had been acknowledged by everyone. For centuries it had been commonly believed that the currently received New Testament text, primarily the Greek text and secondarily the Latin text, was the True New Testament Text which had been preserved by God's special providence. It was out of this common faith, therefore, that the printed

Textus Receptus was born through the editorial labors of Erasmus and his successors under the guiding hand of God. Hence during the Reformation Period the approach to the New Testament text was theological and governed by the common faith in holy Scripture, and for this reason even in those early days the textual criticism of the New Testament was different from the textual criticism of other ancient books.

(b) The Age of Rationalism — The Naturalistic Approach to the New Testament Text

After the commencement of the 17th century rationalists began to arise who laid aside the theological approach to the New Testament text and took up in its stead the naturalistic approach which makes no distinction between the text of the New Testament and that of a purely human book. Denying the common faith, they handled the New Testament text in a wholly secular way. One of the most famous of these rationalists was Hugo Grotius (1583-1645), celebrated Dutch statesman and theologian. In his *Annotations* (pub. 1641-50) Grotius made a number of conjectural emendations in the New Testament text,[2] a procedure which was then customary in the editing of ancient classical authors. And in 1658 Stephen Courcelles, professor at the Arminian College in Amsterdam, continued this trend by publishing an edition of the New Testament containing some of the conjectures of Grotius and also some of his own mixed indiscriminately with variant readings drawn from the New Testament manuscripts.[3] This action on Courcelles' part created alarm among orthodox Christians and awakened new interest in the problem of the New Testament text.

In 1675 John Fell, Dean of Christ Church and later Bishop of Oxford, suggested a new way of attacking this problem. In places in which the New Testament manuscripts differed from each other we should think of the scribes that copied the manuscripts rather than of the original apostolic authors. By noticing all the various ways in which these scribes made mistakes we would be able to detect false readings and thus finally arrive at the true reading by a process of elimination.[4] This suggestion was taken seriously by Gerhard von Maestricht, an official of the city of Bremen, who in 1711 published 43 rules for New Testament textual criticism most of which dealt with the mistakes scribes were likely to make.[5] And this shift of attention from the inspired authors of the New Testament to the uninspired scribes that copied it was another step toward a completely naturalistic New Testament textual criticism.

In 1720 Richard Bentley (1662-1742), famous Cambridge scholar, proposed a thoroughly naturalistic method of New Testament textual criticism. What he advocated was the rejection of the printed Greek New Testament text altogether and of the readings of the majority of the manuscripts and the construction of a new text by comparing the oldest Greek New Testament manuscripts with the oldest manuscripts of the Latin Vulgate. He believed that these ancient Greek and Latin manuscripts would agree very closely and that this close agreement would make it possible to recover the New Testament text in the form in which it existed at the time of the Council of Nicaea (325 A.D.).[6] He also believed that this method of textual criticism would improve the "barbarous" style of the existing New Testament text and "make it more worthy of a revelation."[7]

J. A. Bengel (1687-1752) was an orthodox German Lutheran except in the realm of New Testament textual criticism. Here like Bentley he inclined toward rationalism. He claimed to believe in the providential preservation of the Scriptures, but when he began to deal with the New Testament text he laid this doctrine on the shelf as an unworkable principle. "Concerning the care of the early Church for the purity of the manuscripts and concerning the fruits of this care, whatever is clearly taught must be eagerly and piously maintained. But it is certainly difficult to explain through what churches and ages this care extended, and whatever it was it did not keep from coming into existence those variant readings which circulate today and which are more easily removed when their origin is known."[8]

In his own textual criticism Bengel relied on Bentley's method of comparing various classes of manuscripts with each other.[9] Also he laid great stress on a rule which he himself had formulated: "The hard reading is to be preferred to the easy reading."[10] When there is a choice, Bengel argued, between a reading which is hard to understand and a reading which is easy to understand, the hard reading must be the genuine one, because the orthodox scribes always changed the hard readings to make them easy. Hence, according to Bengel, the orthodox Christians had corrupted their own New Testament text. This hypothesis amounted to a denial of the doctrine that God by His special providence had preserved the True Text down through the ages in the usage of believers. It is no wonder therefore that an outcry was raised against Bengel by conservative Christians in Germany.

(c) The Age of Enlightenment — The Skeptical Approach to the New Testament Text

The last half of the 18th century in Germany was the age of "enlightenment" in which rationalism was positively encouraged by Frederick II, the "philosopher king," who reigned over Prussia 46 years (1740-86). Under these conditions the skepticism inherent in the naturalistic method of New Testament textual criticism was clearly brought out.

Johann Semler (1725-91), professor at Halle, was the first textual critic to suggest that the New Testament manuscripts had been edited, not merely copied, by the ancient scribes.[11] He was bold also in some of his conjectures concerning the New Testament text. For example, he believed that chapter 9 of 2 Corinthians was a fragment inserted by the scribes in its present location and that chapter 16 of Romans was originally a letter to the Corinthians that got attached to Romans by mistake.[12] And in other respects also Semler revealed himself as one of the first modernists. He believed that both the Old and the New Testament canons had grown by degrees and that therefore the Scriptures were not inspired in the traditional sense. According to Semler, the teaching of Jesus and the Apostles contained Jewish conceptions of merely "local" and "temporal" value which it was the task of scientific exegesis to point out.[13]

J. J. Griesbach (1745-1812), pupil of Semler and professor at Jena, early declared himself a skeptic regarding the New Testament text. In 1771 he wrote, "The New Testament abounds in more glosses, additions, and interpolations purposely introduced than any other book."[14] And during his long career there is no indication that he ever changed this view. He was noted for his critical editions of the New Testament and for the comprehensive way in which he worked out a classification of the New Testament manuscripts into three "rescensions" or ancestral groups.[15] He also developed the thought implicit in Bengel's rule, "The hard reading is to be preferred to the easy reading." Like Bengel he interpreted this rule to mean that the orthodox Christians had corrupted their own New Testament text.[16] According to Griesbach, whenever the New Testament manuscripts varied from each other, the orthodox readings were to be ruled out at once as spurious. "The most suspicious reading of all," Griesbach wrote, "is the one that yields a sense favorable to the nourishment of piety (especially monastic piety)." And to this he added another directive: "When there are many variant readings in one place, that reading which more than the others manifestly favors the dogmas of the orthodox is deservedly regarded as suspicious."

Griesbach's skepticism was shared by J. L. Hug (1765-1846), who in 1808 advanced the theory that in the 2nd century the New Testament text had become deeply degenerate and corrupt and that all the extant New Testament texts were merely editorial revisions of this corrupted text.[17] And Carl Lachmann (1793-1851) continued in this same skeptical vein. He believed that from the extant manuscripts it was not possible to construct a text which would reach any farther back than the 4th century. To bridge the gap between this reconstructed 4th-century text and the original text Lachmann proposed to resort to conjectural emendation. In 1831 he published an edition of the Greek New Testament which reflected his views.[18]

(d) Westcott and Hort — The Light That Failed

In the 1860's manuscripts *Aleph* and *B* were made available to scholars through the labors of Tregelles and Tischendorf, and in 1881 Westcott and Hort[19] published their celebrated *Introduction* in which they endeavored to settle the New Testament text on the basis of this new information. They propounded the theory that the original

New Testament text has survived in almost perfect condition in these two manuscripts, especially in *B*. This theory attained almost immediately a tremendous popularity, being accepted everywhere both by liberals and conservatives. Liberals liked it because it represented the latest thing in the science of New Testament textual criticism. Conservatives liked it because it seemed to grant them that security for which they were seeking. But since this security had no foundation in faith, it has not proved lasting. For in the working out of their theory Westcott and Hort followed an essentially naturalistic method. Indeed, they prided themselves on treating the text of the New Testament as they would that of any other book, making little or nothing of inspiration and providence. "For ourselves," Hort wrote, "we dare not introduce considerations which could not reasonably be applied to other ancient texts, supposing them to have documentary attestation of equal amount, variety, and antiquity."[20]

Soon Westcott and Hort's theory began to lose its hold in the liberal and radical camp. In 1899 Burkitt[21] revived Hug's theory that all extant texts are editorial revisions of a lost primitive text, a position later adopted by Streeter[22] and other noted textual critics. The skepticism of Griesbach and other early critics was also revived, and with a vengeance. As early as 1908 Rendel Harris declared that the New Testament text had not at all been settled but was "more than ever, and perhaps finally, unsettled."[23] Two years later Conybeare gave it as his opinion that "the ultimate (New Testament) text, if there ever was one that deserves to be so called, is for ever irrecoverable."[24] And in 1941 Kirsopp Lake, after a lifetime spent in the study of the New Testament text, delivered the following judgment: "In spite of the claims of Westcott and Hort and of von Soden, we do not know the original form of the Gospels, and it is quite likely that we never shall."[25]

Westcott and Hort professed to "venerate" the name of Griesbach "above that of every other textual critic of the New Testament."[26] Like Griesbach they believed that the orthodox Christian scribes had altered the New Testament manuscripts in the interests of orthodoxy. Hence like Griesbach they ruled out in advance any possibility of the providential preservation of the New Testament text through the usage of believers. But at the same time they were very zealous to deny that heretics had made any intentional changes in the New Testament text. "It will not be out of place," they wrote, "to add here a distinct expression cf our belief that even among the numerous unquestionably spurious readings of the New Testament there are no signs of deliberate falsification of the text for dogmatic purposes."[27] The effect of this one-sided theory was to condemn the text found in the majority of the New Testament manuscripts and exonerate that of *B* and *Aleph*. This evident partiality, however, did not appeal to Rendel Harris (1926), who condemned all the manuscripts, including *B* and *Aleph*. All of them, he asserted, were "actually reeking" with "dogmatic falsifications."[28]

As the 20th century progressed, other distinguished scholars grew more and more skeptical. In 1937, for example, F. G. Kenyon revived Griesbach's contention that the text of the New Testament had not been as accurately preserved as the texts of other ancient books. "The textual history of the New Testament," Kenyon wrote, "differs materially from that of other ancient books. The works of classical literature were produced in peaceful conditions. They were copied by professional scribes. . . . They were not exposed to deliberate destruction, at any rate, until, after many centuries, the Christian Church made war on pagan literature. The textual tradition which has come down to us is probably that of the great libraries, where good copies were preserved under the eyes of men of letters. . . . In all these respects the fortunes of the Christian Scriptures were different. In the earliest days the Christians were a poor community, who would seldom have been able to command the services of professional scribes. There were no recognized centres for the promulgation of authorized copies of the Scriptures. . . . Then there was always the danger of destruction. . . . So long as Christianity was at best tolerated and at worst persecuted, the transcription and circulation of the Scriptures were exposed to difficulties from which the pagan literature was free."[29]

(e) New Testament Textual Criticism Since World War II

Since World War II there has been little change of attitude on the part of naturalistic New Testament textual critics. As far as the recovery of the original New Testament text is concerned, pessimism is the order of the day. As G. Zuntz (1953) remarks, "the optimism of the earlier editors has given way to that scepticism which inclines towards regarding 'the original text' as an unattainable mirage."[30] H. Greeven (1960) also has acknowledged the uncertainty of the naturalistic method of New Testament textual criticism. "In general," he says, "the whole thing is limited to probability judgments; the original text of the New Testament, according to its nature, must be and remain a hypothesis."[31] And R. M. Grant (1963) expresses himself still more despairingly. "The primary goal of New Testament textual study," he tells us, "remains the recovery of what the New Testament writers wrote. We have already suggested that to achieve this goal is well nigh impossible."[32] Nor is K. W. Clark (1966) more hopeful. "Great progress has been achieved," he says, "in recovering an early form of text, but it may be doubted that there is evidence of one original text to be recovered."[33] And according to K. Aland (1970), the early New Testament text is "strongly" characterized by variations.[34]

2. Naturalistic Textual Criticism And Modernism

Does naturalistic textual criticism breed modernism? Let us review briefly the history of modernistic Bible study and draw our own conclusions.

(a) The Beginning of Modernism — The Denial of the Biblical Miracles

Modernism may fittingly be said to have begun with the deists, a group of "free-thinkers" who were active during the early part of the 18th century in England, where they founded the Masonic Lodge. They taught that all religions are equally true since all of them, including Christianity, are merely republications of the original religion of nature. Reason, the deists insisted, and not the Bible is the supreme authority, since it is to human reason that the original religion of nature is most clearly revealed. And with this naturalistic outlook it is not surprising that some of the deists denied the reality of the miracles of the Bible. One of those that did so was Thomas Woolston (1669-1731), who ridiculed Christ's miracles and even the biblical account of Christ's resurrection. For this he was convicted of blasphemy and fined one hundred pounds. Being unable to pay, he spent the last four years of his life in prison.[35]

One hundred years later the German rationalists found a less offensive way of denying the miracles of Christ. These miracles, they asserted, were actual events which took place according to the laws of nature. The disciples, however, thought that these remarkable occurrences were miracles because they were ignorant of these natural laws. H. E. G. Paulus (1761-1851), theological professor at Heidelberg, was especially active in devising a naturalistic explanation for each one of the miracles of Christ. Jesus' walking on the water, Paulus explained, was an illusion of the disciples. Actually Jesus was walking on the shore and in the mist was taken for a ghost. In the feeding of the five thousand Jesus and His disciples simply set a good example of sharing which was followed by others, and soon there was food enough for everybody. According to Paulus, Christ's resurrection took place because He did not really die upon the cross but merely swooned. The coolness of the tomb revived Him, and when an earthquake had rolled away the stone at the door of the tomb, He stripped off His grave clothes and put on a gardener's garment which He had managed to procure.[36]

These rationalistic explanations of the miracle-narratives in the Gospels were vigorously attacked by David Strauss (1808-74), who published his famous *Life of Jesus* in 1835. Strauss maintained that in these narratives the miracles are the main thing, the thing for which all the rest exists. Hence the rationalists were absurd in their contention that these narratives had grown up out of utterly trivial events on which a supernaturalistic interpretation had been wrongly placed. On the contrary, Strauss argued, all attempts to find a kernel of historical truth in these narratives must be given up. The miracle-narratives, he insisted, were simply myths. They were popular expressions of certain religious ideas which had been awakened in the minds of early Christians by the impact of Jesus' life.[37]

(b) The Rejection of John's Gospel — The Tuebingen School

After the publication of Strauss' *Life of Jesus* the Gospel of John rapidly lost status in the opinion of naturalistic critics. Soon it was regarded as of little historical value, as a mere collection of unauthentic discourses put in the mouth of Jesus for theological purposes. The leader in this devaluation of the Gospel of John was F. C. Baur (1792-1860), professor at Tuebingen and founder of the "Tuebingen School" of New Testament criticism. According to the Tuebingen School, Matthew and Revelation represented a primitive Jewish gospel; Luke and the four principal Epistles of Paul (Romans, 1 and 2 Corinthians, and Galatians) represented a Pauline gospel; and the rest of the New Testament books, especially the Gospel of John, represented a compromise between these two conflicting tendencies in the early Church. And in order to give time for these doctrinal developments Baur maintained that the Gospel of John had not been written until 170 A.D.[38]

Baur's late date for the writing of the Gospel of John was soon found to be contrary to the evidence. The study of Church history revealed no such doctrinal conflict as Baur's theory required. Also the discovery of Tatian's Gospel Harmony in 1888 and of certain papyrus manuscripts in the 1930's and 1950's all indicated that the Gospel of John must have been written before 100 A.D. Naturalistic critics have long since conceded this, but in spite of this admission they have persisted still in denying that John's Gospel gives us a true picture of the historical Jesus and have supported this denial by various hypotheses.

Because of their zeal for episcopal government and the doctrine of apostolic succession many liberal scholars of the Church of England were reluctant to surrender completely the apostolic authorship of John's Gospel. J. A. Robinson (1902) dean of Westminster, was one of this sort. According to Robinson, the Apostle John wrote his Gospel when he was a very old man, so old that he could no longer distinguish fact from fiction. John's memory had so failed him, Robinson argued, that he confused the authentic words and deeds of Jesus with his own reveries and visions.[39] But could the Christ of John's Gospel have been invented by a doting old man? Is it not easier to believe John's own account of the matter, namely, that the Holy Spirit enabled him to remember Christ's words and to reproduce them accurately (John 14:26)?

The most common hypothesis, however, among naturalistic critics is that the Gospel of John was written not by the Apostle John but by another John called the Elder John, who lived at Ephesus at the end of the first century A. D. and who also wrote the Epistles of John. This would make the Gospel of John a forgery, since it claims to have been written by the disciple whom Jesus loved (John 21:24), that intimate follower who beheld Christ's glory (John 1:14), who leaned on His bosom (John 13:23), and who viewed with wondering eye the blood and water flowing down from His riven side (John 19:35). B. H. Streeter (1924) endeavored to soften the harshness of this consequence by speaking of the Elder John as a mystic, a prophet and a genius,[40] but these efforts at palliation are in vain. The fact still remains that in the verses cited and also in others, such as John 14:26, John's Gospel claims to have been written by a member of the apostolic band and that this would be a false claim if this Gospel had been written by the Elder John rather than the Apostle John. Is it possible that this book of the Bible, which more than any other lays the emphasis on truth, is a forgery? Is such brazen hypocrisy to be looked for in the Gospel of John? Does this paradox which the naturalistic critics would thrust upon us make sense?

Moreover, the evidence even for the existence of an Elder John distinct from the Apostle John is very slender, consisting only of a single reference in the *Church History* of Eusebius (323). In the third book of this *History* Eusebius quotes a statement of an older writer, namely, Papias (d. 160), bishop of Hierapolis. "If anyone ever came," Papias relates, "who had followed the elders, I inquired into the words of the elders, what Andrew or Peter or Philip or Thomas or James or John or Matthew, or any other of the Lord's disciples, had said, and what Aristion and the elder John, the Lord's disciples, were saying."[41]

Eusebius claimed that here Papias was mentioning two different Johns, placing the first John with the Apostles and assigning the second John a place outside the apostolic band by coupling his name with that of Aristion. But in interpreting Papias in this way Eusebius had an axe to grind. He disliked Revelation and was loath to admit that this last book of the Bible had been written by the Apostle John. His discovery of two Johns in this statement of Papias enabled him to suggest that Revelation had been written by Elder John and hence was not truly apostolic. Actually, however, there seems to be no good reason for finding more than one John in this excerpt from Papias. Because the Apostle John had outlived all the other Apostles Papias mentioned him twice, first among the Apostles as one that had spoken and second among the next generation as one that was still speaking at the time he was making his inquiries.

Critics used to believe that the Gospel of John had been written to present Christianity to the Greeks, but since the discovery of the Dead Sea Scrolls in 1947 efforts have been made to connect John's Gospel with the Jewish Sectarians at Qumran, where the scrolls were found. According to R. M. Grant (1963), this Gospel was written about 70 A.D. by a Jerusalem disciple of Jesus for the purpose of presenting Christianity to Jews of this sort.[42] But there is no evidence of any kind that this Jerusalem disciple ever lived. How then could this mighty genius have disappeared so completely from the pages of history? Why would the author of so renowned a Gospel have been forgotten so utterly by the Christian Church?

Is it not better to believe that the beloved disciple who wrote the Gospel of John was the Apostle John, the son of Zebedee? Is not this what the Gospel narrative implies? Is not this the unanimous testimony of the early ecclesiastical writers? What if the Gospel of John differs from the other three Gospels not in presenting a different Jesus but only in presenting a different facet of the infinitely complex character of the Son of God?

(c) The Synoptic Problem — The Two-Document Theory

Since the early 19th century it has been customary to call the first three Gospels (Matthew, Mark and Luke) by a common name, *Synoptic Gospels,* in order to distinguish them from the Gospel of John. This name seems to have been suggested by Griesbach's first edition of the Greek New Testament in which these three Gospels were printed as a *synopsis* in parallel columns. When these Gospels are arranged in this way, the question of their mutual relationship immediately presents itself. How are we to explain the large measure of agreement which exists between these three Gospels not only in content and wording but even in the order in which the subject matter is arranged. The problem of finding an answer to this question is called the "Synoptic problem."

There are three solutions of the Synoptic problem which have found acceptance with scholars. In the first place, there have been those who have believed that Matthew was written first and that Mark and Luke were copied, at least in part, from Matthew. This hypothesis was favored by Griesbach (1783), Hug (1808), and other early 19th century scholars.[43] It is also the official Roman Catholic position, having been decreed by the Pontifical Biblical Commission in 1912.[44]

A second hypothesis, once popular but now abandoned, was that the Synoptic Gospels were written independently of one another but were based on a common oral tradition derived from the Apostles. This view was advocated in Germany by Gieseler (1818)[45] and widely held in England in the mid-19th century, where it was zealously maintained by Alford (1849),[46] Westcott (1860),[47] and other well known scholars.

There is a third hypothesis, however, which for many years has been regarded by most scholars as the correct solution of the Synoptic problem. This is the "two-document" theory which was first promulgated in Germany by C. H. Weisse (1838).[48] According to this hypothesis, the authors of Matthew and Luke made common use of two documents. The first of these was the Gospel of Mark and the second a document usually referred to as *Q* which contained the sayings of Jesus. The common use which the authors of Matthew and Luke made of Mark accounts for the agreement of these two Gospels with each other in passages in which they both agree with Mark, and the common use which these same authors made of Q accounts for the agreement of their Gospels with each other in passages which are not found in Mark.   B. H. Streeter's *The Four Gospels* (1924) is probably still the best presentation of the two-document theory in English.   Indeed Kirsopp Lake (1937)[49] regarded it as the best treatment of the subject in any language.   In this volume Streeter not only defended the two-document hypothesis but went on to expand it into a theory involving several other documentary sources.

The tendency of the two-document theory is obviously to deny the apostolic authorship of the Gospels.   For it is impossible to believe that the Apostle Matthew would have relied on two documents written by others for his information concerning the life of Jesus and not on his own memory of his personal experience with his Lord.   And it is almost equally difficult to suppose that Luke, the disciple and companion of the Apostle Paul, actually preferred to base his Gospel on information gathered up and written down by another rather than on that which he himself had obtained by personal contact with those who had walked and talked with Jesus.   And, finally, the two-document theory is unfavorable also to the traditional view that the Gospel of Mark was written by a personal disciple of Peter.   For if this Gospel had the authority of Peter behind it, it is hard to see how the authors of the other two Synoptic Gospels could have felt at liberty to revise it as drastically as they did, according to the two-document theory.

But the two-document theory is not invulnerable.   B. C. Butler (1951) proved this in his treatise on *The Originality of St. Matthew*.[50] In this volume Butler attacked with admirable clarity certain of the weak spots in Streeter's exposition of the two-document hypothesis. For example, Streeter was driven by the exigencies of his theory to believe that Mark and Q sometimes "overlapped," that is, contained divergent accounts of the same incident or saying.   In these instances of "overlapping," Streeter believed, Luke followed Q, but Matthew "conflated" Mark and Q, that is, pieced them together in a very intricate and laborious manner.   And in the same way Matthew "conflated" Mark with another source M whenever these two documents "overlapped."   Streeter never gave any motive for this curious action on Matthew's part, and in regard to it Butler rightly remarks, "Such a mode of procedure on St. Matthew's part is not indeed impossible. But it is so improbable, that one may be forgiven for asking whether there is no other more satisfactory explanation of the data."[51]   And in regard to another passage Butler observes that Streeter's hypothesis that Matthew "conflated" Mark and Q attributes to the Evangelist "a virtuosity as superhuman as it would be futile."[52]

Unfortunately, however, Butler's own solution of the Synoptic problem was scarcely satisfactory.   According to Butler's hypothesis, Matthew wrote his Gospel in Aramaic during those early years of the Christian Church in which he and the other Apostles were still dwelling together in Palestine.   Matthew's Aramaic Gospel was welcomed by his fellow Apostles and used by them to refresh their memories concerning Jesus' life and teachings. Later, after the Christian mission and movement had begun to take root in Greek-speaking towns and regions, Matthew made a translation of his Aramaic Gospel into Greek. This translation also was welcomed by the other Apostles and used as an aid in their apostolic preaching. When Peter, in his old age, was at Rome, he had with him a copy of this Greek Matthew. When Mark interviewed Peter to gather material for a second Gospel, Peter did not trust his memory but read to Mark selected passages from Matthew's Greek Gospel, making changes here and there. This is why Mark agrees very closely with Matthew in some places and differs in others.[53]

The preceding brief review shows the impossibility of solving the Synoptic problem on a naturalistic basis. The two supposedly underlying documents grow quickly to six or seven, and in addition there are conflations, translations, and editings. This problem can be solved only in a believing way. In dealing with the Gospel writers the fundamental emphasis must be on the inspiration of the Holy Spirit under which they wrote. It is this inspiration that binds the Synoptic Gospels together and is responsible for their agreements and their differences. Whether Matthew, Mark and Luke made use of a common oral tradition or whether they were familiar with one another's writings are interesting questions but not of vital importance. Certainly the Apostles and Evangelists had no need of written documents to refresh their memories of Jesus' words and works. The Holy Spirit brought these matters to their recall in accordance with the promise of the Saviour. *He shall teach you all things, and bring all things to your remembrance, whatsoever I have said unto you* (John 14:26).

(d) Old Testament Higher Criticism — Moses Versus J, E, D and P

The so-called "higher" criticism of the Old Testament began in 1753 with the publication of a treatise written by Jean Astruc, a French physician. In this work Astruc maintained that Moses had used sources in composing the book of Genesis. His argument for this conclusion was founded mainly on the first two chapters of Genesis, in which two distinct accounts of the creation of the world and of man are given. In the first chapter the name *Elohim* is used for God, in the second the name *Jehovah* (often translated *LORD*). According to Astruc, these facts indicated that Moses had used two distinct documents as sources when he wrote the book of Genesis.[54]

Later this same theory was developed more thoroughly in Germany by Eichhorn (1780), Vater (1802), De Wette (1806), Bleek (1822), Ewald (1823), and others. Source analysis was applied to all five books of the Pentateuch, and the conclusion was reached that these books were not written by Moses at all but by three other ancient authors, namely: (1) the *Elohist* (E), who wrote Genesis 1 and the other passages in which God is given the name *Elohim;* (2) *the Jehovist* (J), who wrote Genesis 2 and the other passages in which God is given the name *Jehovah;* (3) the *Deuteronomist* (D), who wrote the book of Deuteronomy. And in addition there was the *Redactor* (R), that is to say, the editor, who, according to the critics, put the documents E and J together long after the death of Moses.[55]

In 1853 Hupfeld divided the E document into two parts, namely, the *first Elohist,* who wrote Genesis 1, and the *second Elohist,* who wrote some of the later portions of the E document.[56] Then in 1865 Graf revolutionized Old Testament higher criticism with his hypothesis that Genesis 1 and the other passages that Hupfeld had assigned to the *first Elohist* had actually been written by priestly writers after the Babylonian Exile and then added to the Pentateuch by a priestly redactor (editor) about 445 B.C. In accordance with Graf's hypothesis these passages were labelled P (*priestly*) and were regarded as the latest rather than the earliest portions of Scripture. In other words, according to Graf and his supporters, the creation account of Genesis 1 was a late development in Jewish thought and one of the last sections to be added to the Old Testament.[57]

But these critics could not substantiate their theory. This inability was demonstrated by conservative scholars of the period and notably by William Henry Green of Princeton Seminary. "The critics," Dr. Green (1895) observed, "are obliged to play fast and loose with the text in a manner and to a degree which renders all their reasoning precarious."[58] The following are a few of the examples which Dr. Green gives of this precarious reasoning.

"Elohim occurs inconveniently for the critics in Gen. 7:9; hence Kautzsch claims that it must have been originally Jehovah, while Dillmann insists that vss. 8-9 were inserted by R (the redactor). The critics wish to make it appear that two accounts of the flood, by P and J respectively, have been blended in the existing text; and that vss. 7-9 is J's account and vss. 13-16 that by P. But unfortunately for them, this is blocked by the occurrence in each one of the verses assigned to J of expressions foreign to J and peculiar to P; and to cap the climax, the divine name is not J's but P's. The repetition cannot, therefore, be wrested into an indication of a duplicate narrative, but simply, as its language clearly shows, emphasizes the fact that the entry into the ark was made on the self-same day that the flood began.

" 'And Jehovah shut him in' (Gen. 7:16b) occurs in the midst of a P paragraph; hence it is alleged that this solitary clause has been inserted from a supposed parallel narrative by J. But this overlooks the significant and evidently intended contrast of the two divine names in this verse, a significance to which Delitzsch calls attention, thus discrediting the basis of the critical analysis which he nevertheless accepts. Animals of every species went into the ark, as Elohim, the God of creation and providence, directed, mindful of the preservation of what He had made; Jehovah, the guardian of His people, shut Noah in.

"Isaac's blessing of Jacob (Gen. 27:27-28) is torn asunder because Jehovah in the first sentence is followed by Elohim in the second. "So Jacob's dream, in which he beholds the angels of Elohim (Gen. 28:12) and Jehovah (Gen. 28:13)" is also torn asunder; "although his waking (Gen. 28:16) from the sleep into which he had fallen (Gen. 28:11-12) shows that these cannot be parted. Jacob's vow (Gen. 28:20-21) is arbitrarily amended by striking out 'then shall Jehovah be my God,' because of his previous mention of Elohim when referring to His general providential benefits.

"The story of the birth of Leah's first four sons (Gen. 29:31-35) and that of the fifth and sixth (Gen. 30:17-20) are traced to different documents notwithstanding their manifest connection, because Jehovah occurs in the former and Elohim in the latter.

"The battle with Amalek (Ex. 17:8-13) is assigned to E because of Elohim (Ex. 17:9); but the direction to record it, the commemorative altar, and the oath of perpetual hostility to Amalek (Ex. 17:14-16), which stand in a most intimate relation to it, are held to be from another document because of Jehovah."[59]

(e) Wellhausen's Reconstruction of the History of Israel

In 1878 Julius Wellhausen published his famous *Prolegomena to the History of Ancient Israel*.[60] This was a complete reconstruction of Old Testament history in agreement with Graf's hypothesis, which accordingly was renamed the Graf-Wellhausen hypothesis. The history of Israel, Wellhausen maintained, began at Mt. Sinai, where Moses persuaded the Israelites to adopt Yahweh (Jehovah) as their tribal god. Ever afterwards they felt themselves to be Yahweh's people, and this feeling gave them a sense of national unity. But Moses gave them no laws. These were developed later after they had settled in the land of Canaan. This primitive legal code was transmitted orally until about 850 B.C. Then it was written down and incorporated in the J narrative and is now found in Exodus 20-23.[61]

Around 750 B.C., according to Wellhausen, a tremendous transformation of the religious thinking of ancient Israel began to take place. Mighty, prophetic reformers arose, such as Amos, Hosea and the first Isaiah, who publicly proclaimed that Yahweh was not a tribal deity but a righteous God who ruled all nations and would punish them for their sins, who would chastise even Israel.[62] This reform movement finally culminated in an exciting event which occurred about 621 B.C. Hilkiah the high priest found in the Temple the book of the law, which had been lost. This book was brought to king Josiah, who accepted it as genuine and called an assembly of the people in which he and the whole nation made a solemn covenant before Yahweh to keep all the commandments written in this book. This action, Wellhausen asserted, marked the entrance of the covenant-concept into Jewish thought. The covenant which Josiah made with Yahweh came to be regarded as typical. Ever after the Jews thought of themselves as Yahweh's covenant people. According to Wellhausen, however, the book that produced this profound effect was not an ancient book, as Josiah was led to believe, but the book of Deuteronomy, which had been written only a short time before by the leaders of the reform movement and placed in the Temple for the express purpose of being "discovered."[63] How Josiah and the people could have been so easily deceived the critics do not say.

And what about the biblical data that contradict Wellhausen's hypothesis? What about those passages which indicate that the book of Deuteronomy was known and obeyed in the days of Joshua and Samuel? In Deuteronomy the Israelites were forbidden to offer up sacrifices in any other location than the place which God should choose for this purpose (Deut. 12:13-14). Accordingly, in Joshua 22:10-34 we find the majority of the people zealous to obey this commandment and ready to punish with the sword those who seemed to have violated it. Also in 1 Samuel, chapters 1 and 2, we find this Deuteronomic law in operation, with pious Israelites coming up every year to offer sacrifices at the Tabernacle in Shiloh. Solomon also, in his prayer of dedication, emphasized that the Temple was that single worship center which had been chosen for the nation by God (1 Kings 8:16). And throughout the sacred history even pious kings are censured for permitting sacrifices to be offered at the high places rather than in the Temple. Do not these facts prove that the book of Deuteronomy was in existence and known from the time of Moses onward?

Wellhausen had a ready answer to this question. These passages, he maintained, were the inventions of later authors and editors who desired to give the false impression that Deuteronomy had been written by Moses and had always been known in Israel.[64] And to prove his thesis Wellhausen pointed to other passages which, in his opinion, demonstrated that Deuteronomy with its commandment to sacrifice at one national worship-center was not known until the time of Josiah. According to Wellhausen, these passages indicated that Gideon, Manoah, Samuel, Saul, Elijah and Elisha all sacrificed wherever they pleased without any thought of a divinely appointed worship-center.[65] It was to put an end to this chaotic state of affairs, Wellhausen argued, and to centralize divine worship at the Temple at Jerusalem that the leaders of the reform movement wrote the book of Deuteronomy and persuaded king Josiah to accept it as a genuine writing of Moses.

In other words, according to Wellhausen, after these Deuteronomic reformers had perpetrated their pious fraud, they and their successors made false entries in the sacred records in order to cover their tracks. But at the same time they were so stupid as to leave untouched all those passages by means of which Wellhausen and other 19th century higher critics were able at last to expose their trickery. Surely this is an incredible paradox rather than a reasonable explanation of the biblical data.

According to the Graf-Wellhausen hypothesis, the Levitical laws of sacrifice and of ceremonial holiness were developed during the

Babylonian exile by Ezekiel and other captive priests, and it was out of these formulations that the present book of Leviticus was put together after the exile by writers of the priestly school (P).[66] Here we have another unconvincing paradox. All during the time in which the glorious Temple of Solomon was standing, with the Ark of God inside it and all the sacred furniture, the priests, according to the critics, had no book of ceremonial law to guide them. Then after the Ark had disappeared, the Temple had been burnt, and the people had been carried away to a foreign land, the complicated ritual of Leviticus was formulated for the first time. How very strange!

But if we recognize Moses as the author of the Pentateuch, the fantastic conjectures of the Graf-Wellhausen hypothesis give way to more balanced views concerning the sacrificial laws of ancient Israel. The first such law of sacrifice was revealed to Moses by God (Exodus 20:23-26) immediately after the giving of the Ten Commandments. Instead of images of gold and silver the Israelites were commanded to erect unto Jehovah an altar of earth and unhewn stone. This divine injunction was placed at the beginning of the Book of the Covenant, which Moses wrote soon after and read to the people and which the people promised to obey. It was the basic law of sacrifice. Later, after the Tabernacle was erected, God modified it so as to place the duty of sacrificing into the hands of the priests whom He had appointed for this purpose. This transfer Moses recorded in the book of Leviticus. Finally, in the book of Deuteronomy Moses instructed the people regarding the national worship-center which God would establish at some future time in the promised land. These modifications were usually in force, but on special occasions and in times of chaos and confusion the law of sacrifice reverted to the original form in which it was first revealed to Moses at Mt. Sinai. For this reason the sacrifices of Gideon, Manoah, Samuel, Saul, Elijah and Elisha were acceptable to God even though they were not offered in the Tabernacle or the Temple.

(f) Modern Archeological Discoveries — Barthianism

Although naturalistic Old Testament scholars still subscribe to the Graf-Wellhausen hypothesis, modern archeological discoveries have greatly weakened this critical reconstruction of Old Testament history. Beginning in the 1920's, a series of investigations in this field has shown that the Old Testament narratives are a good deal more accurate than was once thought possible.[67] This accuracy is hard to explain on the basis of Wellhausen's theory that these stories were transmitted orally until they were finally committed to writing about 850 B.C. Moreover, it has been demonstrated that writing was in common use long before the days of Moses.[68] There is no reason, therefore, on that score why Moses and other ancient Hebrews could not have written books. And, most important of all, Wellhausen's contention that the Israelites worshiped a tribal god has been challenged by the facts, since no instances of this tribal-god concept have been found in the religions of the ancient Orient.[69]

But if the ancient Israelites did not worship a tribal god, what did they worship? In 1933 Walther Eichrodt appealed to Karl Barth's theology for an answer to this question,[70] and since that time many other scholars have done the same. Shifting the covenant-concept back from the reign of Josiah to the time of Moses, these Barthians assert that on Mt. Sinai Moses organized the children of Israel into a covenant community. The Old Testament is the witness of this community to the mighty acts of God, which began with the deliverance from Egyptian bondage. But according to these Barthian critics, it is impossible to tell what these acts of God really were because it is impossible to separate an act of God from the response of the community to that act.[71]

But what does all this mean historically? Were the ancient Israelites Barthians? If not, what was their status, religiously speaking? The critics have no firm answer to this question. According to Albright (1946), Moses was a monotheist.[72] But since 1955 it has been generally maintained that the Sinai covenant was modeled after the treaties of the ancient Hittite kings,[73] and this would imply, it seems, that the ancient Israelites were polytheists after all. If so, when did they become monotheists? Actually, however, the resemblance of these Hittite treaties to the Sinaitic covenant seems very slight. And the theory itself seems very improbable. For if the Israelites were such admirers of these Hittite treaty formulas, why did they not reproduce them in other Old Testament passages also? Why only in Exodus?

If, therefore, we desire to learn the true meaning of the Sinaitic covenant, we must turn neither to the Hittites nor to the Barthian theology nor to the Graf-Wellhausen hypothesis but to the Scriptures as the infallible Word and especially to the New Testament. There we find that at Sinai God introduced His holy Law as a school master to bring His people to Christ (Gal. 3:24).

(g) The Account of Moses' Death — Who Wrote It?

If Moses wrote the Pentateuch, who wrote the account of Moses' death (Deut. 34:1-12)? Many conservative scholars say that it was added by an inspired scribe, but this is an entirely unnecessary hypothesis. If an inspired scribe was needed to write of Moses' death and burial, events which no man witnessed, why couldn't Moses have been that scribe? Why couldn't he have been inspired to write of his own death beforehand? And in regard to the other objections which even before the advent of Old Testament higher criticism were raised by Spinoza (1670), Simon (1685), and LeClerc (1685), a similar answer may be returned. As Witsius (1692), the learned Hebraist, proved long ago, none of the verses pointed out by these 17th century rationalists can be demonstrated decisively to be of post-Mosaic origin.

None of them necessarily implies that the author was looking back from a position in time later than that of Moses.[74]

(h) Jesus and the Critics

Jesus named Moses explicitly as the author of the Pentateuch. *Did not Moses give you the Law?*, He asked the Jews (John 7:19). And again, remonstrating with these hardened unbelievers, He protested, *Had ye believed Moses, ye would have believed Me; for He wrote of Me* (John 5:46). Also in His controversy with the Saducees Jesus calls Exodus the book of Moses (Mark 12:26). And similarly Jesus recognized Moses, not P and D, as the author of Leviticus (Matt. 8:4) and Deuteronomy (Mark 10:5). Hence it is not surprising that critics who have adopted naturalistic views concerning the Pentateuch and the other Old Testament books have also adopted naturalistic views concerning Jesus, charging Him either with deceit or with ignorance and error. Let us now consider some of these views.

(1) *The Aristocratic Jesus.* Spinoza and LeClerc and other 17th-century rationalists assumed an aristocratic attitude in matters of religion. Although they thought themselves to have progressed to a higher state of knowledge, they deemed it best for the common people to continue in the religions in which they had been reared and to cultivate piety and a peaceful and quiet life. And they attributed to Jesus this same aristocratic tolerance of the errors of the masses. "It will be said, perhaps," LeClerc argued, "that Jesus Christ and the Apostles often quote the Pentateuch under the name of Moses, and that their authority should be of greater weight than all our conjectures. But Jesus Christ and the Apostles not having come into the world to teach the Jews criticism, we must not be surprised if they speak in accordance with the common opinion. It was of little consequence to them whether it was Moses or another, provided the history was true; and as the common opinion was not prejudicial to piety, they took no great pains to disabuse the Jews."[75] But to this notion Witsius well replied that if our Lord and His Apostles were not teachers of criticism, at any rate, they were teachers of truth.[76] As teachers of truth they could not have accommodated their doctrine to the errors of their time.

(2) *The Kenotic Jesus.* During the 19th century there were certain theologians and critics who adopted a *kenotic* view of Jesus. They believed that the incarnation of Jesus Christ, the Son of God, took place by means of a *kenosis*, which is the Greek word for *emptying*. At the incarnation, they maintained, Jesus Christ emptied Himself of His divine nature and became entirely human. They based this view on Phil. 2:7, where we are told that Christ *made Himself of no reputation* (literally, *emptied Himself*). In England one of the most prominent advocates of this *kenotic* interpretation of the incarnation of Christ was Charles Gore (1891), later bishop of Oxford. In his Bampton Lectures Gore argued that while on earth Christ had so far

divested Himself of His divine omniscience that He participated not only in human ignorance but also in human error. According to Gore, "our Lord actually committed Himself to an error of fact in regard to the authorship of the 110th Psalm." In matters of Old Testament higher criticism, Gore contended, Jesus chose to be ignorant and mistaken. This, Gore maintained, was part of the *kenosis*, the divine self-emptying of Christ's incarnation.[77]

But if Jesus was so mistaken concerning the Old Testament, how can we trust Him in regard to other matters ? Praise God, then, that the *kenotic* view of Christ's incarnation is not true! While on earth Christ veiled His divine glory, but He did not put it off. This is the true meaning of Phil. 2:7. Christ could not lay aside His Godhead, for His deity is unchangeable.

(3) *The Prophetic Jesus.* During the latter part of the 19th century most naturalistic scholars regarded Jesus as merely a great prophet or moral teacher. One of the best known advocates of this point of view was Adolf Harnack, famous professor of Church History at the University of Berlin. In his lectures on the *Essence of Christianity* (1900) Harnack grouped the teaching of Jesus under three heads: "Firstly, the kingdom of God and its coming. Secondly, God the Father and the infinite value of the human soul. Thirdly, the higher righteousness and the commandment of love."[78] According to Harnack, Jesus' chief concern was to preach the Fatherhood of God. The Gospel, Harnack declared, is "the Fatherhood of God applied to the whole of life."[79]

This, then, was one of the chief reasons why the 19th-century liberals were so eager to find the solution of their Synoptic problem. They believed that if only they could trace the Synoptic Gospels back to their sources they would recover the historical Jesus. They would see Jesus, they thought, as He really was, as merely a very great prophet and moral teacher and not as the divine Son of God that the early Christian Church had depicted Him as being. Such were the expectations of these naturalistic scholars, but their hopes were quickly disappointed. Even the earliest of the supposed sources were found to be theological documents. Even in Mark and Q Jesus appears as a supernatural Person, the Christ of God. William Wrede, a radical German scholar, was one of the first to point this out irrefutably in his celebrated treatise, *The Messianic Secret* (1901).[80] From the standpoint of unbelief this result was very strange, but from the standpoint of Christian faith it was just what might have been anticipated.

(4) *The Apocalyptic Jesus.* In his famous book, *The Quest of the Historical Jesus* (1906), Albert Schweitzer presented Jesus as one whose life was dominated by the prophecy of Daniel and especially by the expression *Son of Man* (Dan. 7:13). According to Schweitzer, Jesus' ministry lasted only one year. All during that year Jesus was expecting that the Kingdom of God would come in a supernatural manner and that He would be revealed as the Messiah,

the heavenly Son of Man. When he sent the twelve disciples out to preach, He thought that this supernatural event would occur before they returned, but He was disappointed in this hope. Finally, He became convinced that in order to bring this present world to an end and to usher in a new supernatural world it would be necessary for Him to die first. With this purpose in mind He went up to Jerusalem at Passover time and was crucified.[81] But in spite of this disaster, so Schweitzer maintained, a "mighty spiritual force" streamed forth from Jesus and became "the solid foundation of Christianity."[82] How could this have been so if Jesus had been the deluded fanatic that Schweitzer depicted Him as being?

(5) *The Kerygmatic Jesus.* Since World War I, and especially since World War II, the *kerygmatic* view of Jesus' life has increasingly dominated the theological scene. According to this view, the Jesus of the Synoptic Gospels is the product of the preaching (*kerygma*) of the Christian community. Early Christian preachers, it is said, used anecdotes of Jesus' life and sayings attributed to Him to drive home the points they were endeavoring to make. Later these anecdotes and sayings were compiled by editors, and from these compilations the Synoptic Gospels were produced. But by the method of *Form-criticism* (Formgeschichte) it is thought possible to analyze these Gospel narratives into their supposedly original fragments. This method, which was used in the study of German folklore, was applied to the New Testament immediately after World War I by K. L. Schmidt, M. Dibelius and R. Bultmann and widely adopted during the inter-war period.[83] And since World War II Form-criticism has thrived greatly, under the leadership of Bultmann and also of younger scholars such as E. Kaesemann, G. Bornkamm and H. Conzelmann.[84]

Since World War II the Form-critics have devoted much attention to the "Son of Man problem." This problem deals with the use of the title *Son of Man* and with the origin and meaning of this designation. In the Synoptic Gospels the Son of Man is spoken of in three ways: (1) as coming, e.g. Mark 13:26; (2) as suffering death and rising again, e.g. Mark 10:33-34; (3) as now at work, e.g. Mark 2:10.[85] What is the basic meaning of this term, and why is it used in these three distinct senses? Did Jesus ever speak of the Son of Man, and if so, did He apply this title to Himself? Many Form-critics answer this last question in the negative. Jesus, they insist, never claimed to be the Son of Man, never even used this expression, some of them add. It was the primitive Christian community, they assert, that introduced this designation, first speaking of Jesus as the coming Son of Man and then extending the term to include Jesus' death and resurrection and the deeds of His earthly ministry.[86] But if Jesus owes the title Son of Man to the usage of the primitive Christian community, why is it that all traces of this popular usage have vanished? Why is it that in the New Testament, with but few exceptions, the expression *Son of Man* is found only on the lips of Jesus? Form-critics confess that they have not been able to solve this problem.[87]

The solution of the "Son of Man problem" is found only in the fact of the incarnation. The term *Son of Man* was Jesus' own way of referring to His human nature as distinguished from His divine nature, to Himself as perfect Man, in which capacity He was active in the deeds of His earthly ministry, suffered and died and rose again, and shall appear in glory at the last day.

Perhaps more than any other group of naturalistic scholars the Form-critics are apt to go to extremes, especially in their attempts to bypass the Apostles and discover the origin of Christianity in the "Christian community." Contrary to the Book of Acts and the unanimous testimony of ancient ecclesiastical writers, they represent the Apostles as receiving instruction from the Christian community rather than founding the Christian community upon their doctrine. This is particularly the case with the Apostle Paul. Although Paul solemnly certified that the gospel which he preached was "not after man" nor "received of man" (Gal. 1:11-12), the Form-critics do not hesitate to contradict him and derive his doctrine from the Christian community. They maintain, for example, that some of Paul's most important doctrinal statements concerning the Person and work of Christ (Rom. 1:3-4; 4:25; Eph. 2:14-16; Phil. 2:6-11; Col. 1:15-20; 1 Tim. 3:16) were quotations from certain Christological hymns which had been composed by the Christian community.[88] In these passages therefore, according to the Form-critics, Paul was not teaching the Christian community anything but merely rehearsing to the community what he had learned from it. But who were these unknown hymn makers of the Christian community who were able to mold the thinking of the Apostle Paul? How could these profound theological geniuses have remained anonymous?

According to Conzelmann (1969), the Christian community was assembled "through the appearances of the Risen One and the preaching of the witnesses to these appearances!"[89] Are we to conclude from this, then, that Jesus' resurrection is a historical event? To this question Conzelmann gives a disappointing answer. A historian, he asserts, cannot prove that Jesus really rose from the dead but only that the disciples believed that Jesus did so.[90] But why did the disciples believe this? To this question the Form-critics merely give the Barthian answer that the disciples chose to believe so. "The Church had to surmount the scandal of the cross," Bultmann tells us, "and did it in the Easter faith."[91] But why did the disciples choose to believe that Jesus rose from the dead? Because He really did so and *shewed Himself* to them *alive after His passion by many infallible proofs* (Acts 1:3). This is the simple answer of the Bible which Form-critics decline to accept but to which they can find no convincing alternative.

3. Naturalistic Textual Criticism And Apologetics

In the preceding pages it has been proved historically that the logic of naturalistic textual criticism leads to complete modernism, to a naturalistic view not only of the biblical text but also of the Bible as a whole and of the Christian faith. For if it is right to ignore the providential preservation of the Scriptures in the study of the New Testament text, why isn't it right to go farther in the same direction? Why isn't it right to ignore other divine aspects of the Bible? Why isn't it right to ignore the divine inspiration of the Scriptures when discussing the authenticity of the Gospel of John or the Synoptic problem or the authorship of the Pentateuch? And why isn't it right to ignore the doctrines of the Trinity and of the incarnation when dealing with the messianic consciousness of Jesus and the Son of Man problem?

Impelled by this remorseless logic, many an erstwhile conservative Bible student has become entirely modernistic in his thinking. But he does not acknowledge that he has departed from the Christian faith. For from his point of view he has not. He has merely traveled farther down the same path which he began to tread when first he studied naturalistic textual criticism of the Westcott and Hort type, perhaps at some conservative theological seminary. From his point of view his orthodox former professors are curiously inconsistent. They use the naturalistic method in the area of New Testament textual criticism and then drop it most illogically, like something too hot to handle, when they come to other departments of biblical study.

(a) Naturalistic Apologetics — The Fallacy of the Neutral Starting Point

This inconsistency in regard to the textual criticism of the Bible and especially of the New Testament has historical roots which reach back three hundred years to the late 17th century. At that time the deists and other unbelievers came up with a novel suggestion. "Let us not," they proposed, "begin our thinking by assuming the truth of Christianity. Let us rather take as our starting point only those truths on which Protestants, Catholics, Jews, Mohammedans, and all good men of every religion and creed agree. Then, standing on this neutral platform of common agreement, let us test all religions and creeds by the light of reason."

Instead of rejecting this proposal as fundamentally unchristian, orthodox Protestant scholars accepted the challenge and during the 18th century developed various apologetic arguments, armed with which they endeavored to meet the unbelievers on their own chosen ground and, fighting in this neutral arena, to demonstrate the truth of historic Christianity and the error of infidelity. Unhappily, however, these orthodox champions did not realize that they had been out-maneuvered and that by the very act of adopting a neutral starting point they had already denied the faith that they intended to defend and had ensured that any argument that they might thereafter advance would be inconsistent.

(b) The Butler-Paley Apologetic System

Joseph Butler (1692-1752) and William Paley (1743-1805) were the two authors of the neutral apologetic system which in many conservative theological seminaries during the 19th and early 20th centuries was taught side by side with the older Reformation faith without any due recognition of the basic difference between these two approaches to Christianity, the one beginning with *reason,* the common truths on which all good men agree, the other beginning with *revelation,* the divine truth on which all men, good or bad, *ought* to agree.

Butler, who later became bishop of Durham, published his famous *Analogy of Religion* in 1736. This book dealt with the *analogy* (similarity) existing between the Christian religion and the facts of nature, as they were known to the science of Butler's day. The book was divided into two parts, the first part dealing with "natural religion," i.e., religious truths revealed in nature as well as in the Bible, and the second part dealing with "revealed religion," i.e., religious truths revealed only in the Bible. The purpose of the book was to show deists and other unbelievers that the same difficulties which they found in the doctrines of Christianity were found also in the facts of nature. Hence Christianity, Butler contended, was, at the very least, just as probable as deism or any other form of unbelief. Therefore it was only prudent to accept Christianity at least on a probability basis, for probability, Butler reminded his readers, was "the very guide of life."[92]   It is said, however, that on his death bed Butler came to recognize that Christianity cannot be received as a probability but only as the truth and that he died triumphantly repeating John 6:37.

Paley, archdeacon of Carlisle, published his *Evidences of Christianity* in 1794. In it he refuted the objections of the deists and of skeptics such as David Hume to the historicity of the miracles of Jesus. "There is satisfactory evidence," he contended, "that many professing to be original witnesses of Christian miracles, passed their lives in labors, dangers, and sufferings, voluntarily undergone in attestation of the accounts which they delivered, and solely in consequence of their belief of those accounts; and that they also submitted, from the same motives, to new rules of conduct." In other words, the sufferings which Jesus' disciples endured and their changed lives were proofs that the miracles to which they bore witness, actually occurred. And to this argument Paley added another, namely, the uniqueness of Jesus. Jesus was not an "enthusiast" or an "impostor," as others were who claimed to be Messiahs, but remained "absolutely original and singular." This uniqueness proved that Jesus was truly the Christ He claimed to be.[93]

No less famous was Paley's *Natural Theology*, published in 1802. In it Paley compared the universe to a watch. If in crossing a field we should find a watch, the intricate machinery of which it was composed would soon convince us that it had not existed from all eternity but had been constructed by a watchmaker. So the much more intricate machinery of the physical world and especially of the bodies of animals and men should convince us that the whole universe has been created by an all-wise God. In discoursing upon this theme Paley exhibited a very considerable knowledge of anatomy and used it to refute the theory of evolution, which in his day was just beginning to raise its head.[94]

Throughout the 19th century annotated editions of these works of Butler and Paley were used as textbooks in the colleges and theological seminaries of Great Britain and America and served as models for later apologetic writings. But although the Butler-Paley apologetic system accomplished much immediate good, in the long run its effect was detrimental to the Christian faith because it presented Christianity as merely a probability and not as the truth. Also it made the starting point of Christian thought dependent on the whims of unbelievers, since, according to the Butler-Paley system, we build our defense of the Christian faith upon the truths on which all men agree. And, finally, the Butler-Paley apologetic system, by its emphasis on probability and on a common starting point with unbelievers, encouraged orthodox Christians to think that they must deal with the text of holy Scripture in the same way in which unbelievers deal with it. Hence the Butler-Paley apologetic system contributed greatly to the spread of naturalistic textual criticism in orthodox Christian circles.

(c) The Need for a Consistently Christian Apologetic System

Today, therefore, there is great need for a consistently Christian apologetic system, for a defense of the Christian faith which takes as its starting point not the facts on which all men agree but the supreme fact on which all men *ought* to agree, namely, God's revelation of Himself in nature, in the holy Scriptures, and in the Gospel of Christ, the saving message of the Scriptures.

God reveals *Himself*, not mere doctrines concerning Himself, but HIMSELF. The Biblical doctrine of salvation reminds us that this is indeed a fact. I am saved by trusting in Jesus personally. But how can I believe in Jesus Christ as a Person unless He first reveal Himself? In the Gospel, therefore, Jesus Christ reveals Himself to me as the triune Saviour God, and not to me only but to all sinners everywhere. And God reveals Himself not only in the Gospel but also in the whole of Scripture as the faithful Covenant God and likewise in this great universe which His hands have made as the almighty Creator God.

This divine revelation is the starting point of a consistently

Christian apologetic system. Taking our stand upon it, we point out the inconsistencies of unbelieving thought and then show how these difficulties can be resolved by a return to God's revealed Truth.

(d) How to Take Our Stand — Through the Logic of Faith

How do we take our stand upon divine revelation? Only in one way, namely, through the logic of faith.

For God so loved the world, that He gave His only begotten Son, that whosoever believeth in Him should not perish, but have everlasting life (John 3:16). Since this Gospel is true, these conclusions logically follow: *First,* the Bible is God's infallibly inspired Word. This must be so, because if our salvation depends on our believing in Christ, then surely God must have left us an infallible record telling us who Jesus Christ is and how we may believe in Him truly and savingly. *Second,* the Bible has been preserved down through the ages by God's special providence. This also must be so, because if God has inspired the holy Scriptures infallibly, then surely He has not left their survival to chance but has preserved them providentially down through the centuries. *Third,* the text found in the majority of the biblical manuscripts is the providentially preserved text. This too must be true, because if God has preserved the Scriptures down through the ages for the salvation of men and the edification and comfort of His Church, then He must have preserved them not secretly in holes and caves but in a public way in the usage of His Church. Hence the text found in the majority of the biblical manuscripts is the true, providentially preserved text. *Fourth,* The providential preservation of the Scriptures did not cease with the invention of printing. For why would God's special, providential care be operative at one time and not at another time, before the invention of printing but not after it? Hence the first printed texts of the Old and New Testament Scriptures were published under the guidance of God's special providence.

Thus when we believe in Christ, the logic of our faith leads us to the true text of holy Scripture, namely, the Masoretic Hebrew text, the Textus Receptus, and the King James Version and other faithful translations. It is on this text, therefore, that we take our stand and endeavor to build a consistently Christian apologetic system.

(For further details regarding the logic of faith consult *Believing Bible Study,* pp. 55-66.)

CHAPTER FOUR

A CHRISTIAN VIEW OF THE BIBLICAL TEXT

In the Bible God reveals Himself in three ways: *First,* He reveals Himself as the God of creation, the almighty Creator God. In revealing Himself in this way God not only repeats the revelation which He has already made of Himself in nature but also amplifies this revelation and makes it clearer. Hence the Scriptures are the God-given eyeglasses which correct our faulty spiritual vision and enable our sin-darkened minds to see aright the revelation which God makes of Himself in the world which He has created. *Second,* God reveals Himself as the God of history, the faithful Covenant God. In the Bible God gives a full account of His dealings with men by way of covenant. *Third,* God reveals Himself as the God of salvation. In the Gospel of Christ He offers Himself to sinners as the triune Saviour God.

But even this is not all that God does for sinners. In addition to revelation there is regeneration. Because of Adam's first transgression all men are sinners (Rom. 5:19). They hate God (Rom. 8:7) and reject His revelation of Himself as foolishness (1 Cor. 2:14). Therefore when God saves sinners, He regenerates them through the power of the Holy Spirit. He raises them up out of their death in sin and gives them the gift of faith (Eph. 2:1,8). Through the Spirit they are born again (John 3:5). They are saved through the renewing of the Holy Ghost (Titus 3:5). They believe in God as He reveals Himself in the holy Bible and trust their souls to Jesus Christ His Son.

When the Holy Spirit gives us the gift of faith, we immediately receive from God three benefits of Christ's redeeming grace. The first of these is *justification.* We are justified by faith (Rom. 3:28). When we believe in Christ His death is reckoned ours (Gal. 2:20), and we receive the gift of His righteousness (2 Cor. 5:21). The second is *adoption.* By faith we become the children of God (John 1:12) and joint heirs with Jesus Christ (Rom. 8:17). The third is *sanctification.* God begins to work within us by His Holy Spirit to will and to do of His good pleasure (Phil. 2:13) and to make us more and more like Christ our Lord (Eph. 4:13).

We are saved by faith! This is a mystery which we cannot fully understand, but it means that there are three things which we can and must do to obtain these benefits which Christ purchased by His atoning sacrifice and to know that we have been born again. In the first place, we must *repent.* Saving faith is a repentant faith. Jesus Christ Himself commands us to repent of our sins and believe the Gospel (Mark 1:15). In the second place, we must *receive* Christ as our only Lord and Saviour (John 1:12). How do we do this? By believing that He died for us upon the cross. *He loved me and gave Himself for me*

(Gal. 2:20). And in the third place, having so received Christ, we must *rest* in Him as He bids us do (Matt. 11:28). When we thus rest in Christ, then we have assurance of faith. Then we know that we have truly received Him as Lord and Saviour.

Does this mean that our assurance comes from ourselves? Do we create our own assurance by our own will power, by our own repenting, receiving, and resting? Not at all! For if our assurance depended on ourselves, we would always be in doubt. We would never know certainly whether we were saved or not. We would never be sure that we had really repented or that we had actually received Christ and were truly resting in Him. Our assurance therefore comes from God. As we continue to trust in Christ, the Holy Spirit bears witness in our hearts that we are truly God's children. *The Spirit itself beareth witness with our spirit, that we are the children of God* (Rom. 8:16).

But how does the Holy Spirit testify to us that we are God's children? Does He do this in some private way apart from Scripture? Not at all! For this would dishonor the Scriptures. Then everyone would be seeking these private revelations of the Spirit and ignoring the revelation which He has given once for all in the holy Bible. The Holy Spirit therefore bears witness not apart from the Word but by and with the Word. He guides believers in their study of the Scriptures, and as He guides them, He persuades them that this blessed Book is truly God's Word and leads them more and more to trust the Saviour who reveals Himself in it. *But the anointing which ye have received of Him abideth in you, and ye need not that any man teach you: but as the same anointing teacheth you of all things, and is truth, and is no lie, and even as it hath taught you, ye shall abide in Him* (1 John 2:27).

1. The Principles Of Believing Bible Study

Three principles of believing Bible study are included in this conviction which we receive from the Holy Spirit that the Bible is truly God's Word. These are as follows: *first*, the infallible inspiration of the Scriptures; *second*, the eternal origin of the Scriptures; *third*, the providential preservation of the Scriptures.

(a) The Infallible Inspiration of the Scriptures

The Holy Spirit persuades us to adopt the same view of the Scriptures that Jesus believed and taught during the days of His earthly ministry. Jesus denied explicitly the theories of the higher critics. He recognized Moses (Mark 12:26), David (Luke 20:42), and Daniel (Matt. 24:15) by name as the authors of the writings assigned to them by the Old Testament believers. Moreover, according to Jesus, all these individual Old Testament writings combined together to form one divine and infallible Book which He called "the Scriptures." Jesus believed that these Scriptures were inspired by the Holy Spirit (Mark 12:36), that not one word of them could be denied (John 10:35), that not one particle of them could perish (Matt. 5:18), and that everything written in them was divinely authoritative (Matt. 4:4, 7, 10).

This same high view of the Old Testament Scriptures was held and taught by Christ's Apostles. *All Scripture,* Paul tells us, *is given by inspiration of God* (2 Tim. 3:16). And Peter adds, *No prophecy of the Scripture is of any private interpretation. For prophecy came not in old time by the will of man: but holy men of God spake as they were moved by the Holy Ghost* (2 Peter 1:20-21). The Scriptures were the living oracles through which God spoke (Acts. 7:38), which had been committed to the Jews for safekeeping (Rom. 3:2), which contained the principles of divine knowledge (Heb. 5:12), and according to which Christians were to pattern their own speech (1 Peter 4:11). To the Apostles, "It is written," was equivalent to, "God says."

Jesus also promised that the New Testament would be infallibly inspired just as the Old had been. *I have yet many things to say unto you,* He told His Apostles, *but ye cannot bear them now. Howbeit when He, the Spirit of truth, is come, He will guide you into all truth: for He shall not speak of Himself; but whatsoever He shall hear, that shall He speak: and He will shew you things to come* (John 16:12-13). The Holy Spirit, Jesus pledged, would enable the Apostles to remember their Lord's teaching and understand its meaning (John 14:26). And these promises began to be fulfilled on the day of Pentecost when Peter was inspired to declare for the first time the meaning of Christ's death and resurrection (Acts 2:14-36). Paul also was conscious of this same divine inspiration. *If any man think himself to be a prophet, or spiritual, let him acknowledge that the things that I write unto you are the commandments of the Lord* (1 Cor. 14:37). And in the last chapter of Revelation John the Apostle asserts the actuality of his inspiration in the strongest possible terms (Rev. 22:18-19).

Jesus, therefore, and His Apostles regarded both the Old and the New Testaments as the infallibly inspired Word of God, and the Holy Spirit, bearing witness in our hearts, assures us that this view was not mistaken.

(b) The Eternal Origin of the Scriptures

When He was on earth Jesus constantly affirmed that His message was eternal, that the very words which He spoke had been given to Him by God the Father before the creation of the world. *For I have not spoken of Myself,* He told the unbelieving multitude, *but the Father which sent Me, He gave Me a commandment, what I should say, and what I should speak. And I know that His commandment is life everlasting: whatsoever I speak therefore, even as the Father said unto Me, so I speak* (John 12:49-50). And in His "high-priestly" prayer Jesus also states emphatically that the words which He had spoken to His Apostles had been given to Him in eternity by God the Father. *For I have given unto them the words which Thou gavest Me* (John 17:8). The Scriptures, therefore, are eternal. When God established His-Covenant of Grace in eternity, He gave to Jesus Christ His Son *the words of eternal life* (John 6:68). These are the words that Christ brought down from heaven for the salvation of His people and now remain inscribed in holy Writ.

The Scriptures are eternal. Does this mean that there is an eternal Bible in heaven, or that the Hebrew and Greek languages in which the Bible is written are eternal? No, but it does mean that Jesus Christ, the divine Word, worked providentially to develop the Hebrew and Greek tongues into fit vehicles for the conveyance of His saving message. Hence in the writing of the Scriptures the Holy Spirit did not have to struggle, as modernists insist, with the limitations of human language. The languages in which the writing was done were perfectly adapted to the expression of His divine thoughts.

For ever, O LORD, Thy Word is settled in heaven (Ps. 119:89). Although the Scriptures were written during a definite historical period, they are not the product of that period but of the eternal plan of God. When God designed the holy Scriptures in eternity, He had the whole sweep of human history in view. Hence the Scriptures are forever relevant. Their message can never be outgrown. *The grass withereth, the flower fadeth: but the Word of our God shall stand for ever* (Isa. 40:8). In the Scriptures God speaks to every age, including our own. *For whatsoever things were written aforetime were written for our learning, that we through patience and comfort of the Scriptures might have hope* (Rom. 15:4).

(c) The Providential Preservation of the Scriptures

Because the Scriptures are forever relevant, they have been preserved down through the ages by God's special providence. The reality of this providential preservation of the Scriptures was proclaimed by the Lord Himself during His life on earth. *Till heaven and earth pass, one jot or one tittle shall in no wise pass from the law, till all be fulfilled* (Matt. 5:18). *And it is easier for heaven and earth to pass, than one tittle of the law to fail* (Luke 16:17). Here our Lord assures us that the Old Testament text in common use among the Jews during His earthly ministry was an absolutely trustworthy reproduction of the original text written by Moses and the other inspired authors. Nothing had been lost from that text, and nothing ever would be lost. It would be easier for heaven and earth to pass than for such a loss to take place.

Jesus also taught that the same divine providence which had preserved the Old Testament would preserve the New Testament too.

In the concluding verses of the Gospel of Matthew we find His "Great Commission" not only to the twelve Apostles but also to His Church throughout all ages, *go ye therefore and teach all nations.* Implied in this solemn charge is the promise that through the working of God's providence the Church will always be kept in possession of an infallible record of Jesus' words and works. And, similarly, in His discourse on the last things He assures His disciples that His promises not only shall certainly be fulfilled but also shall remain available for the comfort of His people during that troubled period which shall precede His second coming. In other words, that they shall be preserved until that time. *Heaven and earth shall pass away, but My words shall not pass away* (Matt. 24:35; Mark 13:31; Luke 21:33).

2. How The Old Testament Text Was Preserved

In discussing the providential preservation of the holy Scriptures we must notice first a very important principle which accounts for the difference between Old Testament textual criticism and New Testament textual criticism. The Old Testament Church was under the care of the divinely appointed Aaronic priesthood, and for this reason the Holy Spirit preserved the Old Testament through this priesthood and the scholars that grouped themselves around it. The Holy Spirit guided these priests and scholars to gather the separate parts of the Old Testament into one Old Testament canon and to maintain the purity of the Old Testament text. In the New Testament Church, on the other hand, this special priesthood has been abolished through the sacrifice of Christ. Every believer is a priest before God, and for this reason the Holy Spirit has preserved the New Testament text not through any special priesthood but through the *universal priesthood of believers,* that is, through the usage of God's people, the rank and file of all those that truly trust in Christ.

With this distinction in mind let us consider briefly the history of the Old Testament text and then pass on to a discussion of the problems of New Testament textual criticism.

(a) How the Priests Preserved the Old Testament Text

The Hebrew Scriptures were written by Moses and the prophets and other inspired men to whom God had given prophetic gifts. But the duty of preserving this written revelation was assigned not to the prophets but to the *priests.* The priests were the divinely appointed guardians and teachers of the law. *And it came to pass, when Moses had made an end of writing the words of this law in a book, until they were finished, that Moses commanded the Levites, which bare the ark of the covenant of the LORD, saying, Take this book of the law, and put it in the side of the ark of the covenant of the LORD your God, that it may be there for a witness against thee* (Deut.

31:24-26). Thus the law "was placed in the charge of the priests to be kept by them along side of the most sacred vessel of the sanctuary, and in its innermost and holiest apartment."[1] Also the priests were commanded, as part of their teaching function, to read the law to the people every seven years (Deut. 31:12). Evidently also the priests were given the task of making correct copies of the law for the use of kings and rulers, or at least of supervising the scribes to whom the king would delegate this work (Deut. 17:18).

Not only the Law of Moses but also the Psalms were preserved in the Temple by the priests, and it was probably the priests who divided the Hebrew psalter into five books corresponding to the five books of Moses. It was David, the sweet singer of Israel who taught the priests to sing psalms as part of their public worship service (1 Chron. 15:16,17). Like David, Heman, Asaph and Ethan were not only singers but also inspired authors, and some of the psalms were written by them. We are told that the priests sang these psalms on various joyful occasions, such as the dedication of the Temple by Solomon (2 Chron. 7:6), the coronation of Joash (2 Chron. 23:18), and the cleansing of the Temple by Hezekiah (2 Chron. 29:30).

How the other Old Testament books were preserved during the reigns of the kings of Israel and Judah we are not told explicitly, but it is likely that the books of Solomon were collected together and carefully kept at Jerusalem. Some of Solomon's proverbs, we are told, were copied out by *the men of Hezekiah king of Judah* (Prov. 25:1).

Except for periodic revivals under godly rulers, such as Asa, Jehoshaphat, Hezekiah, and Josiah, the days of the kings were times of apostasy and spiritual darkness in which the priests neglected almost entirely their God-given task of guarding and teaching God's holy law. This had been the case during the reigns of the ungodly rulers who had preceded the good king Asa. *Now for a long season Israel hath been without the true God, and without a teaching priest and without law* (2 Chron. 15:3). And during the reign of Manasseh the original copy of the Law had been mislaid and was not found again until Josiah's time (2 Kings 22:8). Because the priests were thus unfaithful in their office as teachers, Jerusalem was finally destroyed, and the Jews were carried away captive to Babylon (Mic. 3:11-12). But in spite of everything, God was still watching over His holy Word and preserving it by His special providence. Thus when Daniel and Ezekiel and other true believers were led away to Babylon, they took with them copies of all the Old Testament Scriptures which had been written up to that time.

(b) The Traditional (Masoretic) Hebrew Text of the Old Testament

After the Jews returned from the Babylonian exile, there was a great revival among the priesthood through the power of the Holy Spirit. *Not by might nor by power, but by my Spirit, saith the LORD of hosts* (Zech. 4:6). The Law was taught again in Jerusalem by Ezra the priest who *had prepared his heart to seek the law of the LORD, and to do it, and to teach in Israel statutes and judgments* (Ezra 7:10). By Ezra and his successors, under the guidance of the Holy Spirit, all the Old Testament books were gathered together into one Old Testament canon, and their texts were purged of errors and preserved until the days of our Lord's earthly ministry. By that time the Old Testament text was so firmly established that even the Jews' rejection of Christ could not disturb it. Unbelieving Jewish scribes transmitted this traditional Hebrew Old Testament text, blindly but faithfully, until the dawn of the Protestant Reformation. As Augustine said long ago, these Jewish scribes were the librarians of the Christian Church.[2] In the providence of God they took care of the Hebrew Old Testament Scriptures until at length the time was ripe for Christians to make general use of them.

According to G. F. Moore (1927), the earliest of these scribes were called *Tannaim* (Teachers). These scribes not only copied the text of the Old Testament with great accuracy but also committed to writing their oral tradition, called *Mishna*. These were followed by another group of scribes called *Amoraim* (Expositors). These were the scholars who in addition to their work as copyists of the Old Testament also produced the Talmud, which is a commentary on the Mishna.[3]

The Amoraim were followed in the sixth century by the *Masoretes* (Traditionalists) to whom the Masoretic (Traditional) Old Testament text is due. These Masoretes took extraordinary pains to transmit without error the Old Testament text which they had received from their predecessors. Many complicated safeguards against scribal slips were devised, such as counting the number of times each letter of the alphabet occurs in each book. Also critical material previously perpetuated only by oral instruction was put into writing. It is generally believed that vowel points and other written signs to aid in pronunciation were introduced into the text by the Masoretes.[4]

It was this Traditional (Masoretic) text which was printed at the end of the medieval period. The first portion of the Hebrew Old Testament ever to issue from the press was the Psalms in 1477. In 1488 the entire Hebrew Bible was printed for the first time. A second edition was printed in 1491 and a third in 1494. This third edition was used by Luther in translating the Old Testament into German. Other faithful Protestant translations followed, including in due time the King James Version. Thus it was that the Hebrew Old Testament text, divinely inspired and providentially preserved, was restored to the Church, to the circle of true believers.[5]

(c) The Greek Old Testament (Septuagint)

Although the unbelief of the Jews and their consequent hostility deprived the Church for a time of the Hebrew Old Testament and of the benefits of Hebrew scholarship, still the providence of God did not permit that the Old Testament Scriptures should ever be taken away wholly from His believing people. Even before the coming of Christ God had brought into being the Septuagint, the Greek Old Testament translation which was to serve the Church as a temporary substitute until such a time as the ancient Hebrew Bible could be restored to her. According to tradition, this translation was made at Alexandria for the library of Ptolemy Philadelphus, king of Egypt, by a delegation of seventy Jewish elders, hence the name *Septuagint* (Seventy). According to Irwin (1949), however, and other modern scholars, the Septuagint was not produced in any such official way but arose out of the needs of the Alexandrian Jews.[6] The Pentateuch, it is said, was translated first in the 3rd century B. C., the other Old Testament books following later. From Alexandria the use of the Septuagint rapidly spread until in the days of the Apostles it was read everywhere in the synagogues of the Greek-speaking Jews outside of Palestine. Then, at length, converts from these Greek-speaking synagogues brought their Septuagint with them into the Christian Church.

When one studies the Old Testament quotations in the New Testament, one is struck by the inspired wisdom which the Apostles exhibited in their attitude toward the Septuagint. On the one hand, they did not invariably set this version aside and make new translations from the Hebrew. Such an emphasis on the Hebrew would have been harmful to the gentile churches which had just been formed. It would have brought these gentile Christians into a position of dependence upon the unbelieving Jewish **rabbis,** on whose learning they would have been obliged to rely for an understanding of the Hebrew Old Testament. But on the other hand, the Apostles did not quote from the Septuagint invariably and thus encourage the notion that this Greek translation was equal to the Hebrew Old Testament in authority. Instead, they walked the middle way between these two extremes. Sometimes they cited the Septuagint verbatim, even when it departed from the Hebrew in non-essential ways, and sometimes they made their own translation directly from the Hebrew or used their knowledge of Hebrew to improve the rendering of the Septuagint.

In the Epistle to the Hebrews there are three Old Testament quotations which have been the subject of much discussion. The first of these is Heb. 1:6, *And let all the angels of God worship Him.* This clause is found in *Manuscript B* of the Septuagint as an addition to Deut. 32:43. On this basis the author of the Epistle to the Hebrews has often been accused of citing as Scripture a verse not found in the Hebrew Bible. The text of the Septuagint, however, is not certain at this point. *Manuscript A reads, And let all the angels of God give them (Him) strength,* and this is the reading adopted by Rahlfs (1935), one of the most recent editors of the Septuagint. If the reading of *A* is correct, then the text of *B* must have been changed at this point to agree with Heb. 1:6, and the author of the Epistle to the Hebrews could not be quoting it. He may have had Deut. 32:43 in mind, but the passage which he was actually citing was Psalm 97:7, which is found both in the Hebrew Old Testament and in the Septuagint and which reads (in the Septuagint), *worship Him all ye His angels.*

The second Old Testament quotation causing difficulty is Heb. 10:5, *Sacrifice and offering Thou wouldest not, but a body hast Thou prepared Me.* This is a quotation from Psalm 40:6 and is found in this form in the majority of the manuscripts of the Septuagint. The Hebrew text, however, reads *Mine ears hast Thou opened* instead of *but a body hast Thou prepared Me.* Because of this the author of the Epistle to the Hebrews has been accused also of using a mistranslation of the Hebrew text as a support for the Christian doctrine of Christ's atoning death. But this is not a necessary conclusion. For in Psalm 40 and in Heb. 10 the emphasis is not so much on the sacrifice of Christ's body as on Christ's willing obedience which made the sacrifice of His body effective. Because of this emphasis the inspired author of Hebrews was justified in regarding the Septuagint as sufficiently accurate to express this central meaning of the passage. The opening of Christ's ears to make Him an obedient servant he considered to be the first step in the preparation of Christ's body for His obedient sacrifice.

The third Old Testament quotation to present a problem is Heb. 11:21. *By faith Jacob, when he was a dying, blessed both the sons of Joseph; and worshiped, leaning upon the top of his staff.* This is usually thought to be a reference to Gen. 47:31, where the Hebrew text and the Septuagint differ, the former stating that Jacob *bowed himself upon the bed's head,* the latter that he *bowed himself on the top of his staff.* This difference is attributable to the fact that in Hebrew the words *bed* and *staff* are the same except for their vowel points, so that *bed* could easily be mistaken for *staff* and vice versa. It is usually said that Heb. 11:21 follows the Septuagint reading of Gen. 47:31, but this too is not a necessary conclusion, since actually Heb. 11:21 refers not to Gen. 47:31 but to Gen. 48:1-22. Here Jacob sat, apparently, on the edge of his bed and may very well have had a staff in his hand.

(d) The Latin Old Testament (Vulgate) — The Apocrypha

The earliest Latin version of the Old Testament was a translation of the Septuagint. Scholars think that this translating was probably done at Carthage during the 2nd century. Many other such translations were made during the years that followed. In the fourth century Augustine reported that there was "an infinite variety of Latin translations,"[7] and Jerome that there were as many texts of this version as there were manuscripts.[8] Jerome at first attempted to revise the Latin Old Testament, but in 390 he undertook the labor of producing a new translation directly from the Hebrew. This version, which Jercme completed in 405, later became known as the Latin Vulgate and is the official Bible of the Roman Catholic Church, having been so proclaimed at the Council of Trent (1546).

In his prologue to his translation of the Old Testament Jerome gave an account of the canonical Scriptures of the Hebrew Bible and enumerated them exactly. Then he added: "This prologue to the Scriptures may suit as a helmed preface to all the books which we have rendered from Hebrew into Latin, that we may know that whatever book is beyond these must be reckoned among the Apocrypha."[9] Thus Jerome was one of the first to use the term *Apocrypha* (noncanonical) to designate certain books which were included in the Septuagint and the Latin Old Testament versions but had never been part of the Hebrew Scriptures. The names of these apocryphal books are as follows: Tobit, Judith, Wisdom, Ecclesiasticus, Baruch, First and Second Maccabees, certain additions to the books of Esther and Daniel, First and Second Esdras, and the Prayer of Manasses. These books were written by Jewish authors between 200 B.C. and 100 A.D. Some of them were written in Hebrew or Aramaic and then translated into Greek. Others were written in Greek originally.

The Roman Catholic Church rejects First and Second Esdras and the Prayer of Manasses. Hence in the printed Latin Vulgate they are placed after the New Testament as an appendix and in small type. The other apocryphal books are mentioned by name in the decrees of the Council of Trent, where they are declared sacred and canonical and a solemn curse is pronounced against all those who will not receive them as such. Accordingly, in the printed Latin Vulgate they are interspersed without distinction among the other books of the Latin Old Testament.

Protestants have always opposed this attempt of the Roman Catholic Church to canonize the Apocrypha for several reasons. In the first place, it is contrary to the example of Christ and His Apostles. Never in the New Testament is any passage from the Apocrypha quoted as Scripture or referred to as such. This is admitted by all students of this subject, including present-day scholars such as B. M. Metzger (1957).[10] This fact is decisive for all those who acknowledge the divine authority and infallible inspiration of the New Testament writers. And all the more is this so if it be true, as Metzger and many other scholars have contended, that Paul was familiar with Wisdom, James with Ecclesiasticus, John with Tobit, and the author of Hebrews (who may have been Paul) with 2 Maccabees.[11] For if these Apostles knew these apocryphal books this well and still refrained from quoting or mentioning them as Scripture, then it is doubly certain that they did not accord these books a place in the Old Testament canon. According to C. C. Torrey (1945), however, only in the Epistle to the Hebrews is there clear evidence of a literary allusion to the Apocrypha.[12]

A second reason why the books of the Apocrypha cannot be regarded as canonical is that the Jews, the divinely appointed guardians of the Old Testament Scriptures, never esteemed them such. This fact is freely admitted by contemporary scholars. According to Torrey, the Jews not only rejected the Apocrypha, but after the overthrow of Jerusalem in 70 A.D., they went so far as to "destroy, systematically and thoroughly, the Semitic originals of all extra-canonical literature," including the Apocrypha. "The feeling of the leaders at that time," Torrey tells us, "is echoed in a later Palestinian writing (*Midrash Qoheleth*, 12,12): 'Whosoever brings together in his house more than twenty-four books (the canonical scriptures) brings confusion.' "[13] And additional evidence that the Jews did not recognize the Apocrypha as canonical is supplied by the Talmudic tract Baba Bathra (2nd century) and by the famous Jewish historian Josephus (c. 93 A.D.) in his treatise *Against Apion*. Neither of these sources make any mention of the Apocrypha in the lists which they give of the Old Testament books. For, as Torrey observes, the Jews had but one standard, acknowledged everywhere. Only such books as were believed to have been composed in either Hebrew or Aramaic before the end of the Persian period were received into the Old Testament canon.[14]

There is reason to believe, however, that the Greek-speaking Jews of Alexandria were not so strict as the Palestinian rabbis about the duty of shunning apocryphal books. Although these Alexandrian Jews did not recognize the Apocrypha as Scripture in the highest sense, nevertheless they read these books in Greek translation and included them in their Septuagint. And it was in this expanded form that the Septuagint was transmitted to the early gentile Christians. It is not surprising therefore that those early Church Fathers especially who were ignorant of Hebrew would be misled into placing these apocryphal books on the same plane with the other books of the Septuagint, regarding them all as Scripture. Schuerer (1908) mentions Irenaeus, Tertullian, Clement of Alexandria, Cyprian, and others as having made this mistake.[15] And later investigators, such as Torrey,[16] Metzger,[17] and Brockington (1961),[18] have pointed out another factor which may have led numerous Christians into this error of regarding the Apocrypha as part of the Old Testament. This was the practice which Christians had, and are believed to have initiated, of writing their literature in codex (book) form rather than on rolls. A codex of the Septuagint would contain the Apocrypha bound together indiscriminately with the canonical Old Testament books, and this would induce many gentile Christians to put them all on the same level. Such at least appears to have been the popular tendency in the early and medieval Church.

But whenever early Christians set themselves seriously to consider what books belonged to the Old Testament and what did not, the answer was always in favor of the Hebrew Old Testament.[19] This was the case with Melito (?-172), Julius Africanus (160-240), Origen

(182-251), Eusebius (275-340), Athanasius (293-373) and many later Fathers of the Greek Church. In the Latin Church greater favor was shown toward the Apochrypha, but even here, as we have seen, the Apocrypha were rejected by Jerome (340-420). And in his preface to the books of Solomon Jerome further defined his position. "As the Church reads the books of Judith and Tobit and Maccabees but does not receive them among the canonical Scriptures, so also it reads Wisdom and Ecclesiasticus for the edification of the people, not for the authoritative confirmation of doctrine."[20] Augustine (354-430) at first defended the canonicity of the Apocrypha but later came to a position not much different from Jerome's. There should be a distinction, he came to feel, between the books of the Hebrew canon and the "deuterocanonical" books accepted and read by the churches. Pope Gregory the Great (540-604) also adopted Jerome's position in regard to the Apocrypha, and so did Cardinal Ximenes and Cardinal Cajetan at the beginning of the Protestant Reformation.[21] Hence, the decree of the Council of Trent canonizing the Apocrypha is contrary to the informed conviction of the early and medieval Church. And this is the third reason why Protestants reject it.

But although all Protestants rejected the Apocrypha as canonical Old Testament Scripture, there was still considerable disagreement among them as to what to do with these controversial books. Luther rejected 1 and 2 Esdras, and placed the other apocryphal books in an appendix at the close of the Old Testament, prefacing it with the statement: "Apocrypha — that is, books which are not regarded as equal to the holy Scriptures, and yet are profitable and good to read."[22] The early English Bibles, including finally the King James Version, placed the Apocrypha in the same location, and in addition the Church of England retained the custom of reading from the Apocrypha in its public worship services during certain seasons of the year. In opposition to this practice Puritans and Presbyterians agitated for the complete removal of the Apocrypha from the Bible. In 1825 the British and Foreign Bible Society agreed to this, and since this time the Apocrypha has been eliminated almost entirely from English Bibles (except pulpit Bibles).

(e) The Pseudepigrapha — Enoch, Michael the Archangel, Jannes and Jambres

In addition to the Apocrypha there are also the *Pseudepigrapha*. These are other non-canonical books which were held in high esteem by many early Christians but which, unlike the Apocrypha, were never included in the manuscripts of the Greek Septuagint or of the Latin Vulgate. Because of this circumstance the texts of many of these Pseudepigrapha were lost during the middle-ages and have been found again only in comparatively recent times. They are called Pseudepigrapha because most of them falsely claim to have been written by various Old Testament patriarchs. Actually, however, they were composed between 200 B.C. and 100 A.D., mostly by Jewish authors but in some cases perhaps by Christians.[23]

One of the best known of the Pseudepigrapha is the *Book of Enoch*, an Ethiopic version of which was discovered in Abyssinia by James Bruce (c. 1770). This Book is of special interest because Jude is commonly thought to have quoted it in his Epistle. *And Enoch also, the seventh from Adam, prophesied of these, saying, Behold, the Lord cometh with ten thousands of His saints to execute judgment upon all, and to convince all that are ungodly among them of all their ungodly deeds which they have ungodly committed, and of all their hard speeches which ungodly sinners have spoken against Him.* (Jude 14-15; Enoch 1:9). Among early Christians there were three reactions to this seeming quotation of the Book of Enoch on the part of Jude.[24] First, there were those like Tertullian, who accepted both the Epistle of Jude and the Book of Enoch as canonical. Second, there were those (mentioned by Jerome) who rejected both the Epistle of Jude and the Book of Enoch. Third, there were those like Origen and Augustine, who accepted the Epistle of Jude as canonical but rejected the Book of Enoch. This third position was adopted by the Church at large and is undoubtedly the true one. For it is not certain that Jude actually did quote from the Book of Enoch. He may have been quoting a common source, a traditional saying handed down from remote antiquity. And even if he were quoting from the Book of Enoch, this would not necessarily mean that he was endorsing this book as a whole or vouching for its canonicity.

Jude 9 is another verse which is often attributed to the Pseudepigrapha. *Yet Michael the archangel, when contending with the devil he disputed about the body of Moses, durst not bring against him a railing accusation, but said, the Lord rebuke thee.* According to Origen and Didymus of Alexandria, Jude is here quoting from a non-canonical book called *The Assumption of Moses*. This book was lost for many centuries until in 1861 Ceriani published about a third of it from a manuscript in the Ambrosian Library at Milan. This manuscript comes to an end, however, before reaching the account of the death of Moses, and so there is no way of verifying the statements of Origen and Didymus concerning Jude's use of this book.[25] But even if the manuscript were complete and did contain the desired incident, it would still be preferable to suppose that Jude was quoting not *The Assumption of Moses* but a common source, probably an ancient oral tradition. For a similar instance is related by the prophet Zechariah (Zech. 3:1-3), and this indicates that encounters such as these between the good and evil angels were not fabulous but actual events.

There are also several verses of the Apostle Paul in which he has been accused of citing passages from lost non-canonical books as Scripture. In 1 Cor. 2:9, for example, Paul says, *but as it is written, Eye hath not seen, nor ear heard, neither have entered into the heart*

of man, the things which God hath prepared for them that love Him.
According to Origen, Paul quoted this verse from the *Apocalypse of Elijah*. Jerome denied this allegation but admitted that the verse occurred not only in the *Apocalypse of Elijah* but also in another non-canonical book entitled the *Ascension of Isaiah*. It is probable, however, that Paul is here quoting freely from Isaiah 64:4. Such, at any rate, was the opinion of Clement of Rome (c. 90) and of Jerome. And the same may be said concerning Eph. 5:14, where Paul writes, *Wherefore he saith, Awake thou that sleepest, and arise from the dead, and Christ shall give thee light.* Here again Paul seems to be quoting freely, this time from Isaiah 60:1, in spite of the statement of Epiphanius (c. 390) that these words were also found in the *Apocalypse of Elijah*. For, as Robertson and Plummer (1911) observe, it is more reasonable to suppose that the author or editor of this lost book quoted from Paul than that Paul quoted from him. For if Paul and the other New Testament writers refrained from quoting even the Apocrypha as Scripture, why would they quote other non-canonical books of much lower status in this way.[26]

In 2 Timothy 3:8 Paul refers by name to the magicians who contended with Moses at Pharaoh's court. *Now as Jannes and Jambres withstood Moses, so do these also resist the truth.* Origen asserts that here Paul is quoting from the *Book of Jannes and Jambres*. But there is no need to suppose this. For in the days of Paul the names of these two magicians were well known everywhere both in Jewish and in gentile circles — to Pliny (d. 79), for example, and to Apuleius (c. 130). Hence when Paul identifies these two adversaries of Moses by employing these familiar appellations, we need not conclude that he is quoting from a book.[27]

(f)   Manuscripts of the Hebrew Old Testament — The Dead Sea Scrolls

The Jewish rabbis venerated their copies of the Old Testament so much that they did not allow them to be read to pieces. As soon as their Old Testament manuscripts became too old and worn for ordinary use, they stored them in their synagogues and later buried them. Hence, until rather recently no ancient Hebrew Old Testament manuscripts were available to scholars, the oldest known manuscript dating from no earlier than the 9th century A.D. All the available manuscripts, however, were found to contain the Masoretic (Traditional) text and to agree with one another very closely. The first critic to demonstrate this was Bishop Kennicott, who published at Oxford in 1776-80 the readings of 634 Hebrew manuscripts. He was followed in 1784-88 by De Rossi, who published collations of 825 more manuscripts. No substantial variation among the manuscripts was detected by either of these two scholars.[28]

The discovery of the Dead Sea Scrolls has altered this situation. These scrolls had been placed in earthen jars and deposited in caves near Wadi Qumran by the Dead Sea. They were first brought to light in 1947 by an Arab who was looking for a goat which had wandered away. After a few months some of the scrolls from this first cave were sold by the Arabs to the Syrian Orthodox Monastery of St. Mark and others to the Hebrew University. In 1955 the Monastery of St. Mark sold its share of the Dead Sea Scrolls to the State of Israel. Thus these two lots of ancient writings were finally reunited under the same owners.[29]

This collection includes the following documents: (1) Isaiah A, an almost complete copy of Isaiah in Hebrew; (2) Isaiah B, another copy of Isaiah in Hebrew, reasonably complete from chapter 41 onwards but containing only fragments of earlier chapters; (3) a copy in Hebrew of the first two chapters of Habakkuk with a verse-by-verse commentary also in Hebrew; (4) the *Rule of the Community*, a code of rules of a community written in Hebrew; (5) a collection of hymns in Hebrew; (6) the *Rule of War*, a description in Hebrew of ancient warfare; (7) an Aramaic paraphrase of chapter 5 to 15 of Genesis.[30] Of these seven manuscripts Isaiah A is regarded as the oldest. One expert sets its date at 175-150 B.C.; another expert makes it 50 years younger. The other manuscripts are thought to have been written from 50 to 150 years later than Isaiah A.[31]

After these manuscripts had been discovered in the first cave, ten other caves in the same vicinity were found to contain similar treasures. Of these Cave 4 has proved the most productive. Thousands of fragments, once constituting about 330 separate books, have been taken from this location. These fragments include portions of every Old Testament book except Esther.[32] Rather recently (1972) O'Callaghan has claimed that certain fragments found in Cave 7 are from New Testament manuscripts. This discovery, however, has been rejected by most other scholars.[33]

The discovery of the first Dead Sea Scroll, Isaiah A, was generally regarded by scholars as a victory for the Masoretic (Traditional) Hebrew text of the Old Testament. According to Burrows (1948), this manuscript agreed with the Masoretic text to a remarkable degree in wording.[34] And according to Albright (1955), the second Isaiah scroll (Isaiah B) agreed even more closely with the Masoretic text.[35] But the discovery in 1952 of Cave 4 with its vast store of manuscripts altered the picture considerably. It became apparent that the Proto-Masoretic text of the Isaiah scrolls was not the only type of Old Testament text that had been preserved at Qumran. In the manuscripts from Cave 4 many other text-types have been distinguished. Accordingly, in 1964 F. M. Cross presented some of the conclusions which he had drawn from his Qumran studies. He believed that three distinct ancient texts of Samuel can be identified, namely, (1) an Egyptian text represented by the Septuagint, (2) a Palestinian text represented by manuscript 4Q from Cave 4, and (3) a Proto-Masoretic text represented by a Greek text of Samuel also from Cave 4. And in the Pentateuch also Cross divides the text into the Egyptian, Palestinian, and Proto-Masoretic varieties.[36]   G. R. Driver (1965), however, disagreed with Burrows, Albright, and Cross. According to him, the Dead Sea Scrolls were written in the first and early second centuries A.D.[37]

Thus we see that, despite the new discoveries, our confidence in the trustworthiness of the Old Testament text must rest on some more solid foundation than the opinions of naturalistic scholars. For as the Qumran studies demonstrate, these scholars disagree with one another. What one scholar grants another takes away. Instead of depending on such inconstant allies, Bible-believing Christians should develop their own type of Old Testament textual criticism, a textual criticism which takes its stand on the teachings of the Old Testament itself and views the evidence in the light of these teachings. Such a believing textual criticism leads us to full confidence in the Masoretic (Traditional) Hebrew text which was preserved by the divinely appointed Old Testament priesthood and the scribes and scholars grouped around it.

3. How The New Testament Text Was Preserved

At the Council of Trent the Roman Catholic Church not only added the Apocrypha to the Old Testament but also claimed to be in possession of certain unwritten traditions "which," the Council asserted, "received by the Apostles from the mouth of Christ Himself, or from the Apostles themselves, the Holy Ghost dictating, have come down even unto us, transmitted as it were from hand to hand." A solemn curse was pronounced against anyone who should "knowingly and deliberately" despise these traditions and also against anyone who, "in matters of faith and morals," should "presume to interpret the said sacred Scripture contrary to that sense which holy mother Church hath held and doth hold."[38] According to Roman Catholicism, therefore, a knowledge of the unwritten traditions of the Church is necessary in order to interpret the Scriptures properly. But who has the power to determine what these unwritten traditions are? In 1870 the Vatican Council of bishops answered this question. The Pope, they declared, is infallible when he "defines a doctrine regarding faith or morals to be held by the universal Church." This, however, was a most illogical procedure, for if only the Pope was infallible, then where did the other bishops get the infallibility with which to declare the Pope infallible?

According to Roman Catholic doctrine, then, the authority of the Bible depends upon the authority of the Roman Catholic Church and ultimately of the Pope. But this line of reasoning leads to an endless regression. Why do we believe that the Bible is infallible? Because, Roman Catholics answer, the infallible Pope says that the Bible is infallible and interprets it for us infallibly in accordance with ecclesiastical traditions which only he can define with certainty. But how do Roman Catholics know that the Pope is infallible? To be sure of this they would need an angel to certify that the Pope was truly infallible and then a second angel to establish that the first angel was truly an angel and not the devil in disguise and then a third angel to authenticate the two previous angels, and so on *ad infinitum*.

True Protestants have always rejected these false claims of Roman Catholicism and maintained the very opposite. The true Church derives its authority from the Bible and not the Bible from the Church. In the Bible God reveals Himself, *first*, as the almighty Creator God, *second*, as the faithful Covenant God, and *third*, as the triune Saviour God. And since God thus reveals Himself in the holy Scriptures, we need no human priest to stand between us and Jesus Christ, the great High Priest. Nor do we need an allegedly infallible Pope to assure us that these Scriptures are truly God's Word, for the Holy Ghost Himself gives us this assurance, bearing witness by and with the Word in our hearts.

In order, therefore, to discover the true principles of New Testament textual criticism we must turn neither to the dogmas of the Roman Catholic Church nor to the equally arbitrary dicta of the naturalistic critics but to the teaching of the New Testament itself. The following is a brief outline of this teaching which will be developed more fully in the chapters that follow.

(a) The Universal Priesthood of Believers

As we have seen, the study of the Old Testament indicates that the Old Testament Scriptures were preserved through the divinely appointed Old Testament priesthood. The Holy Spirit guided the priests to gather the separate parts of the Old Testament into one Old Testament canon and to maintain the purity of the Old Testament text. Have the New Testament Scriptures been preserved in this official manner? In the New Testament Church has there ever been a special, divinely appointed organization of priests with authority to make decisions concerning the New Testament text or the books that should belong to the New Testament canon? No! Not at all! When Christ died upon the cross, the veil of the Temple was rent in sunder, and the Old Testament priesthood was done away forever. There has never been a special order of priests in the New Testament Church. Every believer is a priest under Christ, the great High Priest. (1 Peter 2:9, Rev. 1:5-6).

Just as the divine glories of the New Testament are brighter far than the glories of the Old Testament, so the manner in which God has preserved the New Testament text is far more wonderful than the manner in which He preserved the Old Testament text. God preserved the Old Testament text by means of something physical and external, namely, the Aaronic priesthood. God has preserved the New Testament text by means of something inward and spiritual, namely, the universal priesthood of believers, through the leading, that is to say, of the Holy Spirit in the hearts of individual Christians of every walk of life.

(b) The Writing of the New Testament Books

The writing of the New Testament as well as the preservation of it was a fulfillment of the promises of Christ that His Word should be forever preserved. *Heaven and earth shall pass away, but My words shall not pass away* (Matt. 24:35; Mark 13:31; Luke 21-33). As the Saviour was about to return to His heavenly Father, He left His Apostles this blessed assurance: *These things have I spoken unto you being yet present with you. But the Comforter, which is the Holy Ghost, whom the Father will send in my name, He shall teach you all things and bring all things to your remembrance, whatsoever I have said unto you* (John 14:25-26). Here we see that both the agreements of the Four Gospels with one another and their differences are due to the inspiration which the Apostles received from the Holy Spirit and the control which He exercised over their minds and memories.

In the Gospels, therefore, Jesus reveals Himself through the story of His earthly ministry. The rest of the New Testament books are His divine commentary on the meaning of that ministry, and in these books also Jesus reveals Himself. These remaining books were written in accordance with His promise to His Apostles: *I have yet many things to say unto you, but ye cannot bear them now. Howbeit, when He, the Spirit of truth is come, He will guide you into all truth; for He shall not speak of Himself: but whatsoever He shall hear that shall He speak: and He will shew you things to come* (John 16:12-13). It was in fulfillment of this promise that the Holy Spirit descended upon the Apostles at Pentecost, filled their minds and hearts with the message of the risen, exalted Lord, and sent them out to preach this message, first to the Jews at Jerusalem and then to all the world. Then followed the conversion of the Apostle Paul and the Epistles which he wrote under the inspiration of the Holy Spirit. Then James, Peter, John, and Jude were inspired to write their Epistles, and Luke to tell the story of the Acts of the Apostles. Finally, the Revelation proceeded from the inspired pen of John on Patmos, announcing those things that were yet to come. Volumes, of course, could be filled with a discussion of these sacred developments, but here a bare statement of the essential facts must suffice.

(c) The Formation of the New Testament Canon

After the New Testament books had been written, the next step in the divine program for the New Testament Scriptures was the gathering of these individual books into one New Testament canon in order that thus they might take their place beside the books of the Old Testament canon as the concluding portion of God's holy Word. Let us now consider how this was accomplished under the guidance of the Holy Spirit.[39]

The first New Testament books to be assembled together were

the Epistles of Paul. The Apostle Peter, shortly before he died, referred to Paul's Epistles as Scripture and in such a way as to indicate that at least the beginning of such a collection had already been made (2 Peter 3:15-16). Even radical scholars, such as E. J. Goodspeed (1926),[40] agree that a collection of Paul's Epistles was in circulation in the beginning of the 2nd century and that Ignatius (117) referred to it. When the Four Gospels were collected together is unknown, but it is generally agreed that this must have taken place before 170 A.D. because at that time Tatian made his *Harmony of the Gospels* (Diatessaron), which included all four of the canonical Gospels and only these four. Before 200 A.D. Paul, the Gospels, Acts, 1 Peter and 1 John were recognized as Scripture by Christians everywhere (as the writings of Irenaeus, Clement of Alexandria, and Tertullian prove) and accorded an authority equal to that of the Old Testament Scriptures. It was Tertullian, moreover, who first applied the name *New Testament* to this collection of apostolic writings.[41]

The seven remaining books, 2 and 3 John, 2 Peter, Hebrews, James, Jude, and Revelation, were not yet unanimously accepted as Scripture. By the time the 4th century had arrived, however, few Christians seem to have questioned the right of these disputed books to a place in the New Testament canon. Eminent Church Fathers of that era, such as Athanasius, Augustine, and Jerome, include them in their lists of New Testament books. Thus through the Holy Spirit's guidance of individual believers, silently and gradually — but nevertheless surely, the Church as a whole was led to a recognition of the fact that the twenty-seven books of the New Testament, and only these books, form the canon which God gave to be placed beside the Old Testament Scriptures as the authoritative and final revelation of His will.

This guidance of the Holy Spirit was negative as well as positive. It involved not only the selection of canonical New Testament books but also the rejection of many non-canonical books which were mistakenly regarded as canonical by some of the early Christians. Thus the *Shepherd of Hermas* was used as holy Scripture by Irenaeus and Clement of Alexandria, and the same status was wrongly given to the *Teaching of the Twelve Apostles* by Clement and Origen. Clement likewise commented on the *Apocalypse of Peter* and the *Epistle of Barnabas,* to which Origen also accorded the title "catholic." And in addition, there were many false *Gospels* in circulation, as well as numerous false *Acts* ascribed to various Apostles. But although some of these non-canonical writings gained temporary acceptance in certain quarters, this state of affairs lasted for but a short time. Soon all Christians everywhere were led by the Holy Spirit to repudiate these spurious works and to receive only the canonical books as their New Testament Scriptures.

(d) The Preservation of the New Testament Text

Thus the Holy Spirit guided the early Christians to gather the individual New Testament books into one New Testament canon and to reject all non-canonical books. In the same manner also the Holy Spirit guided the early Christians to preserve the New Testament text by receiving the true readings and rejecting the false. Certainly it would be strange if it were otherwise. It would have been passing strange if God had guided His people in regard to the New Testament canon but had withheld from them His divine assistance in the matter of the New Testament text. This would mean that Bible-believing Christians today could have no certainty concerning the New Testament text but would be obliged to rely on the hypotheses of modern, naturalistic critics.

But God in His mercy did not leave His people to grope after the True New Testament Text. Through the leading of the Holy Spirit He guided them to preserve it during the manuscript period. God brought this to pass through the working of His preserving and governing providence. *First*, many trustworthy copies of the original New Testament manuscripts were produced by faithful scribes. *Second*, these trustworthy copies were read and recopied by true believers down through the centuries. *Third*, untrustworthy copies were not so generally read or so frequently recopied. Although they enjoyed some popularity for a time, yet in the long run they were laid aside and consigned to oblivion. Thus as a result of this special providential guidance the True Text won out in the end, and today we may be sure that the text found in the vast majority of the Greek New Testament manuscripts is a trustworthy reproduction of the divinely inspired Original Text. This is the text which was preserved by the God-guided usage of the Greek Church. Critics have called it the *Byzantine* text, thereby acknowledging that it was the text in use in the Greek Church during the greater part of the Byzantine period (452-1453). It is much better, however, to call this text the *Traditional Text*. When we call the text found in the majority of the Greek New Testament manuscripts the Traditional Text, we signify that this is the text which has been handed down by the God-guided tradition of the Church from the time of the Apostles unto the present day.

A further step in the providential preservation of the New Testament was the printing of it in 1516 and the dissemination of it through the whole of Western Europe during the Protestant Reformation. In the first printing of the Greek New Testament we see God's preserving providence working hiddenly and, to the outward eye, accidentally. The editor, Erasmus, performed his task in great haste in order to meet the deadline set by the printer, Froben of Basle. Hence this first edition contained a number of errors of a minor sort, some of which persisted in later editions. But in all essentials the New Testament text first printed by Erasmus and later by Stephanus (1550) and Elzevir (1633) is in full agreement with the Traditional Text providentially preserved in the vast majority of the Greek New Testament manuscripts. This printed text is commonly called the *Textus Receptus* (Received Text). It is the text which was used by the Protestant Reformers during the Reformation and by all Protestants everywhere for three hundred years thereafter. Hence the printing of it was, after all, no accident but the work of God's special providence.

The special providence of God is particularly evident in the fact that the text of the Greek New Testament was first printed and published not in the East but in Western Europe where the influence of the Latin usage and of the Latin Vulgate was very strong. Through the influence of the Latin-speaking Church Erasmus and his successors were providentially guided to follow the Latin Vulgate here and there in those few places in which the Latin Church usage rather than the Greek Church usage had preserved the genuine reading. Hence the Textus Receptus was a further step in the providential preservation of the New Testament. In it the few errors of any consequence occurring in the Traditional Greek Text were corrected by the providence of God operating through the usage of the Latin-speaking Church of Western Europe.

Thus God by His special providence has preserved the New Testament text in a three-fold way through the universal priesthood of believers. In the *first* place, during the fourteen centuries in which the New Testament circulated in manuscript form God worked providentially through the usage of the Greek-speaking Church to preserve the New Testament text in the majority of the Greek New Testament manuscripts. In this way the True New Testament Text became the prevailing *Traditional Text*. In the *second* place, during the 16th century when the New Testament text was being printed for the first time, God worked providentially through the usage of the Latin-speaking Church to influence Erasmus and the other editors and printers of that period to follow the Latin Vulgate in those few places in which the Latin Church usage rather than the Greek Church usage had preserved the genuine reading. Then in the *third* place, during the 450 years which have elapsed since the first printing of the New Testament, God has been working providentially through the usage of Bible-believing Protestants to place and keep the stamp of His approval upon this God-guided printed text. It is upon this Textus Receptus that the King James Version and the other classic Protestant translations are based.

(e) Alternative Views of the Providential Preservation of the New Testament

We see now how Christ has fulfilled His promise always to preserve in His Church the True New Testament Text, namely, through the universal priesthood of believers. In the special providence of God believers down through the ages have been guided to reject false readings and preserve the true, so that today the True New Testament Text is found in the majority of the Greek New Testament manuscripts, in the Textus Receptus, and in the King James Version and the other classic Protestant translations. But because of the opposition of unbelievers conservative Christian scholars have become increasingly reluctant to adopt this view and have offered various alternatives in place of it. Let us therefore consider briefly these alternative views of God's providential preservation of the New Testament text.

(1) *The alleged agreement of all the New Testament manuscripts in matters of doctrine.* In dealing with the problems of the New Testament text most conservatives place great stress on the amount of agreement alleged to exist among the extant New Testament manuscripts. These manuscripts, it is said, agree so closely with one another in matters of doctrine that it does not make much difference which manuscript you follow. The same essential teaching is preserved in them all. This reputed agreement of all the extant New Testament manuscripts in doctrinal matters is ascribed to divine providence and regarded as the fulfillment of the promise of Christ always to preserve in His Church a trustworthy New Testament text.

This is the thought that was emphasized by Richard Bentley (1713) in his celebrated reply to the free-thinker, Anthony Collins, who asserted that New Testament textual criticism had made the sacred text uncertain. This charge, Bentley rejoined, was baseless. "The real text of the sacred writers does not now (since the originals have been so long lost) lie in any single manuscript or edition, but is dispersed in them all. 'Tis competently exact indeed even in the worst manuscript now extant; choose as awkwardly as you can, choose the worst by design, out of the whole lump of readings. . . . Make your 30,000 (variant readings) as many more, if numbers of copies can ever reach that sum: all the better to a knowing and serious reader, who is thereby more richly furnished to select what he sees genuine. But even put them into the hands of a knave or a fool, and yet with the most sinistrous and absurd choice, he shall not extinguish the light of any one chapter, nor so disguise Christianity but that every feature of it will still be the same."[42]

Since the days of Bentley countless conservative scholars have adopted this same apologetic approach to the study of the New Testament text. New Testament textual criticism, they have affirmed, can do no harm to the Christian faith, because the special providence of God has brought it to pass that the differences which exist among the extant New Testament manuscripts do not affect any essential point of doctrine. This theory, however, presupposes an extremely mechanical and unhistorical conception of the providential preservation of Scripture. According to this theory, God in some mechanical way must have prevented heretical scribes from inserting into the New Testament manuscripts which they were copying readings that favored their false views.   Or, if God did now and then allow an heretical reading to creep into a manuscript, He must have quickly brought about the destruction of that manuscript before the false reading could be transferred to another manuscript and thus propagated.   But the testimony of history indicates that God's providential preservation of Scripture did not function in any such mechanical fashion but organically through the Church.   Heretical readings were invented and did circulate for a time, but they were rejected by the universal priesthood of believers under the guidance of God.

(2) *The true reading preserved in at least one of the extant manuscripts.*   Many conservative scholars seem to feel that God's providential care over the New Testament text is adequately defined by the saying that the true reading has been preserved in at least one of the extant New Testament manuscripts.   Theodor Zahn (1909) gave expression to this point of view in the following words: "Though the New Testament text can be shown to have met with varying treatment, it has never as yet been established from ancient citations, nor made really probable on internal grounds, that a single sentence of the original text has disappeared altogether from the text transmitted in the Church, that is, of all the manuscripts of the original and of the ancient translations."[43]   In other words, the true reading is always to be found in some one or other of the extant manuscripts. The only question is, which one.

Zahn's doctrine seems to be comforting at first glance, but on closer analysis this comfort soon disappears.   Has the special providence of God over the New Testament text done no more than to preserve the true readings somewhere, that is to say, in some one or other of the great variety of New Testament manuscripts now existing in the world?   If Christ has done no more than this, how can it be said that He has fulfilled His promise always to preserve in His Church the True New Testament Text?   How can His people ever be certain that they have the True New Testament Text?   For not all the extant New Testament manuscripts have yet been discovered. No doubt many of them still remain in the obscurity into which they were plunged centuries ago, concealed in holes, ruins, and other unknown places.   How can we be sure that many true readings are not hiding in these undiscovered manuscripts?   And even if this is not the case, how can we be certain which of the known manuscripts contain the true reading in places in which these manuscripts differ? For Christians troubled with doubts like these Zahn's theory is no help at all.

(3) *Are naturalistic New Testament textual critics providentially guided?*   Many conservatives have adopted the theory that it is through textual criticism, and especially through the textual criticism of Westcott and Hort, that Christ has fulfilled His promise always to preserve in His Church the True New Testament Text.   In regard to this matter J. H. Skilton (1946) writes as follows: "Textual Criticism, in God's providence, is the means provided for ascertaining

the true text of the Bible."[44]   And half a century earlier Dr. B. B.
Warfield (1893) expressed himself in a very similar manner.   "In the
sense of the Westminster Confession, therefore, the multiplication of
copies of the Scriptures, the several early efforts towards the revision
of the text, the raising up of scholars in our own day to collect and
collate manuscripts, and to reform them on scientific principles —
of our Tischendorfs and Tregelleses, and Westcotts and Horts — are
all parts of God's singular care and providence in preserving His inspired Word pure."[45]

Dr. B. B. Warfield was an outstanding defender of the orthodox
Christian faith, so much so that one hesitates to criticize him in any
way.   Certainly no Bible-believing Christian would wish to say anything disrespectful concerning so venerable a Christian scholar.   But
nevertheless it is a fact that Dr. Warfield's thinking was not entirely
unified.   Through his mind ran two separate trains of thought which
not even he could join together.   The one train of thought was dogmatic, going back to the Protestant Reformation.   When following
this train of thought Dr. Warfield regarded Christianity as true.   The
other train of thought was apologetic, going back to the rationalistic
viewpoint of the 18th century.   When following this train of thought
Dr. Warfield regarded Christianity as merely probable.   And this
same divided outlook was shared by Dr. Warfield's colleagues at
Princeton Seminary and by conservative theologians and scholars
generally throughout the 19th and early 20th century.   Even today
this split-level thinking is still a factor to be reckoned with in conservative circles, although in far too many instances it has passed over
into modernism.

Dr. Warfield's treatment of the New Testament text illustrates
this cleavage in his thinking.   In the realm of dogmatics he agreed
with the Westminster Confession that the New Testament text had
been "kept pure in all ages" by God's "singular care and providence,"
but in the realm of New Testament textual criticism he agreed with
Westcott and Hort in ignoring God's providence and even went so
far as to assert that the same methods were to be applied to the text
of the New Testament that would be applied to the text of a morning
newspaper.   It was to bridge the gap between his dogmatics and his
New Testament textual criticism that he suggested that God had
worked providentially through Tischendorf, Tregelles, and Westcott
and Hort to preserve the New Testament text.   But this suggestion
leads to conclusions which are extremely bizarre and inconsistent.
It would have us believe that during the manuscript period orthodox
Christians corrupted the New Testament text, that the text used by
the Protestant Reformers was the worst of all, and that the True Text
was not restored until the 19th century, when Tregelles brought it forth
out of the Pope's library, when Tischendorf rescued it from a waste
basket on Mt. Sinai, and when Westcott and Hort were providentially
guided to construct a theory of it which ignores God's special providence and treats the text of the New Testament like the text of any

other ancient book. But if the True New Testament Text was lost for 1500 years, how can we be sure that it has ever been found again?

(f) The Principles of Consistently Christian New Testament Textual Criticism

Bentley, Zahn, Warfield, and countless others have tried to devise a theory of the special providential preservation of the Scriptures which leaves room for naturalistic New Testament textual criticism. But this is impossible, for the two concepts are mutually exclusive. Naturalistic New Testament textual criticism requires us to treat the text of the New Testament like the text of any other ancient book, in other words, to ignore or deny the special providential preservation of the Scriptures. Hence if we really believe in the special providential preservation of the Scriptures, then we cannot follow the naturalistic method of New Testament textual criticism.

For a believer, then, the only alternative is to follow a consistently Christian method of New Testament textual criticism in which all the principles are derived from the Bible itself and none is borrowed from the textual criticism of other ancient books. In the preceding pages we have striven to present such a consistently Christian New Testament textual criticism, and now we will recapitulate and summarize its principles briefly:

Principle One: The Old Testament text was preserved by the Old Testament priesthood and the scribes and scholars that grouped themselves around that priesthood.

Principle Two: When Christ died upon the cross, the Old Testament priesthood was abolished. In the New Testament dispensation every believer is a priest under Christ the great High Priest. Hence the New Testament text has been preserved by the universal priesthood of believers, by faithful Christians in every walk of life.

Principle Three: The Traditional Text, found in the vast majority of the Greek New Testament manuscripts, is the True Text because it represents the God-guided usage of this universal priesthood of believers.

Principle Four: The first printed text of the Greek New Testament represents a forward step in the providential preservation of the New Testament. In it the few errors of any consequence occurring in the Traditional Greek Text were corrected by the providence of God operating through the usage of the Latin-speaking Church of Western Europe. In other words, the editors and printers who produced this first printed Greek New Testament text were providentially guided by the usage of the Latin-speaking Church to follow the Latin Vulgate in those few places in which the Latin Church usage rather than the Greek Church usage had preserved the genuine reading.

Principle Five: Through the usage of Bible-believing Protestants God placed the stamp of His approval on this first printed text, and it became the Textus Receptus (Received Text). It is the printed

form of the Traditional Text found in the vast majority of the Greek
New Testament manuscripts.

Principle Six: The King James (Authorized) Version is an
accurate translation of the Textus Receptus. On it God has placed
the stamp of His approval through the long continued usage of English-speaking believers. Hence it should be used and defended today
by Bible-believing Christians.

(g) New Testament Textual Criticism and Evangelism

Why should we Christians study the New Testament text from
a neutral point of view rather than from a believing point of view?
The answer usually given is that we should do this for the sake of
unbelievers. We must start with the neutral point of view in order
that later we may convert unbelievers to the orthodox, believing point
of view. Sir Frederic Kenyon expressed himself to this effect as follows: "It is important to recognize from the first that the problem
is essentially the same, whether we are dealing with sacred or secular
literature, although the difficulty of solving it, and likewise the issues
depending on it are very different. It is important, if for no other
reason, because it is only in this way that we can meet the hostile
critics of the New Testament with arguments, the force of which they
admit. If we assume from the first the supernatural character of
these books and maintain that this affects the manner in which their
text has come down to us, we can never convince those who start with
a denial of that supernatural character. We treat them at first like
any other books, in order to show at last that they are above and
beyond all other books."[46]

Although Kenyon probably advised this oblique approach with
the best of intentions, still the course which he advocated is very
wrong. Orthodox Christians must not stoop to conquer. We must
not first adopt a neutral position toward the Bible in order that later
we may persuade unbelievers to receive the Bible as God's Word.
There are several reasons why we must not do this. In the first place,
if we should take this step, we would be inconsistent. We would be
denying the conclusion that we were seeking to establish. In the second place, we would be ineffective. In taking up this neutral position
we would not be doing anything to convert unbelievers to the orthodox
Christian faith. On the contrary, we would be confirming them in
their confidence in the essential rightness of their unbelieving presuppositions. And in the third place, we would be sinning. To approach
unbelievers from this neutral point of view would be not only allow-
ing them to ignore the divine inspiration and providential preservation of the Scriptures but even doing so ourselves. In other words,
we would be seeking to convert unbelievers by the strange method
of participating in their unbelief.

If we truly believe in Christ, then God is real to us, more real
even than our faith in Him. Otherwise we are not believing but doubt-

ing. Therefore we must begin all our thinking with that which is most real, namely, God and His three-fold revelation of Himself in nature, in the holy Scriptures, and in the Gospel of Christ. This is the system of truth which we must proclaim to others, both to unbelievers and to our fellow Christians. And in this system of truth, as we have seen, the principles of consistently Christian New Testament textual criticism occupy a very necessary and important place.

(h) Believing Bible Study on the Graduate Level — Christ and Grammar

We must make God and Jesus Christ His Son the starting point of all our thinking. But how can we do this on the graduate level at a theological seminary or a university? How can we know for example, whether the King James Version is a correct translation or not? Don't we have to rely on dictionaries, such as Brown-Driver-Briggs, Thayer, Kittel, and Liddel-Scott? And for grammar don't we have to go to the great authorities in this field, such as Gesenius, Bauer, and Blass-Debrunner? And how, really, do we know that the Textus Receptus is a trustworthy reproduction of the majority New Testament text? For our knowledge of the New Testament manuscripts are we not obliged to depend almost entirely on the writings of experts, such as Gregory, Kenyon, Colwell, Metzger, and Aland? When we study the Bible on the graduate level, therefore, how can we begin with God? Must we not rather begin with men? With the information provided by scholars, most of whom are unbelievers?

Questions like these cause many conservative seminary students to panic and become virtual unbelievers in their biblical studies. In order, therefore, to prevent such catastrophes, we must always emphasize the Christian starting point that all our thinking ought to have. If we are Christians, then we must begin our thinking not with the assertions of unbelieving scholars and their naturalistic human logic, but with Christ and the logic of faith.

For example, how do we know that the Textus Receptus is the true New Testament text? We know this through the logic of faith. Because the Gospel is true, the Bible which contains this Gospel was infallibly inspired by the Holy Spirit. And because the Bible was infallibly inspired, it has been preserved by God's special providence. Moreover, this providential preservation was not done privately in secret holes and caves but publicly in the usage of God's Church. Hence the true New Testament text is found in the majority of the New Testament manuscripts. And this providential preservation did not cease with the invention of printing. Hence the formation of the Textus Receptus was God-guided.

And how do we know that the King James Version is a faithful translation of the true New Testament text? We know this also through the logic of faith. Since the formation of the Textus Receptus was God-guided, the translation of it was God-guided also. For as the Textus Receptus was being formed, it was also being translated. The two processes were simultaneous. Hence the early Protestant versions, such as Luther's, Tyndale's, the Geneva, and the King James, were actually varieties of the Textus Receptus. And this was necessarily so according to the principles of God's preserving providence. For the Textus Receptus had to be translated in order that the universal priesthood of believers, the rank and file, might give it their God-guided approval.

In biblical studies, in philosophy, in science, and in every other learned field we must begin with Christ and then work out our basic principles according to the logic of faith. This procedure will show us how to utilize the learning of non-Christian scholars in such a way as to profit by their instruction. Undeniably these unbelievers know a great many facts by virtue of God's common grace. They misinterpret these facts, however, because they ignore and deny God's revelation of Himself in and through the facts. Hence our task is to point out the inconsistencies and absurdities of unbelieving thought and then to take the facts which learned unbelievers have assembled and place them in their proper framework of biblical truth.

For example, if we begin with Christ, then we will understand what language is, namely, the medium by which God reveals the facts unto men and also Himself in and through the facts. And if we adopt this basic position, then the study of Greek grammar, and especially the history of it, will prove immensely profitable to us and will strengthen our faith, for then we will see how God in His providence has preserved the knowledge of Greek grammar from the days of the ancient Alexandrian grammarians down to the time of Erasmus and the Protestant Reformers and even up until now. Such a survey certainly increases our confidence in the King James translators. Judged even by modern standards, their knowledge of the biblical languages was second to none.

Begin with Christ and the Gospel and follow the logic of faith. This is the principle that must guide us in our graduate studies, especially in the biblical field. If we adhere to it, then everything we learn will fit beautifully into its place in the Christian thought-system. But if we ignore Christ and adopt a neutral approach to knowledge, we will soon lose ourselves in a wilderness of details and grow more and more chaotic in our thinking.

(For further discussion see *Believing Bible Study*, pp. 51-52, 214-225. See also *A History of Classical Scholarship*, by J. E. Sandys, vols. 1 & 2.)

CHAPTER FIVE

THE FACTS OF NEW TESTAMENT TEXTUAL CRITICISM

Facts are the temporal truths which God, the eternal Truth, establishes by His works of creation and providence. God reveals facts to men through their thought processes, and in and through the facts God reveals Himself. In the facts of nature God reveals Himself as the almighty Creator God, in the facts of Scripture God reveals Himself as the faithful Covenant God, and in the facts of the Gospel God reveals Himself as the triune Saviour God. Certainty is our clear perception of the clearly revealed facts. Probability is our dimmer perception of the less clearly revealed facts. Error is the sinful rejection of the facts, and especially of God's revelation of Himself in and through the facts.

In New Testament textual criticism, therefore, we must start at the highest point. We must begin with God, the supreme and eternal Truth, and then descend to the lower, temporal facts which He has established by His works of creation and providence. We must take all our principles from the Bible itself and borrow none from the textual criticism of other ancient books. It is only by following this rule that we will be able to distinguish facts from the fictions of unbelievers.

1. An Enumeration Of The New Testament Documents

For information concerning the vast fleet of documents which have transported the New Testament text across the sea of time under the direction of God's special providence let us apply to two of the leading experts in this field, namely, Kurt Aland (1968),[1] who currently assigns official numbers to newly discovered manuscripts of the Greek New Testament, and B. M. Metzger (1968),[2] author of many books and articles concerning the New Testament text.

(a) The Greek New Testament Manuscripts

How many New Testament manuscripts are there? In order to answer this question let us turn to the latest statistics as they are presented by Kurt Aland. According to Aland, there are 5,255 known manuscripts which contain all or part of the Greek New Testament.[3]

The earliest of these Greek New Testament manuscripts are the *papyri.* They are given that name because they are written on papyrus, an ancient type of writing material made from the fibrous pith of the papyrus plant, which in ancient times grew plentifully along the river Nile. Eighty-one of these papyri have now been discovered, many of them mere fragments.[4] The most important of these papyrus manuscripts are the Chester Beatty Papyri and the Bodmer Papyri. The Chester Beatty Papyri were published in 1933-37. They include Papyrus 45 (Gospels and Acts, c. 225 A.D.), Papyrus 46 (Pauline Epistles, c. 225 A.D.), and Papyrus 47 (Revelation, c. 275 A.D.). The Bodmer Papyri were published in 1956-62. The most important of these are Papyrus 66 (John, c. 200 A.D.) and Papyrus 75 (Luke and John 1:15, c. 200 A.D.).

All the rest of the Greek New Testament manuscripts are of *velum* (leather), except for a few late ones in which paper was used. The oldest of the velum manuscripts are written in *uncial* (capital) letters. These uncial manuscripts now number 267.[5] The three oldest complete (or nearly complete) uncial manuscripts are B (*Codex Vaticanus*), Aleph (*Codex Sinaiticus*), and A (*Codex Alexandrinus*). *Codex B* was written about the middle of the 4th century. It is the property of the Vatican Library at Rome. When it arrived there is not known, but it must have been before 1475, since it is mentioned in a catalogue of the library made in that year. *Codex Aleph* was discovered by Tischendorf in 1859 at the Monastery of St. Catherine on Mount Sinai. Tischendorf persuaded the monks to give it as a present (requited with money and favors) to the Czar of Russia. In 1933 it was purchased from the Russian government by the Trustees of the British Museum. It is generally considered by scholars to have been written in the second half of the 4th century. *Codex A* was for many years regarded as the oldest extant New Testament manuscript. It was given to the King of England in 1627 by Cyril Lucar, patriarch of Constantinople, and is now kept in the British Museum. Scholars date it from the first half of the 5th century. Other important uncial manuscripts are W (Gospels, 4th or 5th century), D (Gospels and Acts, 5th or 6th century), and D2 (Pauline Epistles, 6th century).

About the beginning of the 9th century *minuscule* (small letter) handwriting began to be used for the production of books. Thus all the later New Testament manuscripts are *minuscules*. According to Aland, 2,764 minuscules have been catalogued.[6] These date from the 9th to the 16th century.

Another important class of Greek New Testament manuscripts are the *lectionaries*. These are service books which contain in proper sequence the text of the passages of Scripture appointed to be read at the worship services of the Church. These lectionaries are of two kinds, the *synaxaria*, which begin the year at Easter, and the *menologia*, which begin the year at September 1. Aland sets the number of the lectionary manuscripts at 2,143.[7]

(b) Cataloguing the New Testament Manuscripts

To discover and catalogue all these manuscripts was the first task of New Testament textual criticism. As early as 1550 Stephanus began to do this. This scholarly printer placed in the margin of his 3rd edition of the Textus Receptus variant readings taken from 15 manuscripts, which he indicated by Greek numbers. One of these manuscripts was *D* and another *L,* and most of the rest have been identified with minuscule manuscripts in the Royal (National) Library at Paris. Stephanus' pioneer efforts were continued 100 years later by the English scholar Brian Walton. In the 6th volume of his great Polyglot Bible (1657) he included the variant readings of Stephanus and also those of 15 other manuscripts. These were listed along with the libraries in which they were kept. In 1707 John Mill, another English scholar, published his monumental edition of the New Testament in which almost all the available evidence of the Greek manuscripts and the early versions was presented. Scrivener (1883) gives a list of the 82 Greek New Testament manuscripts which Mill knew and catalogued in his epoch making work.[8]

The modern system of cataloguing the New Testament manuscripts was introduced by J. J. Wettstein in his two volume edition of the New Testament, published at Amsterdam in 1751-52. He designated the uncial manuscripts by capital letters and the minuscule manuscripts by Arabic numerals. According to K. W. Clark (1950), Wettstein catalogued about 125 Greek New Testament manuscripts.[9]

After the opening of the 19th century the process of cataloguing New Testament manuscripts speeded up tremendously due to the improved means of travel and communication. During the years 1820-36 J. M. A. Scholz listed 616 manuscripts which had not previously been known. In the four editions of his *Introduction to the Criticism of the New Testament* (1861-94) F. H. A. Scrivener extended the catalogue to almost 3,000 manuscripts. Between the years 1884 and 1912 C. R. Gregory enlarged this list to over 4,000 manuscripts.[10] After Gregory's death in World War I, the task of registering newly discovered manuscripts was taken over by von Dobschuetz, and then by Eltester, and is at present the responsibility of K. Aland. As stated, he lists the total number of Greek New Testament manuscripts at 5,255. In view of these large numbers, it may very well be that almost all the extant New Testament manuscripts have now been discovered and catalogued.

(c) Collating the New Testament Manuscripts

After a manuscript is discovered and catalogued, it must be studied to find out what it says, and its readings must be published. Usually this is done by collating (comparing) the manuscript with some well known printed text and noting the readings in regard to which the manuscript varies from this printed text. If the collation is perfectly accurate, these variant readings, when again compared with the printed text, will exhibit perfectly the text of the manuscript which has been collated. Unfortunately, however, the collations of the earlier New Testament scholars were not very reliable. It was not considered necessary to record every variant reading of the manuscript that was being examined.

It was not until the 19th century that scholars began to aim at perfect accuracy and completeness in the collation of New Testament manuscripts. The most famous of these 19th century publishers and collators of New Testament manuscripts was C. Tischendorf. The 8th edition of his Greek New Testament (1869) is still a mine of information concerning the readings of the New Testament documents and indispensable to the student who desires to examine these matters for himself. Other eminent 19th century investigators of New Testament manuscripts were S. P. Tregelles, F .H. A. Scrivener, and J. W. Burgon.

During the 20th century there have been many who have taken part in the work of collating New Testament manuscripts. Included among these are C. R. Gregory, K. Lake, H. C. Hoskier, and many contemporary scholars. One of the goals, as yet unattained, of 20th century scholarship has been to produce a critical edition of the New Testament which shall take the place of Tischendorf's 8th edition. Von Soden attempted to supply this need in his monumental edition (1902-10), but did not succeed, at least in the judgment of most critics. In 1935 and 1940 S. C. Legg published critical editions of Mark and Matthew respectively, but inaccuracies have also been found in his presentation of the evidence. In 1949 an international committee was formed of British and American scholars, and since that time work on a critical edition of Luke has been in progress. Not long ago (1966) a specimen of this committee's work was rather severely criticized on various counts by K. Aland, who is now working with other European scholars in yet another attempt to produce a new critical edition of the New Testament.[11]

Such then are the impressive results of more than four centuries of New Testament manuscript study. Thousands of manuscripts have been catalogued and many of these manuscripts have been collated and studied. Myriads of facts have been gathered. As believing Bible students we should seek to master these facts. We must remember, however, that facts are never neutral.[12] All facts are temporal truths which God establishes by His works of creation and providence. Hence we must not attempt, as unbelievers do, to force the facts into an allegedly neutral framework but should interpret them in accordance with the divine Truth, namely, God's revelation of Himself in the pages of holy Scripture. When we do this, the consistency of believing thought and the inconsistency of unbelieving thought become evident also in the realm of New Testament textual criticism.

(d) The Ancient New Testament Versions

When and where the New Testament was first translated into Latin has been the subject of much dispute, but, according to Metzger, most scholars now agree that the first Latin translation of the Gospels was made in North Africa during the last quarter of the 2nd century. Only about 50 manuscripts of this Old Latin version survive. These manuscripts are divided into the African Latin group and the European Latin group according to the type of text which they contain. In 382 A.D. Pope Damasus requested Jerome to undertake a revision of the Old Latin version. Jerome complied with this request and thus produced the Latin Vulgate, the official Bible of the Roman Catholic Church. There are more than 8,000 extant manuscripts of the Vulgate.[13]

Of the Syriac versions the most important is the Peshitta, the historic Bible of the whole Syrian Church, of which 350 manuscripts are now extant. The Peshitta was long regarded as one of the most ancient New Testament versions, being accorded a 2nd-century date. In more recent times, however, Burkitt (1904) and other naturalistic critics have assigned a 5th-century date to the Peshitta.[14] But Burkitt's hypothesis is contrary to the evidence, and today it is being abandoned even by naturalistic scholars.[15] All the sects into which the Syrian Church is divided are loyal to the Peshitta. In order to account for this it is necessary to believe that the Peshitta was in existence long before the 5th century, for it was in the 5th century that these divisions occurred.

The Philoxenian Syriac version was produced in 508 A.D. for Philoxenus, bishop of Mabbug, by his assistant Polycarp. In 616 this version was re-issued, or perhaps revised, by Thomas of Harkel, who likewise was bishop of Mabbug. The Philoxenian-Harclean version includes the five books which the Peshitta omits, namely 2 Peter, 2 and 3 John, Jude, and Revelation.[16]

The so-called "Old Syriac" version is represented by only two manuscripts,[17] the Curetonian Syriac manuscript, named after W. Cureton who published it in 1858, and the Sinaitic Syriac manuscript, which was discovered by Mrs. Lewis in 1892 at the same monastery on Mount Sinai in which Tischendorf had discovered *Codex Aleph* almost fifty years before. These manuscripts are called "Old Syriac" because they are thought by critics to represent a Syriac text which is older than the Peshitta. This theory, however, rests on Burkitt's untenable hypothesis that the Peshitta was produced in the 5th century by Rabbula, bishop of Edessa.

The Egyptian New Testament versions are called the Coptic versions because they are written in Coptic, the latest form of the ancient Egyptian language. The Coptic New Testament is extant in two dialects, the Sahidic version of Southern Egypt and the Bohairic version of Northern Egypt. According to Metzger, the Sahidic version dates from the beginning of the 3rd century. The oldest Sahidic manuscript has been variously dated from the mid-4th to the 6th century. The Bohairic version is regarded as somewhat later than the Sahidic. It is extant in many manuscripts, most of which are late. In the 1950's however, M. Bodmer acquired a papyrus Bohairic manuscript containing most of the Gospel of John which was thought by its editor, R. Kasser, to date from the mid-4th century.[18]

In addition to the Latin, Syriac, and Coptic versions, there are a number of other versions which are important for textual criticism. The Gothic version was translated from the Greek in the middle of the 4th century by Ulfilas, the renowned missionary to the Goths. Of this version six manuscripts are still extant. Of the Armenian version, 1,244 manuscripts survive. This version seems to have been made in the 5th century, but by whom is uncertain. Whether it was made from the Greek or from a Syriac version is also a matter of debate among scholars. The Christians of Georgia, a mountainous district between the Black and Caspian seas, also had a New Testament in their own language, several copies of which are still extant.[19]

(e) The Quotations of the Church Fathers

The New Testament quotations found in the writings of the Church Fathers constitute yet another source of information concerning the history of the New Testament text. Some of the most important Fathers, for the purposes of textual criticism, are as follows: the three Western Fathers, Irenaeus (c. 180), Tertullian (150-220), Cyprian (200-258); the Alexandrian Fathers, Clement (c. 200), Origen (182-251); the Fathers who lived in Antioch and in Asia Minor, especially Chrysostom (345-407). Another very important early Christian writer was Tatian, who about 170 A.D. composed a harmony of the Four Gospels called the Diatessaron. This had wide circulation in Syria and has been preserved in two Arabic manuscripts and various other sources.

(f) Families of New Testament Documents

Since the 18th century the New Testament documents have been divided into families according to the type of text which they contain. There are three of these families, namely, the *Western* family, the *Alexandrian* family, and the *Traditional* (Byzantine) family.

The *Western* family consists of those New Testament documents which contain that form of text found in the writings of the Western Church Fathers, especially Irenaeus, Tertullian, and Cyprian. A number of Greek manuscripts contain this text, of which the most important are D and D2. Three other important witnesses to the Western text are the Old Latin version, the Diatessaron of Tatian, and the Curetonian and Sinaitic Syriac manuscripts.

The *Alexandrian* family consists of those New Testament documents which contain that form of text which was used by Origen in some of his writings and also by other Church Fathers who, like Origen, lived at Alexandria. This family includes Papyri 46, 47, 66,

75, *B*, *Aleph.*, and about 25 other Greek New Testament manuscripts. The Coptic versions also belong to the *Alexandrian* family of New Testament documents. Westcott and Hort (1881) distinguished between the text of *B* and the text of other Alexandrian documents. They called the *B* text *Neutral,* thus indicating their belief that it was a remarkable pure text which had not been contaminated by the errors of either the Western or Alexandrian texts. Many subsequent scholars, however, have denied the validity of this distinction.

The *Traditional* (Byzantine) family includes all those New Testament documents which contain the Traditional (Byzantine) text. The vast majority of the Greek New Testament manuscripts belong to this family, including *A* (in the Gospels) and *W* (in Matthew and the last two thirds of Luke). The Peshitta Syriac version and the Gothic version also belong to the Traditional family of New Testament documents. And the New Testament quotations of Chrysostom and the other Fathers of Antioch and Asia Minor seem generally to agree with the Traditional text.

2. The Early History Of The Western Text

The Western text may actually have originated in the East, as Ropes (1926)[20] and other noted scholars have believed, but if so it was probably taken to Rome almost immediately and adopted by the Christian community of that great city as its official text. Then from Rome the use of the Western text spread to all parts of the civilized world, the prestige of the Roman Church securing for it a favorable reception everywhere. As Souter (1912) observed, "The universal diffusion of the Western text can best be explained by the view that it circulated from Rome, the capital and centre of all things."[21]

(a) Western Additions to the New Testament Text

The Western text is singularly long in many places, containing readings which are not found in the Alexandrian or Traditional texts. Some of the most interesting of these Western additions to the New Testament text are as follows:

Matt. 3:15   To the account of Christ's baptism certain Old Latin manuscripts add, *and a great light shone around.*

Matt. 20:28   After the familiar words, *The Son of Man came not to be ministered unto but to minister and to give His life a ransom for many,* D and certain Old Latin manuscripts add, *But as for you, seek to increase from that which is small, and from that which is greater to become less. And when ye come in and are invited to dine, do not sit at the best places; lest some one more honorable than thou approach, and the host come and*

say to thee, Move farther down, and thou be ashamed.
But if thou sit down at the lower place, and some one
less than thou approach, the host also will say to thee,
Move farther up, and this shall be profitable for thee.

Luke 3:22   At Christ's baptism, according to *D* and certain Old
            Latin manuscripts, the heavenly voice states, *Thou*
            art My Son. This day have I begotten Thee.

Luke 6:4   At the end of this verse *D* adds this apochryphal saying
            of Jesus. *On the same day, seeing a certain man work-*
            ing on the sabbath, He said to him, Man, if thou
            knowest what thou doest, thou art blessed, but if thou
            knowest not, thou art cursed and art a transgressor
            of the law.

Luke 23:53 After the words, *wherein never man before was laid,*
            D c Sahidic add, *And when He was laid there, he*
            placed before the tomb a stone, which twenty men
            could scarcely roll.

John 6:56   After Christ's solemn statement, *He that eateth My*
            flesh and drinketh My blood, dwelleth in Me and I
            in him, D and the Old Latin add, *according as the Fa-*
            ther is in Me and I in the Father. Verily, verily I
            say unto you, except ye take the body of the Son of
            Man as the bread of life, ye have not life in Him.

Acts 15:20 To the apostolic decree *D* Sahidic Ethiopic add these
            words (the Golden Rule in negative form), *And*
            whatsoever they do not wish to be done to them-
            selves, not to do to others.

Acts 23:24 Here the Old Latin and the Vulgate give an inter-
            esting explanation why Claudius Lysias sent Paul
            away by night to Felix the governor, *For he feared*
            lest the Jews should seize him and kill him and he
            meanwhile should be accused of having taken a bribe.

These longer Western readings have found few defenders and are
one of the many indications that the Western New Testament text
is a corrupt form of the divine original.

(b) The Western Omissions

In the last portion of Luke there are eight readings which *The*
Revised Standard Version (R.S.V.) and *The New English Bible*
(N.E.B.) remove from the text and consign to the footnotes. These
readings are usually called *Western omissions,* because (with two
exceptions) they are omitted only by a few manuscripts of the Western
group, namely, *D,* certain Old Latin manuscripts, and one or two Old

Syriac manuscripts.   These Western omissions are as follows:

Luke 22:19-20   (the Lord's Supper) from *which is given for you* to *is shed for you,* omitted by *D* and the Old Latin version.

Luke 24:3   (referring to Christ's body) *of the Lord Jesus,* omitted by *D* and the Old Latin version.

Luke 24:6   (the angelic announcement) *He is not here but is risen,* omitted by *D*, the Old Latin version, the Old Syriac version (?), and certain manuscripts of the Armenian version.

Luke 24:12   (Peter's journey to the tomb)   whole verse omitted by *D*, the Old Latin version, and the Old Syriac version (?).

Luke 24:36   (salutation of the risen Christ) *and saith unto them, Peace be unto you,* omitted by *D*, the Old Latin version, and the Old Syriac version (?).

Luke 24:40   (proofs of Christ's resurrection) *And when He had thus spoken, He shewed them His hands and His feet,* omitted by *D* and the Old Latin and Old Syriac versions.

Luke 24:51   (the ascension of Christ) *and was carried up into heaven,* omitted by *Aleph, D,* the Old Latin version and the Sinaitic Syriac manuscript.

Luke 24:52   (recognition of Christ's deity) *worshipped Him, and* omitted by *D*, the Old Latin version and the Sinaitic Syriac manuscript.

The omission of these eight readings in the R.S.V. and the N.E.B. is certainly not a matter that can be taken lightly, for it means, as far as these two modern versions can make it so, that all reference to the atoning work of Christ has been eliminated from Luke's account of the Lord's Supper (Luke 22:19-20) and that the ascension of Christ into heaven (Luke 24:51) has been entirely removed from the Gospels, Mark's account of the ascension having already been rejected by the critics.   Certainly no believing Bible student can remain indifferent to this mutilation of the Gospel record.

In their Greek New Testament text (1881) Westcott and Hort placed these Western omissions in double brackets, thus indicating their opinion that these readings were interpolations which had been added to the text of Luke in all the New Testament manuscripts except *D* and those few others mentioned above.   But the fact that all eight of these readings have recently been found to occur in Papyrus 75 is unfavorable to their hypothesis that these readings are additions to the text. For if this were so, it is hard to see how all these readings could have made their way into so early a witness as Papyrus 75. Surely some of them would have failed to do so and thus would be absent from this papyrus. Hort's answer to objections of this sort was vague and scarcely satisfactory. He believed that these readings were added to the text at a very early date just after the Neutral text "had parted company from the earliest special ancestry of the Western text," perhaps "at the actual divergence,"[22] but where or by whom this was done he didn't say.

Thus Westcott and Hort believed that in Luke's account of the Lord's Supper, for example, all the extant New Testament manuscripts are in error except *D* and a few Old Latin manuscripts. According to these two scholars and also Kilpatrick (1946)[23] and Chadwick (1957),[24] the reading, *which is given for you: this do in remembrance of Me. Likewise the cup after supper, saying, This cup is the new testament in My blood, which is shed for you*, is an interpolation which some very early scribe borrowed from Paul's account of the Lord's Supper (1 Cor. 11:24-25). The scribe's motive, these scholars claim, was to make Luke agree with Matthew and Mark in having the cup come after the bread. This interpolation, these scholars believe, was so extraordinarily successful that it is found today in all the extant New Testament manuscripts except *D* and those few others.

The R.S.V. and the N.E.B. are certainly to be condemned for using such doubtful speculations as a basis for their alterations of the Lucan account of the Lord's Supper. For this theory is rejected even by many liberal scholars. As Kenyon and Legg (1937) and Williams (1951)[25] have pointed out, no scribe would have tried to harmonize Luke's narrative with that of Matthew and Mark by borrowing from 1 Cor. 11:24-25. For this would make the supposed contradiction worse. There would then be two cups where before there had been only one.

The ascension of Christ into heaven is another important Western omission which the R.S.V. and the N.E.B. have wrongly relegated to the footnotes. The words *and was carried up into heaven* are found not in "some" documents or "many" documents, as these two modernistic versions misleadingly state in their footnotes, but in *all* the New Testament documents except those few mentioned above. Westcott and Hort believed that these words were not originally a part of Luke's Gospel but were inserted by a scribe who thought that the ascension was implied by the preceding words, *He was parted from them*. According to Westcott and Hort, Luke did not intend even to hint at the ascension in his Gospel but was saving his account of it for the first chapter of Acts.[26] But, as Zahn (1909) pointed out, this theory is contradicted by the opening verses of Acts, which make it clear that Luke thought that he had already given an account of the ascension in the last chapter of his Gospel.[27]

It is much more reasonable to suppose with Streeter (1924),[28] Williams 1951),[29] and other scholars that the ascension into heaven was omitted by some of the early Christians in order to avoid a seeming conflict with the first chapter of Acts. The account in Luke may have seemed to them to imply that the ascension took place on the very day of the resurrection, and this would seem to be out of harmony with the narrative in Acts, which plainly states that the ascension occurred forty days after the resurrection. In order to eliminate this difficulty they may have omitted the reference to the ascension in Luke 24:51. This drastic remedy, however, was in no wise necessary. For, contrary to the opinion of Streeter and Williams, there is no real contradiction between the Gospel of Luke and Acts in regard to the ascension of Christ. The Gospel of Luke need not be regarded as teaching that the resurrection and ascension of Christ took place on the same day.

Because these eight omitted readings have been found to occur in Papyrus 75, critics are now changing their minds about them. Kurt Aland (1966), for example, has restored these Western omissions to the text of the Nestle New Testament.[30] Hence the R.S.V., the N.E.B., and the other modern versions which omit them are already out of date. And this rapid shifting of opinion shows us how untrustworthy naturalistic textual criticism is. Christians who rely upon it for their knowledge of the New Testament text are to be pitied. Surely they are building their house upon the sands.

(c) The Western and Caesarean Texts in Egypt

The Western text circulated not only in the East and in Italy and North Africa but also in Egypt. This was first proved in 1899 by P. M. Barnard in a study entitled *The Biblical Text of Clement of Alexandria*.[31] Barnard analyzed Clement's quotations from the Four Gospels and Acts and found them to be of a fundamentally Western character. Then in 1926 Papyrus 37, a 3rd-century fragment of Matthew, was shown by H. A. Sanders to be Western in its text,[32] and again in the following year Sanders showed the same thing to be true of Papyrus 38, a 3rd or 4th-century fragment of Acts.[33]

During the 1920's and 30's another type of New Testament text was discovered to have circulated in Egypt, namely, the *Caesarean* text. This text occurs in certain late manuscripts (e.g., *Theta* 1 13 28 565 700) in places in which these manuscripts do not agree with the Traditional (Byzantine) text. In 1924 Streeter gave this newly discovered text the name Caesarean because he believed that Origen used this type of text in Caesarea after he had fled there from Alexandria in 231 A.D.[34] In 1928, however, Kirsopp Lake brought out the possibility that the Caesarean text was an Egyptian text. According to Lake, when Origen first moved to Caesarea, he used the Alexandrian text, not switching to the Caesarean text until later. This might mean that he found the Alexandrian text in Caesarea and used it only temporarily until the Caesarean text could be sent to him out of Egypt.[35] Then, finally, in 1933-37 F. G. Kenyon published the newly discovered Chester Beatty Papyri. In Acts, the Pauline Epistles and Revelation he found them to possess an Alexandrian type of text, but in the Gospels, and especially in Mark, he discovered them to be Caesarean.[36] This discovery provided one more link in the chain binding the Caesarean text to Egypt.

Thus these discoveries and these researches into the New Testament text of ancient Egypt are unfavorable to the theory of Westcott and Hort that the Alexandrian text, and especially the text of *B*, represents the pure original New Testament text. For, as Kenyon pointed out, the evidence shows that the Alexandrian text was not dominant even in Egypt. Clement never used it, and Origen used it only some of the time.[37] Clearly it is wrong to suppose that the Alexandrian text enjoyed an official status that kept it pure.

3. The Early History Of The Alexandrian Text

Concerning the relationship of the Alexandrian New Testament text to the Western New Testament text there has been a difference of opinion dating back to the early days of New Testament textual criticism. Some critics have believed that the Western text was the earlier and that the Alexandrian text came into being as a refinement of this primitive Western text. Among those who have thought this are Griesbach (1796), Hug (1808), Burkitt (1899), A. C. Clark (1914), Sanders (1926), Lake (1928), Glaue (1944), and Black (1954). Other critics have regarded the Alexandrian text as prior and have looked upon the Western Text as a corruption of this purer Alexandrian text-form. Some of those who have held this view are Tischendorf (1868), Westcott and Hort (1881), B. Weiss (1899), Ropes (1926), Lagrange (1935), and Metzger (1964). In the paragraphs that follow we shall bring forth evidence to show that neither of these positions is correct.

(a) Early Alterations in the Alexandrian Text

At a very early date the Alexandrian text was altered in many places. The following are some of these alterations occurring in *B*, which Westcott and Hort (WH) regarded as the purest of all extant manuscripts, and also in the Chester Beatty Papyri and the Bodmer Papyri.

Luke 10:41-42   *One thing is needful.* Traditional Text, Pap 45 (dated 225 A.D.) Pap 75 (dated 200 A.D.).
Few things are needful, or one. B Aleph WH & footnotes of R.V., A.S.V., R.S.V., N.E.B.
This Alexandrian alteration makes Jesus talk about food rather than spiritual realities.

Luke 12:31   *Seek ye the kingdom of God.* Traditional Text, Pap 45.
Seek ye the kingdom. Pap 75.

Seek ye His kingdom. B Aleph, WH, R.V., A.S.V., R.S.V., N.E.B.
A similar Alexandrian alteration is made in Matt. 6:33, where *B* alters the text still further into, *But seek ye first His righteousness and His kingdom.*

Luke 15:21   *B Aleph D* add *Make me as one of thy hired servants.*
As Hoskier observes,[38] this tasteless Alexandrian addition (accepted by WH and placed in the footnotes of modern versions) spoils the narrative. In the true text the prodigal never pronounces the words which he had formulated in vs. 19. As soon as he beholds his father's loving face, they die on his lips. This addition is not found in Pap 75.

Luke 23:35   *saying, He saved others, let him save himself, if this is the Christ, the chosen of God.* Traditional Text.
they said to Him, Thou savedst others, save thyself, if thou art the Son of God, if thou art Christ, the chosen. D c aeth.
saying, He saved others, let him save himself, if this is the Christ, the Son of God, the chosen. Pap 75.
saying, He saved others, let him save himself, if he is the Son, the Christ of God, the chosen. B.
We see here that the Traditional Text was altered by the Western text at a very early date. Then this alteration was adopted in part by Pap 75 and then in still a different form by *B.*

Luke 23:45   *And the sun was darkened.* Here Pap 75, *Aleph B C L* Coptic, WH, R.V., A.S.V., R.S.V., N.E.B., read, *the sun having become eclipsed.* This rationalistic explanation of the supernatural darkness at the crucifixion is ascribed to the Jews in the Acts of Pilate and to a heathen historian Thallus by Julius Africanus, but, as Julius noted, it is impossible, because at Passover time the moon was full.[39]

John 1:15   *John bare witness of Him and cried, saying, This was He of whom I spake, He that cometh after me etc.*
Traditional Text, Pap 66 (dated 200 A.D.), Pap 75.
John bare witness of Him and cried, saying (this was he that said) He that cometh after me etc. B WH & footnotes of R.V., A.S.V.
This Alexandrian alteration, *this was he that said,* makes no sense. It had already been stated that John was speaking.

John 8:39   *If ye were Abraham's children, ye would do the works of Abraham.* Traditional Text.

If ye are Abraham's children, do the works of Abraham. Pap 66 *B*, WH, R.V., A.S.V., and footnotes of N.E.B.

If ye are Abraham's children, ye would do the works of Abraham. Pap 75 *Aleph D*.

Here we see that the Traditional Text has the original reading. This was altered at a very early date by Pap 66, who was followed by *B* and, in modern times, by WH, R.V., A.S.V., and N.E.B. (footnotes). Then, also at a very early date, the scribe of Pap 75 combined the first two readings in an ungrammatical way, and he was followed by *Aleph* and *D*.

John 10:29   *My Father, who gave them to Me, is greater than all.* Traditional Text, Pap 66, Pap 75.

That which My Father hath given unto Me is greater than all. *B Aleph*, WH & footnotes of R.V., A.S.V., R.S.V., N.E.B.

This alteration is of great doctrinal importance, since it makes the preservation of the saints depend on the Church rather than on God. So Westcott expounds it, "The faithful, regarded in their unity, are stronger than every opposing power."[40]

(b) The Alexandrian Text Influenced by the Sahidic (Coptic) Version

Coptic is the latest form of the language of ancient Egypt. At first it was written in native Egyptian characters, but after the beginning of the Christian era Greek capital letters were mainly employed. At least a half a dozen different Coptic dialects were spoken in ancient Egypt, but the most important of these were the Sahidic dialect spoken in southern Egypt and the Bohairic dialect spoken in northern Egypt. At a very early date the Greek New Testament was translated into Sahidic, and some of the distinctive readings of this Sahidic version are found in Papyrus 75, thus supporting the contention of Hoskier (1914) that the Alexandrian text was "tremendously influenced" by the Sahidic version.[41]

For example, in the parable of the Rich Man and Lazarus (Luke 16:19) Papyrus 75 says that the Rich Man's name was *Neves*. The Sahidic version says that the Rich Man's name was *Nineve*. Why was the Rich Man given this name? Metzger (1964) says that it was because there was a wide-spread tradition among the ancient catechists of the Coptic Church that the name of the Rich Man was *Nineveh*, a name which had become the symbol of dissolute riches.[42] Grobel (1964), on the other hand, argues that this name was derived from an old Egyptian folk-tale and that the name *Nineve* in Sahidic means *Nobody*.[43] But, however this may be, it is obvious that this reading was taken early into the text of Papyrus 75 from the Sahidic version.

Another Sahidic reading that found its way into the text of Papyrus 75 occurs in John 8:57. Here the majority of the New Testament documents read, *Hast thou seen Abraham?* But Papyrus 75, *Aleph, T,* Sahidic, Sinaitic Syriac read *Hath Abraham seen thee?*

In John 10:7 Papyrus 75 agrees with the Sahidic version in reading, *I am the shepherd of the sheep,* instead of, *I am the door of the sheep.*

In John 11:12 Papyrus 75 agrees with the Sahidic version against all the rest of the New Testament documents. In the other documents the disciples say (referring to Lazarus), *Lord, if he hath fallen asleep, he will be saved.* Papyrus 75 and the Sahidic version, however, read, *he will be raised.*

(c) Have True Readings Been Hiding for Centuries in the Papyri?

In John 7:52, according to the Traditional Text, the chief priests and Pharisees say to Nicodemus, *Search and look: for out of Galilee hath arisen no prophet.* In the early 19th century the rationalists Bretschneider and Baur insisted that these Jewish rulers could not have said this because they would have known that several prophets, e. g., Elijah, Nahum, Hosea, Jonah, were of Galilean origin.[44] More recently Bultmann (1941) and others have suggested that the true reading is *the Prophet,* referring to the great Prophet whose coming had been foretold by Moses long ago (Deut. 18:18).[45] Still more recently this suggested reading, *the Prophet,* has been found to occur in Papyrus 66 and is regarded by J. R. Michaels (1957) and others as "almost certainly" correct.[46] For support appeal is made to Luke 7:39 where *B* similarly adds *the* before *prophet.* But this appeal cuts both ways, for this *B* reading is accepted only by WH and the footnotes of R.V. and A.S.V. Hence if *B* is wrong in Luke 7:39, it is reasonable to suppose that Papyrus 66 is wrong in John 7:52. And as Fee (1965) observes,[47] a correction appears in this verse in Papyrus 66 which may indicate that even the scribe who wrote it may not, on second thought, have approved of the novelty which he had introduced into the text. Certainly there is no need to change the text to answer the criticism of Bretschneider and Baur. We need only to suppose that the Jewish rulers were so angry that they forgot their biblical history.

There is no compelling reason, therefore, to conclude that in John 7:52 the true reading has been hiding for centuries in Papyrus 66 and has just now come to light. And such a conclusion is contrary to the doctrine of the special providential preservation of the Scriptures, since no one knows where Papyrus 66 comes from. As its name implies, this manuscript is the property of the Bodmer Library in Geneva, Switzerland. According to Kurt Aland (1957), it is part of a collection of more than fifty papyrus documents which was purchased in 1954 by the Bodmer Library from E. N. Adler of London.[48] And to this information Mlle. O. Bongard, secretary of the

Bodmer Library, adds little. "We can only tell you," she writes (1957), "that it was purchased at Geneva by M. Bodmer. The numerous intermediaries are themselves ignorant of the exact source. And so we ourselves have given up looking for it."[49]

The Chester Beatty Papyri, which are housed in the Beatty Museum in Dublin, are in no better position. According to the information which Prof. Carl Schmidt obtained from the dealer, they were found in a pot on the east bank of the Nile south of Cairo.[50] Aland (1963) believes that there may be a connection between the Chester Beatty Papyri and the Bodmer Papyri. According to Aland, "the Bodmer Papyri seem to have been found in one place and to have come from an important Christian educational center, which was very old and which flourished for a long time."[51] Aland thinks it possible that the Chester Beatty Papyri also came from this same place. The reason for supposing this lies in the fact that a fragment of Bodmer Papyrus 66 (from chapter 19 of John) has been found among the Chester Beatty Papyri in Dublin.[52]

But however all this may be, it is evident that as Bible-believing Christians we cannot consistently maintain that there are true readings of the New Testament text which have been hiding in papyri for ages, enclosed in pots, waiting for the light of day, and just now discovered. If we thought this, our faith would be always wavering. We could never be sure that a dealer would not soon appear with something new from somewhere. Thank God that He has not preserved the New Testament text in this secret way but publicly in the usage of His Church and in the Traditional Text and the Textus Receptus which reflect this usage.

(d) Christ's Agony and Bloody Sweat

Luke 22:43-44   "And there appeared an angel unto Him from heaven, strengthening Him. And being in agony He prayed more earnestly: and His sweat was as it were great drops of blood falling down to the ground."

The evidence for these precious verses may be briefly summed up as follows: They are found in the vast majority of the New Testament manuscripts, including *Aleph, D,* and *L.* They are also found in the Old Latin versions and in the Curetonian Syriac. They occur also in the Peshitta and Palestinian Syriac versions and in certain manuscripts of the Armenian and Coptic versions.

The evidence against Luke 22:43-44 is as follows: These verses are omitted by Papyrus 75, *B, A, N, R, T, W,* and a group of later manuscripts called Family 13, which contain the Caesarean text. They are also omitted by one Old Latin manuscript, the Sinaitic Syriac, and Harclean Syriac margin, and the Coptic and Armenian versions.

On the strength of this negative evidence Westcott and Hort decided that the account of Christ's agony and bloody sweat was not part of the original Gospel of Luke but a bit of oral tradition which was inserted into the sacred text somewhere in the western part of the Roman empire. "These verses," they concluded, "and the first sentence of 23:34 (Christ's prayer for His murderers) may safely be called the most precious among the remains of this evangelic tradition which were rescued from oblivion by the scribes of the second century."[53]

In arguing for this theory, however, Westcott and Hort ran into an insoluble difficulty. They insisted that this alleged interpolation was a distinctive feature of the Western text. The early Fathers who cited this reading, they maintained, were all Westerners. "The early patristic evidence on its behalf is purely Western."[54] But if this had been so, how did these verses find acceptance in the 4th century among Eastern Fathers such as Epiphanius, Didymus, Eusebius, and Gregory Nazianzus? For then the Arian controversy was at its height and orthodox Christians were on their guard against anything which detracted from Christ's deity. The account of the Saviour's bloody sweat and of the ministering angel seems, at first sight, to do this, and therefore it would never have been accepted as Scripture by 4th-century Christians if it had come to them as something new and not previously a part of their Bible. According to Epiphanius, precisely the opposite development had taken place. Arius had used these verses to support his low view of Christ, and for this reason some of the orthodox Christians had removed them from their Gospel manuscripts.[55]

In more recent years the genuineness of Luke's account of Christ's agony and bloody sweat has been defended by such well known scholars as Streeter (1924),[56] Goguel, Williams (1951),[57] and especially Harnack (1931).[58] Harnack defended the Lucan authorship of these verses on linguistic grounds. "In the first place," he wrote, "this short passage bears the stamp of the Lucan viewpoint and speech so distinctly that it is in the highest degree mistaken to explain it as an interpolation." Harnack gives two reasons why this passage was offensive to orthodox Christians of the 2nd century and therefore might have been omitted by some of them. "In the first place, it was offensive that an angel strengthened the Lord — especially offensive in the earliest period, when, beginning with the epistles to the Colossians and the Hebrews, it was necessary to fight for the superiority of Jesus over the angels. In the second place, the agony with its bloody consequences was also offensive. . . . The more one emphasized against the Jews and heathen that the Lord endured suffering of His own free will (see Barnabas and Justin), so much the more strange must this fearful soul-struggle have appeared."

The fact that Luke 22:43-44 does not occur in Papyrus 75 indicates that Harnack was right in supposing that it was during the 2nd century that these verses began to be omitted from certain of the New Testament manuscripts. It is not necessary to suppose, however, that this practice originated among orthodox Christians. It may be that the docetists were the first ones to take the decisive step of omitting these verses. These heretics would be anxious to eliminate the account of Christ's agony and bloody sweat, since this passage refuted their contention that Christ's human nature was merely an appearance (phantom) and was one of the biblical texts which Irenaeus (c. 180)[59] and other orthodox writers were urging against them. The easiest way for the docetists to meet this orthodox appeal to scripture was to reject Luke 22:43-44 altogether. And when once this omission was made, it would be accepted by some of the orthodox Christians who for various reasons found these verses hard to reconcile with Christ's deity.

(e) Christ's Prayer for His Murderers

Luke 23:34a   "Then said Jesus, Father forgive them, for they know not what they do."

This disputed reading is found in the vast majority of the New Testament manuscripts, including *Aleph, A, C, L, N,* and also in certain manuscripts of the Old Latin version, in the Curetonian Syriac manuscript and in the Peshitta, Harclean, and Philoxenian versions. It is also cited or referred to by many of the Church Fathers, including the following: in the 2nd century, Tatian [60] and Irenaeus;[61] in the 3rd century, Origen; in the 4th century, Basil, Eusebius, and others. The reading is omitted, on the other hand, by the following witnesses: Papyrus 75, *B, D, W, Theta,* 38, 435, certain manuscripts of the Old Latin version, the Sinaitic manuscript of the Old Syriac version, and the Coptic versions (with the exception of certain manuscripts). Cyril of Alexandria is also listed as omitting the reading, but, as Hort admitted, this is only an inference.

Not many orthodox Christians have agreed with Westcott and Hort in their rejection of this familiar reading which has become hallowed by many centuries of tender association. But these critics were nevertheless positive that this petition ascribed to Christ was not part of the original New Testament text but was interpolated into the Western manuscripts early in the 2nd century. This prayer of our Saviour for His murderers, they insisted, like the agony and bloody sweat, was "a fragment from the traditions, written or oral, which were, for a while at least, locally current beside the canonical Gospels, and which doubtless included matter of every degree of authenticity and intrinsic value. . . . Few verses of the Gospels," they continued, "bear in themselves a surer witness to the truth of what they record than this first of the Words from the Cross: but it need not therefore have belonged originally to the book in which it is now included. We cannot doubt that it comes from an extraneous source."[62]

Westcott and Hort's theory, however, is a most improbable one. This prayer of Christ would be interpreted as referring to the Jews and, thus interpreted, would not be something likely to have been added to the Gospel narrative by 2nd-century Christian scribes. For by that time the relationship between Jews and Christians had hardened into one of permanent hostility, and the average Christian would not have welcomed the thought that the Jews ought to be forgiven or that the Saviour had so prayed. Certainly the general tone of the 2nd-century Christian writers is markedly anti-Jewish. *The Epistle of Barnabas,* written about 130 A.D. reveals this emphasis. "In no other writing of that early time," Harnack tells us, "is the separation of the Gentile Christians from the patriotic Jews so clearly brought out. The Old Testament, he (Barnabas) maintains, belongs only to the Christians. Circumcision and the whole Old Testament sacrificial and ceremonial institution are the devil's work."[63]

For these reasons Harnack (1931) was inclined to accept Luke 23:34a as genuine and to believe that this prayer of Christ for His murderers was omitted from some of the manuscripts because of the offense which it occasioned many segments of the early Christian Church. "The words," he observed, "offered a strong offense to ancient Christendom as soon as they were related to the Jews generally. Indeed the connection, viewed accurately, shows that they apply only to the soldiers; but this is not said directly, and so, according to the far-sighted methods of the exegesis of those days, these words were related to the enemies of Jesus, the Jews generally. But then they conflicted not only with Luke 23:28 but also with the anti-Judaism of the ancient Church generally. . . . The verse ought in no case to be stricken out of the text of Luke; at the very most it must be left a question mark."[64]

Streeter also and Rendel Harris[65] were friendly to the supposition that Christ's prayer for His murderers was purposely deleted from Luke's Gospel by some of the scribes due to anti-Jewish feeling. But again it is not necessary to imagine that orthodox Christian scribes were the first to make this omission. It may be that Marcion was ultimately responsible for this mutilation of the sacred text. For, as Williams observes, "Marcion was anti-Jewish in all his sentiments."[66] It is true that, according to Harnack's analysis, Marcion still included this prayer of Christ in his edition of Luke's Gospel (probably relating it to the Roman soldiers),[67] but some of his followers may have referred it to the Jews and thus come to feel that it ought to be deleted from the Gospel record.

(f) The Only Begotten Son Versus Only Begotten God

John 1:18   "No man hath seen God at any time; *the only begotten Son,* which is in the bosom of the Father, He hath declared Him."

This verse exhibits the following four-fold variation:
(1) *the only begotten Son,* Traditional Text, Latin versions, Curetonian Syriac.
(2) *only begotten God,* Pap 66, *Aleph B C L,* WH.
(3) *the only begotten God,* Pap 75.

(4) *(the) only begotten*, read by one Latin manuscript.

The first reading is the genuine one. The other three are plainly heretical. Burgon (1896) long ago traced these corruptions of the sacred text to their source, namely Valentinus.[68] Burgon pointed out that the first time John 1:18 is quoted by any of the ancients a reference is made to the doctrines of Valentinus. This quotation is found in a fragment entitled *Excerpts from Theodotus*, which dates from the 2nd century. R. P. Casey (1934) translates it as follows:

> The verse, "in the beginning was the Logos and the Logos was with God and the Logos was God," the Valentinians understand thus, for they say that "the beginning" is the "Only Begotten" and that he is also called God, as also in the verses which immediately follow it explains that he is God, for it says, "The *Only-Begotten God* who is in the bosom of the Father, he has declared him."[69]

This passage is very obscure, but at least it is clear that the reading favored by Valentinus was precisely that now found in Papyrus 75, *the only begotten God*. What could be more probable than Dean Burgon's suggestion that Valentinus fabricated this reading by changing *the only begotten Son* to *the only begotten God?* His motive for doing so would be his apparent desire to distinguish between the *Son* and the *Word* (Logos). According to the Traditional reading, the *Word* mentioned in John 1:14 is identified with *the only begotten Son* mentioned in John 1:18. Is it not likely that Valentinus, denying such identification, sought to reinforce his denial by the easy method of altering *Son* to *God* (a change of only one letter in Greek) and using this word *God* in an inferior sense to refer to the *Word* rather than the *Son?* This procedure would enable him to deny that in John 1:14 the *Word* is identified with the *Son*. He could argue that in both these verses the reference is to the *Word* and that therefore the *Word* and the *Son* are two distinct Beings.

Thus we see that it is unwise in present-day translators to base the texts of their modern versions on recent papyrus discoveries or on *B* and *Aleph*. For all these documents come from Egypt, and Egypt during the early Christian centuries was a land in which heresies were rampant. So much was this so that, as Bauer (1934)[70] and van Unnik (1958)[71] have pointed out, later Egyptian Christians seem to have been ashamed of the heretical past of their country and to have drawn a veil of silence across it. This seems to be why so little is known of the history of early Egyptian Christianity. In view, therefore, of the heretical character of the early Egyptian Church, it is not surprising that the papyri, *B, Aleph*, and other manuscripts which hail from Egypt are liberally sprinkled with heretical readings.

(g) Son of God Versus Holy One of God

John 6:68-69   "Then Simon Peter answered Him, Lord, to whom shall we go? Thou hast the words of eternal life. And we believe and are sure that Thou art *the Christ, the Son of the living God."*

This verse exhibits the following four-fold variation:
(1) *the Christ, the Son of the living God,* Traditional Text, Peshitta Syriac, Harclean Syriac, Old Latin (some mss.).
(2) *the Holy One of God,* Papyrus 75, *Aleph B C D L W,* Sahidic, WH, R.V., A.S.V., R.S.V., N.E.B.
(3) *the Christ, the Holy One of God,* Papyrus 66, Sahidic (some mss) Bohairic.
(4) *the Christ, the Son of God, Theta,* 1 33 565, Old Latin, Vulgate, Sinaitic Syriac.

According to the critics, reading (2) *the Holy One of God* was the original reading. This was changed to reading (3) and then to reading (4) and then finally to reading (1). By these easy stages, the critics maintain, John 6:69 was harmonized to Matt. 16:16, which reads, "And Simon Peter answered and said, *Thou art the Christ, the Son of the living God."*

But internal evidence forbids us to adopt this critical conclusion. For if as Bible-believing Christians we regard Matt. 16:16 and John 6:69 as actually spoken by Peter, then it is difficult to explain why on two similar occasions he would make two entirely different affirmations of his faith in Jesus, in one place confessing Him as *the Christ, the Son of God* and in the other as *the Holy One of God.* For in the other Gospels only the demons address Jesus as *the Holy One of God.* (Mark 1:24; Luke 4:34). And even if we should adopt a modernistic approach to John 6:69 and regard it as put in the mouth of Peter by the Gospel writer, still it would be difficult to receive *Holy One of God* as the true reading. For in John 20:31 the evangelist states that his purpose in writing his Gospel is that his readers may believe *that Jesus is the Christ, the Son of God.* Such being his intention, he surely would not have made Peter confess Jesus as *the Holy One of God* rather than as *the Christ the Son of the living God.*

The external evidence also is against the critical hypothesis that *the Holy One of God* is the original reading of John 6:69. For some of the documents which favor this reading have quite evidently gone astray in John 1:34. Here instead of *the Son of God* (which is the reading of most of the New Testament documents) Papyrus 5, *Aleph* 77 218, Old Latin (some mss), Curetonian Syriac read *the Chosen One of God.* This reading is accepted by N.E.B. and placed in the margin by WH, but most critics reject it as false. And if *Chosen One of God* is a false reading in John 1:34, then it is surely reasonable to conclude that *Holy One of God* is a false reading in John 6:69.

Both readings are used as substitutes for the reading *Son of God* and both seem to be supported by the same class of documents. The Gnostic papyri discovered in 1945 at Nag-Hammadi in Egypt seem to indicate that these 2nd-century heretics regarded the term *Son of God* as a mystic name which should not be pronounced except by the initiated, and so it may have been they who introduced these substitutes *Chosen One of God* and *Holy One of God* into the text of John.[72]

(h) Other Heretical Readings in the Alexandrian Text

Other examples of heretical readings in the Alexandrian New Testament text are as follows:

(1) In Mark 1:1 the Traditional Text reads with *B* and most other manuscripts, *The beginning of the Gospel of Jesus Christ, the Son of God. Aleph, Theta,* 28 and several other documents omit *the Son of God.* This seems to be the work of heretics unfriendly to Christ's deity.

(2) In Luke 23:42, according to the Traditional Text and the Old Latin and the Sinaitic Syriac, the prayer of the dying thief was, *Lord, remember me when Thou comest in Thy kingdom.* But according to the Alexandrian text (represented by Papyrus 75, *Aleph B C L,* and the Sahidic), the thief said, *Jesus, remember me when Thou comest in Thy kingdom.* Modern critics insist that this latter reading is the original one, but is this at all a reasonable hypothesis? The dying thief recognizes Jesus as the messianic King; he is praying to Him for pardon and mercy. Would it be at all natural for the thief to address his new found King rudely and familiarly as *Jesus?* Surely not. Surely he must have commenced his dying prayer with the vocative, *Lord!* In the Alexandrian text this prayer has been tampered with by the docetists, who believed that the divine "Christ" returned to heaven just before the crucifixion, leaving only the human Jesus to suffer and die. In accordance with this belief they made the thief address the Saviour not as *Lord* but as *Jesus.*

(3) In John 3:13 the Traditional Text reads with the Old Latin and the Sinaitic Syriac, *No man hath ascended up to heaven but He that came down from heaven, even the Son of Man who is in heaven.* But the Alexandrian text (represented by Papyri 66 and 75, *Aleph B* etc.) omits the clause *who is in heaven.* This mutilation of the sacred text ought also, no doubt, to be charged to heretics hostile to the deity of Christ.

(4) In John 9:35, according to the Traditional Text and the Old Latin version, Jesus asks the blind man, *Dost thou be-*

lieve on the Son of God?   But according to the Western and
Alexandrian texts (represented by Papyri 66 and 75, *Aleph
B D*, the Sinaitic Syriac), Jesus' question is, *Dost thou believe on the Son of Man?*   Tischendorf and von Soden reject
this Western-Alexandrian reading.   Very probably it represents an attempt on the part of heretics to lower Christ's
claim to deity.

(5) John 9:38-39 *And he said, Lord, I believe.   And he worshipped Him.   And Jesus said* . . . These words are omitted
by Papyrus 75, *Aleph W,* Old Latin manuscripts *b l,* and the
4th-century Coptic manuscript Q.   This confession of the
blind man can scarcely have been left out accidentally.
Its absence from these documents goes far toward proving
that this passage was tampered with in ancient times by
heretics.

(6) In John 19:5 Papyrus 66 omits the following famous sentence, *And he saith unto them, Behold the Man.*   Four Old
Latin manuscripts and the Coptic manuscript Q also omit
this reading.   This omission seems to be a mutilation of the
sacred text at the hands of heretics, probably Gnostics.
They seem to have disliked the idea that Christ, whom they
regarded as exclusively a heavenly Being, actually became
a man and was crucified.

(7) In Rom. 14:10 the Traditional Text speaks of the *judgment seat of Christ,* implying that Christ is that Jehovah
spoken of in Isa. 45:23, to whom every knee shall bow.
This Traditional reading is also found in Polycarp, Tertullian, and Marcion.   But the Western and Alexandrian texts
(represented by *Aleph B D2* etc.) take away this testimony
to Christ's deity by substituting *judgment seat of God* for
judgment seat of Christ.   It is difficult to believe that this
substitution was not also made by heretics.

(8) In 1 Tim. 3:16 the Traditional Text reads, *God was manifest in the flesh,* with A (according to Scrivener), C (according to the "almost supernaturally accurate"[73] Hoskier),
(Ignatius), (Barnabas), (Hippolytus), Didymus, Gregory
of Nyssa, and Chrysostom.   The Alexandrian text (represented by *Aleph*) reads, *who was manifest in the flesh,* and
the Western text (represented by *D2* and the Latin versions)
reads, *which was manifest in the flesh.*   Undoubtedly the
Traditional reading, *God was manifest in the flesh,* was the
original reading.   This was altered by the Gnostics into
the Western reading, *which was manifest in the flesh,* in
order to emphasize their favorite idea of mystery.   Then
this Western reading was later changed into the meaningless

Alexandrian reading, *who was manifest in the flesh.*

Since Westcott and Hort, critics have adopted the Alexandrian reading and have translated the word *who* as *He who,* insisting that Paul is here quoting a fragment of an early Christian hymn. But what could Paul have meant by this quotation? Did he mean that the mystery of godliness was the fact that Christ was manifest in the flesh? If he did, why then did he not make his meaning plain by substituting the word *Christ* for the word *He who,* making the quotation read, *Christ was manifest in the flesh, etc.?* Did he mean that Christ was the mystery of godliness? Why then did he not place the word *Christ* in apposition to the word *who,* making the quotation read, *Christ, He who was manifest in the flesh, etc.?* But, according to the critics, Paul did neither of these two things. Instead he quoted an incomplete sentence, a subject without a predicate, and left it dangling. The makers of the R.S.V. adopt the Alexandrian reading and translate it, *He was manifested in the flesh, etc.,* and then place under it a note, Greek, *who.* But if the Greek is *who,* how can the English be *He?* This is not translation but the creation of an entirely new reading. The change, therefore, that the translators felt compelled to make from *who* to *He* comes as a belated admission that the reading, *who was manifest in the flesh,* cannot be interpreted satisfactorily. And ought not unprejudiced students of the problem to regard this as proof that Paul never wrote the verse in this form but rather as it stands in the Traditional Text, *God was manifest in the flesh?*

Two other erroneous Alexandrian readings should also be mentioned:

In Mark 9:29, Acts 10:30 and 1 Cor. 7:5 *Aleph B* and their allies omit *fasting.* These omissions are probably due to the influence of Clement of Alexandria and other Gnostics, who interpreted *fasting* in a spiritual sense and were opposed to literal fasting (Strom. 6:12; 7:12).

In 1 Cor. 11:24 *Aleph B* and their allies read, *This is My body which is for you,* omitting *broken,* either for Gnostic reasons or to avoid a supposed contradiction with John 19:33ff. Many denominations have adopted this mutilated reading in their communion liturgies, but it makes no sense. Even Moffatt and the R.S.V. editors recognized this fact and so retained the traditional reading, *broken for you.*

CHAPTER SIX

DEAN BURGON AND THE TRADITIONAL
NEW TESTAMENT TEXT

Since 1881 many, perhaps most, orthodox Christian scholars have agreed with Westcott and Hort that textual criticism is a strictly neutral science that must be applied in the same way to any document whatever, including the Bible. Yet there have been some orthodox theologians who have dissented from this neutral point of view. One of them was Abraham Kuyper (1894), who pointed out that the publication of the Textus Receptus was "no accident," affirming that the Textus Receptus, "as a foundation from which to begin critical operations, can, in a certain sense, even deserve preference."[1] Another was Francis Pieper (1924), who emphasized the fact that "in the Bible which is in our hands we have the word of Christ which is to be taught by and in the Church until the last day."[2]

It was John W. Burgon (1813-1888), however, who most effectively combatted the neutralism of naturalistic Bible study. This famous scholar spent most of his adult life at Oxford, as Fellow of Oriel College and then as vicar of St. Mary's (the University Church) and Gresham Professor of Divinity. During his last twelve years he was Dean of Chichester. In theology he was a high-church Anglican but opposed to the ritualism into which even in his day the high-church movement had begun to decline. Throughout his career he was steadfast in his defense of the Scriptures as the infallible Word of God and strove with all his power to arrest the modernistic currents which during his lifetime had begun to flow within the Church of England. Because of his learned defense of the Traditional New Testament text he has been held up to ridicule in most of the handbooks on New Testament textual criticism; but his arguments have never been refuted.

Although he lived one hundred years ago, Dean Burgon has the message which we need today in our new Space Age. Since his books have now become difficult to acquire, they should all be reprinted and made available to new generations of believing Bible students. His published works on textual criticism include: *The Last Twelve Verses of Mark* (1871), *The Revision Revised* (1883), and *The Traditional Text of the Holy Gospels* and *The Causes of the Corruption of the Traditional Text*, two volumes which were published in 1896 after Burgon's death.

In his *Revision Revised* Burgon gives us his reconstruction of the history of the New Testament text in the vivid style that was habitual to him. "Vanquished by *THE WORD Incarnate*, Satan next directed his subtle malice against *the Word written*. Hence, as I think, — *hence* the extraordinary fate which befell certain early

139

transcripts of the Gospel. First, heretical assailants of Christianity, — then, orthodox defenders of the Truth, — lastly and above all, self constituted Critics . . . such were the corrupting influences which were actively at work throughout the first hundred years after the death of S. John the Divine. Profane literature has never known anything approaching to it — can show nothing at all like it. Satan's arts were defeated indeed through the Church's faithfulness, because, — (the good Providence of God has so willed it,) — the perpetual multiplication in every quarter of copies required for Ecclesiastical use — not to say the solicitude of faithful men in diverse regions of ancient Christendom to retain for themselves unadulterated specimens of the inspired Text, — proved a sufficient safeguard against the grosser forms of corruption. But this was not all.

"The Church, remember, hath been from the beginning the 'Witness and Keeper of Holy Writ.' Did not her Divine Author pour out upon her in largest measure, 'the SPIRIT of truth,' and pledge Himself that it should be that SPIRIT'S special function to *'guide'* *her children 'into all the Truth' ?* . . . . That, by a perpetual miracle, Sacred Manuscripts would be protected all down the ages against depraving influences of whatever sort, — was not to have been expected; certainly, was never promised. But the Church, in her collective capacity, hath nevertheless — as a matter of fact — been perpetually purging herself of those shamefully depraved copies which once everywhere abounded within her pale: retaining only such an amount of discrepancy in her Text as might serve to remind her children that they carry their 'treasure in earthen vessels,' — as well as to stimulate them to perpetual watchfulness and solicitude for the purity and integrity of the Deposit. Never, however, up to the present hour, hath there been any complete eradication of all traces of the attempted mischief, — any absolute getting rid of every depraved copy extant. These are found to have lingered on anciently in many quarters. *A few such copies linger on to the present day.* The wounds were healed, but the scars remained, — nay, the scars are discernible still.

"What, in the meantime, is to be thought of those blind guides — those deluded ones — who would now, if they could, persuade us to go back to those same codices of which the Church hath already purged herself?"[3]

Burgon's reconstruction of the history of the New Testament text is not only vividly expressed but eminently biblical and therefore true. For if the *true* New Testament text came from God, whence came the *false* texts ultimately save from the evil one? And how could the true text have been preserved save through the providence of God working through His Church?

No doubt most Bible-believing Christians, not being high-church Anglicans, will place less emphasis than Burgon did on the organized Church. Certainly they will not agree with him that the Church must be governed by bishops or that it was through the bishops main-

John Wiliam Burgon (1813-1888)

ly that the New Testament text was preserved. For this would be confusing the Old Testament dispensation with the New Testament dispensation. During the Old Testament dispensation the Church was governed by a divinely appointed priesthood, and it was through that priesthood that the Old Testament Scriptures were preserved. Now, however, in the New Testament dispensation all believers are priests before God, and each congregation of believers has the right to elect its own pastors, elders, and deacons. Hence the New Testament Scriptures were preserved in the New Testament way through the universal priesthood of believers, that is to say, through the God-guided usage of the common people, the rank and file of the true believers.

But these defects in Burgon's presentation do not in any essential way affect the eternal validity of his views concerning the New Testament text. They are eternally valid because they are consistently Christian. In this present chapter, therefore, we will follow Burgon in his defense of the Traditional Text in five passages in which it is commonly thought to be altogether indefensible. If in these five instances the Traditional Text wins a favorable verdict, its general trustworthiness may well be regarded as established.

1. Christ's Reply To The Rich Young Man (Matt. 19:16-17)

As Tregelles (1854) observed long ago,[4] we have in Matt. 19:16-17 a test passage in which the relative merits of the Traditional Text on the one side and the Western and Alexandrian texts on the other can be evaluated. Here, according to the Traditional Text, Matthew agrees with Mark and Luke in stating that Jesus answered the rich man's question, *What good thing shall I do that I may have eternal life*, with the counter-question, *Why callest thou Me good.* But according to Western and Alexandrian texts, Matthew disagrees here with Mark and Luke, affirming that Jesus' counter-question was, *Why askest thou Me concerning the good.* It is this latter reading that is found in *Aleph B D* and eight other Greek manuscripts, in the Old Latin and Old Syriac versions and in Origen, Eusebius, and Augustine.

The earliest extant evidence, however, favors the Traditional reading, *why callest thou Me good.* It is found in the following 2nd-century Fathers: Justin Martyr (c. 150), *He answered to one who addressed Him as Good Master, Why callest thou Me good?*[5] Irenaeus (c. 180), *And to the person who said to Him Good Master, He confessed that God who is truly good, saying, Why callest thou Me good?*[6] Hippolytus (c. 200), *Why callest thou Me good? One is good, My Father who is in heaven.*[7] Modern critics attempt to evade this ancient evidence for the Traditional reading, *Why callest thou Me good*, by claiming that these early Fathers took this reading from Mark and Luke and not from Matthew. But this is a very unnatural supposition. It is very improbable that all three of these 2nd-century Fathers were quoting from Mark and Luke rather than from Matthew, for Matthew was the dominant Gospel and therefore much more likely to be quoted from than the other two.

The internal evidence also clearly favors the Traditional reading, *Why callest thou Me good*. The Western and Alexandrian reading, *Why askest thou Me concerning the good*, has a curiously unbiblical ring. It does not savor of God but of men. It smacks of the philosophy or pseudo-philosophy which was common among the Hellenized gentiles but was probably little known in the strictly Jewish circles in which these words are represented as having been spoken. In short, the Western and Alexandrian reading, *Why askest thou Me concerning the good*, reminds us strongly of the interminable discussions of the philosophers concerning the *summum bonum* (the highest good). How could Jesus have reproved the young man for inviting Him to such a discussion, when it was clear that the youth had in no wise done this but had come to Him concerning an entirely different matter, namely, the obtaining of eternal life?

Modern critics agree that the Western and Alexandrian reading, *Why askest thou Me concerning the good*, does not fit the context and is not what Jesus really said. What Jesus really said, critics admit, was, *Why callest thou Me good*, the reading recorded in Mark. Matthew altered this reading, critics believe, to avoid theological difficulties. W. C. Allen (1907), for example, conjectures, "Matthew's changes are probably intentional to avoid the rejection by Christ of the title 'good', and the apparent distinction made between Himself and God."[8] B. C. Butler (1951), however, has punctured this critical theory with the following well placed objection. "If Matthew had wanted to change the Marcan version, he could have found an easier way of doing so (by simple omission of our Lord's comment on the man's mode of speech)."[9] This remark is very true, and to it we may add that if Matthew had found difficulty with this word of Jesus it would hardly have occurred to him to seek to solve the problem by bringing in considerations taken from Greek philosophy.

Rendel Harris (1891) had this comment to make on the reading, *Why askest thou Me concerning the good*. "A text of which we should certainly say a priori that it was a Gnostic depravation. Most assuredly this is a Western reading, for it is given by *D a b c e ff g h*. But it will be said that we have also to deal with *Aleph B L* and certain versions. Well, according to Westcott and Hort, *Aleph* and *B* were both written in the West, probably at Rome. Did Roman texts never influence one another?"[10] The unbiased student will agree with Harris' diagnosis of the case. It is surely very likely that this reading, redolent as it is of Greek wisdom, originated among Gnostic heretics of a pseudo-philosophic sort. The 2nd-century Gnostic teacher Valentinus and his disciples Heracleon and Ptolemaeus are known to have philosophized much on Matt. 19:17,[11] and it could easily have been one of these three who made this alteration in the sacred text. Whoever it was, he no doubt devised this reading in order to give the passage a more philosophical appearance. Evidently he attempted to model the conversation of Jesus with the rich young man into a Socratic dialogue. The fact that this change made Matthew disagree with Mark and Luke did not bother him much, for, being a heretic, he was not particularly interested in the harmony of the Gospels with each other.

Orthodox Christians, we may well believe, would scarcely have made so drastic a change in the text of Matthew, but when once this new reading had been invented by heretics, they would accept it very readily, for theologically it would be quite agreeable to them. Christ's question, *Why callest thou Me good,* had troubled them, for it seemed to imply that He was not perfectly good. (Not that it actually does imply this when rightly interpreted, but it seemed to.) What a relief to reject this reading and receive in its place the easier one, *Why askest thou Me concerning the good.* It is no wonder, therefore, that this false reading had a wide circulation among orthodox Christians of the 3rd century and later. But the true reading, *Why callest thou Me good,* continued to be read and copied. It is found today in the Sahidic version, in the Peshitta, and in the vast majority of the Greek manuscripts, including *W,* which is probably the third oldest uncial manuscript of the New Testament in existence.

Thus when the Traditional Text stands trial in a test passage such as Matt. 19:17, it not only clears itself of the charge of being spurious but even secures the conviction of its Western and Alexandrian rivals. The reading found in these latter two texts, *Why askest thou Me concerning the good,* is seen to possess all the earmarks of a "Gnostic depravation." The R.V., A.S.V., R.S.V., N.E.B. and other modern versions, therefore, are to be censured for serving up to their readers this stale crumb of Greek philosophy in place of the bread of life.

In his comment on this passage Origen gives us a specimen of the New Testament textual criticism which was carried on at Alexandria about 225 A.D. Origen reasons that Jesus could not have concluded his list of God's commandments with the comprehensive requirement, *Thou shalt love thy neighbor as thyself.* For the reply of the young man was, *All these things have I kept from my youth up,* and Jesus evidently accepted this statement as true. But if the young man had loved his neighbor as himself, he would have been perfect, for Paul says that the whole law is summed up in this saying, *Thou shalt love thy neighbor as thyself.* But Jesus answered, *If thou wilt be perfect, etc.,* implying that the young man was not yet perfect. Therefore, Origen argued, the commandment, *Thou shalt love thy neighbor as thyself,* could not have been spoken by Jesus on this occasion and was not part of the original text of Matthew. This clause, he believed, was added by some tasteless scribe.[12]

Thus it is clear that this renowned Father was not content to abide by the text which he had received but freely engaged in the boldest sort of conjectural emendation. And there were other critics at Alexandria even less restrained than he who deleted many readings of the original New Testament text and thus produced the abbreviated text found in the papyri and in the manuscripts *Aleph* and *B*.

2. The Angel At The Pool (John 5:3b-4)

The next test passage in which the Traditional reading ought to be examined is John 5:3b-4, the account of the descent of the angel into the pool of Bethesda. For the benefit of the reader this disputed reading is here given in its context.

2 Now there is at Jerusalem by the sheep market a pool, which is called in the Hebrew tongue Bethesda, having five porches. 3 In these lay a great multitude of impotent folk, of blind, halt, withered, *waiting for the moving of the water.* 4 *For an angel went down at a certain season into the pool, and troubled the water: whosoever then first after the troubling of the water stepped in was made whole of whatsoever disease he had.* 5 And a certain man was there, which had an infirmity thirty and eight years. 6 When Jesus saw him lie, and knew that he had been now a long time in that case, He saith unto him, Wilt thou be made whole? 7 The impotent man answered Him, Sir, I have no man, when the water is troubled, to put me into the pool: but while I am coming, another steppeth down before me. 8 Jesus saith unto him, Rise, take up thy bed, and walk. 9 And immediately the man was made whole, and took up his bed and walked.

The words in italics (vss. 3b-4) are omitted by Papyri 66 and 75, *Aleph B C*, a few minuscules, the Curetonian Syriac, the Sahidic, the Bodmer Bohairic, and a few Old Latin manuscripts. This disputed reading, however, has been defended not only by conservatives such as Hengstenberg (1861)[13] but also by radicals such as A. Hilgenfeld (1875)[14] and R. Steck (1893).[15] Hengstenberg contends that "the words are necessarily required by the connection," quoting with approval the remark of von Hofmann (an earlier commentator) that it is highly improbable "that the narrator, who has stated the site of the pool and the number of the porches, should be so sparing of his words precisely with regard to that which it is necessary to know in order to understand the occurrence, and should leave the character of the pool and its healing virtue to be guessed from the complaint of the sick man, which presupposes a knowledge of it." Hilgenfeld and Steck also rightly insist that the account of the descent of the angel into the pool in verse 4 is presupposed in the reply which the impotent man makes to Jesus in verse 7.

Certain of the Church Fathers attached great importance to this reference to the angel's descent into the pool (John 5:3b-4), attributing to it the highest theological significance. The pool they regarded as a type of baptism and the angel as the precursor of the Holy Spirit. Such was the interpretation which Tertullian (c. 200) gave to this passage. "Having been washed," he writes, "in the water by the angel, we are prepared for the Holy Spirit."[16] Similarly,

Didymus (c. 379) states that the pool was "confessedly an image of baptism" and the angel troubling the water "a forerunner of the Holy Spirit."[17]   And the remarks of Chrysostom (c. 390) are to the same effect.[18]   These writers, at least, appear firmly convinced that John 5:3b-4 was a genuine portion of the New Testament text.   And the fact that Tatian (c. 175) included this reading in his Diatessaron also strengthens the evidence for its genuineness by attesting its antiquity.[19]

Thus both internal and external evidence favor the authenticity of the allusion to the angel's descent into the pool.   Hilgenfeld[20] and Steck[21] suggest a very good explanation for the absence of this reading from the documents mentioned above as omitting it.   These scholars point out that there was evidently some discussion in the Church during the 2nd century concerning the existence of this miracle working pool.   Certain early Christians seem to have been disturbed over the fact that such a pool was no longer to be found at Jerusalem. Tertullian explained the absence of this pool by supposing that God had put an end to its curative powers in order to punish the Jews for their unbelief.[22]   However, this answer did not satisfy everyone, and so various attempts were made to remove the difficulty through conjectural emendation.   In addition to those documents which omit the whole reading there are others which merely mark it for omission with asterisks and obels.   Some scribes, such as those that produced *A* and *L*, omitted John 5:3b, *waiting for the moving of the water,* but did not have the courage to omit John 5:4, *For an angel . . . whatever disease he had.*   Other scribes, like those that copied out *D* and *W,* omitted John 5:4 but did not see the necessity of omitting John 5:3b. *A* and *L* and about 30 other manuscripts add the genitive *of the Lord* after *angel,* and various other small variations were introduced.   That the whole passage has been tampered with by rationalistic scribes is shown by the various spellings of the name of the pool, *Bethesda, Bethsaida, Bethzatha,* etc.   In spite of this, however, John 5:3b-4 has been preserved virtually intact in the vast majority of the Greek manuscripts (Traditional Text).

3. The Conclusion Of The Lord's Prayer (Matt. 6:13b)

Modern English versions are "rich in omissions," (to borrow a phrase from Rendel Harris).[23]   Time and again the reader searches in them for a familiar verse only to find that it has been banished to the footnotes.   And one of the most familiar of the verses to be so treated is Matt. 6:13b, the doxology with which the Lord's Prayer concludes.

(a) External Evidence in Favor of Matt. 6:13b

For Thine is the kingdom, and the power, and the glory, forever, Amen (Matt. 6:13b).   This conclusion of the Lord's Prayer is found in almost all the Greek New Testament manuscripts (according to Legg,[24] in all but ten), including *W* (4th or 5th century) and *Sigma* and *Phi* (both 6th century). It is also found in the *Apostolic Constitutions*,[25] a 4th century document, and receives further support from Chrysostom (345-407)[26] who comments on it and quotes it frequently, and from Isidore of Pelusium (370-440),[27] who quotes it. But, in spite of this indisputable testimony in its favor, it is universally rejected by modern critics. Is this unanimous disapproval in accord with the evidence?

(b) Is the Conclusion of the Lord's Prayer a Jewish Formula?

Matt. 6:13b is usually regarded as a Jewish prayer-formula that the early Christians took up and used to provide a more fitting termination for the Lord's Prayer, which originally, it is said, ended abruptly with *but deliver us from evil*. According to W. Michaelis (1948), for example, "It (Matt. 6:13b) is obviously modeled after Jewish prayer-formulas, cf. 1 Chron 29:11."[28]

This seems, however, a most improbable way to account for the conclusion of the Lord's Prayer. For if the early Christians had felt the need of something which would provide a smoother ending to this familiar prayer, would they deliberately have selected for that purpose a Jewish prayer-formula in which the name of Jesus does not appear? Even a slight study of the New Testament reveals the difficulty of this hypothesis, for if there was one thing in which the early Christians were united it was in their emphasis on the name of Jesus. Converts were baptized in the name of Jesus Christ (Acts 2:38); miracles were performed in this name (Acts 4:10); by this name alone was salvation possible (Acts 4:12); early Christians were known as those who "called upon this name" (Acts 9:21). Paul received his apostleship "for the sake of His name" (Rom. 1:5), and John wrote his Gospel in order that the readers "might have life through His name" (John 20:31). Is it probable then, (is it at all possible) that these primitive Christians, who on all other occasions were ever mindful of their Saviour's name, should have forgotten it so strangely when selecting a conclusion for a prayer which they regarded as having fallen from His lips? Can it be that they deliberately decided to end the Lord's Prayer with a Jewish formula which makes no mention of Christ?

It is a fact, however, that the Lord's Prayer concludes with a doxology in which the name of Christ is not mentioned. Can this surprising fact be explained? Not, we repeat, on the supposition that this conclusion is spurious. For if the early Christians had invented this doxology or had adopted it from contemporary non-Christian usage, they would surely have included in it or inserted into it their Saviour's name. There is therefore only one explanation of the absence of that adorable name from the concluding doxology of the Lord's Prayer, and this is that this doxology is not spurious but a genuine saying of Christ, uttered before He had revealed unto His disciples His deity and so containing no mention of Himself. At the time He gave this model prayer He deemed it sufficient to direct the praises of His followers toward the Father, knowing that as they grew in their comprehension of the mysteries of their faith their enlightened minds would prompt them so to adore Him also. And the similarity of this doxology to 1 Chron. 29:11 is quite understandable. Might not the words which David used in praise of God be fittingly adapted to the same purpose by One who knew Himself to be the messianic Son of David?

(c) The Testimony of the Ancient Versions and of the Didache

The concluding doxology of the Lord's Prayer is not without considerable testimony in its favor of a very ancient sort. It is found in three Syriac versions, the Peshitta, the Harclean, and the Palestinian. Whether the doxology occurred in the Sinaitic Syriac also is not certain, for the last part of the Lord's Prayer is missing from this manuscript. It is found, however, in the Curetonian manuscript, the other representative of the Old Syriac in the following form, *Because Thine is the kingdom and the glory, for ever and ever, Amen.* The Sahidic also has the doxology of the Lord's Prayer, and so do some manuscripts of the slightly younger Bohairic. In the Sahidic it runs like this, *Because Thine is the power and the glory, unto the ages, Amen.* And in the Old Latin manuscript *k* (which is generally thought to contain the version in its oldest form) the Lord's Prayer ends thus, *Because to Thee is the power for ever and ever.* And the doxology is also found in its customary form in four other Old Latin manuscripts.

Thus the doxology of the Lord's Prayer occurs in five manuscripts of the Old Latin (including the best one), in the Sahidic, and in all the extant Syriac versions. Normally the agreement of three such groups of ancient witnesses from three separate regions would be regarded as an indication of the genuineness of the reading on which they thus agreed. Hort (1881),[29] however, endeavored to escape the force of this evidence by suggesting that the doxologies found (1) in *k*, (2) in the Sahidic version, (3) in the Syriac versions and the vast majority of the Greek manuscripts were three independent developments which had no connection with each other. But by this suggestion Hort multiplied three-fold the difficulty mentioned above. If it is difficult to believe that the early Christians chose for their most familiar prayer a conclusion which made no mention of Christ, it is thrice as difficult to believe that they did this three times independently in three separate regions. Surely it is easier to suppose that these three doxologies are all derived from an original doxology uttered by Christ and that the variations in wording are due to the liturgical use of the Lord's Prayer, which will be described presently.

The Didache (Teaching) of the Twelve Apostles, a work gen-

erally regarded as having been written in the first half of the 2nd century, also bears important witness to the doxology of the Lord's Prayer. This ancient document was not known until 1883, when Bryennios, a Greek Catholic bishop, published it from a copy which he had discovered at Constantinople in 1875. It is a manual of Church instruction in two parts, the first being a statement of Christian conduct to be taught to converts before baptism, and the second a series of directions for Christian worship. Here the following commandment is given concerning prayer. *And do not pray as the hypocrites, but as the Lord commanded in His Gospel, pray thus: Our Father, who art in heaven, hallowed be Thy Name, Thy Kingdom come, Thy will be done, as in heaven so also upon earth; give us this day our daily bread, and forgive us our debt as we forgive our debtors, and lead us not into temptation, but deliver us from evil, for Thine is the power and the glory for ever.*[30]
Here this early-2nd-century writer claims to have taken this model prayer from the Gospel (of Matthew). Is it not reasonable to believe that he took the whole prayer from Matthew, doxology and all? Who would ever have guessed that this ancient author took the preceding portions of the prayer from Matthew but the doxology from *contemporary ecclesiastical usage?* Yet this is the strange hypothesis of Michaelis and others who have come to the Didache with their minds firmly made up beforehand to reject the doxology of the Lord's Prayer. In support of his view Michaelis appeals to the absence of the words *kingdom* and *Amen* from the Didache, but surely these minor verbal differences are not sufficient to justify his contention that the doxology of the Didache was not taken from Matthew. And perhaps it is permissible to point out once more that if the doxology had been taken from contemporary ecclesiastical usage it would have contained the name of Christ, because the other prayers in the Didache, which *were* taken from contemporary ecclesiastical usage, all end with a reference to the Saviour.

(d) The Liturgical Use of the Lord's Prayer

But someone may ask why the doxology of the Lord's Prayer is absent from certain New Testament documents if it was actually a portion of the original Gospel of Matthew. An inspection of Legg's critical edition of this Gospel (1940) discloses that the doxology is omitted by *Aleph B D S* and by six minuscule manuscripts. It is also omitted by all the manuscripts of the Vulgate and by nine manuscripts of the Old Latin. And certain Greek and Latin Fathers omit it in their expositions of the Lord's Prayer. Thus Origen, Tertullian, Cyprian, and Augustine make no mention of it. But these omissions find their explanation in the manner in which the Lord's Prayer was used in the worship services of the early Church.

From very early times the Lord's Prayer was used liturgically in the Church service. This fact is brought home to us by an inspection of C. A. Swainson's volume, *The Greek Liturgies* (1884).[31] Here the learned author published the most ancient Greek liturgies from the oldest manuscripts available. In the 8th-century *Liturgy of St. Basil,* after the worshiping people had repeated the body of the Lord's Prayer, the priest concluded it with these words, *for Thine is the kingdom, and the power, and the glory of the Father,* and the people responded, *Amen.* In two other 8th-century liturgies the wording is the same, except that the doxology repeated by the priest is merely, *for Thine is the kingdom.* Later the doxologies which the priests were directed to pronounce became more and more elaborate. In the 11th-century *Liturgy of St. Chrysostom,* after the people had repeated the Lord's Prayer down to the doxology, the priest was to conclude as follows: *for Thine is the kingdom, and the power, and the glory, of the Father, and of the Son, and of the Holy Ghost, now and always, and for ever and ever.*

Thus we see that from very earliest times in the worship services of the Church the conclusion of the Lord's Prayer was separated from the preceding portions of it. The body of the Prayer was repeated by the people, the conclusion by the priest. Moreover, due to this liturgical use, the conclusion of the Lord's Prayer was altered in various ways in the effort to make it more effective. This, no doubt, was the cause of the minor variations in the doxology which we find in the Didache, the Curetonian Syriac, and the Old Latin manuscript *k.* And furthermore, a distinction soon grew up between the body of the Lord's Prayer and the conclusion of it, a distinction which was made more sharp by the occurrence of the Lord's Prayer in Luke (given by Christ for the second time, on a different occasion) without the concluding doxology. Because the doxology was always separated from the rest of the Lord's Prayer, it began to be regarded by some Christians as a man-made response and not part of the original prayer as it fell from the lips of Christ. Doubtless for this reason it is absent from the ten Greek manuscripts mentioned above and from most of the manuscripts of the Latin versions. And it may also be for this reason that some of the Fathers do not mention it when commenting on the Lord's Prayer.

4. The Woman Taken In Adultery (John 7:53-8:11)

The story of the woman taken in adultery (called the *pericope de adultera*) has been rather harshly treated by the modern English versions. The R.V. and the A.S.V. put it in brackets; the R.S.V. relegates it to the footnotes; the N.E.B. follows Westcott and Hort in removing it from its customary place altogether and printing it at the end of the Gospel of John as an independent fragment of unknown origin. The N.E.B. even gives this familiar narrative a new name, to wit, *An Incident in the Temple.* But as Burgon has reminded us long ago, this general rejection of these precious verses is unjustifiable.

(a) Ancient Testimony Concerning the Pericope de Adultera (John 7:53-8:11)

The story of the woman taken in adultery was a problem also in ancient times.   Early Christians had trouble with this passage. The forgiveness which Christ vouchsafed to the adulteress was contrary to their conviction that the punishment for adultery ought to be very severe.   As late as the time of Ambrose (c. 374), bishop of Milan, there were still many Christians who felt such scruples against this portion of John's Gospel.   This is clear from the remarks which Ambrose makes in a sermon on David's sin.   "In the same way also the Gospel lesson which has been read, may have caused no small offense to the unskilled, in which you have noticed that an adulteress was brought to Christ and dismissed without condemnation . . . Did Christ err that He did not judge righteously?   It is not right that such a thought should come to our minds etc."[32]

According to Augustine (c. 400), it was this moralistic objection to the *pericope de adultera* which was responsible for its omission in some of the New Testament manuscripts known to him.   "Certain persons of little faith," he wrote, "or rather enemies of the true faith, fearing, I suppose, lest their wives should be given impunity in sinning, removed from their manuscripts the Lord's act of forgiveness toward the adulteress, as if He who had said 'sin no more' had granted permission to sin."[33]   Also, in the 10th century a Greek named Nikon accused the Armenians of "casting out the account which teaches us how the adulteress was taken to Jesus . . . saying that it was harmful for most persons to listen to such things."[34]

That early Greek manuscripts contained this *pericope de adultera* is proved by the presence of it in the 5th-century Greek manuscript *D*. That early Latin manuscripts also contained it is indicated by its actual appearance in the Old Latin codices *b* and *e*.   And both these conclusions are confirmed by the statement of Jerome (c. 415) that "in the Gospel according to John in many manuscripts, both Greek and Latin, is found the story of the adulterous woman who was accused before the Lord."[35]   There is no reason to question the accuracy of Jerome's statement, especially since another statement of his concerning an addition made to the ending of Mark has been proved to have been correct by the actual discovery of the additional material in *W*.   And that Jerome personally accepted the *pericope de adultera* as genuine is shown by the fact that he included it in the Latin Vulgate.

Another evidence of the presence of the *pericope de adultera* in early Greek manuscripts of John is the citation of it in the *Didascalia* *(Teaching) of the Apostles* and in the *Apostolic Constitutions*, which are based on the *Didascalia*.

> . . . to do as He also did with her that had sinned, whom the elders set before Him, and leaving the judgment in His hands departed.   But He, the Searcher of Hearts, asked her and said to her, 'Have the elders condemned thee, my daugh-

ter?" She saith to Him, 'Nay, Lord.' And He said unto her, 'Go thy way: Neither do I condemn thee.'[36]

In these two documents (from the 3rd and 4th centuries respectively) bishops are urged to extend forgiveness to penitent sinners. After many passages of Scripture have been cited to enforce this plea, the climax is reached in the supreme example of divine mercy, namely, the compassion which Christ showed to the woman taken in adultery. Tischendorf admitted that this citation was taken from the Gospel of John. "Although," he wrote, "the *Apostolic Constitutions* do not actually name John as the author of this story of the adulteress, in vain would anyone claim that they could have derived this story from any other source."[37] It is true that R. H. Connolly (1929)[38] and other more recent critics insist that the citation was not taken from the canonical Gospel of John but from the apocryphal *Gospel according to the Hebrews*, but this seems hardly credible. During the whole course of the argument only passages from the canonical Scriptures of the Old and New Testaments are adduced. Can we suppose that when the authors of these two works reached the climax of their plea for clemency toward the penitent they would abandon the Scriptures at last and fall back on an apocryphal book?

Another important testimony concerning the *pericope de adultera* is that of Eusebius (c. 324). In his *Ecclesiastical History* Eusebius gives extracts from an ancient treatise written by Papias (d. 150), bishop of Hierapolis, entitled *Interpretation of the Oracles of the Lord*. Eusebius concludes his discussion of Papias' writings with the following statement: "The same writer used quotations from the first Epistle of John, and likewise also from that of Peter, and has expounded another story about a woman who was accused before the Lord of many sins, which the *Gospel according to the Hebrews* contains."[39]

From this statement of Eusebius naturalistic critics have inferred that Eusebius knew the *pericope de adultera* only as a story occurring in the writings of Papias and in the *Gospel according to the Hebrews* and not as a part of the canonical Gospel of John. This conclusion, however, by no means follows necessarily. Eusebius may have been hostile to the story of the woman taken in adultery not only because of moralistic objections but also because it was related by Papias. For Eusebius had a low opinion of Papias and his writings. "He was a man of very little intelligence," Eusebius declared, "as is clear from his books."[40] It may very well be that the disdain which Eusebius felt for Papias made him reluctant to mention the fact that Papias' story occurred also in some of the manuscripts of the Gospel of John. At any rate, an argument against the genuineness of John 7:53-8:11 based on Eusebius is purely an argument from silence, and arguments from silence are always weak. Instead of stressing Eusebius' silence it is more reasonable to lay the emphasis upon his positive testimony, which is that the story of the woman taken in adultery is a very ancient one, reaching back to the days of the Apostles.

Also the Spanish Father Pacian (c. 370), appealed to the *pericope de adultera* when protesting against excessive severity in discipline. "Are you not willing," he asked, "to read in the Gospel that the Lord also spared the adulteress who confessed, whom no man had condemned?"[41]

(b) What the Facts of History Indicate

The facts of history indicate that during the early Christian centuries throughout the Church adultery was commonly regarded as such a serious sin that it could be forgiven, if at all, only after severe penance. For example, Cyprian (c. 250) says that certain bishops who preceded him in the province of North Africa "thought that reconciliation ought not to be given to adulterers and allowed to conjugal infidelity no place at all for repentance."[42] Hence offence was taken at the story of the adulterous woman brought to Christ, because she seemed to have received pardon too easily. Such being the case, it is surely more reasonable to believe that this story was deleted from John's Gospel by over-zealous disciplinarians than to suppose that a narrative so contrary to the ascetic outlook of the early Christian Church was added to John's Gospel from some extra-canonical source. There would be a strong motive for deleting it but no motive at all for adding it, and the prejudice against it would make its insertion into the Gospel text very difficult.

Not only conservatives but also clear thinking radical scholars have perceived that the historical evidence favors the belief that the *pericope de adultera* was deleted from the text of the fourth Gospel rather than added to it. "The bold presentation of the evangelist," Hilgenfeld (1875) observed, "must at an early date, especially in the Orient have seemed very offensive."[43] Hence Hilgenfeld regarded Augustine's statement that the passage had been deleted by over-scrupulous scribes "as altogether not improbable." And Steck (1893) suggested that the story of the adulteress was incorporated in the Gospel of John before it was first published. "That it later," concluded Steck, "was set aside out of moral prudery is easily understandable."[44]

Rendel Harris (1891) was convinced that the Montanists, an ascetic Christian sect which flourished during the 2nd century, were acquainted with the *pericope de adultera*. "The Montanist Churches," he wrote, "either did not receive this addition to the text, or else they are responsible for its omission; but at the same time it can be shown that they knew of the passage perfectly well in the West; for the Latin glossator of the Acts has borrowed a few words from the section in Acts 5:18."[45] In Acts 5:18 we are told that the rulers *laid their hands on the apostles and put them in the common prison.* To this verse the Latin portion of *D* adds, *and they went away each one to his house.* As Harris observes, this addition is obviously taken

from the description of the breaking up of the council meeting in
John 7:53. If the Montanists were the ones who added these words
to Acts 5:18, then the *pericope de adultera* must have been part of
John's Gospel at a very early date.

Naturalistic scholars who insist that John 7:53-8:11 is an addition to the Gospel text can maintain their position only by ignoring
the facts, by disregarding what the ancient writers say about this
pericope de adultera and emphasizing the silence of other ancient
writers who say nothing about it at all. This is what Hort did in his
Introduction (1881). Here the testimony of Ambrose and Augustine
is barely mentioned, and the statement of Nikon concerning the
Armenians is dismissed as mere abuse.[46] Contrary to the evidence
Hort insisted that the *pericope de adultera* was not offensive to the
early Church. "Few in ancient times, there is reason to think, would
have found the section a stumbling block except Montanists and Nova-
tians."[47] With the implications of this sweeping statement, however,
Rendel Harris could not agree. "Evidently," he observed, "Dr. Hort
did not think that the tampering of the Montanists with the text
amounted to much; we, on the contrary, have reason to believe that
it was a very far reaching influence."[48]

Today most naturalistic scholars feel so certain that John 7:53-
8:11 is not genuine that they regard further discussion of the matter
as unprofitable. When they do deal with the question (for the benefit of laymen who are still interested in it) they follow the line of
Westcott and Hort. They dismiss the ancient testimony concerning
this passage as absurd and rely on the "argument from silence." Thus
Colwell (1952) ridicules the reason which Augustine gives for the
deletion of the *pericope de adultera*. "The generality," he declares,
"of the 'omission' in early Greek sources can hardly be explained this
way. Some of those Greek scribes must have been unmarried! Nor
is Augustine's argument supported by the evidence from Luke's Gospel, where even greater acts of compassion are left untouched by the
scribes who lack this story in John."[49]

There is no validity, however, in this point which Colwell tries
to score against Augustine. For there is a big difference between
the story of the adulteress in John 8 and the story in Luke 7 of the
sinful woman who anointed the feet of Jesus and was forgiven. In
Luke the penitence and faith of the woman are stressed; in John
these factors are not mentioned explicitly. In Luke the law of God
is not called in question; in John it, seemingly, is set aside. And in
Luke the sinful woman was a harlot; in John the woman was an
adulteress. Thus there are good reasons why the objections raised
against the story of the adulteress in John would not apply to the
story of the harlot in Luke and why Tertullian, for example, refers
to Luke's story but is silent about John's.

(c) Misleading Notes in the Modern Versions

The notes printed in the modern versions regarding John 7:53-8:11 are completely misleading.   For example, the R.S.V. states that most of the ancient authorities either omit 7:53-8:11 or insert it with variations of text after John 7:52 or at the end of John's Gospel or after Luke 21:38.   And the N.E.B. says the same thing and adds that the *pericope de adultera* has no fixed place in the ancient New Testament manuscripts.   These notes imply that originally the story of the adulteress circulated as an independent narrative in many forms and that later, when scribes began to add it to the New Testament, they couldn't agree on where to put it, some inserting it at one place and others at another.

Von Soden (1902) showed long ago that the view implied by these notes is entirely erroneous.   Although this scholar denied the genuineness of John 7:53-8:11, nevertheless, in his monumental study of this passage he was eminently fair in his presentation of the facts. After mentioning that this section is sometimes found at the end of the Gospel of John and sometimes in the margin near John 7:52 and that in one group of manuscripts (the Ferrar group) the section is inserted after Luke 21:38, von Soden continues as follows: "But in the great majority of the manuscripts it stands in the text between 7:52 and 8:12 except that in at least half of these manuscripts it is provided with deletion marks in the margin."[50]   Thus the usual location of the *pericope de adultera* is in John between 7:52 and 8:12. The manuscripts which have it in any other place are exceptions to the rule.

"The pericope," says Metzger (1964), "is obviously a piece of floating tradition which circulated in certain parts of the Western Church.   It was subsequently inserted into various manuscripts at various places."[51]   But Metzger's interpretation of the facts is incorrect, as von Soden demonstrated long ago by his careful scholarship. Von Soden showed that the usual location of the *pericope de adultera* was also its original location in the New Testament text.   The other positions which it sometimes occupies and the unusually large number of variant readings which it contains were later developments which took place after it became part of the New Testament.   "In spite of the abundance of the variant readings," he declared, "it has been established with certainty that the *pericope* was not intruded into the Four Gospels, perhaps in various forms, in various places. This hypothesis is already contradicted by the fixed place which the section has, against which the well known, solitary exception of the common ancestor of the so-called Ferrar group can prove nothing. On the contrary, when the *pericope,* at a definite time and at a definite place was first incorporated into the Four Gospels, in order then to defend its place with varying success against all attacks, it had the following wording."[52]   And then von Soden goes on to give his reconstruction of the original form of the *pericope de adultera.*   This does not differ materially from the form printed in the Textus Receptus and the King James Version.

Also the opening verses (John 7:53-8:2) of the *pericope de adultera* indicate clearly that its original position in the New Testament was in John between 7:52 and 8:12, for this is the only location in which these introductory verses fit the context. The first of them (John 7:53) describes the breaking up of the stormy council meeting which immediately precedes. The next two verses (John 8:1-2) tell us what Jesus did in the meantime and thereafter. And thus a transition is made to the story of the woman taken in adultery. But in those other locations mentioned by N.E.B., which the *pericope de adultera* occupies in a relatively few manuscripts, these introductory verses make no sense and thus prove conclusively that the *pericope* has been misplaced.

Long ago Burgon pointed out how untrustworthy some of those manuscripts are which misplace the *pericope de adultera*. "The Critics eagerly remind us that in four cursive copies (the Ferrar group) the verses in question are found tacked on to the end of Luke 21. But have they forgotten that 'these four codexes are derived from a common archetype,' and therefore represent one and the same ancient and, I may add, corrupt copy? The same Critics are reminded that in the same four Codexes 'the agony and bloody sweat' (St. Luke 22:43-44) is found thrust into St. Matthew's Gospel between ch. 26:39 and 40. Such licentiousness on the part of a solitary exemplar of the Gospels no more affects the proper place of these or of those verses than the superfluous digits of a certain man of Gath avail to disturb the induction that to either hand of a human being appertain but five fingers and to either foot but five toes."[53]

(d) The Silence of the Greek Fathers Explained

The arguments of naturalistic critics against the genuineness of John 7:53-8:11 are largely arguments from silence, and the strongest of these silences is generally thought to be that of the Greek Church Fathers. Metzger (1964) speaks of it as follows: "Even more significant is the fact that no Greek Church Father for a thousand years after Christ refers to the pericope, including even those who, like Origen, Chrysostom, and Nonnus (in his metrical paraphrase), dealt with the entire Gospel verse by verse. Euthymius Zigabenus, who lived in the first part of the twelfth century, is the first Greek writer to comment on the passage, and even he declares that the accurate copies of the Gospel do not contain it."[54]

This argument, however, is not nearly so strong as Metzger makes it seem. In the first place, as Burgon pointed out long ago, we must knock off at least three centuries from this thousand year period of which Metzger speaks so ominously. For Tischendorf lists 9 manuscripts of the 9th century which contain the *pericope de adultera* in its usual place and also one which may be of the 8th century. And so the silence of the Greek Church Fathers during the last third of this thousand year period couldn't have been because they didn't know of manuscripts which contained John 7:53-8:11 in the position which it now occupies in the great majority of the New Testament manuscripts. The later Greek Fathers didn't comment on these verses mainly because the earlier Greek Fathers hadn't done so.

But neither does the silence of the earlier Greek Fathers, such as Origen (c. 230), Chrysostom (c. 400), and Nonnus (c. 400), necessarily imply that these ancient Bible scholars did not know of the *pericope de adultera* as part of the Gospel of John. For they may have been influenced against it by the moralistic prejudice of which we have spoken and also by the fact that some of the manuscripts known to them omitted it. And Burgon mentions another very good reason why these early Fathers failed to comment on this section. Their commenting was in connection with their preaching, and their preaching would be affected by the fact that the *pericope de adultera* was omitted from the ancient Pentecostal lesson of the Church.

"Now for the first time, it becomes abundantly plain, why Chrysostom and Cyril, in publicly commenting on St. John's Gospel, pass straight from ch. 7:52 to ch. 8:12. Of course they do. Why should they, — how could they, — comment on what was not publicly read before the congregation? The same thing is related (in a well-known 'scholium') to have been done by Apolinarius and Theodore of Mopsuestia. Origen also, for aught I care, — though the adverse critics have no right to claim him, seeing that his commentary on all that part of St. John's Gospel is lost, — but Origen's name, as I was saying, for aught I care, may be added to those who did the same thing." [55]

At a very early date it had become customary throughout the Church to read John 7:37-8:12 on the day of Pentecost. This lesson began with John 7:37-39, verses very appropriate to the great Christian feast day in which the outpouring of the Holy Spirit is commemorated: *In the last day, that great day of the feast, Jesus stood and cried saying, If any man thirst, let him come unto Me and drink . . . But this spake He of the Spirit which they that believe on Him should receive.* Then the lesson continued through John 7:52, omitted John 7:53-8:11, and concluded with John 8:12, *Again therefore Jesus spake unto them, saying, I am the light of the world: he that followeth Me shall not walk in darkness, but shall have the light of life.* Thus the fact that the *pericope de adultera* was not publicly read at Pentecost was an additional reason why the early Greek Church Fathers did not comment on it.

Why was the story of the adulteress omitted from the Pentecostal lesson? Obviously because it was inappropriate to the central idea of Pentecost. But critics have another explanation. According to them, the passage was not part of the Gospel of John at the time that the Pentecostal lesson was selected. But, as Burgon pointed

out, this makes it more difficult than ever to explain how this passage
came to be placed after John 7:52. Why would a scribe introduce this
story about an adulteress into the midst of the ancient lesson for
Pentecost? How would it occur to anyone to do this?

Moreover, although the Greek Fathers were silent about the
pericope de adultera, the Church was not silent. This is shown by
the fact that John 8:3-11 was chosen as the lesson to be read publicly each year on St. Pelagia's day, October 8. Burgon points out
the significance of this historical circumstance. "The great Eastern
Church speaks out on this subject in a voice of thunder. In all her
Patriarchates, as far back as the written records of her practice reach,
— and they reach back to the time of those very Fathers whose silence
was felt to be embarrassing, — the Eastern Church has selected nine
out of these twelve verses to be the special lesson for October 8."[56]

(e) The Internal Evidence

Naturalistic critics have tried to argue against the genuineness
of John 7:53-8:11 on the basis of the internal evidence. Colwell
(1952), for example, claims that the story of the woman taken in
adultery does not fit its context and that it differs in its vocabulary
and general tone from the rest of John's Gospel.[57] But by these arguments the critics only create new difficulties for themselves. For
if the *pericope de adultera* is an interpolation and if it is so markedly
out of harmony with its context and with the rest of the Gospel of
John, why was it ever placed in the position which it now occupies?
This is the question which Steck (1893)[58] asked long ago, and it
has never been answered.

Actually, however, there is little substance to these charges.
Arguments from literary style are notoriously weak. They have been
used to prove all sorts of things. And Burgon long ago pointed out
expressions in this passage which are characteristic of John's Gospel.
"We note how entirely in St. John's manner is the little explanatory
clause in ver. 6, — 'This they said, tempting Him that they might
have to accuse Him.' We are struck besides by the prominence given
in verses 6 and 8 to the act of writing, — allusions to which, are
met with in every work of the last Evangelist."[59]

As for not fitting the context, Burgon shows that the actual
situation is just the reverse. When the *pericope de adultera* is omitted, it leaves a hole, a gaping wound that cannot be healed. "Note
that in the oracular Codexes *B* and *Aleph* immediate transition is
made from the words 'out of Galilee ariseth no prophet,' in ch. 7:52, to
the words 'Again therefore JESUS spake unto them, saying,' in ch.
8:12. And we are invited by all the adverse Critics alike to believe
that so the place stood in the inspired autograph of the Evangelist.

"But the thing is incredible. Look back at what is contained
between ch. 7:37 and 52, and note — (a) That two hostile parties
crowded the Temple courts (ver. 40-42); (b) That some were for

laying violent hands on our LORD (ver. 44); (c) That the Sanhedrin, being assembled in debate, were reproaching their servants for not having brought Him prisoner, and disputing one against another (ver. 45-52). How can the Evangelist have proceeded, — 'Again therefore JESUS spake unto them, saying, I am the light of the world'? What is it supposed then that St. John meant when he wrote such words?"[60]

Surely the Dean's point is well taken. Who can deny that when John 7:53-8:11 is rejected, the want of connection between the seventh and eighth chapters is exceedingly strange? The reader is snatched from the midst of a dispute in the council chamber of the Sanhedrin back to Jesus in the Temple without a single word of explanation. Such impressionistic writing might possibly be looked for in some sophisticated modern book but not in a book of the sacred Scriptures.

(f) The Negative Evidence of the Manuscripts and Versions Explained

It is not surprising that the *pericope de adultera* is omitted in Papyri 66 and 75, *Aleph B W* and *L*. For all these manuscripts are connected with the Alexandrian tradition which habitually favored omissions. When once the Montanists or some other extreme group had begun to leave the story of the adulteress out of their copies of John's Gospel, the ascetic tendencies of the early Church were such that the practice would spread rapidly, especially in Egypt, and produce just the situation which we find among the Greek manuscripts. For the same reason many manuscripts of the Coptic (Egyptian) versions, including the recently discovered Bodmer Papyrus III, omit this passage, as do also the Syriac and Armenian versions. All these versions reflect the tendency to omit a passage which had become offensive. And the fact that the section had been so widely omitted encouraged later scribes to play the critic, and thus were produced the unusually large number of variant readings which appear in this passage in the extant manuscripts. And for the same cause many scribes placed deletion marks on the margin opposite this section.

None of these phenomena proves that the *pericope de adultera* is not genuine but merely that there was a widespread prejudice against it in the early Church. The existence of this prejudice makes it more reasonable to suppose that the story of the adulteress was omitted from the text of John than to insist that in the face of this prejudice it was added to the text of John. There would be a motive for omitting it but no motive for adding it.

5. The Last Twelve Verses Of Mark

Burgon's best known work in the field of textual criticism was his treatise on *The Last Twelve Verses of Mark*, which he published in 1871 after years of preliminary study.[61] For over a century this volume has deservedly been held in high esteem by believing Bible students, and its basic arguments all this while have remained irre-futable. In the following paragraphs, therefore, an effort will be made to summarize Burgon's discussion of this disputed passage and to bring his work up to date by the inclusion of new material which has been discovered since Burgon's day.

(a) The Critics Unable to Develop a Satisfactory Theory

And they went out quickly and fled from the sepulchre; for they trembled and were amazed: neither said they any thing to any man; for they were afraid. All the naturalistic critics agree that with this verse (Mark 16:8) the genuine portion of Mark's Gospel ends. But this negative conclusion is the only thing upon which critics are able to agree in regard to the conclusion of Mark. When we ask how it came about that Mark's Gospel ends here without any mention of the post-resurrection appearances of Christ, immediately the critics begin to argue among themselves. For over one hundred years (since the publication of Burgon's book) they have been discussing this question and have been unable to come up with a theory which is acceptable to all or even to most of them.

According to some critics, Mark intentionally ended his Gospel with the words *for they were afraid*. J. M. Creed (1930),[62] for example, and R. H. Lightfoot (1950)[63] have argued that all other attempts to explain why the Gospel of Mark ends here have failed, and that therefore we *must* believe that Mark purposely concluded his Gospel at this point. The scholars who hold this view have ad-vanced various theories to explain why Mark would have done so strange a thing. According to Creed, the story of the empty tomb was new when Mark wrote his Gospel, and by ending with the silence of the women Mark was explaining why this story had never been told before.[64] According to Lohmeyer (1936), the purpose of Mark in ending his Gospel at 16:8 was to hint at a glorious second coming of Christ which was to take place in Galilee.[65] Lightfoot (1937) had a Barthian theory of this passage. He thought that Mark's purpose in concluding with 16:8 was to leave the reader in a state of reverent awe which anticipated an "event" or "crisis" which was "found to have the quality of absolute finality"[66] (whatever that means).

But the theory that Mark purposely ended his Gospel at 16:8 has never been widely held, in spite of Creed's and Lightfoot's argu-ments that this is the only possible view. As Beach (1959) rightly observes, "It seems unlikely that Mark would end the Gospel on a note of fear, for the whole purpose and import of the Gospel is that men should not be afraid."[67] And it is even less likely that Mark concluded his Gospel without any reference to the appearance of the risen Christ to His disciples. For this, as W. L. Knox (1942) re-minds us, would be to leave unmentioned "the main point of his Gospel, and the real 'happy ending' on which the whole faith of the Church depended."[68]

Many of those who hold that the Gospel of Mark ends at 16:8 endeavor to account for this alleged fact by supposing that Mark intended to finish his Gospel but was prevented from doing so, perhaps by death. "At Rome," remarks Streeter (1924), "in Nero's reign this might easily happen."[69] But to suppose that Mark died thus prematurely is to contradict the express statements of Papias, Irenaeus, Clement of Alexandria, and Origen that Mark lived to publish his Gospel. And even if all these ancient writers were wrong and Mark did die before he had finished his Gospel, would his associates have published it in this incomplete state? Would they not have added something from their recollections of Mark's teaching to fill in the obvious gap in the narrative? Only by doing thus could they show their regard for their deceased friend.

Hence the only remaining alternative open to the critics is that the original ending of Mark's Gospel has completely disappeared. Juelicher (1894)[70] and C. S. C. Williams (1951)[71] suggest that it was intentionally removed by certain of those who disapproved of its teaching concerning Christ's resurrection. Other scholars believe that the original conclusion of Mark's Gospel was lost accidentally. Since it was the last page, they argue, it might easily have been torn off. But although these theories explain the absence of this hypothetical "lost ending" from *some* of the manuscripts, it can hardly account for its complete disappearance from *all* the known copies of Mark. Creed (1930) pointed this out some years ago. "Once the book was in circulation, the conclusion would be known and a defective copy could be completed without difficulty. And there would be an overwhelming interest in a restoration of the complete text at this crucial point. It would seem better, therefore, to push back the supposed mutilation to the very beginning of the book's history. But the earlier we suppose the mutilation to have taken place, the greater the likelihood that the author was himself within reach to supply what was wanting."[72]

(b) Ancient Evidence Favorable to Mark 16:9-20

Thus it is an easy thing to say that the genuine portion of the Gospel of Mark ends at 16:8, but it is a difficult task to support this statement with a satisfactory explanation as to how the Gospel came to end there, a task so difficult that it has not yet been adequately accomplished. But the last twelve verses of Mark cannot be disowned on the strength of an unsupported statement, even when it is made by the most eminent of modern scholars. For these verses have an enormous weight of testimony in their favor which cannot be lightly set aside. They are found in all the Greek manuscripts except *Aleph* and *B* and in all the Latin manuscripts except *k*. All the Syriac versions contain these verses, with the exception of the Sinaitic Syriac, and so also does the Bohairic version. And, even more important, they were quoted as Scripture by early Church Fathers who lived one hundred and fifty years before *B* and *Aleph* were written, namely, Justin Martyr (c. 150),[73] Tatian (c. 175),[74] Irenaeus (c. 180),[75] and Hippolytus (c. 200).[76] Thus the earliest extant testimony is on the side of these last twelve verses. Surely the critical objections against them must be exceedingly strong to overcome this evidence for their genuineness.

(c) Documents That Omit Mark 16:9-20

No doubt the strongest argument that can be brought against the last twelve verses of Mark is that there are extant documents that omit them. In Legg's apparatus these are listed as follows: the Greek manuscripts *Aleph* and *B*, the Sinaitic Syriac manuscript, the Adysh and Opiza manuscripts of the Old Georgian version, and 8 manuscripts of the Armenian version. Colwell (1937), however, has enlarged this list of Armenian manuscripts to 62.[77]

In place of Mark 16:9-20 the Old Latin manuscript *k* has the so-called "short ending" of Mark, which reads as follows:

And all things whatsoever that had been commanded they explained briefly to those who were with Peter; after these things also Jesus Himself appeared and from the east unto the west sent out through them the holy and uncorrupted preaching of eternal salvation. Amen.

L, Psi, and a few other Greek manuscripts have this "short ending" placed between 16:8 and 16:9. P. Kahle (1951) reports that 5 Sahidic manuscripts also contain both this "short ending" and Mark 16:9-20.[78] The "short ending" is also found in the margins of 2 Bohairic manuscripts and in 7 Ethiopic ones.

(d) The Negative Evidence of the Documents Inconclusive

Long ago Burgon demonstrated that this negative evidence of the documents is inconclusive. In the first place, he pointed out that in the early Church there were those who had difficulty in reconciling Mark 16:9 with Matthew 28:1. For, at first sight, these two passages seem to contradict each other. Mark says that Christ rose "early the first day of the week," that is, *Sunday morning;* while Matthew seems to say that Christ rose "in the end of the Sabbath," which, strictly interpreted, means *Saturday evening.* It is true that Matthew's expression can be more loosely construed to mean *the end of Saturday night,* and thus the conflict with Mark can be avoided, but there were some early Christians, it seems, who did not realize this and were seriously troubled by the apparent disagreement. Eusebius (c. 325), in his *Epistle to Marinus,* discusses this problem at considerable length. His solution was to place a comma after the word *risen* in Mark 16:9 and to regard the phrase *early the first day of the week* as referring to the time at which Jesus appeared to Mary Magdalene rather than as indicating the hour in which He rose from the dead.[79]

In the second place, Burgon called attention to the fact that in many ancient manuscripts of the Four Gospels the Western order was followed. Matthew was placed first, then John, then Luke, and finally Mark. Thus Mark 16:9-20 was often, no doubt, written on the very last page of the manuscript and could easily be torn off.[80] Suppose some early Christian, who was already wrestling with the problem of harmonizing Mark 16:9 with Matthew 28:1, should find a manuscript which had thus lost its last page containing Mark 16:9-20. Would not such a person see in this omission an easy solution of his difficulties? He would argue as modern critics do that the genuine text of Mark ended at 16:8 and that verses 16:9-20 were a later addition to the Gospel narrative. Thus a tendency on the part of certain ancient scribes to omit the last twelve verses of Mark could easily develop, especially at Alexandria where the scribes were accustomed to favor the shorter reading and reject the longer as an interpolation.

(e) The Alleged Difference in Literary Style

One of the negative arguments employed by the critics is the alleged difference in literary style which distinguishes these last twelve verses from the rest of Mark's Gospel. This argument is still used by critics today. Thus Metzger (1964) claims that "seventeen non-Marcan words or words used in a non-Marcan sense" are present in these verses.[81] Long ago, however, Tregelles (1854) admitted "that arguments on *style* are often very fallacious, and that by themselves they prove very little."[82] And Burgon (1871) demonstrated this to be true. In a brilliant chapter of his treatise on Mark he showed that the alleged differences of style were mere nothings. For example, Meyer (1847) and other critics had made much of the fact that two typically Marcan words, namely, *euthus* (straightway) and *palin* (again) were not found in Mark 16:9-20. Burgon showed that *euthus* did not occur in chapters 12 and 13 of Mark and *palin* did not occur in chapters 1, 6, 9, and 13 of Mark. Thus the fact that these words did not occur in Mark 16:9-20 proved nothing in regard to the genuineness of this section.[83]

(f) The Alleged Discrepancy Between Mark 16:9-20 and Mark 16:1-8

For over one hundred years also it has been said that there is a discrepancy, a remarkable lack of continuity, between the last twelve verses of Mark and the preceding eight verses. Mark 16:9-20, we are told, differs so radically from Mark 16:1-8 that it could not have been written by the Evangelist himself but must have been added by a later hand. Why, the critics ask, are we not told what happened to the women, and why is no account given of the appearance of the risen Christ to Peter and the other disciples in Galilee, a meeting which is promised in Mark 16:7? These objections, however, are not as serious as at first they seem to be. For it was evidently not Mark's intention to satisfy our curiosity about the women or to report that meeting of Christ and His disciples which is promised in Mark 16:7. His purpose was to emphasize the importance of faith in the risen Christ. *He that believeth and is baptized shall be saved; but he that believeth not shall be damned. And these signs shall follow them that believe* (Mark 16:16-17). Thus he passes over everything else and concentrates on those appearances of the risen Christ in which belief (or unbelief) is especially involved.

Thus there is nothing in these arguments from internal evidence which need give the defender of Mark 16:9-20 any real cause for concern. On the contrary, the critics themselves are the ones who must bear the sting of these objections. They are caught in their own trap. For if the last twelve verses of Mark are in such obvious disagreement with what immediately precedes, how could they ever have been added by a later hand? Why didn't the person who added them remove such glaring contradictions?

Hort answered this question by supposing that Mark 16:9-20 was taken by some scribe from a lost document and added to Mark's Gospel without change.[84] Similarly, Streeter suggested that Mark 16:9-20 was originally "a summary intended for catechetical purposes; later on the bright idea occurred to some one of adding it as a sort of appendix to his copy of Mark."[85] This theory of Hort and Streeter, however, is far from a satisfactory explanation of the facts. For if Mark 16:9-20 was taken from an independent document and if the discontinuity between this section and the preceding verses is as great as these scholars say it is, then why were no efforts made to smooth over the discrepancy? The manuscripts reveal no signs of any such attempts.

(g) Eusebius' Epistle to Marinus

Eusebius (c. 325) did not include Mark 16:9-20 in his *canons*, a cross reference system which he had devised for the purpose of making it easier to look up parallel passages in the Four Gospels. This does not necessarily mean, however, that Eusebius rejected these last twelve verses of Mark. Burgon demonstrated this long ago in his study of Eusebius' *Epistle to Marinus*. The relevant portions of this Epistle are translated by Burgon as follows:

"He who is for getting rid of the entire passage will say that it is not met with in all the copies of Mark's Gospel: the accurate copies at all events *circumscribe the end* of Mark's narrative at the words of the young man who appeared to the women and said, 'Fear not ye! Ye seek Jesus of Nazareth,' etc.: to which the Evangelist adds, — 'And when they heard it, they fled, and said nothing to any man, for they were afraid.' For at these words, in almost all copies of the Gospel according to Mark, *the end has been circumscribed.* What follows, (which is met with seldom, and only in some copies, certainly not in all,) might be dispensed with.

"But another, on no account daring to reject anything what-ever which is, under whatever circumstance, met with in the text of the Gospels, will say that here are two readings (as is so often the case elsewhere;) and that *both* are to be received, — inasmuch as by the faithful and pious, *this* reading is not held to be genuine rather than *that* nor *that* than *this*."[86]

This passage from Eusebius was repeated by Jerome (c. 400), Hesychius of Jerusalem (c. 430), and Victor of Antioch (c. 550). On the basis of it modern critics claim that Eusebius rejected the last twelve verses of Mark, but this is plainly an exaggeration. The second paragraph of this passage shows that Eusebius regarded Mark 16:9-20 as at least possibly genuine. Critics also have interpreted Eusebius as stating that "the accurate copies" and "almost all copies" end Mark's Gospel at 16:8. But Burgon pointed out that Eusebius doesn't say this. Eusebius says that the accurate copies *cir-cumscribe the end* at 16:8 and that in almost all copies *the end has been circumscribed* at this point. What did Eusebius mean by this unusual expression? Burgon's explanation seems to be the only possible one.

Burgon reminded his readers that it was customary, at least in the later manuscript period, to indicate in the New Testament manuscripts the beginning and the end of the Scripture lesson ap-pointed to be read in the worship services of the Church. The beginning of the Scripture lesson was marked by the word beginning (Greek *arche*), written in the margin of the manuscript, and the end of the reading by the word *end* (Greek *telos*), written in the text. Burgon argued that this practice began very early and that it was this to which Eusebius was referring when he said that the most accurate copies and almost all copies *circumscribe the end* at Mark 16:8. Eusebius was not talking about the end of the Gospel of Mark but about the liturgical sign indicating the end of a Scripture lesson. He is simply saying that this liturgical sign *end* (*telos*) was present after Mark 16:8 in many of the manuscripts known to him.[87]

This may explain why some of the New Testament documents omit Mark 16:9-20. It may be that some scribe saw the liturgical sign *end* (*telos*) after Mark 16:8 and, misinterpreting it to mean that Mark's Gospel ended at this point, laid down his pen. And this would be especially likely to happen if the last page, containing Mark 16:9-20, had accidentally been torn off. "Of course," Burgon argued, "it will have *sometimes* happened that S. Mark 16:8 came to be written at the bottom of the left hand page of a manuscript. And we have but to suppose that in the case of one such Codex the next leaf, which should have been *the last*, was missing, — (*the very thing which has happened in respect of one of the Codices at Moscow*) — and what else *could* result when a copyist reached the words, FOR THEY WERE AFRAID. THE END, but the very phenomenon which has exercised critics so sorely and which gives rise to the whole of the present discussion? The copyist will have brought S. Mark's Gospel to an end there, *of course.* What else could he possibly do?"[88]

When once this omission of Mark 16:9-20 was made, it would be readily adopted by early Christians who were having difficulty harmonizing Mark 16:9 with Matthew 28:1. "That some," Burgon observes, "were found in very early times eagerly to acquiesce in this omission; to sanction it; even to multiply copies of the Gospel so mutilated; (critics or commentators intent on nothing so much as reconciling the apparent discrepancies in the Evangelical narratives;) — appears to me not at all unlikely."[89]

Burgon also suggested that just as Jerome and other later writers copied Eusebius' *Epistle to Marinus* so in this Epistle Eusebius himself was merely copying some lost treatise of Origen (c. 230),[90] and this was one of the very few points on which Westcott and Hort were inclined to agree with Burgon.[91] If this suggestion is correct and Origen was the original author of the *Epistle to Marinus,* then the consequences for textual criticism are very important. For all documents that omit Mark 16:9-20 are in some way connected with Alexandria or Caesarea, the two localities in which Origen, the great textual critic of antiquity, lived and labored. The absence of Mark 16:9-20 from these documents and the doubts which Eusebius seems to have felt about them may all be due to an error of judgment on the part of Origen.

(h) Were Heretics Responsible for the Omission of Mark 16:9-20?

Burgon died in 1888, too soon to give us the benefit of his comment on a development which had taken place shortly before his death, namely, the discovery in 1884 of the apocryphal *Gospel of Peter* in a tomb at Akhmim in Egypt.[92] Had Burgon lived longer, he would not have failed to point out the true significance of the agreement of this *Gospel of Peter* with the Old Latin New Testament manuscript *k* in the last chapter of the Gospel of Mark.

According to modern scholars, the original *Gospel of Peter* was written about 150 A.D. by docetic heretics who denied the reality of Christ's sufferings and consequently the reality of His human body. This false view is seen in the account which this apocryphal writing gives of Christ's crucifixion. In it we are told that when our Lord hung upon the cross, the divine Christ departed to heaven and left only the human Jesus to suffer and die.

> And the Lord cried out aloud saying: My power, *my* power, thou hast forsaken me. And when he had so said, he was taken up.[93]

Also the account which the *Gospel of Peter* gives of the resurrection of Christ is uniquely docetic.

> . . . and they saw the heavens opened and two men descend thence having a great light, and drawing near unto the sepulchre

. . . and the sepulchre was opened, and both of the young men entered in . . . and while they were yet telling them the things which they had seen, they saw again three men come out of the sepulchre, and two of them sustaining the other, and a cross following after them. And of the two they saw that their heads reached unto heaven, but of him that was led by them that it overpassed the heavens. And they heard a voice out of the heavens saying, Hast thou preached unto them that sleep? And an answer was heard from the cross, *saying*:   Yea.[94]

In the Gospel of Mark the Old Latin New Testament manuscript *k* gives a heretical, docetic account of the resurrection of Christ similar to that found in the apocryphal *Gospel of Peter*. In Mark 16:4 manuscript *k* reads as follows:

Suddenly, moreover, at the third hour of the day, darkness fell upon the whole world, and angels descended from heaven, and as the Son of God was rising in brightness, they ascended at the same time with him, and straightway it was light.[95]

It is generally believed by scholars that *k* represents an early form of the Old Latin version, which, like the *Gospel of Peter*, dates from the 2nd century. If this is so, the fact that *k* agrees with the *Gospel of Peter* in giving a docetic account of the resurrection of Christ indicates that Irenaeus (c. 180) was correct in pointing out a special connection between the Gospel of Mark and docetism. This ancient Father observed that docetic heretics "who separate Jesus from Christ, alleging that Christ remained incapable of suffering, but that it was Jesus who suffered," preferred the Gospel of Mark.[96]

In chapter 16 of Mark, then, the Old Latin *k* contains a text which has been tampered with by docetic heretics who, like the author of the apocryphal *Gospel of Peter*, denied the reality of Christ's sufferings and of His human body. And this same *k* also omits the last twelve verses of Mark and substitutes in their place the so-called "short ending," which omits the post-resurrection appearances of Christ.

And all things whatsoever that had been commanded they explained briefly to those who were with Peter; after these things also Jesus Himself appeared and from the east unto the west sent out through them the holy and uncorrupted preaching of eternal salvation. Amen.[97]

Do not these facts fit together perfectly and explain each other? The same docetic heretics who tampered with the first half of Mark 16 in *k* also abbreviated the second half of Mark 16 in this same manuscript. They evidently thought that in the last twelve verses of Mark too great emphasis was placed on the bodily appearances of Christ to His disciples. They therefore rejected these concluding verses of Mark's Gospel and substituted a "short ending" of their own devising, a docetic conclusion in which Christ's post-resurrection appearances are almost entirely eliminated.

In addition to these docetists who abbreviated the conclusion of Mark's Gospel there were also other heretics, probably Gnostics, who expanded it by adding after Mark 16:14 a reading which was known to Jerome (415)[98] and which appears as follows in *Codex W*:

> And they answered and said, 'This age of lawlessness and unbelief is under Satan, who doth not allow the truth of God to prevail over the unclean things of the spirits. Therefore reveal thy righteousness now.' So spake they to Christ. And Christ answered them, 'The term of the years of Satan's dominion hath been fulfilled, but other terrible things draw near. And for those who have sinned I was delivered over unto death, that they may return to the truth and sin no more, that they may inherit the spiritual and incorruptible glory of righteousness which is in heaven.'[99]

Hence, in addition to the causes which Dean Burgon discussed so ably, the tampering of heretics must have been one of the factors which brought about the omission of Mark 16:9-20 in the few New Testament documents which do omit this passage.

We see, then, that believing scholars who receive the last twelve verses of Mark as genuine are more reasonable than naturalistic scholars who reject them. For there are many reasons why these verses might have been omitted by the few New Testament documents which do omit them, but no reason has yet been invented which can explain satisfactorily either how a hypothetical "lost ending" of Mark could have disappeared from all the extant New Testament documents or how the author of Mark's Gospel could have left it incomplete without any ending at all.

It is sometimes said that the last twelve verses of Mark are not really important, so that it makes little difference whether they are accepted or rejected. This, however, is hardly the case. For Mark 16:9-20 is the only passage in the Gospels which refers specifically to the subject which is attracting so much attention today, namely, tongues, healings, and other spiritual gifts. The last verse of this passage is particularly decisive (Mark 16:20). Here we see that the purpose of the miracles promised by our Lord was to confirm the preaching of the divine Word by the Apostles. Of course, then, these signs ceased after the Apostles' death. Today we have no need of them. The Bible is the all-sufficient miracle. And if we take this high view of the Bible, we cannot possibly suppose that the ending of one of the Gospels has been completely lost.

CHAPTER SEVEN

THE TRADITIONAL NEW TESTAMENT TEXT

The Bible is the Book of the Covenant. Its origin is eternal, its inspiration infallible, its preservation providential and sure. In it God reveals Himself as the almighty Creator God, the faithful Covenant God, and the triune Saviour God. In it Christ reveals Himself to sinners as Prophet, Priest, and King. Hence the Bible is unique! divine! No other book is like the Bible. And because this is so, we must reject every type of naturalistic Bible study, every tendency to deal with the Bible as other ancient books are dealt with. Above all we must be alert to the dangers of naturalistic New Testament textual criticism. For this is naturalistic Bible study of a most insidious sort. It begins by persuading an unsuspecting Christian to ignore God's providential preservation of the Scriptures and then leads him on to ignore other divine aspects of the Bible until almost before he knows it he finds himself bereft of faith and almost completely modernistic in outlook.

Therefore, as Bible-believing Christians, we reject all forms of naturalistic New Testament textual criticism and adopt and advocate in their place a consistently Christian method which derives all its principles from the Bible itself and none from the textual criticism of other ancient books. And because this consistently Christian approach leads us to accept the Traditional New Testament Text, found in the vast majority of the manuscripts, as a trustworthy reproduction of the divinely inspired Originals, we shall now endeavor to defend this Traditional Text against the attacks of naturalistic critics and especially of Westcott and Hort. Such a defense may possibly contribute to the beginning of a new Reformation.

1. The Traditional Text Not The Invention Of Editors

Although naturalistic textual critics differ from one another in regard to many matters, they all agree in regarding the Traditional Text, found in the vast majority of the Greek New Testament manuscripts, as a late invention. They believe that there were editors who deliberately created the Traditional Text by selecting *readings* (words, phrases, and sentences) from the various texts already in existence and then recombining these readings in such a way as to form an altogether new text. This naturalistic view, however, is contrary to the evidence, as we shall endeavor to show in the following paragraphs.

(a) The Evidence of Codex W

In demonstrating the antiquity of the Traditional Text it is well to begin with the evidence of *Codex W*, the Freer Manuscript of the Gospels, named after C. L. Freer of Detroit, who purchased it in 1906 from an Arab dealer at Gizeh, near Cairo. It is now housed in the Freer Gallery of Art in Washington, D.C. In 1912 it was published under the editorship of H. A. Sanders.[1] It contains the Four Gospels in the Western order, Matthew, John, Luke, Mark. In John and the first third of Luke the text is Alexandrian in character. In Mark the text is of the Western type in the first five chapters and of a mixed "Caesarean" type in the remaining chapters. The especial value of *W*, however, lies in Matthew and the last two thirds of Luke. Here the text is Traditional (Byzantine) of a remarkably pure type. According to Sanders, in Matthew the text of *W* is of the *Kappa* 1 type, which von Soden (1906) regarded as the oldest and best form of the Traditional (Byzantine) Text.[2]

The discovery of *W* tends to disprove the thesis of Westcott and Hort that the Traditional Text is a fabricated text which was put together in the 4th century by a group of scholars residing at Antioch. For *Codex W* is a very ancient manuscript. B. P. Grenfell regarded it as "probably fourth century."[3] Other scholars have dated it in the 5th century. Hence *W* is one of the oldest complete manuscripts of the Gospels in existence, possibly of the same age as *Aleph*. Moreover, *W* seems to have been written in Egypt, since during the first centuries of its existence it seems to have been the property of the Monastery of the Vinedresser, which was located near the third pyramid.[4] If the Traditional Text had been invented at Antioch in the 4th century, how would it have found its way into Egypt and thence into *Codex W* so soon thereafter? Why would the scribe of *W*, writing in the 4th or early 5th century, have adopted this newly fabricated text in Matthew and Luke in preference to other texts which (according to Hort's hypothesis) were older and more familiar to him? Thus the presence of the Traditional Text in *W* indicates that this text is a very ancient text and that it was known in Egypt before the 4th century.

(b) The Evidence of Codex A

Another witness to the early existence of the Traditional Text is *Codex A* (*Codex Alexandrinus*). This venerable manuscript, which dates from the 5th century, has played a very important role in the history of New Testament textual criticism. It was given to the King of England in 1627 by Cyril Lucar, patriarch of Constantinople, and for many years was regarded as the oldest extant New Testament manuscript. In Acts and the Epistles *Codex A* agrees most closely with the Alexandrian text of the *B* and *Aleph* type, but in the Gospels it agrees generally with the Traditional Text. Thus in the

Gospels *Codex A* testifies to the antiquity of the Traditional Text. According to Gregory (1907) and Kenyon (1937), *Codex A* was probably written in Egypt. If this is so, then *A* is also another witness to the early presence of the Traditional Text upon the Egyptian scene.

(c) The Evidence of the Papyri

When the Chester Beatty Papyri were published (1933-37), it was found that these early 3rd century fragments agree surprisingly often with the Traditional (Byzantine) Text against all other types of text. "A number of Byzantine readings," Zuntz (1953) observes, "most of them genuine, which previously were discarded as 'late', are anticipated by Pap. 46." And to this observation he adds the following significant note, "The same is true of the sister-manuscript Pap. 45; see, for example, Matt. 26:7 and Acts. 17:13."[5] And the same is true also of the Bodmer Papyri (published 1956-62). Birdsall (1960) acknowledges that "the Bodmer Papyrus of John (Papyrus 66) has not a few such Byzantine readings."[6] And Metzger (1962) lists 23 instances of the agreements of Papyri 45, 46, and 66 with the Traditional (Byzantine) Text against all other text-types.[7] And at least a dozen more such agreements occur in Papyrus 75.

(d) Traditional (Byzantine) Readings in Origen

One of the arguments advanced by Westcott and Hort and other naturalistic critics against the early existence and thus against the genuineness of the Traditional (Byzantine) Text is the alleged fact that "distinctively" Traditional readings are never found in the New Testament quotations of Origen and other 2nd and 3rd-century Church Fathers. In other words, it is alleged that these early Fathers never agree with the Traditional Text in places in which it stands alone in opposition to both the Western and Alexandrian texts. For example, in Matt. 27:34 the Traditional Text tells us that before the soldiers crucified Jesus they gave Him *vinegar* mingled with gall, thus fulfilling the prophecy of Psalm 69:21. Hort thought this to be a late reading suggested by the Psalm. The true reading, he contended, is that found in *Aleph B D etc., wine* mingled with gall. Burgon (1896), however, refuted Hort's argument by pointing out that the Traditional reading *vinegar* was known not only to Origen but also to the pagan philosopher Celsus (c. 180), who used the passage to ridicule Jesus.[8] In his treatise *Against Celsus* Origen takes note of this blasphemy and reproves it, but he never suggests that Celsus has adopted a false reading. "Those that resist the word of truth," Origen declares, "do ever offer to Christ the Son of God the gall of their own wickedness, and the *vinegar* of their evil inclinations; but though He tastes of it, yet He will not drink it."[9]

Hence, contrary to the assertions of the naturalistic critics, the distinctive readings of the Traditional (Byzantine) Text were known to Origen, who sometimes adopted them, though perhaps not usually. Anyone can verify this by scanning the apparatus of Tischendorf. For instance, in the first 14 chapters of the Gospel of John (that is, in the area covered by Papyrus 66 and Papyrus 75) out of 52 instances in which the Traditional Text stands alone Origen agrees with the Traditional Text 20 times and disagrees with it 32 times. These results make the position of the critics that Origen knew nothing of the Traditional Text difficult indeed to maintain.

Naturalistic critics, it is true, have made a determined effort to explain away the "distinctively" Traditional readings which appear in the New Testament quotations of Origen (and other early Fathers). It is argued that these Traditional readings are not really Origen's but represent alterations made by scribes who copied Origen's works. These scribes, it is maintained, revised the original quotations of Origen and made them conform to the Traditional Text. The evidence of the Bodmer Papyri, however, indicates that this is not an adequate explanation of the facts. Certainly it seems a very unsatisfactory way to account for the phenomena which appear in the first 14 chapters of John. In these chapters 7 out of 20 "distinctively" Traditional readings which occur in Origen occur also in Papyrus 66 and/or in Papyrus 75. These 7 readings at least must have been Origen's own readings, not those of the scribes who copied Origen's works, and what is true of these 7 readings is probably true of the other 13, or at least of most of them. Thus it can hardly be denied that the Traditional Text was known to Origen and that it influenced the wording of his New Testament quotations.

(e) The Evidence of the Peshitta Syriac Version

The Peshitta Syriac version, which is the historic Bible of the whole Syrian Church, agrees closely with the Traditional Text found in the vast majority of the Greek New Testament manuscripts. Until about one hundred years ago it was almost universally believed that the Peshitta originated in the 2nd century and hence was one of the oldest New Testament versions. Hence because of its agreement with the Traditional Text the Peshitta was regarded as one of the most important witnesses to the antiquity of the Traditional Text. In more recent times, however, naturalistic critics have tried to nullify this testimony of the Peshitta by denying that it is an ancient version. Burkitt (1904), for example, insisted that the Peshitta did not exist before the 5th century but "was prepared by Rabbula, bishop of Edessa (the capital city of Syria) from 411-435 A.D., and published by his authority."[10]

Burkitt's theory was once generally accepted, but now scholars are realizing that the Peshitta must have been in existence before Rabbula's episcopate, because it was the received text of both the two sects into which the Syrian Church became divided. Since this division took place in Rabbula's time and since Rabbula was the

B.F. Westcott (1825-1901)

F.J.A. Hort (1828-1892)

leader of one of these sects, it is impossible to suppose that the Peshitta was his handiwork, for if it had been produced under his auspices, his opponents would never have adopted it as their received New Testament text. Indeed A. Voobus, in a series of special studies (1947-54),[11] has argued not only that Rabbula was not the author of the Peshitta but even that he did not use it, at least not in its present form. If this is true and if Burkitt's contention is also true, namely, that the Syrian ecclesiastical leaders who lived before Rabbula also did not use the Peshitta, then why *was* it that the Peshitta was received by all the mutually opposing groups in the Syrian Church as their common, authoritative Bible? It must have been that the Peshitta was a very ancient version and that because it was so old the common people within the Syrian Church continued to be loyal to it regardless of the factions into which they came to be divided and the preferences of their leaders. It made little difference to them whether these leaders quoted the Peshitta or not. They persevered in their usage of it, and because of their steadfast devotion this old translation retained its place as the received text of the Syriac-speaking churches.

(f) The Evidence of the Sinaitic Syriac Manuscript

The Sinaitic Syriac manuscript was discovered by two sisters, Mrs. Lewis and Mrs. Gibson, in the monastery of St. Catherine on Mount Sinai, hence the name. It contains a type of text which is very old, although not so old as the text of the Peshitta. Critics assign an early 3rd-century date to the text of the Sinaitic Syriac manuscript. If they are correct in this, then this manuscript is remarkable for the unexpected support which it gives to the Traditional Text. For Burkitt (1904) found that "not infrequently" this manuscript agreed with the Traditional Text against the Western and Alexandrian texts.[12] One of these Traditional readings thus supported by the Sinaitic Syriac manuscript is found in the angelic song of Luke 2:14. Here the Traditional Text and the Sinaitic Syriac read, *good will among (toward) men*, while the Western and Alexandrian texts read, *among men of good will.*

(g) The Evidence of the Gothic Version

The Gothic version also indicates that the Traditional Text is not a late text. This New Testament translation was made from the Greek into Gothic shortly after 350 A.D. by Ulfilas, missionary bishop to the Goths. "The type of text represented in it," Kenyon (1912) tells us, "is for the most part that which is found in the majority of Greek manuscripts."[13] The fact, therefore, that Ulfilas in A.D. 350 produced a Gothic version based on the Traditional Text proves that this text must have been in existence before that date. In other words, there must have been many manuscripts of the Traditional type on hand in the days of Ulfilas, manuscripts which since that time have perished.

(h) The "Conflate Readings"

Westcott and Hort found proof for their position that the Traditional Text was a "work of attempted criticism performed deliberately by editors and not merely by scribes" in eight passages in the Gospels in which the Western text contains one half of the reading found in the Traditional Text and the Alexandrian text the other half.[14] These passages are Mark 6:33; 8:26; 9:38; 9:49; Luke 9:10; 11:54; 12:18; 24:53. Since Hort discusses the first of these passages at great length, it may serve very well as a sample specimen.

Mark 6:33 *And the people saw them departing, and many knew Him, and ran together there on foot out of all the cities,*

(Then follow three variant readings.)

(1) *and came before them and came together to Him.* Traditional Reading.

(2) *and came together there.* Western Reading.

(3) *and came before them.* Alexandrian Reading.

Hort argued that here the Traditional reading was deliberately created by editors who produced this effect by adding the other two readings together. Hort called the Traditional reading a "conflate reading," that is to say, a mixed reading which was formed by combining the Western reading with the Alexandrian reading. And Hort said the same thing in regard to his seven other specimen passages. In each case he maintained that the Traditional reading had been made by linking the Western reading with the Alexandrian. And this, he claimed, indicated that the Traditional Text was the deliberate creation of an editor or a group of editors.

Dean Burgon (1882) immediately registered one telling criticism of this hypothesis of conflation in the Traditional Text. Why, he asked, if conflation was one of the regular practices of the makers of the Traditional Text, could Westcott and Hort find only *eight* instances of this phenomenon? "Their theory," Burgon exclaimed, "has at last forced them to make an appeal to Scripture and to produce some actual specimens of their meaning. After ransacking the Gospels for 30 years, they have at last fastened upon *eight*."[15]

Westcott and Hort disdained to return any answer to Burgon's objection, but it remains a valid one. If the Traditional Text was created by 4th-century Antiochian editors, and if one of their habitual practices had been to conflate (combine) Western and Alexandrian readings, then surely more examples of such conflation ought to be discoverable in the Gospels than just Hort's *eight*. But only a few more have since been found to add to Hort's small deposit. Kenyon (1912) candidly admitted that he didn't think that there were very many more.[16] And this is all the more remarkable because not only the Greek manuscripts but also the versions have been carefully canvassed by experts, such as Burkitt and Souter and Lake, for readings which would reveal conflation in the Traditional Text.

Moreover, even the eight alleged examples of conflation which Westcott and Hort did bring forward are not at all convincing. At least they did not approve themselves as such in the eyes of Bousset (1894). This radical German scholar united with the conservatives in rejecting the conclusions of these two critics. In only one of their eight instances did he agree with them. In four of the other instances he regarded the Traditional reading as the original reading, and in the three others he regarded the decision as doubtful. "Westcott and Hort's chief proof," he observed, "has almost been turned into its opposite."[17]

In these eight passages, therefore, it is just as easy to believe that the Traditional reading is the original and that the other texts have omitted parts of it as to suppose that the Traditional reading represents a later combination of the other two readings.

(i) Alleged Harmonizations in the Traditional Text

According to the naturalistic critics, the Traditional Text is characterized by harmonizations, especially in the Gospel of Mark. In other words, the critics accuse the Traditional Text of being altered in Mark and made to agree with Matthew. Actually, however, the reverse is the case. The boldest harmonizations occur not in the Traditional Text but in the Western and Alexandrian texts and not in Mark but in Matthew. For example, after Matt. 27:49 the following reading is found in *Aleph B C L* and a few other Alexandrian manuscripts: *And another, taking a spear, pierced His side, and there flowed out water and blood.* Because this reading occurs in *B*, Westcott and Hort were unwilling to reject it completely,[18] but less prejudiced critics admit that it is a harmonization taken from John 19:34.

A similar harmonization occurs in Matt. 24:36. Here *Aleph B D Theta* and a few other manuscripts read: *But of that day and hour knoweth no man, no not the angels of heaven, neither the Son, but the Father only.* The Traditional text, however, omits, *neither the Son.* Naturalistic critics say that this omission was made by orthodox scribes who were loath to believe that Christ could be ignorant of anything. But if this were so, why didn't these scribes omit this same reading in Mark 13:32? Why would they omit this reading in Matthew and leave it stand in Mark? Obviously, then, this is not a case of omission on the part of the Traditional Text but of harmonization on the part of the Western and Alexandrian texts, represented by *Aleph B D Theta* etc.

There is no evidence, therefore, to prove that the Traditional Text is especially addicted to harmonization.

(j) Why the Traditional Text Could Not Have Been Created by Editors

Thus discoveries since the days of Westcott and Hort have continued steadily to render less and less reasonable their hypothesis that the Traditional Text was created by editors. For if it originated thus, then it must consist of readings taken not only from the Western and Alexandrian texts but also many others, including the "Caesarean," the Sinaitic Syriac, Papyrus 45, Papyrus 46, Papyrus 66, and even Papyrus 75. In short, if the Traditional Text was created by editors, then we must agree with Hutton (1911) that it is a magpie's nest. The Traditional Text, he asserted, "is in the true sense of the word eclectic, drawing 'Various readings' of various value from various sources. Often times it picked up a diamond, and sometimes a bit of broken glass, sometimes it gives us brass or lacquer without distinction from the nobler metal. It was for all the world like a magpie, and the result is not unlike a magpie's nest."[19] But was Hutton really reasonable in supposing that the Traditional Text was created by editors who went about their work in the same irrational manner in which a magpie goes about selecting materials for her nest? Surely the hypothesis that the Traditional Text was created by editors breaks down if it is necessary to assume that those who performed this task were as whimsical as that witless bird.

And in the second place, to create the Traditional (Byzantine) Text by blending three or four or five older texts into one would be an amazingly difficult feat. It would be hard to do this even under modern conditions with a large desk on which to spread out your documents and a chair to sit on. Modern scholars who attempt this usually construct a critical apparatus by comparing all the documents with one standard, printed text and noting the variant readings. Ancient scribes, however, would be laboring under great disadvantages. They would have no printed text to serve as a standard of comparison, no desks, and not even any chairs! According to Metzger (1964), they sat on stools or on the ground and held the manuscripts which they were writing on their knees.[20] Under such conditions it would surely be difficult to be continually comparing many documents while writing. It seems unlikely that ancient scribes would be able to work with more than two documents at once. A scribe would compare his manuscript with another manuscript and write in some of the variant readings, usually in the margin. Another scribe would copy this corrected manuscript and adopt some of the corrections. Hence the mixture would be sporadic and unsystematic and not at all of the kind that would be required to produce the Traditional (Byzantine) New Testament Text.

Thus the theory that the Traditional Text was created by editors breaks down when carefully considered. No reason can be given why the supposed editors should have gone about their tremendous task in the irrational manner that the alleged evidence would require.

2. The Traditional Text Not An Official Text

Why is it that the Traditional (Byzantine) Text is found in the vast majority of the Greek New Testament manuscripts rather than some other text, the Western text, for example, or the Alexandrian? What was there about the Traditional (Byzantine) Text which enabled it to conquer all its rivals and become the text generally accepted by the Greek Church?

(a) Westcott and Hort's Theory of the Traditional (Byzantine) Text

The classic answer to this question was given by Westcott and Hort in their celebrated *Introduction* (1881). They believed that from the very beginning the Traditional (Byzantine) Text was an *official* text with official backing and that this was the reason why it overcame all rival texts and ultimately reigned supreme in the usage of the Greek Church. They regarded the Traditional Text as the product of a thorough-going revision of the New Testament text which took place at Antioch in two stages between 250 A.D. and 350 A.D. They believed that this text was the deliberate creation of certain scholarly Christians at Antioch and that the presbyter Lucian (d. 312) was probably the original leader in this work. According to Westcott and Hort, these Antiochian scholars produced the Traditional Text by mixing together the Western, Alexandrian, and Neutral (*B-Aleph*) texts. "Sometimes they transcribed unchanged the reading of one of the earlier texts, now of this, now of that. Sometimes they in like manner adopted exclusively one of the readings but modified its form. Sometimes they combined the readings of more than one text in various ways, pruning or modifying them if necessary. Lastly, they introduced many changes of their own where, so far as appears, there was no previous variation."[21]

What would be the motive which would prompt these supposed editors to create the Traditional New Testament Text? According to Westcott and Hort, the motive was to eliminate hurtful competition between the Western, Alexandrian, and Neutral (*B-Aleph*) texts by the creation of a compromise text made up of elements of all three of these rival texts. "The guiding motives of their (the editors') criticism are transparently displayed in its effects. It was probably initiated by the distracting and inconvenient currency of at least three conflicting texts in the same region. The alternate borrowing from all implies that no selection of one was made, — indeed it is difficult to see how under the circumstances it could have been made, — as entitled to supremacy by manifest superiority of pedigree. Each text may perhaps have found a patron in some leading personage or see, and thus have seemed to call for a conciliation of rival claims."[22]

In other words, Westcott and Hort's theory was that the Traditional Text was an official text created by a council or conference of bishops and leading churchmen meeting for the express purpose of constructing a New Testament text on which all could agree, and in their discussion of the history of the Traditional Text they continue to emphasize its official character. This text, they alleged, was dominant at Antioch in the second half of the 4th century, "probably by authority."[23] It was used by the three great Church Fathers of Antioch, namely, Diodorus (d. 394), Chrysostom (345-407), and Theodore of Mopsuestia (350-428). Soon this text was taken to Constantinople and became the dominant text of that great, imperial city, perhaps even the official text. Then, due to the prestige which it had obtained at Constantinople, it became the dominant text of the whole Greek-speaking Church. "Now Antioch," Westcott and Hort theorized, "is the true ecclesiastical parent of Constantinople; so that it is no wonder that the traditional Constantinopolitan text, whether formally official or not, was the Antiochian text of the fourth century. It was equally natural that the text recognized at Constantinople should eventually become in practice the standard New Testament of the East."[24]

(b) Westcott and Hort's Theory Disproved

Thus Westcott and Hort bore down heavily on the idea that the Traditional (Byzantine) Text was an *official* text. It was through ecclesiastical authority, they believed, that this text was created, and it was through ecclesiastical authority that this text was imposed upon the Church, so that it became the text found in the vast majority of the Greek New Testament manuscripts. This emphasis on ecclesiastical authority, however, has been abandoned by most present-day scholars. As Kenyon (1912) observed long ago, there is no historical evidence that the Traditional Text was created by a council or conference of ancient scholars. History is silent concerning any such gathering. "We know," he remarks, "the names of several revisers of the Septuagint and the Vulgate, and it would be strange if historians and Church writers had all omitted to record or mention such an event as the deliberate revision of the New Testament in its original Greek."[25]

Recent studies in the Traditional (Byzantine) Text indicate still more clearly that this was not an official text imposed upon the Church by ecclesiastical authority or by the influence of any outstanding leader. Westcott and Hort, for example, regarded Chrysostom as one of the first to use this text and promote its use in the Church. But studies by Geerlings and New (1931)[26] and by Dicks (1948)[27] appear to indicate that Chrysostom could hardly have performed this function, since he himself does not seem always to have used the Traditional Text. Photius (815-897) also, patriarch of Constantinople, seems to have been no patron of the Traditional Text, for according to studies by Birdsall (1956-58), he customarily used a mixed type of text thought to be Caesarean.[28] The lectionaries also indicate that the Traditional Text could not have been imposed on the Church by ecclesiastical authority. These, as has been stated, are manuscripts containing the New Testament Scripture lessons appointed to be read at the various worship services of the ecclesiastical year. According to the researches of Colwell (1933) and his associates, the oldest of these lessons are not Traditional but "mixed" in text.[29] This would not be the case if Westcott and Hort's theory were true that the Traditional Text from the very beginning had enjoyed official status.

(c) The True Text Never an Official Text

Thus recent research has brought out more clearly the fact that the true New Testament text has never been an official text. It has never been dependent on the decisions of an official priesthood or convocation of scholars. All attempts to deal with the New Testament text in this way are bound to fail, for this is a return to Old Testament bondage. Nay, this is worse than Old Testament bondage! For God appointed the priests of the Old Testament dispensation and gave them authority to care for the Old Testament Scriptures, but who appointed the priests and pundits of our modern ecclesiastical scene and gave them the right to sit in judgment on the New Testament text? It was not in this way that the New Testament text was preserved but rather through the testimony of the Holy Spirit operating in the hearts of individual Christians and gradually leading them, by common consent, to reject false readings and to preserve the true.

3. Have Modern Studies Disintegrated The Traditional Text?

In the more recent years certain scholars have been saying that modern studies have disintegrated the Traditional (Byzantine) Text. Not only (so they say) has its use by Chrysostom been disproved but also its uniformity. Birdsall (1956) expresses himself on this head as follows: "Since the publication of Hort's Introduction in 1881 it has been assumed in most quarters, as handbooks reflect, that the text was uniform from the time of John Chrysostom and that this uniform text (called by a variety of names, and here Byzantine) is to be found in his quotations. . . . However, more recent investigation has questioned both the uniformity of the Byzantine text and its occurrence in Chrysostom's citations."[30] And earlier Colwell (1935) gave voice to the same opinion and appealed for support to the investigations of von Soden and Kirsopp Lake. "This invaluable pioneer work of von Soden greatly weakened the dogma of the dominance of a homogeneous Syrian (Traditional) text. But the fallacy received its death blow at the hands of Professor Lake. In an excursus published in his study of the Caesarean text of Mark, he annihilated the theory that the middle ages were ruled by a single recension which attained a high degree of uniformity."[31]

Have the studies of von Soden and Lake disintegrated the Traditional (Byzantine) Text, or is this a misinterpretation of the researches of the two scholars? This is the question which we will consider in the following paragraphs.

(a) The Researches of von Soden

Von Soden (1906) made the most extensive study of the Traditional (Byzantine) Text that has ever yet been undertaken.[32] He called the Traditional Text the *Kappa* (Common) text, thereby indicating that it is the text most commonly found in the New Testament manuscripts. He divided the Traditional manuscripts into three classes, *Kappa* 1, *Kappa* x, and *Kappa* r. The manuscripts in the *Kappa* 1 class (as the numeral 1 implies) he regarded as containing the earliest form of the Traditional (Byzantine) Text. Among the best representatives of this class he placed *Omega* (8th century), *V* (9th century), and *S* (10th century). In 1912, as has been stated, Sanders found that *Codex W* contained the *Kappa* 1 text in Matthew.

Von Soden considered the *Kappa* r text to be a revision of the Traditional Text (the letter r signifying *revision*). In between the *Kappa* 1 manuscripts and the *Kappa* r manuscripts in respect to time von Soden located the great majority of the Traditional (Byzantine) manuscripts. These he named *Kappa* x (the letter x signifying *unknown*) to indicate that the small differences which distinguish them from each other had not yet been thoroughly studied. And in addition von Soden distinguished several other families of manuscripts the texts of which had originated in the mixture of the Traditional and Western texts. One of the earliest of these was the *Kappa* a family, the chief representatives of which are *Codex A* (5th century) and *K* and *Pi* (both 9th century).

Thus von Soden divided the vast family of Traditional (Byzantine) manuscripts (which he called the *Kappa* manuscripts) into three main varieties. Unlike Colwell, however, he did not regard this variety as affecting the essential agreement existing between the Traditional manuscripts, i.e., the uniformity of their underlying text. "The substance of the text," he wrote, "remains intact throughout the whole period of perhaps 1,200 years. Only very sporadically do readings found in other text-types appear in one or another of the varieties."[33]

(b) The Researches of Kirsopp Lake

Von Soden's conclusions have, in general, been confirmed by the researches of Kirsopp Lake. In 1928 Lake and his associates published the results of a careful examination which they had made in the 11th chapter of Mark of all the manuscripts on Mt. Sinai, at Patmos, and in the Patriarchal Library and the collection of St. Saba at Jerusalem.[34]   On the basis of this examination Lake was even more disposed than von Soden to stress the unity of the Traditional (Byzantine) Text, going even so far as to deny that the *Kappa* 1 text and the *Kappa* r text were really distinct from the *Kappa* x text (which Lake preferred to call the *Ecclesiastical* text). "We cannot," he wrote, "at present distinguish anything which can be identified with von Soden's *Kappa* r, nor do we feel any confidence in his *Kappa* 1 as a really distinct text."[35]

In a later study (1940), however, Lake agreed with von Soden that the *Kappa* 1 and *Kappa* x manuscripts are distinguishable from each other even though they differ from each other very little. "*Kappa* 1 and *Kappa* x," he reported, "each show a certain amount of individual variation, by which they can be identified — but it is surprisingly little. The scribes who were responsible for the variations in the Byzantine text introduced remarkably few and unimportant changes, they shunned all originality."[36]

Thus Lake came to the same conclusions as von Soden in regard to the uniformity of text exhibited by the vast majority of the New Testament manuscripts. Both these noted scholars discovered that in spite of the divisions which exist among these manuscripts they all have the same fundamental text. This agreement, however, is not so close as to indicate that these manuscripts have been copied from each other. On this point Lake (1928) is very explicit. "Speaking generally," he says, "the evidence in our collations for the grouping of the codices which contain this text is singularly negative. There is extraordinarily little evidence of close family relationship between the manuscripts even in the same library. They have essentially the same text with a large amount of sporadic variation."[37]

And the more recent studies of Aland (1964) have yielded the same result. He and his associates collated 1,000 minuscule manuscripts of the Greek New Testament in 1,000 different New Testament passages. According to him, 90% of these minuscules contain the Traditional (Byzantine) text, which he calls, "the majority text."[38]

(c) The God-guided Usage of the Church

We see, then, that Birdsall and Colwell are quite mistaken in suggesting that modern studies have "disintegrated" (so Birdsall) the Traditional (Byzantine) Text. Certainly von Soden and Lake themselves entertained no such opinion of the results of their work. On the contrary, the investigations of these latter two scholars seem to have established the essential uniformity of the Traditional (Byzantine) text on a firmer basis than ever. They have shown that the vast majority of the Greek New Testament manuscripts exhibit precisely that amount of uniformity of text which one might expect the God-guided usage of the Church to produce. They agree with one another closely enough to justify the contention that they all contain essentially the same text, but not so closely as to give any grounds for the belief that this uniformity of text was produced by the labors of editors, or by the decrees of ecclesiastical leaders, or by mass production on the part of scribes at any one time or place. It was not by any of these means that the vast majority of the Greek New Testament manuscripts came to agree with each other as closely as they do, but through the God-guided usage of the Church, through the leading of the Holy Spirit in the hearts of individual believers.

4. Why Did The Traditional Text Triumph?

In the eyes of many naturalistic critics the history of the Traditional (Byzantine) New Testament Text has become a puzzling enigma that requires further study. "It is evident," says Birdsall (1956), "that all presuppositions concerning the Byzantine text — or texts — except its inferiority to other types, must be doubted and investigated *de novo*."[39] One wonders, however, why Birdsall makes this single exception. Every other presupposition concerning the Traditional (Byzantine) Text must be doubted. But there is one presupposition, Birdsall says, which must never be doubted, namely, the inferiority of the Traditional (Byzantine) Text to all other texts. Yet it is just this presupposition which makes the history of the Traditional Text so puzzling to naturalistic textual critics. If the Traditional Text was late and inferior, how could it have so completely displaced earlier and better texts in the usage of the Church. Westcott and Hort said that this was because the Traditional Text was an official text, put together by influential ecclesiastical leaders and urged by them upon the Church, but this view has turned out to be contrary to the evidence. Why, then, did the Traditional Text triumph?

Naturalistic textual critics will never be able to answer this question until they are ready to think "unthinkable thoughts." They must be willing to lay aside their prejudices and consider seriously the evidence which points to the Traditional (Byzantine) Text as the True Text of the New Testament. This is the position which the believing Bible student takes by faith and from which he is able to provide a consistent explanation of all the phenomena of the New Testament.

(a) The Early History of the True Text

If we accept the Traditional Text as the True New Testament Text, then the following historical reconstruction suggests itself:

Beginning with the Western and Alexandrian texts, we see that they represent two nearly simultaneous departures from the True Text which took place during the 2nd century. The making of these two texts proceeded, for the most part, according to two entirely different plans. The scribes that produced the Western text regarded themselves more as interpreters than as mere copyists. Therefore they made bold alterations in the text and added many interpolations. The makers of the Alexandrian text, on the other hand, conceived of themselves as grammarians. Their chief aim was to improve the style of the sacred text. They made few additions to it. Indeed, their fear of interpolation was so great that they often went to the opposite extreme of wrongly removing genuine readings from the text. Because of this the Western text is generally longer than the True Text and the Alexandrian is generally shorter.

Other texts, such as the Caesarean and Sinaitic Syriac texts, are also best explained as departures from the True, that is to say, the Traditional (Byzantine) Text. This is why each of them in turn agrees at times with the Traditional Text against all other texts. No doubt also much mixture of readings has gone into the composition of these minor texts.

As all scholars agree, the Western text was the text of the Christian Church at Rome and the Alexandrian text that of the Christian scribes and scholars of Alexandria. For this reason these two texts were prestige-texts, much sought after by the wealthier and more scholarly members of the Christian community. The True Text, on the other hand, continued in use among the poorer and less learned Christian brethren. These humble believers would be less sensitive to matters of prestige and would no doubt prefer the familiar wording of the True Text to the changes introduced by the new prestige-texts. Since they were unskilled in the use of pen and ink, they would be little tempted to write the variant readings of the prestige-texts into the margins of their own New Testament manuscripts and would be even less inclined to make complete copies of these prestige-texts. And since they were poor, they would be unable to buy new manuscripts containing these prestige-texts.

For all these reasons, therefore, the True Text would continue to circulate among these lowly Christian folk virtually undisturbed by the influence of other texts. Moreover, because it was difficult for these less prosperous Christians to obtain new manuscripts, they put the ones they had to maximum use. Thus all these early manuscripts of the True Text were eventually worn out. None of them seems to be extant today. The papyri which do survive seem for the most part to be prestige-texts which were preserved in the libraries of ancient Christian schools. According to Aland (1963),[40] both the Chester Beatty and the Bodmer Papyri may have been kept at such an institution. But the papyri with the True Text were read to pieces by the believing Bible students of antiquity. In the providence of God they were used by the Church. They survived long enough, however, to preserve the True (Traditional) New Testament Text during this early period and to bring it into the period of triumph that followed.

(b) The Triumph of the True New Testament Text (300-1000 A.D.)

The victorious march of the True New Testament Text toward ultimate triumph began in the 4th century. The great 4th-century conflict with the Arian heresy brought orthodox Christians to a theological maturity which enabled them, under the leading of the Holy Spirit, to perceive the superior doctrinal soundness and richness of the True Text. In ever increasing numbers Christians in the higher social brackets abandoned the corrupt prestige-texts which they had been using and turned to the well worn manuscripts of their poorer brethren, manuscripts which, though meaner in appearance, were found in reality to be far more precious, since they contained the True New Testament Text. No doubt they paid handsome sums to have copies made of these ancient books, and this was done so often that these venerable documents were worn out through much handling by the scribes. But before these old manuscripts finally perished, they left behind them a host of fresh copies made from them and bearing witness to the True Text. Thus it was that the True (Traditional) Text became the standard text now found in the vast majority of the Greek New Testament manuscripts.

(c) Lost Manuscripts of the Traditional Text

During the march of the Traditional (Byzantine) Text toward supremacy many manuscripts of the Traditional type must have perished. The investigations of Lake (1928) and his associates indicate that this was so. "Why," he asked, "are there only a few fragments (even in the two oldest of the monastic collections, Sinai and St. Saba) which come from a date earlier than the 10th century? There must have been in existence many thousands of manuscripts of the gospels in the great days of Byzantine prosperity, between the 4th and the 10th centuries. There are now extant but a pitiably small number. Moreover, the amount of direct genealogy which has been detected in extant codices is almost negligible. Nor are many known manuscripts sister codices."[41] As a result of these investigations, Lake found it "hard to resist the conclusion that the scribes usually destroyed their exemplars when they copied the sacred books."[42] If Lake's hypothesis is correct, then the manuscripts most likely to be destroyed would be those containing the Traditional Text. For these were the ones which were copied most during the period between the 4th and the 10th centuries, as is proved by the fact that the vast majority of the later Greek New Testament manuscripts are of the Traditional type. The Gothic version, moreover, was made about 350 A.D. from manuscripts of the Traditional type which are no longer extant. Perhaps Lake's hypothesis can account for their disappearance.

By the same token, the survival of old uncial manuscripts of the Alexandrian and Western type, such as *Aleph, B,* and *D,* was due to the fact that they were rejected by the Church and not read or copied but allowed to rest relatively undisturbed on the library shelves of ancient monasteries. Burgon (1883) pointed this out long ago, and it is most significant that his observation was confirmed more than 40 years later by the researches of Lake.

(d) The Church as an Organism

When we say that the Holy Spirit guided the Church to preserve the True New Testament Text, we are not speaking of the Church as an organization but of the Church as an *organism*. We do not mean that in the latter part of the 4th century the Holy Spirit guided the bishops to the True Text and that then the bishops issued decrees for the guidance of the common people. This would have been a return to Old Testament bondage and altogether out of accord with the New Testament principle of the universal priesthood of believers. Investigations indicate that the Holy Spirit's guidance worked in precisely the opposite direction. The trend toward the True (Traditional) Text began with the common people, the rank and file, and then rapidly built up such strength that the bishops and other official leaders were carried along with it. Chrysostom, for example, does not seem to have initiated this trend, for, as stated above, studies by Geerlings and New and by Dicks indicate that Chrysostom did not always use the Traditional Text.

There is evidence that the triumphal march of the Traditional (Byzantine) Text met with resistance in certain quarters. There were some scribes and scholars who were reluctant to renounce entirely their faulty Western, Alexandrian, and Caesarean texts. And so they compromised by following sometimes their false texts and sometimes the True (Traditional) Text. Thus arose those classes of mixed manuscripts described by von Soden and other scholars. This would explain also the non-Traditional readings which Colwell and his associates have found in certain portions of the lectionary manuscripts.[43] And if Birdsall is right in his contention that Photius (815-897), patriarch of Constantinople, customarily used the Caesarean text,[44] this too must be regarded as a belated effort on the part of this learned churchman to keep up the struggle against the Traditional Text. But his endeavor was in vain. Even before his time the God-guided preference of the common people for the True (Traditional) New Testament Text had prevailed, causing it to be adopted generally throughout the Greek-speaking Church.

5. The Ancient Versions And The Providence of God

It was the Greek-speaking Church especially which was the object of God's providential guidance regarding the New Testament text because this was the Church to which the keeping of the *Greek* New Testament had been committed. But this divine guidance was by no means confined to those ancient Christians who spoke Greek. On the contrary, indications can be found in the ancient New Testament versions of this same God-guided movement of the Church away from readings which were false and misleading and toward those which were true and trustworthy. This evidence can be summarized as follows:

(a) The Providence of God in the Syrian Church

In the Syrian Church this God-guided trend away from false New Testament texts and toward the True is clearly seen. According to all investigators from Burkitt (1904) to Voobus (1954),[45] the Western text, represented by Tatian's Diatessaron (Gospel Harmony) and the Curetonian and Sinaitic Syriac manuscripts, circulated widely in the Syrian Church until about the middle of the 4th century. After this date, however, this intrusive Western text was finally rejected, and the whole Syrian Church returned to the use of the ancient Peshitta Syriac version, which is largely of the Traditional (Byzantine) text-type. In other words, the Syrian Church as well as the Greek was led by God's guiding hand back to the True Text.

(b) The Providence of God in the Latin Church

Among the Latin-speaking Christians of the West the substitution of Jerome's Latin Vulgate for the Old Latin version may fairly be regarded as a movement toward the Traditional (Byzantine) Text. The Vulgate New Testament is a revised text which Jerome (384) says that he made by comparing the Old Latin version with "old Greek" manuscripts. According to Hort, one of the Greek manuscripts which Jerome used was closely related to *Codex A*, which is of the Traditional text-type. "By a curious and apparently unnoticed coincidence the text of *A* in several books agrees with the Latin Vulgate in so many peculiar readings devoid of Old Latin attestation as to leave little doubt that a Greek manuscript largely employed by Jerome in his revision of the Latin version must have had to a great extent a common original with *A*."[46]

In this instance, Hort's judgment seems undoubtedly correct, for the agreement of the Latin Vulgate with the Traditional Text is obvious, at least in the most important passages, such as, Christ's agony (Luke 22:43-44), Father forgive them (Luke 23:34), and the ascension (Luke 24:51). Kenyon (1937)[47] lists 24 such passages in the Gospels in which the Western text (represented by *D*, Old Latin) and the Alexandrian text (represented by *Aleph B*) differ from each other. In these 24 instances the Latin Vulgate agrees 11 times with the Western text, 11 times with the Alexandrian text, and 22 times with the Traditional Text (represented by the Textus Receptus). In fact, the only important readings in regard to which the Latin Vulgate disagrees with the Traditional New Testament

Text are the conclusion of the Lord's Prayer (Matt. 6:13), certain clauses of the Lord's Prayer (Luke 11:2-4), and the angel at the pool (John 5:4). In this last passage, however, the official Roman Catholic Vulgate agrees with the Traditional Text. Another telltale fact is the presence in the Latin Vulgate of four of Hort's eight so-called "conflate readings." Although these readings are not at all "conflate", nevertheless, they do seem to be one of the distinctive characteristics of the Traditional Text, and the presence of four of them in the Latin Vulgate is most easily explained by supposing that Jerome employed Traditional (Byzantine) manuscripts in the making of the Latin Vulgate text.

There are also a few passages in which the Latin Vulgate has preserved the true reading rather than the Greek Traditional New Testament Text. As we shall see in the next chapter, these few true Latin Vulgate readings were later incorporated into the Textus Receptus, the first printed Greek New Testament text, under the guiding providence of God.

(c) The Providence of God in the Coptic (Egyptian) Church

Thus during the 4th and 5th centuries among the Syriac-speaking Christians of the East, the Greek-speaking Christians of the Byzantine empire, and the Latin-speaking Christians of the West the same tendency was at work, namely, a God-guided trend away from the false Western and Alexandrian texts and toward the True Traditional Text. At a somewhat later date, moreover, this tendency was operative also among the Coptic Christians of Egypt. An examination of Kenyon's 24 passages, for example, discloses 12 instances in which some of the manuscripts of the Bohairic (Coptic) version agree with the Textus Receptus against Aleph B and the remaining Bohairic manuscripts. This indicates that in these important passages the readings of the Traditional Text had been adopted by some of the Coptic scribes.

(d) The Trend Toward the Orthodox Traditional Text — How to Explain It?

During the Middle Ages, therefore, in every land there appeared a trend toward the orthodox, Traditional (Byzantine) Text. Since the days of Griesbach naturalistic textual critics have tried to explain this fact by attributing it to the influence of "monastic piety." According to these critics, the monks in the Greek monasteries invented the orthodox readings of the Traditional Text and then multiplied copies of that text until it achieved supremacy. But if the Traditional (Byzantine) Text had been the product of Greek monastic piety, it would not have remained orthodox, for this piety included many errors such as the worship of Mary, of the saints, and of images and pictures. If the Greek monks had invented the Traditional Text, then surely they would have invented readings favoring these errors and superstitions. But as a matter of fact no such heretical readings occur in the Traditional Text.

Here, then, we have a truly astonishing fact which no naturalistic historian or textual critic can explain. Not only in the Greek Church but also throughout all Christendom the medieval period was one of spiritual decline and doctrinal corruption. But in spite of this growth of error and superstition the New Testament text most widely read and copied in the medieval Greek Church was the orthodox, Traditional (Byzantine) Text. And not only so but also in the other regions of Christendom there was a trend toward this same Traditional Text. How shall we account for this unique circumstance? There is only one possible explanation, and this is found in God's special, providential care over the New Testament text. All during this corrupt medieval period God by His providence kept alive in the Greek Church a priesthood of believers characterized by a reverence for and an interest in the holy Scriptures. It was by them that most of the New Testament manuscripts were copied, and it was by them that the Traditional New Testament Text was preserved. In this Traditional Text, found in the vast majority of the Greek New Testament manuscripts, no readings occur which favor Mary-worship, saint-worship, or image-worship. On the contrary, the Traditional Text was kept pure from these errors and gained ground everywhere. Was this not a manifestation of God's singular care and providence operating through the universal priesthood of believers?

(e) The Protestant Reformation — A Meeting of East and West

In spite of the corruption of the medieval Greek Church, the True Text of the Greek New Testament was preserved in that Church through the God-guided priesthood of believers. These were pious folk, often laymen, who though sharing in many of the errors of their day, still had a saving faith in Christ and a reverence for the holy Scriptures. But, someone may ask, if there were such a group of believers in the medieval Greek Church, why did not this group finally produce the Protestant Reformation? Why did the Protestant Reformation take place in Western Europe rather than in Eastern Europe, in the territory of the Roman Church rather than in that of the Greek Church?

This question can be answered, at least in part, linguistically. From the very beginning the leaders of the Greek Church, being Greeks, were saturated with Greek philosophy. Hence in presenting the Gospel to their fellow Greeks they tended to emphasize those doctrines which seemed to them most important philosophically and to neglect the doctrines of sin and grace, a neglect which persisted throughout the medieval period. Hence, even if the Greek Church had not been overrun by the Turks at the end of the Middle Ages, it still could not have produced the Protestant Reformation, since it lacked the theological ingredients for such a mighty, spiritual explosion.

In the Western Church the situation was different. Here the two theological giants, Tertullian and Augustine, were Latin-speaking and not at home, apparently, in the Greek language. Consequently they were less influenced by the errors of Greek philosophy and left more free to expound the distinctive doctrines of the Christian faith. Hence from these two great teachers there entered into the doctrinal system of the Roman Church a slender flame of evangelical truth which was never entirely quenched even by the worst errors of the medieval period and which blazed forth eventually as the bright beacon of the Protestant Reformation.[48] This occurred after the Greek New Testament Text had finally been published in Western Europe. Hence the Protestant Reformation may rightly be regarded as a meeting of the East and West.

(f) A New Reformation — Why the Ingredients Are Still Lacking

The length to which Hort would go in his rejection of the Traditional Text is seen in his treatment of Mark 6:22. Here the Western manuscript *D* agrees with the Alexandrian manuscripts *B Aleph L Delta* 238 565 in relating that the girl who danced before Herod and demanded the Baptist's head as payment for her shameful performance was not the daughter of Herodias, as the Traditional Text (in agreement with all the other extant manuscripts and the ancient versions) states, but Herod's own daughter named Herodias. Hort actually adopted this reading, but subsequent scholars have not approved his choice. As M. R. Vincent (1899) truly remarked concerning this strange reading, " . . . it is safe to say that Mark could not have intended this. The statement directly contradicts Josephus, who says that the name of the damsel was Salome, and that she was the daughter of Herod Philip, by Herodias, who did not leave her husband until after Salome's birth. It is, moreover, most improbable that even Herod the Tetrarch would have allowed his own daughter thus to degrade herself."[49] And even Goodspeed (1923), who usually follows Hort religiously, here reads with the Traditional Text, "Herodias' own daughter."

Thus even Hort's disciples and admirers have admitted that here in Mark 6:22 he by no means exhibits that "almost infallible judgment" which Souter (1912) attributed to him.[50] Isn't it strange therefore that for almost one hundred years so many conservative Christian scholars have followed the Westcott and Hort text so slavishly and rejected and vilified the text of the Protestant Reformation? Unless this attitude is changed, the ingredients of a new Reformation will still be lacking.

CHAPTER EIGHT

THE TEXTUS RECEPTUS AND THE KING JAMES VERSION

What about all the modern Bible versions and paraphrases which are being sold today by bookstores and publishing houses? Are all these modern-speech Bibles "holy" Bibles? Does God reveal Himself in them? Ought Christians today to rely on them for guidance and send the King James Version into honorable retirement? In order to answer these questions let us first consider the claims of the Textus Receptus and the King James Version and then those of the modern versions that seek to supplant them.

1. Three Alternative Views Of The Textus Receptus (Received Text)

One of the leading principles of the Protestant Reformation was the sole and absolute authority of the holy Scriptures. The New Testament text in which early Protestants placed such implicit reliance was the *Textus Receptus* (Received Text), which was first printed in 1516 under the editorship of Erasmus. Was this confidence of these early Protestants misplaced? There are three answers to this question which may be briefly summarized as follows:

(a) The Naturalistic, Critical View of the Textus Receptus

Naturalistic textual critics, of course, for years have not hesitated to say that the Protestant Reformers were badly mistaken in their reliance upon the Textus Receptus. According to these scholars, the Textus Receptus is the worst New Testament text that ever existed and must be wholly discarded. One of the first to take this stand openly was Richard Bentley, the celebrated English philologian. In an apology written in 1713 he developed the party line which naturalistic critics have used ever since to sell their views to conservative Christians.[1] New Testament textual criticism, he asserted, has nothing to do with Christian doctrine, since the substance of doctrine is the same even in the worst manuscripts. Then he added that the New Testament text has suffered less injury by the hand of time than the text of any profane author. And finally, he concluded by saying that we cannot begin the study of the New Testament text with any definite belief concerning the nature of God's providential preservation of the Scriptures. Rather we must begin our study from a neutral standpoint and then allow the results of this neutral method to teach us what God's providential preservation of the New Testament text actually has been. In other words, we begin with agnosticism and work ourselves into faith gradually. Some seminaries still teach this party line.

(b) The High Anglican View of the Textus Receptus

This was the view of Dean J. W. Burgon, Prebendary F. H. A. Scrivener, and Prebendary Edward Miller. These conservative New Testament textual critics were not Protestants but high Anglicans. Being high Anglicans, they recognized only three ecclesiastical bodies as true Christian churches, namely, the Greek Catholic Church, the Roman Catholic Church, and the Anglican Church, in which they themselves officiated. Only these three communions, they insisted, had the "apostolic succession." Only these three, they maintained, were governed by bishops who had been consecrated by earlier bishops and so on back in an unbroken chain to the first bishops, who had been consecrated by the Apostles through the laying on of hands. All other denominations these high Anglicans dismissed as mere "sects."

It was Burgon's high Anglicanism which led him to place so much emphasis on the New Testament quotations of the Church Fathers, most of whom had been bishops. To him these quotations were vital because they proved that the Traditional New Testament Text found in the vast majority of the Greek manuscripts had been authorized from the very beginning by the bishops of the early Church, or at least by the majority of these bishops. This high Anglican principle, however, failed Burgon when he came to deal with the printed Greek New Testament text. For from Reformation times down to his own day the printed Greek New Testament text which had been favored by the bishops of the Anglican Church was the Textus Receptus, and the Textus Receptus had not been prepared by bishops but by Erasmus, who was an independent scholar. Still worse, from Burgon's standpoint, was the fact that the particular form of the Textus Receptus used in the Church of England was the third edition of Stephanus, who was a Calvinist. For these reasons, therefore, Burgon and Scrivener looked askance at the Textus Receptus and declined to defend it except in so far as it agreed with the Traditional Text found in the majority of the Greek New Testament manuscripts.

This position, however, is illogical. If we believe in the providential preservation of the New Testament text, then we must defend the Textus Receptus as well as the Traditional Text found in the majority of the Greek manuscripts. For the Textus Receptus is the only form in which this Traditional Text has circulated in print. To decline to defend the Textus Receptus is to give the impression that God's providential preservation of the New Testament text ceased with the invention of printing. It is to suppose that God, having preserved a pure New Testament text all during the manuscript period, unaccountably left this pure text hiding in the manuscripts and allowed an inferior text to issue from the printing press and circulate among His people for more than 450 years. Much, then, as we admire Burgon for his general orthodoxy and for his defense of the Traditional New Testament Text, we cannot follow him in his high Anglican emphasis or in his disregard for the Textus Receptus.

(c) The Orthodox Protestant View of the Textus Receptus

The defense of the Textus Receptus, therefore, is a necessary part of the defense of Protestantism. It is entailed by the logic of faith, the basic steps of which are as follows: *First,* the Old Testament text was preserved by the Old Testament priesthood and the scribes and scholars grouped themselves around that priesthood (Deut. 31:24-26). *Second,* the New Testament text has been preserved by the universal priesthood of believers, by faithful Christians in every walk of life (1 Peter 2:9). *Third,* the Traditional Text, found in the vast majority of the Greek New Testament manuscripts, is the True Text because it represents the God-guided usage of this universal priesthood of believers. *Fourth,* The first printed text of the Greek New Testament was not a blunder or a set-back but a forward step in the providential preservation of the New Testament. Hence the few significant departures of that text from the Traditional Text are only God's providential corrections of the Traditional Text in those few places in which such corrections were needed. *Fifth,* through the usage of Bible-believing Protestants God placed the stamp of His approval on this first printed text, and it became the Textus Receptus (Received Text).

Hence, as orthodox Protestant Christians, we believe that the formation of the Textus Receptus was guided by the special providence of God. There were *three* ways in which the editors of the Textus Receptus, Erasmus, Stephanus, Beza, and the Elzevirs, were providentially guided. In the *first* place, they were guided by the manuscripts which God in His providence had made available to them. In the *second* place, they were guided by the providential circumstances in which they found themselves. Then in the *third* place, and most of all, they were guided by the *common faith.* Long before the Protestant Reformation, the God-guided usage of the Church had produced throughout Western Christendom a common faith concerning the New Testament text, namely, a general belief that the currently received New Testament text, primarily the Greek text and secondarily the Latin text, was the True New Testament Text which had been preserved by God's special providence. It was this common faith that guided Erasmus and the other early editors of the Textus Receptus.

2. How Erasmus And His Successors Were Guided By The Common Faith

When we believe in Christ, the logic of faith leads us *first,* to a belief in the infallible inspiration of the original Scriptures, *second,* to a belief in the providential preservation of this original text down through the ages, and *third,* to a belief in the Bible text current among believers as the providentially preserved original text. This is the common faith which has always been present among Christians. For Christ and His Word are inseparable, and faith in Him and in the holy Scriptures has been the common characteristic of all true believers from the beginning. Always they have regarded the current Bible text as the infallibly inspired and providentially preserved True Text. Origen, for example, in the 3rd century, was expressing the faith of all when he exclaimed to Africanus, "Are we to suppose that that Providence which in the sacred Scriptures has ministered to the edification of all the churches of Christ had no thought for those bought with a price, for whom Christ died!"[2]

This faith, however, has from time to time been distorted by the intrusion of unbiblical ideas. For example, many Jews and early Christians believed that the inspiration of the Old Testament had been repeated three times. According to them, not only had the original Old Testament writers been inspired but also Ezra, who rewrote the whole Old Testament after it had been lost. And the Septuagint likewise, they maintained, had been infallibly inspired. Also the Roman Catholics have distorted the common faith by their false doctrine that the authority of the Scriptures rests on the authority of the Church. It was this erroneous view that led the Roman Church to adopt the Latin Vulgate rather than the Hebrew and Greek Scriptures as its authoritative Bible. And finally, many conservative Christians today distort the common faith by their adherence to the theories of naturalistic New Testament textual criticism. They smile at the legends concerning Ezra and the Septuagint, but they themselves have concocted a myth even more absurd, namely, that the true New Testament text was lost for more than 1,500 years and then restored by Westcott and Hort.

But in spite of these distortions due to human sin and error this common faith in Christ and in His Word has persisted among believers from the days of the Apostles until now, and God has used this common faith providentially to preserve the holy Scriptures. Let us now consider how it guided Erasmus and his successors in their editorial labors on the Textus Receptus.

(a) The Life of Erasmus — A Brief Review

Erasmus was born at Rotterdam in 1466, the illegitimate son of a priest but well cared for by his parents. After their early death he was given the best education available to a young man of his day at first at Deventer and then at the Augustinian monastery at Steyn. In 1492 he was ordained priest, but there is no record that he ever functioned as such. By 1495 he was studying in Paris. In 1499 he went to England, where he made the helpful friendship of John Colet, later dean of St. Paul's, who quickened his interest in biblical studies. He then went back to France and the Netherlands. In 1505 he again visited England and then passed three years in Italy. In 1509 he returned to England for the third time and taught at Cambridge University until 1514. In 1515 he went to Basel, where he published his New Testament in 1516, then back to the Netherlands for a sojourn at the University of Louvain. Then he returned to Basel in 1521 and remained there until 1529, in which year he removed to the imperial town of Freiburg-im-Breisgau. Finally, in 1535, he again returned to Basel and died there the following year in the midst of his Protestant friends, without relations of any sort, so far as known, with

Desiderius Erasmus (1466-1536)

the Roman Catholic Church.[3]

One might think that all this moving around would have interfered with Erasmus' activity as a scholar and writer, but quite the reverse is true. By his travels he was brought into contact with all the intellectual currents of his time and stimulated to almost superhuman efforts. He became the most famous scholar and author of his day and one of the most prolific writers of all time, his collected works filling ten large volumes in the Leclerc edition of 1705 (phototyped by Olms in 1962).[4] As an editor also his productivity was tremendous. Ten columns of the catalogue of the library in the British Museum are taken up with the bare enumeration of the works translated, edited, or annotated by Erasmus, and their subsequent reprints. Included are the greatest names of the classical and patristic world, such as Ambrose, Aristotle, Augustine, Basil, Chrysostom, Cicero, and Jerome.[5] An almost unbelievable showing.

To conclude, there was no man in all Europe better prepared than Erasmus for the work of editing the first printed Greek New Testament text, and this is why, we may well believe, God chose him and directed him providentially in the accomplishment of this task.

(b) Erasmus Guided by the Common Faith — Factors Which Influenced Him

In order to understand how God guided Erasmus providentially let us consider the three alternative views which were held in Erasmus' days concerning the preservation of the New Testament text, namely, the *humanistic* view, the *scholastic* view, and the *common* view, which we have called the *common faith*.

The *humanistic* view was well represented by the writings of Laurentius Valla (1405-57), a famous scholar of the Italian renaissance. Valla emphasized the importance of language. According to him, the decline of civilization in the dark ages was due to the decay of the Greek and Latin languages. Hence it was only through the study of classical literature that the glories of ancient Greece and Rome could be recaptured. Valla also wrote a treatise on the Latin Vulgate, comparing it with certain Greek New Testament manuscripts which he had in his possession. Erasmus, who from his youth had been an admirer of Valla, found a manuscript of Valla's treatise in 1504 and had it printed in the following year. In this work Valla favored the Greek New Testament text over the Vulgate. The Latin text often differed from the Greek, he reported. Also there were omissions and additions in the Latin translation, and the Greek wording was generally better than that of the Latin.[6]

The *scholastic* theologians, on the other hand, warmly defended the Latin Vulgate as the only true New Testament text. In 1514 Martin Dorp of the University of Louvain wrote to Erasmus asking him not to publish his forthcoming Greek New Testament. Dorp argued that if the Vulgate contained falsifications of the original Scriptures and errors, the Church would have been wrong for many centuries, which was impossible. The references of most Church Councils to the Vulgate, Dorp insisted, proved that the Church considered this Latin version to be the official Bible and not the Greek New Testament, which, he maintained, had been corrupted by the heretical Greek Church.[7] And after Erasmus' Greek New Testament had been published in 1516, Stunica, a noted Spanish scholar, accused it of being an open condemnation of the Latin Vulgate, the version of the Church.[8] And about the same time Peter Sutor, once of the Sorbonne and later a Carthusian monk, declared that "If in one point the Vulgate were in error, the entire authority of holy Scripture would collapse."[9]

Believing Bible students today are often accused of taking the same extreme position in regard to the King James Version that Peter Sutor took more than 450 years ago in regard to the Latin Vulgate. But this is false. We take the third position which we have mentioned, namely, the *common* view. In Erasmus' day this view occupied the middle ground between the humanistic view and the scholastic view. Those that held this view acknowledged that the Scriptures had been providentially preserved down through the ages. They did not, however, agree with the scholastic theologians in tying this providential preservation to the Latin Vulgate. On the contrary, along with Laurentius Valla and other humanists, they asserted the superiority of the Greek New Testament text.

This common view remained a faith rather than a well articulated theory. No one at that time drew the logical but unpalatable conclusion that the Greek Church rather than the Roman Church had been the providentially appointed guardian of the New Testament text. But this view, though vaguely apprehended, was widely held, so much so that it may justly be called the common view. Before the Council of Trent (1546) it was favored by some of the highest officials of the Roman Church, notably, it seems, by Leo X, who was pope from 1513 to 1521 and to whom Erasmus dedicated his New Testament. Erasmus' close friends also, John Colet, for example, and Thomas More and Jacques Lefevre, all of whom like Erasmus sought to reform the Roman Catholic Church from within, likewise adhered to this common view. Even the scholastic theologian Martin Dorp was finally persuaded by Thomas More to adopt it.[10]

In the days of Erasmus, therefore, it was commonly believed by well informed Christians that the original New Testament text had been providentially preserved in the current New Testament text, primarily in the current Greek text and secondarily in the current Latin text. Erasmus was influenced by this common faith and probably shared it, and God used it providentially to guide Erasmus in his editorial labors on the Textus Receptus.

(c) Erasmus' Five Editions of the Textus Receptus

Between the years 1516 and 1535 Erasmus published five editions of the Greek New Testament. In the first edition (1516) the text was preceded by a dedication to Pope Leo X, an exhortation to the reader, a discussion of the method used, and a defense of this method. Then came the Greek New Testament text accompanied by Erasmus' own Latin translation, and then this was followed by Erasmus' notes, giving his comments on the text. In his 2nd edition (1519) Erasmus revised both his Greek text and his own Latin translation. His substitution in John 1:1 of *sermo* (speech) for *verbum* (word), the rendering of the Latin Vulgate, aroused much controversy. The 3rd edition (1522) is chiefly remarkable for the inclusion of 1 John 5:7, which had been omitted in the previous editions. The 4th edition (1527) contained the Greek text, the Latin Vulgate, and Erasmus' Latin translation in three parallel columns. The 5th edition (1535) omitted the Vulgate, thus resuming the practice of printing the Greek text and the version of Erasmus side by side.[11]

(d) The Greek Manuscripts Used by Erasmus

When Erasmus came to Basel in July, 1515, to begin his work, he found five Greek New Testament manuscripts ready for his use. These are now designated by the following numbers: 1(an 11th-century manuscript of the Gospels, Acts, and Epistles), 2(a 15th-century manuscript of the Gospels), 2ap (a 12th-14th-century manuscript of Acts and the Epistles), 4ap (a 15th-century manuscript of Acts and the Epistles), and 1r (a 12th-century manuscript of Revelation). Of these manuscripts Erasmus used 1 and 4ap only occasionally. In the Gospels, Acts, and Epistles his main reliance was on 2 and 2ap.[12]

Did Erasmus use other manuscripts beside these five in preparing his Textus Receptus? The indications are that he did. According to W. Schwarz (1955), Erasmus made his own Latin translation of the New Testament at Oxford during the years 1505-6. His friend, John Colet, who had become Dean of St. Paul's, lent him two Latin manuscripts for this undertaking, but nothing is known about the Greek manuscripts which he used.[13] He must have used some Greek manuscripts or other, however, and taken notes on them. Presumably therefore he brought these notes with him to Basel along with his translation and his comments on the New Testament text. It is well known also that Erasmus looked for manuscripts everywhere during his travels and that he borrowed them from everyone he could. Hence although the Textus Receptus was based mainly on the manuscripts which Erasmus found at Basel, it also included readings taken from others to which he had access. It agreed with the common faith because it was founded on manuscripts which in the providence of God were readily available.

(e) Erasmus' Notes — His Knowledge of Variant Readings and Critical Problems

Through his study of the writings of Jerome and other Church Fathers Erasmus became very well informed concerning the variant readings of the New Testament text. Indeed almost all the important variant readings known to scholars today were already known to Erasmus more than 460 years ago and discussed in the notes (previously prepared) which he placed after the text in his editions of the Greek New

Testament. Here, for example, Erasmus dealt with such problem passages as the conclusion of the Lord's Prayer (Matt. 6:13), the interview of the rich young man with Jesus (Matt. 19:17-22), the ending of Mark (Mark 16:9-20), the angelic song (Luke 2:14), the angel, agony, and bloody sweat omitted (Luke 22:43-44), the woman taken in adultery (John 7:53-8:11), and the mystery of godliness (1 Tim. 3:16).

In his notes Erasmus placed before the reader not only ancient discussions concerning the New Testament text but also debates which took place in the early Church over the New Testament canon and the authorship of some of the New Testament books, especially Hebrews, James, 2 Peter, 2 and 3 John, Jude and Revelation. Not only did he mention the doubts reported by Jerome and the other Church Fathers, but also added some objections of his own. However, he discussed these matters somewhat warily, declaring himself willing at any time to submit to "The consensus of public opinion and especially to the authority of the Church."[14] In short, he seemed to recognize that in reopening the question of the New Testament canon he was going contrary to the common faith.

But if Erasmus was cautious in his notes, much more was he so in his text, for this is what would strike the reader's eye immediately. Hence in the editing of his Greek New Testament text especially Erasmus was guided by the common faith in the current text. And back of this common faith was the controlling providence of God. For this reason Erasmus' humanistic tendencies do not appear in the Textus Receptus which he produced. Although not himself outstanding as a man of faith, in his editorial labors on this text he was providentially influenced and guided by the faith of others. In spite of his humanistic tendencies Erasmus was clearly used of God to place the Greek New Testament text in print, just as Martin Luther was used of God to bring in the Protestant Reformation in spite of the fact that, at least at first, he shared Erasmus' doubts concerning Hebrews, James, Jude and Revelation.[15]

(f) Latin Vulgate Readings in the Textus Receptus

The God who brought the New Testament text safely through the ancient and medieval manuscript period did not fumble when it came time to transfer this text to the modern printed page. This is the conviction which guides the believing Bible student as he considers the relationship of the printed Textus Receptus to the Traditional New Testament text found in the majority of the Greek New Testament manuscripts.

These two texts are virtually identical. Kirsopp Lake and his associates (1928) demonstrated this fact in their intensive researches in the Traditional text (which they called the Byzantine text). Using their collations, they came to the conclusion that in the 11th chapter of Mark "the most popular text in the manuscripts of the tenth to the fourteenth century"[16] differed from the Textus Receptus only four times. This small number of differences seems almost negligible in view of the fact that in this same chapter *Aleph, B,* and *D* differ from the Textus Receptus 69, 71, and 95 times respectively. Also add to this the fact that in this same chapter *B* differs from *Aleph* 34 times and from *D* 102 times and that *Aleph* differs from *D* 100 times.

There are, however, a few places in which the Textus Receptus differs from the Traditional text found in the majority of the Greek New Testament manuscripts. The most important of these differences are due to the fact that Erasmus, influenced by the usage of the Latin-speaking Church in which he was reared, sometimes followed the Latin Vulgate rather than the Traditional Greek text.

Are the readings which Erasmus thus introduced into the Textus Receptus necessarily erroneous? By no means ought we to infer this. For it is inconceivable that the divine providence which had preserved the New Testament text during the long ages of the manuscript period should blunder when at last this text was committed to the printing press. According to the analogy of faith, then, we conclude that the Textus Receptus was a further step in God's providential preservation of the New Testament text and that these few Latin Vulgate readings which were incorporated into the Textus Receptus were genuine readings which had been preserved in the usage of the Latin-speaking Church. Erasmus, we may well believe, was guided providentially by the common faith to include these readings in his printed Greek New Testament text. In the Textus Receptus God corrected the few mistakes of any consequence which yet remained in the Traditional New Testament text of the majority of the Greek manuscripts.

The following are some of the most familiar and important of those relatively few Latin Vulgate readings which, though not part of the Traditional Greek text, seem to have been placed in the Textus Receptus by the direction of God's special providence and therefore are to be retained. The reader will note that these Latin Vulgate readings are also found in other ancient witnesses, namely, old Greek manuscripts, versions, and Fathers.

Matt. 10:8   *raise the dead,* is omitted by the majority of the Greek manuscripts. This reading is present, however, in *Aleph B C D* 1, the Latin Vulgate, and the Textus Receptus.

Matt. 27:35   *that it might be fulfilled which was spoken by the prophet, They parted My garments among them, and upon My vesture did they cast lots.* Present in Eusebius (c. 325), 1 and other "Caesarean" manuscripts, the Harclean Syriac, the Old Latin, the Vulgate, and the Textus Receptus. Omitted by the majority of the Greek manuscripts.

John 3:25   *Then there arose a questioning between some of John's disciples and the Jews about purifying.* Pap 66, *Aleph,* 1 and other "Caesarean" manuscripts, the Old Latin, the Vulgate, and the Textus Receptus read *the Jews.* Pap 75, *B,* the Peshitta, and the majority of the Greek manuscripts read *a Jew.*

Acts 8:37   *And Philip said, If thou believest with all thine heart, thou mayest. And he answered and said, I believe that Jesus Christ is the Son of God.* As J. A. Alexander (1857) suggested, this verse, though genuine, was omitted by many scribes, "as unfriendly to the practice of delaying baptism, which had become common, if not prevalent, before the end of the 3rd century."[17] Hence the verse is absent from the majority of the Greek manuscripts. But it is present in some of them, including *E* (6th or 7th century). It is cited by Irenaeus (c. 180) and Cyprian (c. 250) and is found in the Old Latin and the Vulgate. In his notes Erasmus says that he took this reading from the margin of 4ap and incorporated it into the Textus Receptus.

Acts 9:5   *it is hard for thee to kick against the pricks.* This reading is absent here from the Greek manuscripts but present in Old Latin manuscripts and in the Latin Vulgate known to Erasmus. It is present also at the end of Acts 9:4 in *E*, 431, the Peshitta, and certain manuscripts of the Latin Vulgate. In Acts 26:14, however, this reading is present in all the Greek manuscripts. In his notes Erasmus indicates that he took this reading from Acts 26:14 and inserted it here.

Acts 9:6   *And he trembling and astonished said, Lord, what wilt Thou have me to do? and the Lord said unto him,* This reading is found in the Latin Vulgate and in other ancient witnesses. It is absent, however, from the Greek manuscripts, due, according to Lake and Cadbury (1933), "to the paucity of Western Greek texts and the absence of *D* at this point."[18] In his notes Erasmus indicates that this reading is a translation made by him from the Vulgate into Greek.

Acts 20:28   *Church of God.* Here the majority of the Greek manuscripts read, *Church of the Lord and God.* The Latin Vulgate, however, and the Textus Receptus read, *Church of God,* which is also the reading of *Aleph B,* and other ancient witnesses.

Rom. 16:25-27 In the majority of the manuscripts this doxology is placed at the end of chapter 14. In the Latin Vulgate and the Textus Receptus it is placed at the end of chapter 16, and this is also the position it occupies in *Aleph B C* and *D*.

Rev.   22:19   *And if any man shall take away from the words of the*
                  book of this prophecy, God shall take away his part out
                  of the book of life. According to Hoskier, all the Greek
                  manuscripts, except possibly one or two, read, *tree of*
                  life. The Textus Receptus reads, *book of life,* with the
                  Latin   Vulgate   (including   the   very   old   Vulgate
                  manuscript *F*), the Bohairic verson, Ambrose (d. 397),
                  and the commentaries of Primasius (6th century) and
                  Haymo (9th century). This is one of the verses which
                  Erasmus is said to have translated from Latin into
                  Greek. But Hoskier seems to doubt that Erasmus did
                  this, suggesting that he may have followed Codex 141.[19]

(g) The Human Aspect of the Textus Receptus

God works providentially through sinful and fallible human beings,
and therefore His providential guidance has its human as well as its
divine side. And these human elements were evident in the first edition
(1516) of the Textus Receptus. For one thing, the work was performed so
hastily that the text was disfigured with a great number of typographical
errors. These misprints, however, were soon eliminated by Erasmus
himself in his later editions and by other early editors and hence are not a
factor which need to be taken into account in any estimate of the abiding
value of the Textus Receptus.

The few typographical errors which still remain in the Textus
Receptus of Revelation do not involve important readings. This fact,
clearly attributable to God's special providence, can be demonstrated by
a study of H. C. Hoskier's monumental commentary on Revelation
(1929),[19] which takes the Textus Receptus as its base. Here we see that the
only typographical error worth noting occurs in Rev. 17:8, *the beast that*
was, and is not, and yet is. Here the reading *kaiper estin (and yet is)* seems
to be a misprint for *kai paresti (and is at hand),* which is the reading of
Codex 1r, the manuscript which Erasmus used in Revelation.

The last six verses of Codex 1r (Rev. 22:16-21) were lacking, and its
text in other places was sometimes hard to distinguish from the
commentary of Andreas of Caesarea in which it was embedded.
According to almost all scholars, Erasmus endeavored to supply these
deficiencies in his manuscript by retranslating the Latin Vulgate into
Greek. Hoskier, however, was inclined to dispute this on the evidence of
manuscript 141.[19] In his 4th edition of his Greek New Testament (1527)
Erasmus corrected much of this translation Greek (if it was indeed such)
on the basis of a comparison with the Complutensian Polyglot Bible
(which had been printed at Acala in Spain under the direction of Cardinal
Ximenes and published in 1522), but he overlooked some of it, and this
still remains in the Textus Receptus. These readings, however, do not
materially affect the sense of the passages in which they occur. They are
only minor blemishes which can easily be removed or corrected in
marginal notes. The only exception is *book* for *tree* in Rev. 22:19, a
variant which Erasmus could not have failed to notice but must have

retained purposely. Critics blame him for this but here he may have been guided providentially by the common faith to follow the Latin Vulgate.

There is one passage in Revelation, however, in which the critics, rather inconsistently, blame Erasmus for *not* moving in the direction of the Latin Vulgate. This is Rev. 22:14a, *Blessed are they that do His commandments, etc.* Here, according to Hoskier,[19] *Aleph* and *A* and a few Greek minuscule manuscripts read, *wash their robes*, and this is the reading favored by the critics. A few other Greek manuscripts and the Sahidic version read, *have washed their robes.* The Latin Vulgate reads, *wash their robes in the blood of the Lamb.* But the Textus Receptus reading of Erasmus, *do His commandments*, is found in the majority of the Greek manuscripts and in the Bohairic and Syriac versions and is undoubtedly the Traditional reading.

It is customary for naturalistic critics to make the most of human imperfections in the Textus Receptus and to sneer at it as a mean and almost sordid thing. These critics picture the Textus Receptus as merely a money-making venture on the part of Froben the publisher. Froben, they say, heard that the Spanish Cardinal Ximenes was about to publish a printed Greek New Testament text as part of his great Complutensian Polyglot Bible. In order to get something on the market first, it is said, Froben hired Erasmus as his editor and rushed a Greek New Testament through his press in less than a year's time. But those who concentrate in this way on the human factors involved in the production of the Textus Receptus are utterly unmindful of the providence of God. For in the very next year, in the plan of God, the Reformation was to break out in Wittenberg, and it was important that the Greek New Testament should be published first in one of the future strongholds of Protestantism by a book seller who was eager to place it in the hands of the people and not in Spain, the land of the Inquisition, by the Roman Church, which was intent on keeping the Bible from the people.

(h) Robert Stephanus — His Four Editions of the Textus Receptus

After the death of Erasmus in 1536 God in His providence continued to extend the influence of the Textus Receptus. One of the agents through which He accomplished this was the famous French printer and scholar Robert Stephanus (1503-59). Robert's father Henry and his stepfather Simon de Colines were printers who had published Bibles, and Robert was not slow to follow their example. In 1523 he published a Latin New Testament, and two times he published the Hebrew Bible entire. But the most important were his four editions of the Greek New Testament in 1546, 1549, 1550, and 1551 respectively. These activities aroused the opposition of the Roman Catholic Church, so much so that in 1550 he was compelled to leave Paris and settle in Geneva, where he became a Protestant, embracing the Reformed faith.[20]

Stephanus' first two editions (1546 and 1549) were pocket size (large pockets) printed with type cast at the expense of the King of France. In text they were a compound of the Complutensian and Erasmian editions. Stephanus' 4th edition (1551) was also pocket size. In it the text was for the first time divided into verses. But most important was Stephanus' 3rd edition. This was a small folio (8½ by 13 inches) likewise printed at royal expense. In the margin of this edition Stephanus entered variant readings taken from the Complutensian edition and also 14 manuscripts, one of which is thought to have been *Codex D*. In text the 3rd and 4th editions of Stephanus agreed closely with the 5th edition of Erasmus, which was gaining acceptance everywhere as the providentially appointed text. It was the influence no doubt of this common faith which restrained Stephanus from adopting any of the variant readings which he had collected.[21]

(i) Calvin's Comments on the New Testament Text

The mention of Geneva leads us immediately to think of John Calvin (1509-64), the famous Reformer who had his headquarters in this city. In his commentaries (which covered every New Testament book except 2 and 3 John and Revelation) Calvin mentions Erasmus by name 78 times, far more often than any other contemporary scholar. Most of these references (72 to be exact) are criticisms of Erasmus' Latin version, and once (Phil. 2:6) Calvin complains about Erasmus' refusal to admit that the passage in question teaches the deity of Christ. But five references deal with variant readings which Erasmus suggested in his notes, and of these Calvin adopted three. On the basis of these statistics therefore it is perhaps not too much to say that Calvin disapproved of Erasmus as a translator and theologian but thought better of him as a New Testament textual critic.

In John 8:59 Calvin follows the Latin Vulgate in omitting *going through the midst of them, and so passed by.* Here he accepts the suggestion of Erasmus that this clause has been borrowed from Luke 4:30. And in Heb. 11:37 he agrees with Erasmus in omitting *were tempted.* But in readings of major importance Calvin rejected the opinions of Erasmus. For example, Calvin dismisses Erasmus' suggestion that the conclusion of the Lord's Prayer is an interpolation (Matt. 6:13). He ignores Erasmus' discussion of the ending of Mark (Mark 16:9-20). He is more positive than Erasmus in his acceptance of the *pericope de adultera* (John 7:53-8:11). He opposes Erasmus' attack on the reading *God was manifest in the flesh* (1 Tim. 3:16). And he receives 1 John 5:7 as genuine.

To the three variant readings taken from Erasmus' notes Calvin added 18 others. The three most important of these Calvin took from the Latin Vulgate, namely, *light* instead of *Spirit* (Eph. 5:9), *Christ* instead of *God* (Eph. 5:21), *without thy works* instead of *by thy works* (James 2:18). Calvin also made two conjectural emendations. In James 4:2 he followed Erasmus (2nd edition) and Luther in changing *kill* to *envy.* Also he suggested that 1 John 2:14 was an interpolation because to him it seemed repetitious.[22]

In short, there appears in Calvin as well as in Erasmus a humanistic tendency to treat the New Testament text like the text of any other book. This tendency, however, was checked and restrained by the common faith in the current New Testament text, a faith in which Calvin shared to

Robert Stephanus (1503-1559)

a much greater degree than did Erasmus.

(j) Theodore Beza's Ten Editions of the New Testament

Theodore Beza (1519-1605), Calvin's disciple and successor at Geneva, was renowned for his ten editions of the Greek New Testament, nine published during his lifetime and one after his death. He is also famous for his Latin translation of the New Testament, first published in 1556 and reprinted more than 100 times. Four of Beza's Greek New Testaments are independent folio editions, but the six others are smaller reprints. The folio editions contain Beza's critical notes, printed not at the end of the volume, as with Erasmus, but under the text. The dates of these folio editions are usually given as 1565, 1582, 1588-9, and 1598 respectively. There seems to be some confusion here, however, because there is a copy at the University of Chicago dated 1560, and Metzger (1968), following Reuss (1872), talks about a 1559 edition of Beza's Greek New Testament.[23]

In his edition of 1582 (which Beza calls his *third* edition) Beza listed the textual materials employed by him. They included the variant readings collected by Robert Stephanus, the Syriac version published in 1569 by Tremellius, a converted Jewish scholar, and also the Arabic New Testament version in a Latin translation prepared by Francis Junius, later a son-in-law of Tremellius. Beza also mentioned two of his own manuscripts. One of these was *D*, the famous *Codex Bezae* containing the Gospels and Acts, which had been in his possession from 1562 until 1581, in which year he had presented it to the University of Cambridge. The other was *D2*, *Codex Claromontanus*, a manuscript of the Pauline Epistles, which Beza had obtained from the monastery of Clermont in Northern France. But in spite of this collection of materials, Beza in his text rarely departs from the 4th edition of Stephanus, only 38 times according to Reuss (1872).[24] This is a remarkable fact which shows the hold which the common faith had upon Beza's mind.

In his notes Beza defended the readings of his text which he deemed doctrinally important. For example, he upheld the genuineness of Mark 16:9-20 against the adverse testimony of Jerome. "Jerome says this," he concludes. "But in this section I notice nothing which disagrees with the narratives of the other Evangelists or indicates the style of a different author, and I testify that this section is found in all the oldest manuscripts which I happen to have seen." And in 1 Tim. 3:16 Beza defends the reading *God was manifest in the flesh*. "The concept itself," he declares, "demands that we receive this as referring to the very person of Christ." And concerning 1 John 5:7 Beza says, "It seems to me that this clause ought by all means to be retained."

On the other hand, Beza confesses doubt concerning some other passages in his text. In Luke 2:14 Beza places *good will toward men* in his text but disputes it in his notes. "Nevertheless, following the authority of Origen, Chrysostom, the Old (Vulgate) translation, and finally the sense itself, I should prefer to read *(men) of good will*." In regard also to the *pericope de adultera* (John 7:53-8:11) Beza confides, "As far as I am

Theodore Beza (1519-1605)

concerned, I do not hide the fact that to me a passage which those ancient writers reject is justly suspect." Also Beza neither defends nor rejects the conclusion of the Lord's Prayer (Matt. 6:13) but simply observes, "This clause is not written in the Vulgate edition nor had been included in a second old copy *(D?)*."

The diffident manner in which Beza reveals these doubts shows that he was conscious of running counter to the views of his fellow believers. Just as with Erasmus and Calvin, so also with Beza there was evidently a conflict going on within his mind between his humanistic tendency to treat the New Testament like any other book and the common faith in the current New Testament text. But in the providence of God all was well. God used this common faith providentially to restrain Beza's humanism and lead him to publish far and wide the true New Testament text.

Like Calvin, Beza introduced a few conjectural emendations into his New Testament text. In the providence of God, however, only two of these were perpetuated in the King James Version, namely, Romans 7:6 *that being dead wherein* instead of *being dead to that wherein*, and Revelation 16:5 *shalt be* instead of *holy*. In the development of the Textus Receptus the influence of the common faith kept conjectural emendation down to a minimum.

(k) The Elzevir Editions — The Triumph of the Common Faith

The Elzevirs were a family of Dutch printers with headquarters at Leiden. The most famous of them was Bonaventure Elzevir, who founded his own printing establishment in 1608 with his brother Matthew as his partner and later his nephew Abraham. In 1624 he published his first edition of the New Testament and in 1633 his 2nd edition. His texts followed Beza's editions mainly but also included readings from Erasmus, the Complutensian, and the Latin Vulgate. In the preface to the 2nd edition the phrase *Textus Receptus* made its first appearance. "You have therefore the text now received by all (textum ab omnibus receptum) in which we give nothing changed or corrupt."[25]

This statement has often been assailed as a mere printer's boast or "blurb", and no doubt it was partly that. But in the providence of God it was also a true statement. For by this time the common faith in the current New Testament text had triumphed over the humanistic tendencies which had been present not only in Erasmus but also Luther, Calvin, and Beza. The doubts and reservations expressed in their notes and comments had been laid aside and only their God-guided texts had been retained. The Textus Receptus really was the text received by all. Its reign had begun and was to continue unbroken for 200 years. In England Stephanus' 3rd edition was the form of the Textus Receptus generally preferred, on the European continent Elzevir's 2nd edition.

Admittedly there are a few places in which the Textus Receptus is supported by only a small number of manuscripts, for example, Eph. 1:18, where it reads, *eyes of your understanding,* instead of *eyes of your heart;* and Eph. 3:9, where it reads, *fellowship of the mystery,* instead of *dispensation of the mystery.* We solve this problem, however, according to the logic of faith. Because the Textus Receptus was God-guided as a whole, it was probably God-guided in these few passages also.

3. The Johannine Comma (1 John 5:7)

In the Textus Receptus 1 John 5:7-8 reads as follows:

7 For there are three that bear witness IN HEAVEN, THE FATHER, THE WORD, AND THE HOLY SPIRIT: AND THESE THREE ARE ONE. 8 AND THERE ARE THREE THAT BEAR WITNESS IN EARTH, the spirit, and the water, and the blood: and these three agree in one.

The words printed in capital letters constitute the so-called *Johannine comma*, the best known of the Latin Vulgate readings of the Textus Receptus, a reading which, on believing principles, must be regarded as possibly genuine. This *comma* has been the occasion of much controversy and is still an object of interest to textual critics. One of the more recent discussions of it is found in Windisch's *Katholischen Briefe* (revised by Preisker, 1951);[26] a more accessible treatment of it in English is that provided by A. D. Brooke (1912) in the *International Critical Commentary*.[27] Metzger (1964) also deals with this passage in his handbook, but briefly.[28]

(a) How the Johannine Comma Entered the Textus Receptus

As has been observed above, the Textus Receptus has both its human aspect and its divine aspect, like the Protestant Reformation itself or any other work of God's providence. And when we consider the manner in which the *Johannine comma* entered the Textus Receptus, we see this human element at work. Erasmus omitted the *Johannine comma* from the first edition (1516) of his printed Greek New Testament on the ground that it occurred only in the Latin version and not in any Greek manuscript. To quiet the outcry that arose, he agreed to restore it if but one Greek manuscript could be found which contained it. When one such manuscript was discovered soon afterwards, bound by his promise, he included the disputed reading in his third edition (1522), and thus it gained a permanent place in the Textus Receptus. The manuscript which forced Erasmus to reverse his stand seems to have been 61, a 15th or 16th-century manuscript now kept at Trinity College, Dublin. Many critics believe that this manuscript was written at Oxford about 1520 for the special purpose of refuting Erasmus, and this is what Erasmus himself suggested in his notes.

The *Johannine comma* is also found in *Codex Ravianus*, in the margin of 88, and in 629. The evidence of these three manuscripts, however, is not regarded as very weighty, since the first two are thought to have taken this disputed reading from early printed Greek texts and the latter (like 61) from the Vulgate.

But whatever may have been the immediate cause, still, in the last analysis, it was not trickery which was responsible for the inclusion of the *Johannine comma* in the Textus Receptus but the usage of the Latin-speaking Church. It was this usage which made men feel that this reading ought to be included in the Greek text and eager to keep it there after its inclusion had been accomplished. Back of this usage, we may well believe, was the guiding providence of God, and therefore the *Johannine comma* ought to be retained as at least possibly genuine.

(b) The Early Existence of the Johannine Comma

Evidence for the early existence of the *Johannine comma* is found in the Latin versions and in the writings of the Latin Church Fathers. For example, it seems to have been quoted at Carthage by Cyprian (c. 250), who writes as follows: "And again concerning the Father and the Son and the Holy Spirit it is written: *and the Three are One.*"[29] It is true that Facundus, a 6th-century African bishop, interpreted Cyprian as referring to the following verse,[30] but, as Scrivener (1883) remarks, it is "surely safer and more candid" to admit that Cyprian read the *Johannine comma* in his New Testament manuscript "than to resort to the explanation of Facundus."[31]

The first undisputed citations of the *Johannine comma* occur in the writing of two 4th-century Spanish bishops, Priscillian,[32] who in 385 was beheaded by the Emperor Maximus on the charge of sorcery and heresy, and Idacius Clarus,[33] Priscillian's principal adversary and accuser. In the 5th century the *Johannine comma* was quoted by several orthodox African writers to defend the doctrine of the Trinity against the gainsaying of the Vandals, who ruled North Africa from 439 to 534 and were fanatically attached to the Arian heresy.[34] And about the same time it was cited by Cassiodorus (480-570), in Italy.[35] The *comma* is also found in *r* an Old Latin manuscript of the 5th or 6th century, and in the *Speculum*, a treatise which contains an Old Latin text. It was not included in Jerome's original edition of the Latin Vulgate, but around the year 800 it was taken into the text of the Vulgate from the Old Latin manuscripts. It was found in the great mass of the later Vulgate manuscripts and in the Clementine edition of the Vulgate, the official Bible of the Roman Catholic Church.

(c) Is the Johannine Comma an Interpolation?

Thus on the basis of the external evidence it is at least possible that the *Johannine comma* is a reading that somehow dropped out of the Greek New Testament text but was preserved in the Latin text through the usage of the Latin-speaking Church, and this possibility grows more and more toward probability as we consider the internal evidence.

In the first place, how did the *Johannine comma* originate if it be not genuine, and how did it come to be interpolated into the Latin New Testament text? To this question modern scholars have a ready answer. It arose, they say, as a trinitarian interpretation of 1 John 5:8, which originally read as follows: *For there are three that bear witness, the spirit, and the water, and the blood: and these three agree in one.* Augustine was one of those who interpreted 1 John 5:8 as referring to the Trinity. "If we wish to inquire about these things, what they signify, not absurdly does the Trinity suggest Itself, who is the one, only, true, and highest God, Father, Son, and Holy Spirit, concerning whom it could most truly be said, *Three are Witnesses, and the Three are One.* By the word *spirit* we consider God the Father to be signified, concerning the worship of whom the Lord spoke, when He said, *God is a spirit.* By the word *blood* the Son is signified, because *the Word was made flesh.* And by the word *water* we understand the Holy Spirit. For when Jesus spoke concerning the water which He was about to give the thirsty, the evangelist says, *This He spake concerning the Spirit whom those that believed in Him would receive.*"[36]

Thus, according to the critical theory, there grew up in the Latin-speaking regions of ancient Christendom a trinitarian interpretation of *the spirit, the water, and the blood* mentioned in 1 John 5:8, *the spirit* signifying the Father, *the blood* the Son, and *the water* the Holy Spirit. And out of this trinitarian interpretation of 1 John 5:8 developed the *Johannine comma*, which contrasts the witness of the Holy Trinity in heaven with the witness of the spirit, the water, and the blood on earth.

But just at this point the critical theory encounters a serious difficulty. If the *comma* originated in a trinitarian interpretation of 1 John 5:8, why does it not contain the usual trinitarian formula, namely, the Father, the *Son,* and the Holy Spirit. Why does it exhibit the singular combination, never met with elsewhere, the Father, the *Word,* and the Holy Spirit? According to some critics, this unusual phraseology was due to the efforts of the interpolator who first inserted the *Johannine comma* into the New Testament text. In a mistaken attempt to imitate the style of the Apostle John, he changed the term *Son* to the term *Word.* But this is to attribute to the interpolator a craftiness which thwarted his own purpose in making this interpolation, which was surely to uphold the doctrine of the Trinity, including the eternal generation of the Son. With this as his main concern it is very unlikely that he would abandon the time-honored formula, Father, *Son,* and Holy Spirit, and devise an altogether new one, Father, *Word,* and Holy Spirit.

In the second place, the omission of the *Johannine comma* seems to leave the passage incomplete. For it is a common scriptural usage to present solemn truths or warnings in groups of three or four, for example, the repeated *Three things, yea four* of Proverbs 30, and the constantly recurring refrain, *for three transgressions and for four,* of the prophet Amos. In Genesis 40 the butler saw *three branches* and the baker saw *three baskets.* And in Matt. 12:40 Jesus says, *As Jonas was three days and three nights in the whale's belly; so shall the Son of Man be three days and three nights in the heart of the earth.* It is in accord with biblical usage, therefore, to expect that in 1 John 5:7-8 the formula, *there are three that bear witness,* will be repeated at least twice. When the *Johannine comma* is included, the formula is repeated twice. When the *comma* is omitted, the formula is repeated only once, which seems strange.

In the third place, the omission of the *Johannine comma* involves a grammatical difficulty. The words *spirit, water,* and *blood* are neuter in gender, but in 1 John 5:8 they are treated as masculine. If the *Johannine comma* is rejected, it is hard to explain this irregularity. It is usually said

that in 1 John 5:8 *the spirit, the water, and the blood* are personalized and
that this is the reason for the adoption of the masculine gender. But it is
hard to see how such personalization would involve the change from the
neuter to the masculine. For in verse 6 the word Spirit plainly refers to the
Holy Spirit, the Third *Person* of the Trinity. Surely in this verse the word
Spirit is "personalized," and yet the neuter gender is used. Therefore,
since personalization did not bring about a change of gender in verse 6, it
cannot fairly be pleaded as the reason for such a change in verse 8. If,
however, the *Johannine comma* is retained, a reason for placing the
neuter nouns *spirit, water,* and *blood* in the masculine gender becomes
readily apparent. It was due to the influence of the nouns *Father* and
Word, which are masculine. Thus the hypothesis that the *Johannine
comma* is an interpolation is full of difficulties.

(d) Reasons for the Possible Omission of the Johannine Comma

For the absence of the *Johannine comma* from all New Testament
documents save those of the Latin-speaking West the following
explanations are possible.

In the first place, it must be remembered that the *comma* could easily
have been omitted accidentally through a common type of error which is
called *homoioteleuton* (similar ending). A scribe copying 1 John 5:7-8
under distracting conditions might have begun to write down these
words of verse 7, *there are three that bear witness,* but have been forced to
look up before his pen had completed this task. When he resumed his
work, his eye fell by mistake on the identical expression in verse 8. This
error would cause him to omit all of the *Johannine comma* except the
words *in earth,* and these might easily have been dropped later in the
copying of this faulty copy. Such an accidental omission might even have
occurred several times, and in this way there might have grown up a
considerable number of Greek manuscripts which did not contain this
reading.

In the second place, it must be remembered that during the 2nd and
3rd centuries (between 220 and 270, according to Harnack)[37] the heresy
which orthodox Christians were called upon to combat was not Arianism
(since this error had not yet arisen) but Sabellianism (so named after
Sabellius, one of its principal promoters), according to which the Father,
the Son, and the Holy Spirit were one in the sense that they were
identical. Those that advocated this heretical view were called
Patripassians (Father-sufferers), because they believed that God the
Father, being identical with Christ, suffered and died upon the cross, and
Monarchians, because they claimed to uphold the Monarchy (sole-
government) of God.

It is possible, therefore, that the Sabellian heresy brought the
Johannine comma into disfavor with orthodox Christians. The statement, *these three are one,* no doubt seemed to them to teach the Sabellian
view that the Father, the Son and the Holy Spirit were identical. And if
during the course of the controversy manuscripts were discovered which
had lost this reading in the accidental manner described above, it is easy

to see how the orthodox party would consider these mutilated manuscripts to represent the true text and regard the *Johannine comma* as a heretical addition. In the Greek-speaking East especially the *comma* would be unanimously rejected, for here the struggle against Sabellianism was particularly severe.

Thus it was not impossible that during the 3rd century amid the stress and strain of the Sabellian controversy, the *Johannine comma* lost its place in the Greek text but was preserved in the Latin texts of Africa and Spain, where the influence of Sabellianism was probably not so great. In other words, it is not impossible that the *Johannine comma* was one of those few true readings of the Latin Vulgate not occurring in the Traditional Greek Text but incorporated into the Textus Receptus under the guiding providence of God. In these rare instances God called upon the usage of the Latin-speaking Church to correct the usage of the Greek-speaking Church.[38]

4. The King James Version

Not only modernists but also many conservatives are now saying that the King James Version ought to be abandoned because it is not contemporary. The Apostles, they insist, used contemporary language in their preaching and writing, and we too must have a Bible in the language of today. But more and more it is being recognized that the language of the New Testament was biblical rather than contemporary. It was the Greek of the Septuagint, which in its turn was modeled after the Old Testament Hebrew. Any biblical translator, therefore, who is truly trying to follow in the footsteps of the Apostles and to produce a version which God will bless, must take care to use language which is above the level of daily speech, language which is not only intelligible but also biblical and venerable. Hence in language as well as text the King James Version is still by far superior to any other English translation of the Bible.

(a) The Forerunners of the King James Version

Previous to the Reformation a number of translations were made of the Latin Vulgate into Anglo-Saxon and early English. One of the first of these translators was Caedmon (d.680), an inmate of the monastery of Whitby in northern England, who retold in alliterative verse the biblical narratives which had been related to him by the monks. Bede (672-735), the most renowned scholar of that period, not only wrote many commentaries on various books of the Bible, but also translated the Gospel of John into Anglo-Saxon. King Alfred (848-901) did the same for several other portions of Scripture, notably the Ten Commandments and the Psalms. And eclipsing all these earlier translations in importance was that made by John Wyclif (d. 1384) of the entire Latin Bible into the English of his day, the New Testament appearing in 1380 and the Old in 1382. Not long after Wyclif's death a second edition of his English Bible, more satisfactory in language and style than the first, was prepared by his close associate, John Purvey.

The first printed English version of the Bible was that of William Tyndale, one of England's first Protestant martyrs. Tyndale was born in Gloucestershire in 1484 and studied both at Oxford and Cambridge. About 1520 he became attached to the doctrines of the Reformation and conceived the idea of translating the Scriptures into English. Unable to do so in England, he set out for the Continent in the spring of 1524 and seems to have visited Hamburg and Wittenberg. In that same year (probably at Wittenberg) he translated the New Testament from Greek into English for dissemination in his native land. It is estimated that 18,000 copies of this version were printed on the Continent of Europe between 1525 and 1528 and shipped secretly to England. After this Tyndale continued to live on the Continent as a fugitive, constantly evading the efforts of the English authorities to have him tracked down and arrested. But in spite of this ever present danger his literary activity was remarkable. In 1530-31 he published portions of the Old Testament which he had translated from the Hebrew and in 1534 a revision both of this translation and also of his New Testament. In this same year he left his place of concealment and settled in Antwerp, evidently under the impression that the progress of the Reformation in England had made this move a safe one. In so thinking, however, he was mistaken. Betrayed by a friend, he was imprisoned in 1535 and executed the following year. According to Foxe, his dying prayer was this: "Lord, open the King of England's eyes." But his life's work had been completed. He had laid securely the foundations of the English Bible. A comparison of Tyndale's Version with the King James Version is said to indicate that from five sixths to nine tenths of the latter is derived from the martyred translator's work.

After the initial impulse had been given by Tyndale, a number of other English translations of the Bible appeared in rapid succession. The first of these was published in 1535 by Myles Coverdale, who translated not from the Hebrew and Greek but from the Latin Vulgate and from contemporary Latin and German versions, relying heavily all the while on Tyndale's version. In 1537 John Rogers, a close friend of Tyndale, published an edition of the Bible bearing on its title page the name "Thomas Matthew", probably a pseudonymn for Rogers himself. This "Matthew Bible" contained Tyndale's version of the Old and New Testaments and Coverdale's version of those parts of the Old Testament which had not been translated by Tyndale. Then in 1539, under the auspices of Thomas Cromwell, the king's chamberlain, Coverdale published a revision of the Matthew Bible, which because of its large size was called the Great Bible. This Cromwell established as the official Bible of the English Church and deposited it in ecclesiastical edifices throughout the kingdom. In the reign of Queen Elizabeth two revisions were made of the Great Bible. The first was prepared by English Protestants in exile at Geneva and published there in 1560. The second was the Bishops' Bible, published in 1568 by the English prelates under the direction of Archbishop Parker. And finally, the Roman Catholic remnant in England were provided by their leaders with a translation of the Latin Vulgate into English, the New Testament being published in 1582 and the Old in 1609-10. This is known as the Douai Version, since it was prepared at Douai in Flanders, an important center of English Catholicism during the Elizabethan age.[39]

(b) How the King James Version Was Made — The Six Companies

Work on the King James Version began in 1604. In that year a group of Puritans under the leadership of Dr. John Reynolds, president of Corpus Christi College, Oxford, suggested to King James I that a new translation of the Bible be undertaken. This suggestion appealed to James, who was himself a student of theology and of the Scriptures, and he immediately began to make the necessary arrangements for carrying it out. Within six months the general plan of procedure had been drawn up and a complete list made of the scholars who were to do the work. Originally 54 scholars were on the list, but deaths and withdrawals reduced it finally to 47. These were divided into six companies which checked each other's work. Then the final result was reviewed by a select committee of six and prepared for the press. And because of all this careful planning the whole project was completed in less than seven years. In 1611 the new version issued from the press of Robert Barker in a large folio volume bearing on its title page the following inscription: "The Holy Bible, containing the Old Testament and the New: Newly Translated out of the Original tongues; & with the former Translations diligently compared and revised by his Majesties special Commandment. Appointed to be read in Churches." The original tongues referred to in the title were the current printed Hebrew Bibles for the Old Testament and Beza's printed Greek Testament for the New. The "former translations" mentioned there include not only the five previous English versions mentioned above but also the Douai Version, the Latin versions of Tremellius and Beza, and several Spanish, French, and Italian versions. The King James Version, however, is mainly a revision of the Bishops' Bible, which in turn was a slightly revised edition of Tyndale's Bible. Thus the influence of Tyndale's translation upon the King James Version was very strong indeed.[40]

(c) The King James Version Translators Providentially Guided — Preface to the Reader

The translators of the King James Version evidently felt themselves to have been providentially guided in their work. This belief plainly appears in the 'Preface of the Translators', written by Dr. Miles Smith, one of the leaders of this illustrious band of scholars. Concerning his co-laborers he speaks as follows: "Truly, good Christian Reader, we never thought from the beginning that we should need to make a new translation, nor yet to make of a bad one a good one; but to make a good one better, or out of many good ones one principal good one, not justly to be excepted against; that hath been our endeavor, that our mark. To that purpose there were many chosen, that were greater in other men's eyes

than in their own, and that sought the truth rather than their own praise.
. . And in what sort did these assemble? In the trust of their own
knowledge, or of their sharpness of wit, or deepness of judgment, as it
were an arm of flesh? At no hand. They trusted in him that hath the key of
David, opening, and no man shutting; they prayed to the Lord, the Father
of our Lord, to the effect that *St. Augustine* did; *O let thy Scriptures be my
pure delight; let me not be deceived in them, neither let me deceive by
them*. In this confidence and with this devotion, did they assemble
together; not too many, lest one should trouble another; and yet many,
lest many things haply might escape them."[41]

God in His providence has abundantly justified this confidence of the
King James translators. The course of history has made English a world-
wide language which is now the native tongue of at least 300 million
people and the second language of many millions more. For this reason
the King James Version is known the world over and is more widely read
than any other translation of the holy Scriptures. Not only so, but the
King James Version has been used by many missionaries as a basis and
guide for their own translation work and in this way has extended its
influence even to converts who know no English. For more than 350 years
therefore the reverent diction of the King James Version has been used by
the Holy Spirit to bring the Word of life to millions upon millions of
perishing souls. Surely this is a God-guided translation on which God,
working providentially, has placed the stamp of His approval.

(d) How the Translators Were Providentially Guided —
The Marginal Notes

The marginal notes which the translators attached to the King
James Version indicate how God guided their labors providentially.
According to Scrivener (1884), there are 8,422 marginal notes in the 1611
edition of the King James Version, including the Apocrypha. In the Old
Testament, Scrivener goes on to say, 4,111 of the marginal notes give the
more literal meaning of the original Hebrew or Aramaic, 2,156 give
alternative translations, and 67 give variant readings. In the New
Testament 112 of the marginal notes give literal rendering of the Greek,
582 give alternative translations, and 37 give variant readings. These
marginal notes show us that the translators were guided providentially
through their thought processes, through weighing every possibility and
choosing that which seemed to them best.[42]

The 1611 edition of the King James Version also included 9,000
"cross references" to parallel passages. These are still very useful,
especially for comparing the four Gospels with each other. These "cross
references" show that from the very start the King James Version was
intended not merely as a pulpit Bible to be read in church, but also as a
study Bible to guide the private meditations of God's people.[43]

As the marginal notes indicate, the King James translators did not
regard their work as perfect or inspired, but they did consider it to be a
trustworthy reproduction of God's holy Word, and as such they
commended it to their Christian readers: "Many other things we might

give thee warning of, gentle Reader, if we had not exceeded the measure of a preface already. It remaineth that we commend thee to God, and to the Spirit of His grace, which is able to build further than we can ask or think. He removeth the scales from our eyes, the veil from our hearts, opening our wits that we may understand His Word, enlarging our hearts, yea, correcting our affections, that we may love it above gold and silver, yea, that we may love it to the end. Ye are brought unto fountains of living water which ye digged not; do not cast earth into them, neither prefer broken pits before them. Others have laboured, and you may enter into their labours. O receive not so great things in vain: O despise not so great salvation."[44]

(e) Revisions of the King James Version — Obsolete Words Eliminated

Two editions of the King James Version were published in 1611. The first is distinguished from the second by a unique misprint, namely, *Judas* instead of *Jesus* in Matt. 26:36. The second edition corrected this mistake and also in other respects was more carefully done. Other editions followed in 1612, 1613, 1616, 1617, and frequently thereafter. In 1629 and 1638 the text was subjected to two minor revisions. In the 18th century the spelling and punctuation of the King James Version were modernized, and many obsolete words were changed to their modern equivalents. The two scholars responsible for these alterations were Dr. Thomas Paris (1762), of Cambridge, and Dr. Benjamin Blayney (1769), of Oxford, and it is to their efforts that the generally current form of the King James Version is due. In the 19th century the most important edition of the King James Version was the *Cambridge Paragraph Bible* (1873), with F. H. A. Scrivener as its editor. Here meticulous attention was given to details, such as, marginal notes, use of Italic type, punctuation, orthography, grammar, and references to parallel passages. In 1884 also Scrivener published his *Authorized Edition of the English Bible,* a definitive history of the King James Version in which all these features and many more are carefully discussed.[45] Since that time, however, comparatively little research has been done on the history of the King James Version, due probably to loss of interest in the subject.

(f) Obsolete Words in the King James Version — How to Deal with Them

But are there still obsolete words in the King James Version or words that have changed their meaning? Such words do indeed occur, but their number is relatively small. The following are some of these archaic renderings with their modern equivalents:

by and by, Mark 6:25		at once
carriages, Acts 21:15		baggage
charger, Mark 6:25		platter
charity, 1 Cor. 13:1		love

chief estates, Mark 6:21 .... chief men
coasts, Matt. 2:16 .... borders
conversation, Gal. 1:13................................... conduct
devotions, Acts 17:23 .... objects of worship
do you to wit, 2 Cor. 8:1 .... make known to you
fetched a compass, Acts 28:13 .... circled
leasing, Psalm 4:2; 5:6...................................... lying
let, 2 Thess. 2:7 .... restrain
lively, 1 Peter 2:5... living
meat, Matt. 3:4 .... food
nephews, 1 Tim. 5:4 .... grandchildren
prevent, 1 Thess. 4:15 .... precede
room, Luke 14:7-10................................... seat, place
scrip, Matt. 10:10 .... bag
take no thought, Matt. 6:25 .... be not anxious

There are several ways in which to handle this matter of obsolete words and meanings in the King James Version. Perhaps the best way is to place the modern equivalent in the margin. This will serve to increase the vocabulary of the reader and avoid disturbance of the text. Another way would be to place the more modern word in brackets beside the older word. This would be particularly appropriate in Bibles designed for private study.

(g) Why the King James Version Should be Retained

But, someone may reply, even if the King James Version needs only a few corrections, why take the trouble to make them? Why keep on with the old King James and its 17th-century language, its *thee* and *thou* and all the rest? Granted that the Textus Receptus is the best text, but why not make a new translation of it in the language of today? In answer to these objections there are several facts which must be pointed out.

In the first place, the English of the King James Version is not the English of the early 17th century. To be exact, it is not a type of English that was ever spoken anywhere. It is biblical English, which was not used on ordinary occasions even by the translators who produced the King James Version. As H. Wheeler Robinson (1940) pointed out, one need only compare the preface written by the translators with the text of their translation to feel the difference in style.[46] And the observations of W. A. Irwin (1952) are to the same purport. The King James Version, he reminds us, owes its merit, not to 17th-century English — which was very different — but to its faithful translation of the original. Its style is that of the Hebrew and of the New Testament Greek.[47] Even in their use of *thee* and *thou* the translators were not following 17th-century English usage but biblical usage, for at the time these translators were doing their work these singular forms had already been replaced by the plural *you* in polite conversation.[48]

In the second place, those who talk about translating the Bible into the "language of today" never define what they mean by this expression.

What is the *language of today*? The language of 1881 is not the language of today, nor the language of 1901, nor even the language of 1921. In none of these languages, we are told, can we communicate with today's youth. There are even some who feel that the best way to translate the Bible into the language of today is to convert it into "folk songs." Accordingly, in many contemporary youth conferences and even worship services there is little or no Bible reading but only crude kinds of vocal music accompanied by vigorous piano and strumming guitars. But in contrast to these absurdities the language of the King James Version is enduring diction which will remain as long as the English language remains, in other words, throughout the foreseeable future.

In the third place, the current attack on the King James Version and the promotion of modern-speech versions is discouraging the memorization of the Scriptures, especially by children. Why memorize or require your children to memorize something that is out of date and about to be replaced by something new and better? And why memorize a modern version when there are so many to choose from? Hence even in conservative churches children are growing up densely ignorant of the holy Bible because they are not encouraged to hide its life-giving words in their hearts.

In the fourth place, modern-speech Bibles are unhistorical and irreverent. The Bible is not a modern, human book. It is not as new as the morning newspaper, and no translation should suggest this. If the Bible were this new, it would not be the Bible. On the contrary, the Bible is an ancient, divine Book, which nevertheless is always new because in it God reveals Himself. Hence the language of the Bible should be venerable as well as intelligible, and the King James Version fulfills these two requirements better than any other Bible in English. Hence it is the King James Version which converts sinners soundly and makes of them diligent Bible students.

In the fifth place, modern-speech Bibles are unscholarly. The language of the Bible has always savored of the things of heaven rather than the things of earth. It has always been biblical rather than contemporary and colloquial. Fifty years ago this fact was denied by E. J. Goodspeed and others who were pushing their modern versions. On the basis of the papyrus discoveries which had recently been made in Egypt it was said that the New Testament authors wrote in the everyday Greek of their own times.[49] This claim, however, is now acknowledged to have been an exaggeration. As R. M. Grant (1963) admits,[50] the New Testament writers were saturated with the Septuagint and most of them were familiar with the Hebrew Scriptures. Hence their language was not actually that of the secular papyri of Egypt but biblical. Hence New Testament versions must be biblical and not contemporary and colloquial like Goodspeed's version.

Finally, in the sixth place, the King James Version is the historic Bible of English-speaking Protestants. Upon it God, working providentially, has placed the stamp of His approval through the usage of many generations of Bible-believing Christians. Hence, if we believe in God's providential preservation of the Scriptures, we will retain the King James

Version, for in so doing we will be following the clear leading of the Almighty.

5. The Text Of The King James Version — Questions And Problems

When a believer begins to defend the King James Version, unbelievers immediately commence to bring up various questions and problems in the effort to put the believer down and silence him. Let us therefore consider some of these alleged difficulties.

(a) The King James Version a Variety of the Textus Receptus

The translators that produced the King James Version relied mainly, it seems, on the later editions of Beza's Greek New Testament, especially his 4th edition (1588-9). But also they frequently consulted the editions of Erasmus and Stephanus and the Complutensian Polyglot. According to Scrivener (1884),[51] out of the 252 passages in which these sources differ sufficiently to affect the English rendering, the King James Version agrees with Beza against Stephanus 113 times, with Stephanus against Beza 59 times, and 80 times with Erasmus, or the Complutensian, or the Latin Vulgate against Beza and Stephanus. Hence the King James Version ought to be regarded not merely as a translation of the Textus Receptus but also as an independent variety of the Textus Receptus.

The King James translators also placed variant readings in the margin, 37 of them according to Scrivener.[52] To these 37 textual notes 16 more were added during the 17th and 18th centuries,[53] and all these variants still appear in the margins of British printings of the King James Version. In the special providence of God, however, the text of the King James Version has been kept pure. None of these variant readings has been interpolated into it. Of the original 37 variants some are introduced by such formulas as, "Many ancient copies add these words"; "Many Greek copies have"; "Or, as some copies read"; "Some read". Often, however, the reading is introduced simply by "Or", thus making it hard to tell whether a variant reading or an alternative translation is intended.

One of these variant readings is of special interest. After John 18:13 the Bishops' Bible (1568) had added the following words in italics, *And Annas sent Christ bound unto Caiaphas the high priest.* This was a conjectural emendation similar to one which had been suggested by Luther and to another which had been adopted by Beza in his Latin version on the authority of Cyril of Alexandria (d. 444). The purpose of it was to harmonize John 18:13 with Matt. 26:57, which states that the interrogation of Jesus took place at the house of Caiaphas rather than at the house of Annas. The King James translators, however, along with Erasmus and Calvin, solved the problem by translating John 18:24 in the pluperfect, *Now Annas HAD sent Him bound unto Caiaphas the high priest.* This made it unnecessary to emend the text at John 18:13 after the manner of the Bishops' Bible. Hence the King James translators took this conjectural emendation out of the text and placed it in their margin, where it has retained its place unto this day.[54]

Sometimes the King James translators forsook the printed Greek text and united with the earlier English versions in following the Latin Vulgate. One well known passage in which they did this was Luke 23:42, the prayer of the dying thief. Here the Greek New Testaments of Erasmus, Stephanus, and Beza have, *Lord, remember me when Thou comest IN Thy kingdom,* with the majority of the Greek manuscripts. But all the English Bibles of that period (Tyndale, Great, Geneva, Bishops', Rheims, King James) have, *Lord, remember me when Thou comest INTO Thy kingdom,* with the Latin Vulgate and also with Papyrus 75 and B.

At John 8:6 the King James translators followed the Bishops' Bible in adding the clause, *as though He heard them not.* This clause is found in *E G H K* and many other manuscripts, in the Complutensian, and in the first two editions of Stephanus. After 1769 it was placed in italics in the King James Version.

Similarly, at 1 John 2:23 the King James translators followed the Great Bible and the Bishops' Bible in adding the clause, *he that acknowledgeth the Son hath the Father also,* and in placing the clause in italics, thus indicating that it was not found in the majority of the Greek manuscripts or in the earlier editions of the Textus Receptus. Beza included it, however, in his later editions, and it is found in the Latin Vulgate and in *Aleph* and *B.* Hence modern versions have removed the italics and given the clause full status. The Bishops' Bible and the King James Version join this clause to the preceding by the word *but,* taken from Wyclif. With customary scrupulosity the King James translators enclosed this *but* in brackets, thus indicating that it was not properly speaking part of the text but merely a help in translation.

(b) The Editions of the Textus Receptus Compared — Their Differences Listed

The differences between the various editions of the Textus Receptus have been carefully listed by Scrivener (1884)[55] and Hoskier (1890).[56] The following are some of the most important of these differences.

Luke 2:22   *their purification,* Erasmus, Stephanus, majority of the Greek manuscripts. *her purification,* Beza, King James, Elzevir, Complutensian, 76 and a few other Greek minuscule manuscripts, Latin Vulgate (?).

Luke 17:36   *Two men shall be in the field: the one shall be taken and the other left.* Erasmus, Stephanus 1 2 3 omit this verse with the majority of the Greek manuscripts. Stephanus 4, Beza, King James, Elzevir have it with *D,* Latin Vulgate, Peshitta, Old Syriac.

John 1:28   *Bethabara beyond Jordan,* Erasmus, Stephanus 3 4, Beza, King James, Elzevir, *Pi* 1 13, Old Syriac, Sahidic.

Bethany beyond Jordan, Stephanus 1 2, majority of Greek manuscripts including Pap 66 & 75 *Aleph A B,* Latin Vulgate.

John   16:33   *shall have tribulation,* Beza, King James, Elzevir, *D* 69 many other Greek manuscripts, Old Latin, Latin Vulgate. *have tribulation,* Erasmus, Stephanus, majority of Greek manuscripts.

Rom.   8:11   *by His Spirit that dwelleth in you.* Beza, King James, Elzevir, *Aleph A C,* Coptic. *because of His Spirit that dwelleth in you.* Erasmus, Stephanus, majority of Greek manuscripts including *B D,* Peshitta, Latin Vulgate.

Rom.   12:11   *serving the Lord,* Erasmus 1, Beza, King James, Elzevir, majority of Greek manuscripts including Pap 46 *Aleph A B,* Peshitta, Latin Vulgate. *serving the time,* Erasmus 2 3 4 5, Stephanus, *D G.*

1 Tim.   1:4   *godly edifying,* Erasmus, Beza, King James, Elzevir, *D,* Peshitta, Latin Vulgate. *dispensation of God,* Stephanus, majority of Greek manuscripts including *Aleph A G.*

Heb.   9:1   Here Stephanus reads *first tabernacle,* with the majority of the Greek manuscripts. Erasmus, Beza, Luther, Calvin omit *tabernacle* with Pap 46 *Aleph B D,* Peshitta, Latin Vulgate. The King James Version omits *tabernacle* and regards *covenant* as implied.

James   2:18   *without thy works,* Calvin, Beza (last 3 editions), King James *Aleph A B,* Latin Vulgate. *by thy works,* Erasmus, Stephanus, Beza 1565, majority of Greek manuscripts.

   This comparison indicates that the differences which distinguish the various editions of the Textus Receptus from each other are very minor. They are also very few. According to Hoskier, the 3rd edition of Stephanus and the first edition of Elzevir differ from one another in the Gospel of Mark only 19 times.[57] *Codex B,* on the other hand, disagrees with *Codex Aleph* in Mark 652 times and with *Codex D* 1,944 times. What a contrast!
   The texts of the several editions of the Textus Receptus were God-guided. They were set up under the leading of God's special providence. Hence the differences between them were kept down to a minimum. But these disagreements were not eliminated altogether, for this would require not merely providential guidance but a miracle. In short, God chose to preserve the New Testament text providentially rather than miraculously, and this is why even the several editions of the Textus

Receptus vary from each other slightly.

But what do we do in these few places in which the several editions of the Textus Receptus disagree with one another? Which text do we follow? The answer to this question is easy. We are guided by the common faith. Hence we favor that form of the Textus Receptus upon which more than any other God, working providentially, has placed the stamp of His approval, namely, the King James Version, or, more precisely, the Greek text underlying the King James Version. This text was published in 1881 by the Cambridge University Press under the editorship of Dr. Scrivener, and there have been eight reprints, the latest being in 1949.[58] In 1976 also another edition of this text was published in London by the Trinitarian Bible Society.[59] We ought to be grateful that in the providence of God the best form of the Textus Receptus is still available to believing Bible students. For the sake of completeness, however, it would be well to place in the margin the variant readings of Erasmus, Stephanus, Beza, and the Elzevirs.

(c) The King James Old Testament — Variant Readings

Along side the text, called *kethibh* (written), the Jewish scribes had placed in the margin of their Old Testament manuscripts certain variant readings, which they called *keri* (read). Some of these *keri* appear in the margin of the King James Old Testament. For example, in Psalm 100:3 the King James text gives the *kethibh, It is He that hath made us and not we ourselves,* but the King James margin gives the *keri, It is He that hath made us, and His we are.* And sometimes the *keri* is placed in the King James text (16 times, according to Scrivener). For example, in Micah 1:10 the King James text gives the *keri, in the house of Aphrah roll thyself in the dust.* The Hebrew *kethibh,* however, is, *in the house of Aphrah I have rolled myself in the dust.*

Sometimes also the influence of the Septuagint and the Latin Vulgate is discernible in the King James Old Testament. For example, in Psalm 24:6 the King James text reads, *O Jacob,* with the Hebrew *kethibh,* but the King James margin reads, *O God of Jacob,* which is the reading of the Septuagint, the Latin Vulgate, and also of Luther's German Bible. In Jer. 3:9 the King James margin reads *fame (qol)* along with the Hebrew *kethibh,* but the King James text reads *lightness (qal)* in agreement with the Septuagint, and the Latin Vulgate. And in Psalm 22:16 the King James Version reads with the Septuagint, the Syriac, and the Latin Vulgate, *they pierced my hands and my feet.* The Hebrew text, on the other hand, reads, *like a lion my hands and my feet,* a reading which makes no sense and which, as Calvin observes, was obviously invented by the Jews to deny the prophetic reference to the crucifixion of Christ.

(d) The Headings of the Psalms — Are They Inspired?

Many of the Psalms have headings. For example, *To the chief Musician, A Psalm and Song of David* (Psalm 65). The King James translators separated these headings and printed them in small type, each one above the Psalm to which it belonged. Some conservative scholars, such as J. A. Alexander (1850),[60] have criticized the King James translators for doing this. These headings, they have insisted, should be regarded as the first verses of their respective Psalms. They give three reasons for this opinion: first, in the Hebrew Bible no distinction is made between the Psalms and their headings; second, the New Testament writers recognized these headings as true; third, each heading is part of the Psalm which it introduces and hence is inspired. This position, however, may go beyond the clear teaching of Scripture. In any case, it is better to follow the leading of the King James translators and recognize the obvious difference between the heading of a Psalm and the Psalm itself.

The King James translators handled the subscriptions of the Pauline Epistles similarly, printing each one after its own epistle in small type. But this has never been a problem, since these subscriptions have never been regarded as inspired.

(e) Maximum Certainty Versus Maximum Uncertainty

God's preservation of the New Testament text was not miraculous but providential. The scribes and printers who produced the copies of the New Testament Scriptures and the true believers who read and cherished them were not inspired but God-guided. Hence there are some New Testament passages in which the true reading cannot be determined with absolute certainty. There are some readings, for example, on which the manuscripts are almost equally divided, making it difficult to determine which reading belongs to the Traditional Text. Also in some of the cases in which the Textus Receptus disagrees with the Traditional Text it is hard to decide which text to follow. Also, as we have seen, sometimes the several editions of the Textus Receptus differ from each other and from the King James Version. And, as we have just observed, the case is the same with the Old Testament text. Here it is hard at times to decide between the *kethibh* and the *keri* and between the Hebrew text and the Septuagint and Latin Vulgate versions. Also there has been a controversy concerning the headings of the Psalms.

In other words, God does not reveal every truth with equal clarity. In biblical textual criticism, as in every other department of knowledge, there are still some details in regard to which we must be content to remain uncertain. But the special providence of God has kept these uncertainties down to a *minimum*. Hence if we believe in the special providential preservation of the Scriptures and make this the leading principle of our biblical textual criticism, we obtain *maximum certainty*, all the certainty that any mere man can obtain, all the certainty that we need. For we are led by the logic of faith to the Masoretic Hebrew text, to the New Testament Textus Receptus, and to the King James Version.

But what if we ignore the providential preservation of the Scriptures and deal with the text of the holy Bible in the same way in which we deal with the texts of other ancient books? If we do this, we are following the logic of unbelief, which leads to *maximum uncertainty*. When we handle the text of the holy Bible in this way, we are behaving as unbelievers behave. We are either denying that the providential preservation of the Scriptures is a fact, or else we are saying that it is not an important fact, not important enough to be considered when dealing with the text of the holy Bible. But if the providential preservation of the Scriptures is not important, why is the infallible inspiration of the original Scriptures important? If God has not preserved the Scriptures by His special providence, why would He have infallibly inspired them in the first place? And if it is not important that the Scriptures be regarded as infallibly inspired, why is it important to insist that Gospel is completely true? And if this is not important, why is it important to believe that Jesus is the divine Son of God?

In short, unless we follow the logic of faith, we can be certain of nothing concerning the Bible and its text. For example, if we make the Bodmer and Chester Beatty Papyri our chief reliance, how do we know that even older New Testament papyri of an entirely different character have not been destroyed by the recent damming of the Nile and the consequent flooding of the Egyptian sands?[61]

6. Modern English Bible Versions — Are They Of God?

Modern-speech English Bible versions were first prepared during the 18th century by deists who were irked by the biblical language of the King James Version. In 1729 Daniel Mace published a Greek New Testament text with a translation in the language of his own day. The following are samples of his work: *When ye fast, don't put on a dismal air, as the hypocrites do* (Matt. 6:16). *Social affection is patient, is kind* (1 Cor. 13:4). *The tongue is a brand that sets the whole world in a combustion . . . tipp'd with infernal sulphur it sets the whole train of life in a blaze* (James 3:6). Similarly, in 1768 Edward Harwood published a New Testament translation which he characterized as "a liberal and diffusive version of the sacred classics." His purpose, he explained, was to allure the youth of his day "by the innocent stratagem of a modern style to read a book, which is now, alas! too generally neglected and disregarded by the young and gay." And about the same time Benjamin Franklin offered a specimen of "Part of the First Chapter of Job modernized."[62]

Serious efforts, however, to dislodge the King James Version from its position of dominance and to replace it with a modern version did not begin until a century later, and it is with these that we would now deal briefly.

(a) The R. V., the A. S. V., and the N. E. B.

By the middle of the 19th century the researches and propaganda of Tischendorf and Tregelles had convinced many British scholars that the Textus Receptus was a late and inferior text and that therefore a revision of the King James Version was highly necessary. This clamor for a new revision of the English Bible was finally met in 1870, when a Revision

Committee was appointed by the Church of England to carry out the project. This Committee consisted of 54 members, half of them being assigned to the Old Testament and half to the New. One of the most influential members of the New Testament section was Dr. F. J. A. Hort, and the text finally adopted by the revisers was largely the Westcott and Hort text. The New Testament was finished November 11, 1880, and published May 17, 1881, amid tremendous acclaim. Within a few days 2,000,000 copies had been sold in London, 365,000 in New York, and 110,000 in Philadelphia. The Old Testament was completed in 1884 and published in 1885. By this time, however, popular demand had died down, and the market for the entire Revised Bible was merely fair, the sale of it reaching no such phenomenal heights as the Revised New Testament had attained.

While this work of revision had been going on in England a committee of American scholars had been organized to cooperate in the endeavor. They promised not to publish their own revised edition of the Bible until 14 years after the publication of the English Revised Version (R.V.), and in exchange for this concession were given the privilege of publishing in an appendix to this version a list of the readings which they favored but which the British revisers declined to adopt. In accordance with this agreement, the American Committee waited until 1901 before they published their own Revised Version, which was very like its English cousin except that there was a more thorough elimination of antiquated words and of words specifically English and not American in meaning. By the publishers, Thomas Nelson and Sons, it was called the Standard Version, and from this circumstance it is commonly known as the American Standard Version (A.S.V.).[63]

Neither the R.V. nor the A.S.V. fared as well as their promoters had hoped. They were never widely used, due largely to their poor English style, which, according to F. C. Grant (1954), "was, in many places, unbelievably wooden, opaque, or harsh."[64] Because of this lack of success these two versions have been largely abandoned, and their place has been filled by the Revised Standard Version (1946) in America and the New English Bible (1961) in England. Both are in modern speech. The R.S.V. was prepared by a committee appointed by the International Council of Religious Education, representing 40 Protestant denominations in the United States and Canada. The N.E.B. was prepared by a similar committee representing nine denominations in Great Britain.

The modernism of the R.S.V. and the N.E.B. appears everywhere in them. For example, both of them profess to use *thou* when referring to God and *you* when referring to men. Yet the disciples are made to use *you* when speaking to Jesus, implying, evidently, that they did not believe that He was divine. Even when they confess Him to be the Son of God, the disciples are still made to use *you. You are the Christ,* Peter is made to say, *the Son of the living God* (Matt. 16:16). In both the R.S.V. and the N.E.B. opposition to the virgin birth of Christ is plainly evident. Thus the N.E.B. calls Mary a *girl* (Luke 1:27) rather than a *virgin,* and at Matt. 1:16 the N.E.B. and some editions of the R.S.V. include in a footnote a reading found only in the Sinaitic Syriac manuscript which states that Joseph was the father of Jesus.

The N.E.B. exhibits all too plainly a special hostility to the deity of Christ. This is seen in the way in which the Greek word *proskyneo* is translated. When it is applied to God, the N.E.B. always translates it *worship,* but when it is applied to Jesus, the N.E.B. persistently translates it *pay homage* or *bow low.* Thus the translators refuse to admit that Jesus was worshipped by the early Church. Even the Old Testament quotation, *Let all the angels of God worship Him* (Heb. 1:6), is rendered by the N.E.B., *Let all the angels of God pay him homage.* The only passage in which *proskyneo* is translated *worship* when applied to Jesus is in Luke 24:52. But here this clause is placed in a footnote as a late variant reading. By using the word *worship* here these modernistic translators give expression to their belief that the worship of Jesus was a late development which took place in the Church only after the true New Testament text had been written.

(b) Contemporary Modern-speech English Bibles

In addition to the R.S.V. and the N.E.B. at least 25 other modern-speech English Bibles and New Testaments have been published. Some of these, notably the Weymouth (1903), the Moffatt (1913), and the Goodspeed (1923), enjoyed great popularity in their own day but now are definitely out of date. We will confine our remarks therefore to contemporary modern-speech versions which are being widely used today by evangelicals.

(1) *The New Testament In the Language of the People,* by Charles B. Williams (1937). As he states in his preface, Williams follows the text of Westcott and Hort. He not only adopts all their errors but even goes beyond them in omitting portions of the New Testament text. For example, he omits Luke 22:43-44 (Christ's agony and bloody sweat) and Luke 23:34a (Christ's prayer for His murderers) instead of putting these passages in brackets as Westcott and Hort do. As for John 7:53-8:11 (the woman taken in adultery), he does not place this passage at the end of John's Gospel, as Westcott and Hort do, but omits it altogether. In addition, Williams interjects bits of higher criticism into his introductions to the various New Testament books. For example, he tells us that the author of John's Gospel is likely John the Apostle but some scholars think another John wrote it. It is usually thought, he says, that Paul wrote 2 Thessalonians, 1 and 2 Timothy, but some deny it, etc.

(2) *New American Standard New Testament* (1960), Lockman Foundation. As its name implies, this is a modernization of the A.S.V. It follows the text of the A.S.V. very closely and even goes farther in its omissions. For example, in Luke 24:51 it omits Christ's ascension into heaven, which the A.S.V. had left standing in the text. In the "Way of Life Edition" of this modern-speech version we have an illogical mixture of pietism and naturalistic thinking. In the text there are verses in black letter which a sinner is to believe to the saving of his soul, while at the bottom of the page are frequent notes which destroy all confidence in the

sacred text, stating that such and such readings are not found in the best manuscripts, etc. How can such a Bible convert a thinking college student? No wonder it has to be supplemented by much music and mysticism, fun and frolic.

(3) *The New Testament in the Language of Today* (1963), by William F. Beck. This modern-speech version makes much of Papyrus 75, mentioning it frequently. In John 8:57 the translator adopts the unusual reading of Papyrus 75, *Has Abraham seen You?* instead of the common reading, *Have You seen Abraham?* Consistency requires that Dr. Beck adopt the other unusual readings of Papyrus 75, such as *Neves* for the name of the Rich Man (Luke 16:19), *shepherd* for *door* (John 10:7), *raised* for *saved* (John 11:12). But in these passages Dr. Beck adopts the common readings, forsaking Papyrus 75, and he doesn't even mention the fact that this recently discovered authority omits the blind man's confession of faith (John 9:38). In short, as a textual critic Dr. Beck seems rather capricious in his choices.

(4) *Good News For Modern Man, The New Testament in Today's English Version* (1966), American Bible Society. This version claims to be based on a Greek text published specially by the United Bible Societies in 1966 with the aid of noted scholars. The translation was prepared by Dr. Robert G. Bratcher. In it some verses are omitted and others marked with brackets. But this is done capriciously without regard even to naturalistic principles. For example, Christ's agony and bloody sweat (Luke 22:43-44) is bracketed, while Christ's prayer for His murderers (Luke 23:34a) is left unbracketed. This version has been called "the bloodless Bible," since it shuns the mention of Christ's *blood*, preferring instead to speak of Christ's *death*.

(5) *The Living New Testament, Paraphrased* (1967), by Ken Taylor. This paraphrase uses the A.S.V. as its basic text. Like so many other modern-speech Bibles in vogue among evangelicals, it is arbitrary in its renderings. The name, *Son of Man*, for example, which Jesus applied to Himself is rendered six different ways. Sometimes it is translated *I*, sometimes *He*, sometimes *Son of Mankind*, sometimes *Man from Heaven*, sometimes *Man of Glory*, and sometimes *Messiah*. And this variation is kept up even in parallel passages in which the Greek wording is identical. For example, in Matt. 9:6 *Son of Man* is translated *I*, while in Mark 2:10 it is translated *I, the Man from Heaven*. What reason is there for this whimsical treatment of one of our Saviour's sacred titles? Taylor gives none. Doctrinally also Taylor wrests the Scriptures with his paraphrase. For instance, in Rom. 8:28 Taylor tells us that all things work for our good, if only we love God and fit into His plans.

(6) *The Jerusalem Bible* (1966), Doubleday. This Bible was originally a French modern-speech version prepared by French Roman Catholic scholars at L'Ecole Biblique (The Biblical School) at Jerusalem and published in Paris in 1955. It sold so widely in the French-speaking world that a few years later commercial publishers in England and America jointly undertook an equivalent English version, which they published in 1966 under the sensational and misleading title *Jerusalem Bible*. The modernism of this Bible also is offensive to orthodox Christians.

(7) *The New American Bible* (1970), Confraternity of Christian Doctrine. This official, Roman Catholic, modern-speech Bible, with a prefatory letter of approval from Pope Paul VI, has been authorized as a source of readings in the Mass. In the text and notes and in the introductions to the New Testament books many critical positions formerly regarded as official have been sharply reversed. For example, it is now permissible for Roman Catholics to hold that the Gospel of Matthew is an expanded version of the Gospel of Mark and later than the Gospel of Luke. Permission is also given to maintain that the Gospel of John was not written by the Apostle John but by a disciple-evangelist and then was later revised by a disciple-redactor. It is also suggested that 2 Peter was not written by the Apostle Peter and even that 1 Peter may likewise have been pseudonymous. Mark 16:9-20 and John 7:53-8:11 are not regarded as original portions of their respective Gospels, and the *Johannine comma* (1 John 5:7-8) is omitted without comment. This complete about-face is ominous, for it shows how far Roman Catholic authorities are willing to go in their efforts to give themselves a "new image" and to make room for modernists in their ecclesiastical structure. Liberal Protestantism is about to collapse and fall into the waiting arms of Roman Catholicism. And many inconsistent Fundamentalists will be involved in this disaster because of their addiction to naturalistic New Testament textual criticism and naturalistic modern-speech versions.

(8) *New International Version* (1973), New York Bible Society. This translation follows the critical (Westcott and Hort) text. There seems to be nothing particularly remarkable about it. However, it is falsely called *International*. Obviously it is wholly American, sometimes painfully so. For example, it joins *Beck's version* and *Good News for Modern Man* in consistently substituting *rooster* for *cock*. But this is American barnyard talk. Is there anything wrong with our American barnyard talk? As good Americans we answer, of course not. Nevertheless, however, such talk is not literary enough to be given a place in holy Scripture.

(c) The King James Version — The Providentially Appointed English Bible

Do we believing Bible Students "worship" the King James Version? Do we regard it as inspired, just as the ancient Jewish philosopher Philo (d. 42 A.D.) and many early Christians regarded the Septuagint as inspired? Or do we claim the same supremacy for the King James Version that Roman Catholics claim for the Latin Vulgate? Do we magnify its authority above that of the Hebrew and Greek Old and New Testament Scriptures? We have often been accused of such excessive veneration for the King James Version, but these accusations are false. In regard to Bible versions we follow the example of Christ's Apostles. We adopt the same attitude toward the King James Version that they maintained toward the Septuagint.

In their Old Testament quotations the Apostles never made any distinction between the Septuagint and the Hebrew Scriptures. They never said, "The Septuagint translates this verse thus and so, but in the original Hebrew it is this way." Why not? Why did they pass up all these opportunities to display their learning? Evidently because of their great respect for the Septuagint and the position which it occupied in the providence of God. In other words, the Apostles recognized the Septuagint as the providentially approved translation of the Old Testament into Greek. They understood that this was the version that God desired the gentile Church of their day to use as its Old Testament Scripture.

In regard to Bible versions, then, we follow the example of the Apostles and the other inspired New Testament writers. Just as they recognized the Septuagint as the providentially appointed translation of the Hebrew Old Testament into Greek, so we recognize the King James Version and the other great historic translations of the holy Scriptures as providentially approved. Hence we receive the King James Version as the providentially appointed English Bible. Admittedly this venerable version is not absolutely perfect, but it is trustworthy. No Bible-believing Christian who relies upon it will ever be led astray. But it is just the opposite with modern versions. They are untrustworthy, and they do lead Bible-believing Christians astray.

It is possible, if the Lord tarry, that in the future the English language will change so much that a new English translation of the Bible will become absolutely necessary. But in that case any version which we prepare today would be equally antiquated. Hence this is a matter which we must leave to God, who alone knows what is in store for us. For the present, however, and the foreseeable future no new translation is needed to take the place of the King James Version. Today our chief concern must be to create a climate of Christian thought and learning which God can use providentially should the need for such a new English version ever arise. This would insure that only the English wording would be revised and not the underlying Hebrew and Greek text.

(For further discussion see *Believing Bible Study*, pp. 81-88, 214-228).

(d) Which King James Version? — A Feeble Rebuttal

Opponents of the King James Version often try to refute us by asking us which edition of the King James Version we receive as authoritative. For example, a professor in a well known Bible school writes as follows: "With specific reference to the King James translation, I must ask you which revision you refer to as the one to be accepted? It has been revised at least three times. The first translation of 1611 included the Apocrypha, which I do not accept as authoritative."

This retort, however, is very weak. All the editions of the King James Version from 1611 onward are still extant and have been examined minutely by F. H. A. Scrivener and other careful scholars. Aside from printers errors, these editions differ from each other only in regard to spelling, punctuation, and, in a few places, italics. Hence any one of them may be used by a Bible-believing Christian. The fact that some of them include the Apocrypha is beside the point, since this does not affect their accuracy in the Old and New Testaments.

CHAPTER NINE

CHRIST'S HOLY WAR WITH SATAN

As Dean Burgon (1883) pointed out, the history of the New Testament text is the history of a conflict between God and Satan. Soon after the New Testament books were written Satan corrupted their texts by means of heretics and misguided critics whom he had raised up. These assaults, however, on the integrity of the Word were repulsed by the providence of God, who guided true believers to reject these false readings and to preserve the True Text in the majority of the Greek New Testament manuscripts. And at the end of the middle ages this True Text was placed in print and became the Textus Receptus, the foundation of the glorious Protestant Reformation.

But Satan was not defeated. Instead he staged a clever come-back by means of naturalistic New Testament textual criticism. Old corrupt manuscripts, which had been discarded by the God-guided usage of the believing Church, were brought out of their hiding places and re-instated. Through naturalistic textual criticism also the fatal logic of unbelief was set in motion. Not only the text but every aspect of the Bible and of Christianity came to be regarded as a purely natural phenomenon. And today thousands of Bible-believing Christians are falling into this devil's trap through their use of modern-speech versions which are based on naturalistic textual criticism and so introduce the reader to the naturalistic point of view. By means of these modern-speech versions Satan deprives his victims of both the shield of faith and the sword of the Spirit and leaves them unarmed and helpless before the terrors and temptations of this modern, apostate world. What a clever come-back! How Satan must be hugging himself with glee over the seeming success of his devilish strategy.

1. The Gospel And The Logic Of Faith

How can we dispel these dark clouds of error which the devil has generated and bring a new Reformation to our modern age? In only one way, namely, through the preaching of the Gospel. But the Gospel which we preach must be the pure Gospel, and we must preach it not according to the dictates of our own human logic but according to the logic of faith. We must preach the Gospel, *first,* as a message that must be believed, *second,* as a command that must be obeyed, and, *third,* as an assurance that comforts and sustains. Let us therefore discuss these three concepts briefly.

(a) The Gospel Is a Message that Must Be Believed

The Gospel is a message that must be believed. Our Lord Jesus Himself teaches us this in the Gospel of Mark. *Now after that John was put in prison, Jesus came into Galilee, preaching the gospel of the kingdom of God, and saying, The time is fulfilled, and the kingdom of God is at hand, repent ye and believe the gospel* (Mark 1:14-15). And what was this Gospel which Jesus commanded all who heard Him to believe? That He should die upon the cross for sinners. Jesus explained this also to His disciples on the road to Caesarea Philippi. *And He began to teach them, that the Son of Man must suffer many things, and be rejected of the elders, and of the chief priests, and scribes, and be killed, and after three days rise again. . . . And when He had called the people unto Him with His disciples also, He said unto them, Whosoever will come after Me, let him deny himself, and take up his cross and follow Me. For whosoever will save his life shall lose it; but whosoever shall lose his life for My sake and the gospel's, the same shall save it* (Mark 8:31, 34-35).

There are four things especially which we must believe concerning Christ's atoning death for sinners:

First, Christ died for many sinners. *For even the Son of Man came not to be ministered unto, but to minister, and to give His life a ransom for many* (Mark 10:45).

Second, Christ died for all kinds of sinners, for all sorts and conditions of men. *And I, if I be lifted up from the earth, will draw all men unto Me. This He said, signifying what death He should die* (John 12:32-33).

Third, Christ died for sinners the world over. *For God so loved the world, that He gave His only begotten Son, that whosoever believeth in Him should not perish, but have everlasting life. For God sent not His Son into the world to condemn the world; but that the world through Him might be saved* (John 3:16-17).

Fourth, Christ died for all those sinners who down through the ages would be converted through the preaching of the Gospel. *Neither pray I for these* (the Apostles) *alone, but for them also which shall believe on Me through their word; that they all may be one; as Thou, Father, art in Me, and I in Thee, that they all may be one in Us; that the world may believe that Thou has sent Me* (John 17:20-21).

(b) The Gospel Is a Command that Must Be Obeyed

We must believe the message of the Gospel that Christ died for sinners, but we cannot really do so until we apply this message to ourselves and believe in Jesus personally. And this is what Jesus commands us to do in the Gospel. *What must we do,* the Jews asked Him hypocritically, *that we might work the works of God? This is the work of God,* He answered sternly, *that ye believe on Him whom He hath sent* (John 6:29). And Jesus repeated this command again and again throughout the course of His earthly ministry. *I am the bread of life: he that cometh to Me shall never hunger; and he that believeth on Me shall never thirst* (John 6:35). *I am the resurrection, and the life: he that believeth in Me, though he were dead, yet shall he live; and whosoever liveth and believeth in Me shall never die* (John 11:25-26). *Ye believe in God, believe also in Me* (John 14:1).

But how do we obey the command of the Gospel? How do we believe in

Jesus? How do we receive Him? By repenting and applying the message of the Gospel to ourselves (Mark 1:15). By believing that Jesus died for us personally on the cross. This is what Jesus told Nicodemus when he came to Him by night seeking salvation. *And as Moses lifted up the serpent in the wilderness, even so must the Son of Man be lifted up: that whosoever believeth in Him should not perish, but have eternal life* (John 3:14-15). We must receive Jesus as our perfect sacrifice. *Whoso eateth My flesh, and drinketh My blood, hath eternal life: and I will raise him up at the last day* (John 6:54). We must trust wholly in His body given and His blood shed for us at Calvary. *And He took bread, and gave thanks, and brake it, and gave unto them, saying, This is My body which is given for you: this do in remembrance of Me. Likewise also the cup after supper, saying, This cup is the new testament in My blood, which is shed for you* (Luke 22:20).

(c) The Gospel Is an Assurance that Comforts and Sustains

We are saved, first, by believing the message of the Gospel that Jesus died for sinners and, second, by applying this message to ourselves so that we repent and believe that Jesus died for us personally upon the cross. But there is also a third requirement. We must persevere, we must abide in Christ. Jesus reminds His Apostles of this obligation in His famous metaphor. *I am the vine, ye are the branches: He that abideth in Me, and I in him the same bringeth forth much fruit: for without Me ye can do nothing. If a man abide not in Me, he is cast forth as a branch, and is withered; and men gather them, and cast them into the fire, and they are burned* (John 15:5-6). How about this third requirement? Will we persevere? In the future will we still believe and be saved, or will we cease to believe and become unsaved? Will we abide in Christ, or will we be cast forth as a broken branch and perish?

The Gospel gives us the assurance which we need to comfort us and calm our fears. In the Gospel Jesus teaches us that the sinners for whom He died were given unto Him by God the Father in the eternal Covenant of Grace before the foundation of the world. *All that the Father giveth Me shall come to Me; and him that cometh to Me I will in no wise cast out. For I came down from heaven not to do Mine own will, but the will of Him that sent Me. And this is the Father's will which hath sent Me, that of all which He hath given Me I should lose nothing, but should raise it up again at the last day* (John 6:37-39). Because true believers have been given to Christ by God the Father, they shall never perish. *My sheep hear My voice, and I know them, and they follow Me: And I give unto them eternal life; and they shall never perish, neither shall any man pluck them out of My hand. My Father, which gave them Me is greater than all; and no man is able to pluck them out of My Father's hand* (John 10:27-29).

I am the good shepherd, Jesus says, *the good shepherd giveth His life for the sheep* (John 10:11). Christ died for the elect, for those that had been given to Him by God the Father before the foundation of the world. *I am the good shepherd, and know My sheep, and am known of Mine. As the Father knoweth Me, even so know I the Father: and I lay down My life for the sheep* (John 10:14-15). There are three ways especially in which this doctrine comforts believers. In the *first* place, this doctrine teaches us that Jesus loved us not only on the cross but from all eternity. He *loved me and gave Himself for me* (Gal. 2:20). In the *second* place, this doctrine reveals to us that on the cross Jesus not only fully satisfied for all our sins but also purchased for us the gift of the Holy Spirit and of faith. *Therefore being by the right hand of God exalted, and having received of the Father the promise of the Holy Ghost, He hath shed forth this, which ye now see and hear* (Acts 2:33). And in the *third* place, this doctrine assures us that we will never lose our eternal redemption, which was obtained for us by Jesus through His sufferings and death. *Neither by the blood of goats and calves, but by His own blood He entered in once into the holy place, having obtained eternal redemption for us* (Heb. 9:12).

2. Hyper-Calvinism and Arminianism Versus the Logic Of Faith

Christ died for sinners of every sort (John 12:32). Repent and believe that He died for you personally (John 3:14-15). Christ died for His elect (John 10:11). Believe and be comforted (John 14:1). Know that Jesus loved you not only on the cross but from all eternity (Gal. 2:20). Know that on the cross He not only fully satisfied for all your sins but also purchased for you the gift of the Holy Spirit and of faith (Acts 2:33). Know that you shall never perish because no man is able to pluck you out of your heavenly Father's hand (John 10:29). Such is the Gospel when it is preached according to the logic of faith.

Many modern Christians, however, reject this logic of faith on the ground that it does not solve the problem of the non-elect (the reprobate). "What about the non-elect," they clamor, "how do these reprobates fit into the logic of faith? For if Christ died for the elect only, then how can God command all men to repent and believe that Christ died for them personally? For then He would be asking the non-elect to believe something that is not true in their case. And how can God find fault with the non-elect for not believing that Christ died for them personally? For how can He blame them for not believing something that is not true in regard to them?"

There are three answers to this objection (WHICH NO CONVICTED SINNER WILL EVER RAISE): *first*, the hyper-Calvinistic answer; *second*, the Arminian answer; *third*, the biblical answer, which is founded on the logic of faith.

(a) Hyper-Calvinism — An Error of Human Logic

Hyper-Calvinists base their presentation of the Gospel upon a faulty human logic. They reason that because Christ died for the elect only salvation is offered to the elect only. Hence before a sinner can believe that Christ died for him personally upon the cross, he must try to find out whether he has any right to believe this. In other words, according to the hyper-Calvinists, before a sinner can receive Jesus as his Saviour, he must have good grounds for believing that he is one of God's elect.

How can we determine whether we are members of God's elect? How can we find out whether we have the right to believe that Jesus died for us upon the cross? According to the hyper-Calvinists, there are two tests by which we can discover this. The first test is repentance. Do we truly repent, are we genuinely sorry for our sins? The second test is willingness. *Thy people shall be willing in the day of Thy power* (Psalm 110:3). Are we truly willing to receive Jesus as our Saviour? Do we really wish to be saved? According to hyper-Calvinism, we have no right to believe that Jesus died for us personally until we can answer these questions in the affirmative. Only if we pass these preliminary tests, do we have any reason for supposing that we belong to the elect for whom the Saviour laid down His life.

Hyper-Calvinism appeals to some because at first sight it seems to be logical and to promote earnestness. Actually, however, it is illogical. On the one hand, it requires us to know that we are elect before we believe in Christ, and, on the other hand, it teaches us that the only way we can know that we are elect is to begin to believe in Christ by repenting and being willing to have Him as our Saviour. And even the earnestness of hyper-Calvinism is often detrimental. It takes our eyes off our Saviour and turns them inward on ourselves and our mental state. It fills us with doubt as to whether we are saved or even can be saved. And, finally, hyper-Calvinism makes the conversion of a sinner very difficult, almost impossible. For it teaches him that he cannot believe in Christ savingly until he is sure that he is one of the elect. But how can a sinner ever be sure of this apart from Christ?

(b) Arminianism — Another Error of Human Logic

But what if we drop the doctrine of election altogether and assert that Christ died for all human beings? Arminians do this and are very pleased with themselves. They claim that this makes the way of salvation very simple. First you take as your major premise the proposition, "Christ died for all human beings." Then you supply the minor premise, "I am a human being." Then you draw the conclusion, "Christ died for me." Then on the basis of this conclusion you receive Christ as your Saviour.

But this "simple Gospel" is not so simple after all. There are difficulties. As an exposition of the way of salvation it is faulty in three respects. In the first place, I cannot first believe that Jesus died for others and then as a consequence believe that Jesus died for me. For how can I really be sure that Jesus died for others unless I first am sure that He died for me? In the second place, if I believe this proposition, "Jesus died for me," merely as the conclusion of a logical syllogism, then I do not truly believe it and hence have no basis for receiving Jesus as my Saviour. But on the other hand, if I truly believe that Jesus died for me, then I have already received Him as my Saviour. In the third place, I cannot first believe that Jesus died for me and then on this basis receive Jesus as my Saviour. For repenting, believing, and receiving are all aspects of one act of faith. They go together and cannot be separated from one another. I receive Jesus as my Saviour by repenting and believing that He died for me. If I try to receive Him in any other way, then I am not a Christian but a mystic.

Hence it is a mistake to tell a sinner first to believe that Jesus died for all human beings numerically, and then to believe that Jesus died for him because he is a human being, and finally to receive Jesus as his Saviour on this basis. For this implies that there is no difference between saved saints and lost sinners from the standpoint of faith. Both saved saints and lost sinners could unite in the same confession, "Jesus died for all human beings. Therefore Jesus must have died for me because I am a human being." In this case both the saved saint and the lost sinner would believe the same thing, and the only difference between the two would be that the saved saint *receives* Christ as his Saviour while the lost sinner doesn't. And this would imply that we are saved not by *believing* but by a *receiving* which is different from believing, by a "yielding" to Christ perhaps, or a "surrendering" to Him, or a "turning over of our lives" to Him. But all this is salvation by works and contrary to the Bible. For the Scriptures plainly teach that to receive Christ as Saviour is to believe on Him. *Believe on the Lord Jesus Christ, and thou shalt be saved* (Acts 16:31). *But as many as received Him, to them gave He power to become the sons of God, even to them that believe on His name* (John 1:12).

These, then, are some of the cardinal errors of Arminianism. It tends to break down the distinction between the saved and the lost. It substitutes an unbiblical *receiving* for the *believing* commanded in the Gospel. Hence it minimizes the doctrine of justification by faith and promotes an unscriptural mysticism.

(c) The Logic of Faith — Christ's Death Sufficient for All Men but Efficient for the Elect

"Christ died sufficiently for all men but efficiently only for the elect." This is an ancient saying which is not found in Scripture but which sums up very well the teaching of the Bible concerning the death of Christ. It emphasizes three points especially:

First, the doctrine of election and God's universal command to all men to repent and trust in Jesus' blood are not contrary. For our Lord Jesus Christ Himself taught both. On the one hand, He taught the doctrine of election with great plainness, especially in His high priestly prayer. *Father, the hour is come; glorify Thy Son, that Thy Son also may glorify Thee. As Thou hast given Him power over all flesh, that He should give eternal life to as many as Thou hast given Him* (John 17:1-2). On the other hand, Jesus offered salvation to all men without distinction and even mourned over the non-elect that refused to believe in Him. Consider, for example, His lamentation over the apostate city of Jerusalem. *O Jerusalem, Jerusalem, thou that killest the prophets and stonest them which are sent unto thee, how often would I have gathered thy children together, even as a hen gathereth her chickens under her wings, and ye would not* (Matt. 23:37). But how do we reconcile these two strands in our Lord's teaching? Only God knows the answer to this question. *The secret things belong unto the LORD our God: but those things which are revealed belong unto us and to our children* (Deut. 29:29).

Second, we cannot receive Christ by human logic but only by the logic of faith. Both the hyper-Calvinists and the Arminians try to reason their way to Christ by means of logical syllogisms. The hyper-Calvinist says, "Christ died for the elect. I am one of the elect. Therefore Christ must have died for me." The Arminian says, "Christ died for all human beings. I am a human being. Therefore Christ must have died for me." But it is not in this way that we believe that Christ died for us upon the cross. If we truly believe this, then this belief is the *foundation* of all our reasoning and not a conclusion which we arrive at through logical reasoning. In other words, the belief that Jesus died for us upon the cross is the beginning of the logic of faith. We arrive at this belief not through reasoning but through an act of faith. And this act of faith makes us truly reasonable because it brings us into immediate contact with Christ *in whom are hid all the treasures of wisdom and knowledge* (Col. 2:3).

Third, we perform this act of faith through the effectual calling of the Holy Spirit. How do we break through the encirclement of our human experience and reach out and lay hold on Christ? How are we able to believe that Jesus died for us upon the cross? This we do not know exactly. We only know that the Holy Spirit makes us able. *No man can say that Jesus is the Lord, but by the Holy Ghost* (1 Cor. 12:3). We are saved through the Holy Spirit's regenerate power. *Not by works of righteousness which we have done, but according to His mercy He saved us, by the washing of regeneration, and renewing of the Holy Ghost* (Titus 3:5). The Holy Spirit, sent by God the Father, draws me to God's Son and teaches me that Jesus died for me. *No man can come to Me except the Father which hath sent Me draw him: and I will raise him up at the last day. It is written in the prophets, And they shall be all taught of God. Every one therefore that hath heard, and hath learned of the Father, cometh unto Me* (John 6:44-45). Thus it is the Holy Spirit that introduces us to the logic of faith.

3. The Logic Of Faith And The Christian Thought-System

"Lord Jesus, I repent. O blessed Redeemer, I believe that Thou didst die for me personally upon the cross. Forgive me and take me, O Thou my Saviour." When a sinner receives Jesus in this manner by the power of the Holy Spirit, he has taken the first step in the logic of faith. And this first step leads to *three* momentous changes in his life and thinking:

First, the converted sinner exchanges a sinful life for a godly life. This was the emphasis of the Ancient Church. Justin Martyr (165 A.D.) thus describes the striking change which Christianity made in the lives of these early believers. "We who once served lust now find our delight only in pure morals; we who once followed sorcery, now have consecrated ourselves to the good and unbegotten God; we who once loved gain above all, now give what we have for the common use and share with every needy one. We who once hated and destroyed one another, and on account of their different manners would not live with men of a different tribe, now, since the coming of Christ, live with them, pray for our enemies, and seek to convince those who hate us unjustly that they may live according to the good precepts of Christ, to the end that they may become partakers with us of the same joyful hope of a reward from God, the Ruler of all" (First Apology, Chap. 14).

Second, the converted sinner exchanges a guilty, evil conscience for a good and peaceful conscience. This was the emphasis of the Reformation Church under the leadership of Martin Luther. During the middle ages professing Christians tried to rid themselves of guilt and secure peace of conscience through penances, pilgrimages, crusades, the building of great cathedrals, and finally through the purchase of indulgences from the pope. It was at this point that Luther arose and nailed his Ninety-five Theses on the church door in Wittenberg. In them he insisted that an indulgence can never remove guilt, for God has kept this authority in His own hand. Only by true faith in Christ can guilt be taken away, justification granted, and peace of conscience obtained (Rom. 3:28). This was the message that ushered in the Protestant Reformation.

Third, the converted sinner exchanges a carnal mind for a spiritual mind. This must be our emphasis today in the Modern Church if we truly desire to bring in a New Reformation. *For to be carnally minded is death; but to be spiritually minded is life and peace* (Rom. 8:6). This is a favorite Bible verse with many pious, modern Christians. The only trouble is that they take far too narrow and restricted a view of the spiritual-mindedness which God requires. It is not sufficient for us to be spiritually minded only in our private devotions or when doing mission work or talking with Christian friends or speaking in a Church. Many modern Christians are spiritually minded in these respects but are carnally minded in their New Testament textual criticism, in their philosophy and science, and in their economic and political views. In these areas their thinking is the same as the thinking of unbelievers.

To be truly spiritually minded, therefore, is something much bigger and more comprehensive than these pietists suppose. To be spiritually minded in the largest and best sense is to follow the logic of faith out into every realm of thought and life and thus to work out biblical views concerning the nature of faith, concerning the holy Scriptures, concerning philosophy and science, and concerning politics and economics. In order, now, to see how all this fits together, let us review very briefly the teaching of the Bible in these four fields.

(a) The Biblical View of Faith — The Difference Between Faith and Mere Belief

What is the difference between faith and doubting? Many Christians are unable to answer this question because they confuse divine, God-given faith with mere animal or human belief. Animal belief arises spontaneously out of habit. If you put your dog's food in a certain bowl, he will soon believe that this is the place to go when hungry. But if you stop putting food in the bowl, his belief will begin to give place to doubt and will eventually cease. Our human beliefs likewise arise involuntarily out of our experience. For example, unless we are very ill or in great danger, we cannot help believing that we will be alive tomorrow, because this has always been our experience. Yet we cannot be sure. So when we believe anything, we partly doubt it, and when we doubt anything we partly believe it.

But our faith in God is different from all our other beliefs. For otherwise this faith would be in part a doubting, and our thinking would be no better than a dog's. God is the Truth, the Supreme Reality on which all other realities depend. *A God of truth and without iniquity, just and right is He* (Deut. 32:4). And because God is most real, we must believe in Him as such. We must let nothing else be more real to us than God. For this is faith! Anything less than this would be doubting. We must make God and Jesus Christ His Son the starting point of all our thinking.

We see, then, the difference between the carnally minded man and the spiritually minded man. The carnally minded man begins his thinking with something other than God and then believes in God merely as a probability or a possibility. Hence he cannot distinguish between believing and doubting. All his beliefs are doubtful. The spiritual man takes God and Jesus Christ His Son as the starting point of all his thinking. When anything else becomes more real to him than God and Christ, then he knows that he is doubting and must repent and return to the feet of his Saviour.

(b) The Biblical View of the Holy Scriptures — Their Content and History

The spiritual man is drawn to the holy Bible by the logic of faith as by a magnet. For how else can he take God as the starting point of all his thinking save through the diligent study of the sacred Scriptures. They are God's revelation of HIMSELF, the eyeglasses through which we may view aright God's revelation of Himself in nature, the key to God's revelation of Himself in history, the pure well of salvation to which the preachers of the Gospel must continually repair for fresh supplies of living water. In the Scriptures God reveals Himself as the God of Creation, the God of History, and the God of Salvation. In the first chapter of Genesis God reveals Himself as the almighty Creator God. In the Prophets He reveals Himself as the faithful Covenant God. In the Four Gospels and the other New Testament books He reveals Himself as the triune Saviour God.

Right views of the content of the Bible lead to right views of the history of its text. Because the Gospel is true and necessary for the salvation of souls, the Bible which contains this Gospel must have been infallibly inspired. And since the Bible was infallibly inspired, it must have been preserved down through the ages by God's special providence. And this providential preservation took place not in holes and caves but in the usage of the Church. And it did not cease with the invention of printing. Hence the true text of holy Scripture is found today in the printed Masoretic text, in the Textus Receptus, and in the King James Version and other faithful translations.

The logic of faith also shows us the inconsistencies and absurdities of unbelieving Bible study. The Old Testament critics, for example, admit that the art of writing had been known for centuries before the time of Moses, but they still insist that the Old Testament material was transmitted orally for hundreds of years after the death of Moses, not being written down until the 8th century B.C. And in the New Testament field unbelieving scholars tell us that the books of the New Testament were written not by the Apostles but by anonymous persons in the Early Church and that Christianity, including even Jesus Himself, was also the invention of such anonymous persons. But if these anonymous persons had so much ability as this, how could they possibly have remained anonymous?

(c) The Biblical View of Philosophy and Science — Truth and Fact

Through the study of the Scriptures also we are led to a biblical view of philosophy and science and especially of truth and fact. It is in this last respect that modern unbelievers fail notably. For the most part they are positivists. They insist that we must begin our thinking with *facts,* facts which (they claim) are independent of God, facts (they say) that are so no matter whether God exists or not. But when you ask them what facts are, they cannot tell you. Hence they are beginning their thinking blindly. The Bible, on the other hand, tells us what facts are. Facts are *temporal truths* which God, the eternal Truth (John 14:6), has established by His works of creation and providence. God reveals these facts in nature and in the holy Scriptures, and in and through the facts He reveals Himself. The facts which God clearly reveals are certain, the facts which He less clearly reveals are probable, and the facts which He does not reveal at all are His secrets (Deut. 29:29), forever hidden from the mind of man. Error and falsehood, however, are not from God but from Satan, the evil one.

By virtue of God's common grace unbelieving scientists know many facts, but because they ignore God's revelation of Himself in and through these facts, they too fall into many inconsistencies. For example, they say that the universe has been expanding into infinite space from all eternity. Why then hasn't it disappeared long ago? Some try to answer this question by supposing that the universe is constantly being replenished by hydrogen atoms which come from nothing. Others say that the universe is alternately expanding and contracting like an accordion. They admit, however, that this oscillation could not have gone on from all eternity but would have eventually "damped out" and come to a halt.[1]

In other scientific fields also unbelievers contradict themselves in fundamental ways. In geology, for example, the uniformitarians admit that the fossils were buried quickly, but at the same time they insist that the strata in which the fossils are buried were laid down very slowly. And similarly, evolutionists appeal to reason in the effort to justify their theory, but at the same time they overthrow the authority of human reason by assigning it an animal origin. And nuclear physicists also contradict themselves, professing to believe in scientific law but at the same time maintaining that the atom is governed by the laws of chance.

We see therefore that in spite of the many marvelous achievements the history of modern science has been one of apostasy and rebellion against God. Newton, the father of modern science, believed in God, but he was led by his rationalism to give first place in his thinking to four independent, disconnected absolutes which he had set up, namely, time, space, inertia, and gravity. To God, creation, providence, and the Bible Newton gave only second place in his thinking. And later scientists dropped these religious concepts, retaining only Newton's rationalistic absolutes. Hence the contradictions which we have noticed.

Einstein revised Newtonian science (on his own confession) in a pantheistic direction. He made simultaneity relative to the human observer. This led to two different kinds of simultaneity, namely, the simultaneity of events near at hand in which the observer is present (mathematically plus), and the simultaneity of events far away in which the observer is absent (mathematically minus). But Einstein ignored this discrepancy. And Einstein also ignored the observable fact that simultaneous events do not occur in exactly the same space but do occur at exactly the same time. Hence simultaneity is coincidence in time only and does not at all depend on the human observer and his position in space.

On what then does simultaneity depend? On the eternal plan of God. In the Bible God reveals Himself as the only Absolute. *I am God, and there is none else; I am God, and there is none like Me* (Isaiah 46:9). God's eternal plan for all things is the only ultimate continuum. *Declaring the end from the beginning, and from ancient times the things that are not yet done, saying, My counsel shall stand, and I will do all My pleasure* (Isaiah 46:10). Hence God created time when He began to fulfill His eternal plan, and God created space when He created the world. Simultaneity, therefore, depends on the eternal decree of God, *who worketh all things after the counsel of His own will* (Eph. 1:11). Such is the comprehensive framework which the Bible affords for all the details of science.

The Bible, therefore, enables us to interpret scientific experiments properly. For example, the Michelson-Morley experiment, which Einstein tried to explain away, actually indicates that the earth is not travelling in space but is stationary. In other words, the earth cannot be *removed* out of its place (Psalm 104:5). It has an absolute inertia which cannot be overcome. This absolute inertia of the earth, combined with the earth's gravity, probably guides the motion of the sun and moon. It would not control the movements of the planets, however, since these are governed by the gravity of the sun. Hence it is probable that the sun, like the moon, revolves about the earth, while the planets revolve about the sun. This hypothesis was advanced 400 years ago by Tycho Brahe. Unfortunately, it was rejected by his pupil Kepler, who for mystic reasons preferred a sun-centered universe.

(For further discussion see *Believing Bible Study,* pp. 165-71, 223-24.)

(d) The Biblical View of Politics and Economics — Occupy Till I Come

On September 25, 1961, President John F. Kennedy made an address before the United Nations General Assembly in which he committed the United States of America to an eventual surrender to the United Nations Peace Force. "The program to be presented to this Assembly for general and complete disarmament under effective international control moves to bridge the gap between those who insist on a gradual approach and those who talk only of the final and total achievement. It would create machinery to keep the peace as it destroys the machinery of war. It would proceed through balanced and safeguarded stages designed to give no state a military advantage over another. It would place the final responsibility for verification and control where it belongs, not with the big powers alone, not with one's adversary or one's self, but in an international organization within the framework of the United Nations."[2]

For almost two decades this policy of unilateral disarmament and surrender has been relentlessly pursued by the forces of the Liberal-left, until now the end of the road is clearly in sight. Humanly speaking, the United States has only a few more years to exist as an independent nation. Soon riots and insurrections will take place. Then the Russians will move in with overwhelming force in the name of the United Nations, and the United States Government will surrender as planned. Then world government, the goal of the Liberal-left, will have been achieved. Christians, however, will be bitterly persecuted even unto death.

Most American citizens are completely carnal, absorbed in their fleshly pursuits and oblivious to their country's impending doom. And, tragically, this carnal carelessness is shared by many professing Christians. They take a balcony view of these threatening dangers and will not lift a finger to avert them, insisting that the rapture will take place before these disasters overtake America. But this is a misuse of biblical prophecy. Christ's word to us is, *Occupy till I come* (Luke 19:13). We must not use the doctrine of the second coming of our Lord as an excuse for failure to do our present duty now. As spiritually minded Christians we must work for the re-arming of our country and do everything we can to roll back the tide of atheism and communism which is now engulfing the world. But in order to accomplish this we must first arm ourselves with *the sword of the Spirit* (Eph. 6:17), namely, the true Word of God, which is found today in the printed Masoretic text, the Textus Receptus, and the King James Version and other faithful translations.

(e) Why Believing Bible Students Must Use the King James Version — A Recapitulation

In regard to Bible versions many contemporary Christians are behaving like spoiled and rebellious children. They want a Bible version that pleases them no matter whether it pleases God or not. "We want a Bible version in our own idiom," they clamor. "We want a Bible that talks to us in the same way in which we talk to our friends over the telephone. We want an informal God, no better educated than ourselves, with a limited vocabulary and a taste for modern slang." And having thus registered their preference, they go their several ways. Some of them unite with the modernists in using the R.S.V. or the N.E.B. Others deem the N.A.S.V. or the N.I.V. more "evangelical". Still others opt for the T.E.V. or the *Living Bible.*

But God is bigger than you are, dear friend, and the Bible version which you must use is not a matter for you to decide according to your whims and prejudices. It has already been decided for you by the workings of God's special providence. If you ignore this providence and choose to adopt one of the modern versions, you will be taking the first step in the logic of unbelief. For the arguments which you must use to justify your choice are the same arguments which unbelievers use to justify theirs, the same method. If you adopt one of these modern versions, you must adopt the naturalistic New Testament textual criticism upon which it rests. This naturalistic textual criticism requires us to study the New Testament text in the same way in which we study the texts of secular books which have *not* been preserved by God's special providence. In other words, naturalistic textual criticism regards the special, providential preservation of the Scriptures as of no importance for the study of the New Testament text. But if we concede this, then it follows that the infallible inspiration of the Scriptures is likewise unimportant. For why is it important that God should infallibly inspire the Scriptures, if it is not important that He should preserve them by His special providence?

Where, oh where, dear brother or sister, did you ever get the idea that it is up to you to decide which Bible version you will receive as God's holy Word. As long as you harbor this false notion, you are little better than an unbeliever. As long as you cherish this erroneous opinion, you are entirely on your own. For you the Bible has no real authority, only that which your rebellious reason deigns to give it. For you there is no comfort, no assurance of faith. Cast off, therefore, this carnal mind that leads to death! Put on the spiritual mind that leads to life and peace! Receive by faith the True Text of God's holy Word, which has been preserved down through the ages by His special providence and now is found in the Masoretic Hebrew text, the Greek Textus Receptus, and the King James Version and other faithful translations!

4. Why Satan Can Not Win — God's Eternal Purpose

Today Satan seems successful as never before not only in raising up adversaries to persecute and destroy God's people but also in depriving them of their faith in the Word of God through naturalistic New Testament textual criticism and the resultant modernism. Will Satan's clever come-back be finally successful? No, for this is but a phase of his losing battle. The Bible indicates that Satan was once the fairest of God's creatures. He was *the anointed cherub* (Ezek. 28:14). He was *Lucifer, son of the morning* (Isaiah 14:12), bright as the morning star. But he fell through pride (1 Tim. 3:6) and dragged down a multitude of rebellious spirits with him (2 Peter 2:4, Jude 6). Then, after his fall, Satan began his long and stubborn guerrilla-warfare against God. In the Garden of Eden he persuaded our first parents to violate the Covenant of Works and thus involved the whole human race in his ruinous conspiracy.

But God was ready for this stratagem of Satan. Even before He created the world God had provided the remedy for Adam's sin. In the eternal Covenant of Grace He had appointed Jesus Christ His Son to be the Second Adam and to do what the first Adam failed to do, namely, to fulfill the broken Covenant of Works and save His people from its condemnation. *As in Adam all die, even so in Christ shall all be made alive* (1 Cor. 15:22). By His life of perfect obedience and by His sufferings and death Jesus completely fulfilled the requirements of the Covenant of Works and paid the penalty of its violation. Through His obedience Christ earned for His people the gift of righteousness and delivered them from the guilt of Adam's sin. *For as by one man's disobedience many were made sinners, so by the obedience of One shall many be made righteous* (Rom. 5:19). By the regenerating power of the Holy Spirit Christ unites His people to Himself and constitutes them one new human race. *If any man be in Christ, he is a new creature* (2 Cor. 5:17). And finally, His saving work shall culminate in the restoration of the whole universe. *Behold, I make all things new (Rev. 21:5).*

God in His eternal plan and purpose decreed the fall of Satan and the sin of Adam in order that He might reveal His wrath, His power, His longsuffering, and His redeeming love and mercy. *What if God, willing to shew His wrath, and to make His power known, endured with much longsuffering the vessels of wrath fitted to destruction: And that He might make known the riches of His glory on the vessels of mercy, which He had afore prepared unto glory, even us whom He hath called, not of the Jews only, but also of the Gentiles?* (Rom. 9:22-24).

Satan's attack upon the holy Bible is bound to fail, because the Bible is the *Book of the Covenant* (Exodus 24:7). The Bible is eternal, infallible, pure and sure, and in it God reveals *Himself,* not mere information concerning Himself but HIMSELF. In the Bible God reveals Himself as the almighty Creator God, the faithful Covenant God, and the triune Saviour God. The God of Creation, the God of History, and the God of Salvation! In the Bible Christ reveals Himself to sinners as Prophet, Priest, and King.

"I believe that Jesus died for me!" This confession is the foundation of the Christian thought-system, the beginning of the logic of faith. Because the Gospel is true and necessary for the salvation of souls, the Bible, which contains the Gospel, was infallibly inspired and has been providentially preserved down through the ages. Therefore, dear Christian Readers, continue in this life-giving logic. Be spiritually minded in all your thinking, especially in your New Testament textual criticism. Take your stand with Christ and receive from His hands the True Text of holy Scripture which He has preserved for you by His special providence. Then, armed with the sword of the Spirit and sheltered by the shield of faith, press on to victory.

HEAVEN AND EARTH SHALL PASS AWAY, BUT MY WORDS SHALL NOT PASS AWAY (Matt. 24:35).

THE
HOLY
BIBLE,

Conteyning the Old Testament,
AND THE NEW.

Newly Translated out of the Originall
tongues: & with the former Translations
diligently compared and reuised by his
Maiesties speciall Comandement.

Appointed to be read in Churches.

Imprinted at London by Robert
Barker Printer to the Kings
most Excellent Maiestie.

ANNO DOM. 1611.

**KING JAMES VERSION
FIRST EDITION 1611
TITLE PAGE**

ABBREVIATIONS

BASOR ....Bulletin of the American Schools of Oriental Research.
Berlin ....Die Griechischen Christlichen Schriftsteller, Preussisch.
Akademie der Wissenschaften.
HTR ....Harvard Theological Review (Harvard University Press).
ICC ....The International Critical Commentary (Scribner's).
JBL ....The Journal of Biblical Literature.
JTS ....The Journal of Theological Studies (Oxford University Press).
LCL ....The Loeb Classical Library.
MPG ....Migne, Patrologiae Cursus Completus, Series Graeca.
MPL ....Migne, Patrologiae Cursus Completus, Series Latina.
NSHE ....The New Schaff-Herzog Encyclopedia of Religious Knowledge (Funk & Wagnalls).
NTS ....New Testament Studies (Cambridge University Press).
TS ....Texts and Studies (Cambridge University Press).
TU ....Texte und Untersuchungen zur Geschichte der altchristlichen Literatur.
Vienna ....Corpus Scriptorum Ecclesiasticorum Latinorum, Academia Litterarum Vindobonensis.
ZNW ....Zeitschrift fur die neutestamentliche Wissenschaft und die Kunde des Urchristentums.

INTRODUCTION

Note 1 ....MPG, vol. 7, col. 805, col. 844.
Note 2 ....De La Rue, vol. 1, p. 16.

CHAPTER ONE

Note 1 ....Paul Radin, *Monotheism Among Primitive Peoples*, Basel: Ethnographical Museum, 1954, Preface.
Note 2 ....W. Schmidt, *The Origin and Growth of Religion*, trans. by H. J. Rose, London: Methuen, 1931, p. 191.
Note 3 ....Idem, p. 208.
Note 4 ....Calvin, *Institutes*, Book I, Chapter 6, Section 1.
Note 5 ....Rudolph Thiel (1957), *And There Was Light*, New York: Mentor Book, 1960, p. 356.
Note 6 ....Harlow Shapley, "On the Evidences of Inorganic Evolution," *Evolution After Darwin*, vol. 1, *The Evolution of Life*, Chicago: University of Chicago Press, Copyright 1960 by the University of Chicago, pp. 25-26.
Note 7 ....Albert Einstein, *The Evolution of Physics*, New York: Simon & Schuster, 1938, p. 224.

Note 8 .... Ernst Mach, *Die Mechanik,* Leipzig: Brockhaus, 1908, p. 238.
Bertrand Russell, *The ABC of Relativity,* New York: Signet Science Library Book, 1962, pp. 13-14.
Max Born, *Einstein's Theory of Relativity,* New York: Dover, 1962, p. 345.

Note 9 .... *The Growth of Physical Science,* James Jeans, New York: Fawcett, 1961, pp. 125-28.

Note 10 ....Bible-Science Newsletter, Vol. 15 (1977), Nos. 1 & 2.

Note 11 ....Bible-Science Newsletter, Vol. 14 (1976), No. 1.

Note 12 ....*Climatic Change,* Harlow Shapley (Ed.), Cambridge, Mass.: Harvard University Press, 1954.

Note 13 ....F. Hoyle (1955), *Frontiers of Astronomy,* New York: Mentor Book, 1962, p. 19.

Note 14 ....J. C. Whitcomb & H. M. Morris, *The Genesis Flood,* Grand Rapids: Baker, 1961, p. 127.

Note 15 ....George G. Simpson, "The History of Life," *Evolution After Darwin,* vol. 1, *The Evolution of Life,* Chicago: University of Chicago Press, Copyright 1960 by the University of Chicago, p. 125.

Note 16 ....William Howells, *Mankind in the Making,* Garden City, N. Y.: Doubleday, 1959, p. 149.

Note 17 ....F. H. T. Rhodes, *The Evolution of Life,* Baltimore: Penguin Books, 1962, p. 38, 43.

Note 18 ....F. E. Zeuner, *Dating the Past,* London: Methuen, 1952, pp. 311, 313.

Note 19 ...."The Petrified Forests of Yellowstone Park," by Erling Dorf, *The Scientific American,* April, 1964, pp. 104-108.

Note 20 ....*The Genesis Flood,* Whitcomb & Morris, p. 161.

Note 21 ....J. M. Macfarlane, *Fishes the Source of Petroleum,* New York: Macmillan, 1923, pp. 384-400.

Note 22 ....Archibald Geikie, *Text-Book of Geology,* 4th ed. London: Macmillan, 1903, vol. 1, p. 678.

Note 23 ...."The Mechanics of Appalachian Structure," by Bailey Willis, *U. S. Geological Survey,* 1893, pp. 227-228.

Note 24 ....*The Genesis Flood,* Whitcomb & Morris, pp. 185-187.

Note 25 ....Idem. pp. 265-266.

Note 26 ....L. D. Leet & S. Judson, *Physical Geology,* New York: Prentice-Hall, 1954, p. 266.

Note 27 ....Idem, pp. 291-292.

Note 28 ...."Continental Drift," by J. Tuzo Wilson, *The Scientific American,* April, 1963, pp. 86-99.

Note 29 ....*Physical Geology,* pp. 269-270.

Note 30 ....*The Genesis Flood,* Whitcomb & Morris, pp. 153-154.

Note 31 ....Idem, pp. 77, 122, 267, 269.

Note 32 ....Idem, p. 294.

Note 33 ....Idem, pp. 303-311.

Note 34 ....George G. Simpson, "The History of Life," *Evolution*

After Darwin, vol. 1, *The Evolution of Life*, Chicago: University of Chicago Press, Copyright 1960 by the University of Chicago, p. 149.

Note 35 ....*The Evolution of Life*, p. 153.

Note 36 ...."Correlation of Change in the Evolution of Higher Primates," by S. Zuckerman, *Evolution As A Process*, Julian Huxley editor, London: Allen & Unwin, 1954, pp. 304-349.

Note 37 ...."Further Evidence of Lower Pleistocene Hominids from East Rudolf, North Kenya," *Nature*, vol. 231 (1971), pp. 244-245.

Note 38 ....E. A. Hooton, *Up From The Ape*, New York: Macmillan, 1946, p. 346.

Note 39 ....Cesare Emeliani et al., *Evolution After Darwin*, vol. 3, Chicago: University of Chicago Press, 1960, p. 164.

Note 40 ...."Age of Bed I, Olduvai Gorge, Tanganyika," by L. S. B. Leakey, J. F. Evernden and G. H. Curtis, *Nature*, vol. 191 (1961), p. 479.

Note 41 ....*Nature*, vol. 226 (1970), p. 223.

Note 42 ....*Scientific American*, vol. 224, April, 1971, p. 52.

Note 43 ....*Sir Isaac Newton's Mathematical Principles*, translated by Andrew Motte in 1729, Berkeley, Calif.: University of California Press, 1960, p. 6.

Note 44 ....*Opticks*, by Sir Isaac Newton, New York: Dover, 1952, pp. 403-404.

Note 45 ....*ABC of Relativity*, Russell, p. 44.

Note 46 ....Hans Reichenbach, *From Copernicus To Einstein*, New York: Philosophical Library, 1942, p. 45.

Note 47 ...."Contribution to the Co-rotating Magnetic Field Model of the Pulsar," by V. G. Endean and J. E. Allen, *Nature*, vol. 228 (1970), pp. 346-349.

Note 48 ....*An Introduction To Astronomy*, by C. M. Huffer, E. Trinklein, M. Bunge, New York: Holt, Rinehart & Winston, 1967, pp. 17, 342.

Note 49 ....*Dynamic Astronomy*, by Robert T. Dixon, Englewood Cliffs, N. J.: Prentice-Hall, Inc., 1971, p. 307.

Note 50 ...."Anti-Matter," by Geoffrey Burbridge and Fred Hoyle, *Scientific American*, April, 1958, pp. 34-39.

Note 51 ...."Gravity," by George Gamow, *Scientific American*, March, 1961, p. 106.

Note 52 ....Albert Einstein, *Essays In Science*, trans. by Alan Harris, New York: Philosophical Library, 1934, p. 30.

Note 53 ....*Reflections Of A Physicist*, by P. W. Bridgman, New York: Philosophical Library, 1955, pp. 178-179.

Note 54 ....Werner Heisenberg, *Physics And Philosophy*, New York: Harper, 1958, pp. 42-43.

Note 55 ....James Jeans (1947), *The Growth Of Physical Science*, New York: Fawcett World Library, 1961, pp.

294-295.

Note 56 ....*Physics And Philosophy,* Heisenberg, p. 90.
Note 57 ....*Reflections Of A Physicist,* Bridgman, p. 179.
Note 58 ....Max Born, *The Restless Universe,* New York: Dover, 1951, p. 19.
Note 59 ....J. M. Keynes, *A Treatise On Probability,* London: Macmillan, 1921, pp. 332-336.
Note 60 ....*The Elements of Probability Theory,* by Harald Cramer, New York: Wiley, 1955, pp. 11-20.
Note 61 ....*The Restless Universe,* Born, p. 18.
Note 62 ....*Essays In Science,* Einstein, pp. 20-21.
Note 63 ....*The Way Things Are,* by P. W. Bridgman, Cambridge, Mass.: Harvard University Press, 1959, p. 121.
Note 64 ....Martin Luther, *Commentary On Galatians,* Gal. 2:20.
Note 65 ....Samuel Rutherford, *Religious Letters,* To Mr. Henry Stewart, his wife, and two daughters, all prisoners of Christ at Dublin, 1640.

CHAPTER TWO

Note 1 ....*History of Religions,* by G. F. Moore, New York: Scribners, 1913, p. 270.
Note 2 ....Idem, p. 434.
Note 3 ....Idem, p. 210.
Note 4 ....Idem, pp. 221-228.
Note 5 ....Idem, pp. 447-450.
Note 6 ....Idem, pp. 174-178.
Note 7 ....Idem, pp. 380-405.
Note 8 ....Idem, pp. 272-275.
Note 9 ....Idem, pp. 283-301.
Note 10 ....Idem, pp. 48-64.
Note 11 ....Idem, pp. 31-37.
Note 12 ....Idem, pp. 6-7.
Note 13 ....*History Of Ancient Philosophy,* by W. Windelband (1893), trans. by H. E. Cushman (1899), New York: Dover Publications, 1956, p. 38.
Note 14 ....Idem, p. 40.
Note 15 ....*Greek Philosophy,* Part I, Thales to Plato, by John Burnet, London, Macmillan, 1928, p. 25.
Note 16 ....*Ancient Philosophy,* Windelband, pp. 51-55.
Note 17 ....Idem, pp. 315-215.
Note 18 ....Idem, pp. 114-118.
Note 19 ....*Greek Philosophy,* Burnet, pp. 87-93.
Note 20 ....*Ancient Philosophy,* Windelband, pp. 130-132.
Note 21 ....*A History Of Philosophy,* by F. Ueberweg, trans. by G. S. Morris, New York: Scribner, 1876, vol. 1, pp. 115-117.
Ancient Philosophy, Windelband, pp. 190-223.

Greek Philosophy, Burnet, pp. 333-350.

Note 22 ....*Aristotle,* by A. E. Taylor (1919), New York: Dover, 1956, pp. 5-113.

History Of Philosophy, Ueberweg, vol. 1, pp. 139-180.

Ancient Philosophy, Windelband, pp. 224-292.

Note 23 ....*History Of Philosophy,* Ueberweg, vol. 1, pp. 222-232.

Ancient Philosophy, Windelband, pp. 346-348.

Note 24 ....NSHE, Articles, "Gnosticism," "Docetism," "Adoptionism," "Monarchianism," "Arianism."

Note 25 ....*Creeds Of Christendom,* Schaff, vol. 2, pp. 57-60, 62-63.

Note 26 ....NSHE, Article, "Indulgences."

Note 27 ....Surah LXI, 6.

Note 28 ....Surah, IV, 171.

Note 29 ....*The Meaning Of The Glorious Koran,* by M. M. Pickthall, New York: New American Library, 1953, p. xxviii.

Note 30 ....*The Koran Translated Into English,* by George Sale, Chandos Classic, London: F. Warne & Co., pp. 50-54.

Note 31 ....*History Of Philosophy,* Ueberweg, vol. 1, pp. 402-428.

Note 32 ....Idem, pp. 429-439 - 452-457.

Note 33 ....NSHE, Articles, "Scholasticism," "Thomas Aquinas." "Current Roman Catholic Thought on Evolution." by J. Franklin Ewing, S. J., *Evolution After Darwin,* University of Chicago Press, 1960, vol. 93, pp. 25-28.

Note 34 ....*Proslogium,* Chapter I.

Note 35 ....*Canon Of The New Testament,* by B. W. Westcott, 4th ed., London: Macmillan, 1875, p. 477.

Note 36 ....*Creeds Of Christendom,* Schaff, vol. 3, p. 96.

Note 37 ....Idem, p. 361.

Note 38 ....Idem, pp. 589-490.

Note 39 ....Idem, p. 808.

Note 40 ....Idem, p. 605-606.

Note 41 ....Idem, p. 718.

Note 42 ....Idem, p. 738.

Note 43 ....*A History Of Modern Philosophy, by Harald Hoeffding,* trans. by B. E. Meyer, New York: Dover, 1955, vol. 1, pp. 212-241.

Note 44 ....*The Philosophical Works Of Descartes,* trans. by E. S. Haldane and G. R .H. Ross (1911), New York: Dover, 1955, vol. 1, p. 101, "Discourse on the method of rightly conducting the reason and seeking for truth in the sciences."

Note 45 ....Idem, vol. 1, pp. 144-199, "Meditations on the First Philosophy."

Note 46 ....*History of Modern Philosophy,* Hoeffding, vol. 1, pp. 292-331.

Works of Spinoza, trans. by R. H. M. Elwes (1883), New York: Dover, 1951, vol. 2, "Improvement of the

Understanding," and "Ethics."

Note 47 ....*History Of Modern Philosophy*, Hoeffding, vol. 1, pp. 332-368.

Note 48 ....Idem, vol. 1, pp. 377-391.

Note 49 ....*The Works Of John Locke*, London: Bohn, 1854, vol. 1, p. 205, Book II, chap. 1, sec. 2.

Note 50 ....Idem, vol. 1, p. 207, Book II, chap. 1, sec. 4.

Note 51 ....Idem, vol. 2, p. 129, Book IV, chap. 1, sec. 1.

Note 52 ....*History Of Modern Philosophy*, Hoeffding, vol. 1, pp. 414-423.

George Berkeley, *Three Dialogues Between Hylas And Philonous*, New York: Liberal Arts Press, 1954, especially Dialogue III.

Note 53 ....*History Of Modern Philosophy*, Hoeffding, vol. 1, pp. 424-440.

David Hume, *An Inquiry Concerning Human Understanding* and Selections from *A Treatise Of Human Nature*, Chicago: Open Court Publishing Co., 1927.

Note 54 ....*History Of Modern Philosophy*, Hoeffding, vol. 2, pp. 29-109.

Note 55 ....Immanuel Kant, *Critique Of Pure Reason*, trans. by J. M. D. Meiklejohn, New York: Colonial Press, 1900. Immanuel Kant, *Prolegomena To Any Future Metaphysics*, trans. by L. W. Beck, New York: Liberal Arts Press, 1950.

Note 56 ....Immanuel Kant, *Fundamental Principles Of The Metaphysics Of Morals*, trans. by T. K. Abbott, New York: Liberal Arts Press, 1949. Immanuel Kant, *Critique Of Practical Reason*, trans. by L. W. Beck, New York: Liberal Arts Press, 1956.

Note 57............Immanuel Kant, *Religion Within The Limits Of Reason Alone*, trans. by T. M. Greene and H. H. Hudson, 2nd edition, La Salle, Ill.: Open Court Publishing Co., 1960.

Note 58 ....*History Of Modern Philosophy*, Hoeffding, vol. 2, pp. 174-192. *The Philosophy Of Hegel*, by W. T. Stace, (1923), New York: Dover, 1955.

Note 59 ....*The Logic of Hegel*, trans. by W. Wallace, 2nd edition, Oxford University Press, 1892, p. 17.

Note 60 ....Idem, p. 24

Note 61 ....Idem, p. 29.

Note 62 ....G. W. F. Hegel, *The Philosophy Of History*, trans. by J. Sibree, New York: Dover, 1956, p. 39.

Note 63 ....*Kant's Weltanschauung*, by Richard Kroner, trans. by John E .Smith, University of Chicago Press, Foreword, pp. vii-viii. *The Philosophy Of (As If)*, by H. Vaihinger, trans.

by C. K. Ogden, London: Kegan Paul, 1934.

Note 64 ....*The Ritschlian Theology And The Evangelical Faith,*
by James Orr, London: Hodder & Stoughton, 1897.
A History Of Christian Thought, by L. J. Neve &
O. W. Heick, Philadelphia: Muhlenberg Press, vol.
2, pp. 148-154.

Note 65 ....W. Rauschenbusch, *Christianity And The Social Cri-
sis,* New York: Macmillan, 1907.
W. Rauschenbusch, *Christianizing The Social Order,*
New York: Macmillan, 1913.

Note 66 ....Soren Kierkegaard, *Either/Or,* vol. 1, trans. by D. F.
& L. M. Swenson, vol. 2, trans. by W. Lowrie, Gar-
den City, N. Y.: Doubleday, 1959.

Note 67 ....*History Of Modern Philosophy,* Hoeffding, vol. 2, pp.
285-289.

Note 68 ....Karl Jaspers, *Man In The Modern Age,* trans. by
Eden & Cedar Paul, London: Routledge & Kegan
Paul, 1933.

Note 69 ....Martin Heidegger, *Existence And Being,* trans. by
Scott, Hull & Crick, Chicago: Henry Regnery Co.,
1949.

Note 70 ....Jean-Paul Sartre, *Being And Nothingness,* trans. by
Hazel E. Barnes, New York: Philosophical Library,
1956.

Note 71 ....Karl Barth, *The Epistle To The Romans,* trans. by
Edwyn C. Hoskins, Oxford University Press, 1933.
Karl Barth, *The Doctrine Of The Word Of God,*
trans. by G. T. Thomson, Edinburgh: T & T Clark,
1936.

Note 72 ....La Mettrie, *Man A Machine,* trans. by G. C. Bussey,
Chicago: Open Court Publishing Co., 1927.

Note 73 ....*History Of Modern Philosophy,* Hoeffding, vol 1, pp.
472-484.

Note 74 ....Idem, vol. 2, pp. 500-501.

Note 75 ....*The Origin Of Life,* by A. I. Oparin, trans. by S.
Morgulis, 2nd edition, New York: Dover, 1953, pp.
1-18.

Note 76 ....Idem, pp. 19-28.
"On the Origin of Life," by John Keosian, *Science,*
vol. 131 (1960), pp. 479-482.

Note 77 ....Charles Darwin, *Origin Of Species,* 1959, concluding
sentence.

Note 78 ....*Origin Of Life,* Oparin, Introduction, p. x.

Note 79 ....*What Science Knows About Life,* by Heinz Woltereck,
trans. by Mervin Savill, New York: Association Press,
1963, p. 28.

Note 80 ...."Organic Compound Sythesis Of The Primitive Earth,"
by Stanley L. Miller and Harold C. Urey, *Science,* vol.

130 (1959), p. 251.

Note 81 ...."Evolution of Enzymes and the Photosynthetic Apparatus," by Melvin Calvin, *Science*, vol. 130 (1959), p. 1173.

Note 82 ...."Voyage to the Planets," by K. F. Weaver, *National Geographic*, August, 1970, p. 158.
"The Planet Venus," by R. Jastrow, *Science*, vol. 160 (1968), pp. 1403-1410.

Note 83 ...."Mars and the Absent Organic Molecules," Science News, vol. 110, Oct. 9, 1976, pp. 228-29.
N. Y. Times, Oct. 1, 1976.

Note 84 ...."The Structure of Viruses," by R. W. Horne, *The Scientific American*, January, 1963, p. 48.

Note 85 ...."Rebuilding a Virus," by H. Fraenkel-Conrat, *The Scientific American*, June, 1956, pp. 42-44.

Note 86 ...."Nucleic Acids," by F. H. C. Crick, *The Scientific American*, September, 1957, pp. 188-191.
Virus Hunters, by Greer Williams, New York: Knopf, 1959, pp. 483-484.

Note 87 ....*The Scientific American*, November, 1965, p. 5.

Note 88 ....*Heredity And The Nature Of Man*, by T. Dobzhansky, New York: Harcourt Brace, 1964, pp. 34-35.

Note 89 ....*History Of Modern Philosophy*, Hoeffding, vol. 2, pp. 320-360.
Cours de Philosophie Positive, par Auguste Comte, 2 vols., Paris: La Societe Positiviste, 1892.

Note 90 ....*The Meaning Of Meaning*, by C. K. Ogden & I. A. Richards, London: K. Paul, Trench, Trubner & Co., 1923.

Note 91 ....*A History Of Western Philosophy*, by Bertrand Russell, New York: Simon & Schuster, 1945, pp. 828-836.
An Inquiry Into Meaning And Truth, by Bertrand Russell, London: Allen & Unwin, 1940, pp. 327-347.

Note 92 ....*The Vienna Circle*, by Victor Kraft, trans. by Arthur Pap, New York: Philosophical Library, 1953.

Note 93 ....*Tractatus Logico-Philosophicus*, by Ludwig Wittgenstein (1921), trans. by D. F. Pears and B. F. McGuinness, London: Routledge & Kegan Paul, 1961.

Note 94 ....*Logic, Semantics, Mathematics, Papers from* 1923-1938, by Alfred Tarski, trans. by J. H. Woodger, Oxford, 1956.

Note 95 ....*Science and Sanity*, by Alfred Korzybski, Lancaster, Pa.: Science Press, 1933.
The Tyranny Of Words, by Stuart Chase, New York: Harcourt, Brace & Co., 1938.
Language In Action, by S. I. Hayakawa, New York: Harcourt, Brace & Co., 1939.

Note 96 ....*Introduction To Semantics*, and *Formalization Of Logic*, by Rudolph Carnap, Harvard University Press,

1959.
Meaning And Necessity, by Rudolph Carnap, University of Chicago Press, 1947.

Note 97 ....Norbert Wiener, *Cybernetics,* 2nd edition, New York: John Wiley & Sons, 1961, pp. 169-203.
Norbert Wiener, *I Am A Mathematician,* Garden City, N.Y.: Doubleday, 1956, pp. 240-269.
Norbert Wiener, *The Human Use Of Human Beings,* 2nd edition, Garden City, N. Y.: Doubleday, 1954, pp. 48-73.

Note 98 ....*Design For A Brain,* by W. Ross Ashby, 2nd edition, New York: John Wiley & Sons, 1960, p. 55.

Note 99 ...."The New Style of Science," by Henry Margenau, *Yale Alumni Magazine,* February, 1962, pp. 8-17.

Note 100 ....*Experience And Prediction,* by Hans Reichenbach, Chicago: University of Chicago Press, Copyright 1938 by the University of Chicago, p. 192.

Note 101 ....Adam Smith, *Wealth Of Nations,* edited by J. E. T. Rogers, Oxford, 1880, vol. 2, p. 272.

Note 102 ...."The Threat of Russia's Rising Strategic Power," by John G. Hubbell, *Reader's Digest,* Feb. 1968, p. 54.

Note 103 ....N. Y. Times, May 27, 1972.

Note 104 ....N. Y. Times, Aug. 15 & 16, 1958.

Note 105 ....*Freedom from War; The United States Program for General and Complete Disarmament in a Peaceful World,* Department of State Publication 7277, Sept. 1961. The same proposal was made by President Kennedy in an address to the United Nations, Sept. 25, 1961. N. Y. Times, Sept. 26, 1961.

Note 106 ....*Congressional Record,* Vol. 108, Part 1, Jan. 29, 1962, p. 1043. Vol. 108, Part 3, March 1, 1962, p. 3216.

Note 107 ....*Science,* vol. 151 (1966), pp. 53-57.

Note 108 ....N. Y. Times, Feb. 10, 1967.

Note 109 ....N. Y. Times, Mar. 22, 1967.

Note 110 ..........N.Y. Times, Nov. 25, 1975..
N. Y. Times, Aug. 4, 1976.

CHAPTER THREE

Note 1 ...."Should Conservatives Abandon Textual Criticism?," by Marchant A. King, *Bibliotheca Sacra,* vol. 130 (January-March, 1973), pp. 35-40.

Note 2 ....Hugonis Grotii, *Annotationes,* vol. 1, Amsterdam, 1641; vol. 2, Paris, 1646; vol. 3, Paris, 1650.

Note 3 ....S. Curcellaei, *Novum Testamentum,* Amsterdam, 1658.

Note 4 ....*Novi Testamenti Libri Omnes,* Oxford, 1675, Preface.

Note 5 ....J. A. Bengel, *Gnomon Of The New Testament,* trans. by J. Bandinel, Edinburgh; T. & T. Clark, 1840, vol. 1, pp. 20-37.

Note 6 ....*Novum Testamentum Graece*, Tischendorf, vol. 3, Prolegomena, Leipzig: Hinrichs', 1894, pp. 231-240.

Note 7 ....R. Bentley, "Letter to Archbishop Wake," *Works,* Dyce, London: Macpherson, 1838.

Note 8 ....J. A. Bengel, *Novum Testamentum, Graecum,* Tubingae: George Cotta, p. 420.

Note 9 ....Idem, p. 429.

Note 10 ....Idem, p. 385.

Note 11 ....*Apparatus ad Liberalem Novi Testamenti Interpretationem,* Halae, 1767, pp. 44-50.

Note 12 ....D. Io. Sal. Semleri, *Paraphrasis II. Epistolae ad Corinthos,* Halae, 1776, Preface.

Note 13 ....NSHE, Article, "Semler."

Note 14............J. J. Griesbach, *Opuscula Academica,* Jena, 1824, vol. 1, p. 317.

Note 15 ....J. J. Griesbach, *Novum Testamentum Graece,* editio secunda, Londinin, 1809, vol. 1, pp. 75-82.

Note 16 ....Idem, pp. 63-71.

Note 17 ....*Einleitung in die Schriften des Neuen Testaments,* (2nd edition), Stuttgart 1821, vol. 1, pp. 145-216.

Note 18 ....*Theologische Studien und Kritieken,* Hamburg: 1830, pp. 817-845
Novum Testamentum, Graece et Latine, Berlin: 1942, p. v. xxxi.

Note 19 ....*The New Testament in the Original Greek,* vol. 2, Introduction and Appendix, London: Macmillan, 1881.

Note 20 ....Idem, p. 277.

Note 21 ....TS, vol. 5 (1899), p. xviii.

Note 22 ....*The Four Gospels,* by B. H. Streeter, London: Macmillan, 1924, pp. 111-127.

Note 23 ....*Side Lights on New Testament Research,* by J. Rendel Harris, London: James Clarke & Co., 1908, p. 3.

Note 24 ....*History of New Testament Criticism,* by F. C. Conybeare, London; Watts & Co., 1910, p. 129.

Note 25 ....*Family 13 (The Ferrar Group),* by K. & S. Lake, Philadelphia: University of Pennsylvania Press, 1941, p. vii.

Note 26 ....*N. T. in Greek,* vol. 2, p. 185.

Note 27 ....Idem, p. 282.

Note 28 ....*Bulletin of the Bezan Club,* III: Nov., 1926, p. 5.

Note 29 ....*The Text of the Greek Bible,* by F. G. Kenyon, London: Duckworth, 1937, pp. 244-246.

Note 30 ....*The Text of the Epistles,* by G. Zuntz, London: Oxford University Press, 1953, p. 9.

Note 31 ....*Der Urtext des Neuen Testaments,* Kiel: Hirt, 1960, p. 20.

Note 32 ....*A Historical Introduction To The New Testament,* by R. M. Grant, New York: Harper & Rowe, 1963, p. 51.

Note 33 ...."The Theological Relevance of Textual Variation in Current Criticism of the Greek New Testament," by K. W. Clark, JBL, vol. 85 (1966), p. 16.

Note 34 ...."Bemerkungen zu den gegenwartigen Moglichkeiten textkritischer Arbeit," by Kurt Aland, NTS, vol. 17 (1970), p. 3.

Note 35 ....*History of New Testament Criticism*, Conybeare, pp. 41-47.

Note 36 ....*The Quest Of The Historical Jesus*, by Albert Schweitzer, trans. by W. Montgomery, London: A. & C. Black, 1910, pp. 48-57.

Note 37 ....Idem, pp. 68-96.

Note 38 ....NSHE, Article, "Baur, Ferdinand Christian."

Note 39 ....*Study Of The Gospels*, by J. A. Robinson, London: 1902, p. 128ff.

Note 40 ....*Four Gospels*, Streeter, pp. 465-481.

Note 41 ....*Ecclesiastical History*, Eusebius, LCL, vol. 1, p. 293.

Note 42 ....*Historical Introduction To The New Testament*, R. M. Grant, p. 160.

Note 43 ....*Introduction To The New Testament*, by Theodor Zahn, trans. by M. W. Jacobus, Edinburgh: T. & T. Clark, 1909, vol. 2, pp. 405-408.

Note 44 ....*Introduction To The New Testament*, by A. H. McNeile, 2nd edition, Oxford, 1953, pp. 64-65.

Note 45 ....*Introduction To The New Testament*, Zahn, vol. 2, p. 408.

Note 46 ....*Greek New Testament*, by Henry Alford, 7th edition, London: Longmans, Green, 1898, vol. 1, pp. 8-9.

Note 47 ....*Study Of The Gospels*, by B. F. Westcott, 5th edition, London: Macmillan, 1875, pp. 164-180.

Note 48 ....*Quest Of The Historical Jesus*, Schweitzer, pp. 121-136.

Note 49 ....*An Introduction To The New Testament*, by K. & S. Lake, New York: Harper, 1937, p. 6, note.

Note 50 ....*The Originality Of St. Matthew*, by B. C. Butler, Cambridge: Cambridge University Press, 1951.

Note 51 ....Idem, p. 4.

Note 52 ....Idem, p. 11.

Note 53 ....Idem, pp. 157-171.

Note 54 ....*An Introduction To The Old Testament*, by E. J. Young, Grand Rapids: Eerdmans, 1949, pp. 120-123.

Note 55 ....*The Five Books Of Moses*, by O. T. Allis, Philadelphia: Presbyterian & Reformed Pub. Co., 1943, pp. 14-15.

Note 56 ....Idem, pp. 15-17.

Note 57 ....Idem, pp. 17-18.

Note 58 ....W. H. Green, *The Higher Criticism Of The Pentateuch*, New York: Scribner's, 1906, p. 90.

Note 59 ....Idem, pp. 92-95.

Note 60 ....*Prolegomena To The History Of Ancient Israel,* With a Reprint of the Article, *Israel,* from the *Encyclopedia Britannica,* by Julius Wellhausen, *Preface* by Prof. Robertson Smith, Cleveland: World Publishing Co., 1961.

Note 61 ....Idem, pp. 430-440, 464.

Note 62 ....Idem, pp. 472-476.

Note 63 ....Idem, pp. 24-28, 32-34, 402.

Note 64 ....Idem, pp. 20-21.

Note 65 ....Idem, pp. 21-22.

Note 66 ....Idem, pp. 34-39, 294.

Note 67 ....*History Of Israel,* by John Bright, Philadelphia: Westminster Press, 1959, p. 63.

Note 68 ....Idem, pp. 62-63.

Note 69 ....Idem, pp. 129-130.

Note 70 ....*Theology Of The Old Testament,* by Walther Eichrodt, trans. by J. A. Baker from 6th German edition, Philadelphia: Westminster Press, 1961, pp. 36-38.

Note 71 ....*Understanding The Old Testament,* by B. W. Anderson, 2nd edition, Englewood Cliffs, N. J.: Prentice-Hall, 1966, pp. 61-65.

Note 72 ....*From The Stone Age To Christianity,* by W. F. Albright (2nd edition), Baltimore: Johns Hopkins Press, 1946, p. 207.

Note 73 ...."Law and Covenant in Israel and the Ancient Near East," by G. E. Mendenhall, *The Biblical Colloquium,* 1955, pp. 32-34.
Old Testament Theology, by *G. Von Rad, trans. by* D. M. G. Stalker, Edinburgh: Oliver & Boyd, 1962, pp. 132-133.

Note 74 ....W. H. Green, *Higher Criticism Of The Pentateuch,* pp. 47-52.

Note 75 ....Idem, p. 49.

Note 76 ....Idem, p. 51.

Note 77 ....*The Incarnation Of The Son Of God,* by Charles Gore, New York: Scribners', 1891, pp. 166, 212-217.

Note 78 ....*What Is Christianity?,* by Adolf Harnack, Trans. by T. B. Saunders, New York: Putnam, 1901, p. 51.

Note 79 ....Idem, p. 65.

Note 80 ....W. Wrede, *Des Messiasgeheimnis in den Evangelien,* Goettingen, 1901.

Note 81 ....*Quest Of The Historical Jesus,* Schweitzer, pp. 328-395.

Note 82 ....Idem, p. 397.

Note 83 ....*The Meaning Of Jesus Christ,* by Martin Dibelius, trans. by F. C. Grant, New York: Scribners', 1939.

Note 84 ....*The New Testament In Current Study,* by Reginald Fuller, New York: Scribners', 1962.

Note 85 ....*Theology Of The New Testament,* by Rudolph Bultmann, Vol. 1, trans. by Frederick Grobel, New York:
Scribners', 1951, p. 30.

Note 86 ...."The Synoptic Son of Man Sayings in Recent Discussion," by I. H. Marshall, NTS, vol. 12 (1966),
pp. 327-351.
The Son Of Man In Myth And History," by F. H.
Borsch, Philadelphia: Westminster Press, 1967.

Note 87 ....Recent Articles on "the Son of Man problem" include
the following:
"Exit the Apocalyptic Son of Man," by R. Leivestad,
NTS, vol. 18 (1972), pp. 243-67.
"The Man from Heaven in Johannine Sectarianism,"
by W. A. Meeks, JBL, vol. 91 (1972), pp. 44-72.
"The Origin of the Son of Man Concept as Applied
to Jesus," by W. O. Walker, JBL, vol. 91 (1972),
pp. 482-490.

Note 88 ....*New Testament Christological Hymns,* by Jack T.
Sanders, Cambridge University Press, 1971.
"Pauline Theology in the Letter to the Colossians,"
by E. Lohse, NTS, vol. 15 (1969), pp. 211-220.
"The Problem of Pre-existence in Philippians 2:6-11,"
by Charles H. Talbert, JBL, vol. 86, (1967), pp. 141-
153.

Note 89 ....*An Outline Of The Theology Of The New Testament,*
by Hans Conzelmann, trans. by John Bowden, Evans-
ton: Harper & Row, 1969, p. 32.

Note 90 ....Idem, p. 68.

Note 91 ....*Theology Of The New Testament,* Bultmann, vol. 1,
p. 45.

Note 92 ....Joseph Butler, *The Analogy Of Religion,* with an introduction and notes by Howard Malcom, D. D., Phila-
delphia: Lippincott, 1881.

Note 93 ....*Paley's Evidences Of Christianity,* with notes by C.
M. Narne, M.A., New York: Carter & Bros., 1854.

Note 94 ....*Natural Theology,* by William Paley, D.D., *Works,*
vol. 1, Boston: Joshua Belcher, 1810.

CHAPTER FOUR

Note 1 ....W. H. Green, *General Introduction To The Old Testament, The Canon,* New York: Scribners', 1898, pp.
11-18.

Note 2 ....*De Civ. Dei,* xviii, 36.

Note 3 ....*Judaism,* by G. F. Moore, Cambridge, Mass.: Harvard University Press, 1927, vol. 1, p. 4.

Note 4 ....*The Ancestry Of Our English Bible,* by Ira Price, 2nd
Revised Edition, by W. A. Irwin & A. P. Wikgren,

New York: Harper, 1949, pp. 23-27.

Note 5 ....Idem, p. 35.

Note 6 ....Idem, p. 52.

Note 7 ....*Handbook To The Textual Criticism Of The New Testament*, by F. G. Kenyon, London: Macmillan, 1912, p. 210.

Note 8 ....Ibid.

Note 9 ....*Prologus Galeatus.*

Note 10 ....*An Introduction To The Apocrypha*, by Bruce M. Metzger, New York: Oxford University Press, 1957, p. 171.

Note 11 ....Idem, pp. 158-170.

Note 12 ....*The Apocryphal Literature*, by Charles C. Torrey, New Haven: Yale University Press, 1945, pp. 20-21.

Note 13 ....Idem, p. 15.

Note 14 ....Idem, p. 17.

Note 15 ....NSHE, Article, "Apocrypha."

Note 16 ....*The Apocryphal Literature*, Torrey, p. 23.

Ncte 17 ....*Introduction To The Apocrypha*, Metzger, p. 177-178.

Note 18 ....*A Critical Introduction To The Apocrypha*, by L. H. Brockington, London: Duckworth, 1961, p. 136.

Note 19 ....*The Apocryphal Literature*, Torrey, pp. 24-35.
Introduction To The Apocrypha, Metzger, pp. 178-180.

Note 20 ....*Pref. ad Libros Sol.*

Note 21 ....*The Bible In The Church*, by B. F. Westcott, London: Macmillan, 1901, pp. 163-198, 249-255.
General Introduction To The Old Testament, The Canon, W. F. Green, pp. 157-177.

Ncte 22 ....*Introduction To The Apocrypha*, Metzger, p. 183.

Note 23 ....*The Apocrypha And Pseudepigrapha Of The Old Testament*, by R. H. Charles, vol 2, *Pseudepigrapha*, Oxford: Clarendon Press, 1913.

Note 24 ....*Jewish And Christian Apocalypses*, by F. C. Burkitt, London: Oxford University Press, 1914, pp. 17-18.
Epistles Of St. James And St. Jude, by Alfred Plummer, London: Hodder & Stoughton, 1897, p. 441.

Note 25 ....*Jewish And Christian Apocalypses*, Burkitt, pp. 37-40.
Epistles Of St. James And St. Jude, Plummer, pp. 419-425.

Note 26 ....*Jewish And Christian Apocalypses*, Burkitt, pp. 45-46.
First Fpistle Of St. Paul To The Corinthians, Robertson & Plummer, ICC, New York: Scribners', 1911, pp. 41-42.

Note 27 ...."Jannes And Jambres," by John Rutherford, *International Standard Bible Encyclopedia*, Chicago: 1937.
Origen, *Contra Celsum*, IV, 51.

Note 28 ....*Our Bible And The Ancient Manuscripts*, by F. G. Kenyon, London: Eyre & Spottiswoode, 1898, p. 41.

Note 29 ....*Second Thoughts On The Dead Sea Scrolls,* by F. F.
Bruce, Grand Rapids: Eerdman's, 1956, p. 21.
Note 30 ....Idem, pp. 22-25.
Note 31 ....Idem, pp. 38-42.
Note 32 ....Idem, pp. 28-33.
Note 33 ....*Newsletter No.* 11, *American Schools of Oriental Re-
search,* Cambridge, Mass., June, 1972.
Note 34 ...."Variant Readings in the Isaiah Manuscripts," by
Millar Burrows, BASOR, October, 1948, p. 16.
Note 35 ...."New Light on Early Recensions of the Hebrew Bi-
ble," by W. F. Albright, BASOR, December, 1955,
p. 30.
Note 36 ...."The History of the Biblical Text in the Light of Dis-
coveries in the Judean Desert," by F. M. Cross, HTR,
vol. 57 (1964) pp. 296-297.
Note 37 ....*The Judean Scrolls, The Problem And A Solution,* by
G. R. Driver, Oxford: Blackwell, 1965, pp. 3-6, 239-241,
371.
Note 38 ....*Creeds Of Christendom,* Schaff, vol. 2, pp. 79-83.
Note 39 ....Some of the best known English works on the history
of the New Testament Canon are as follows:
History Of The New Testament Canon, B. F. West-
cott, London; Macmillan, 4th edition, 1875.
Canon And Text Of The New Testament, C. R. Greg-
ory, New York, Scribners' 1907.
Text And Canon Of The New Testament, A. Souter,
London: Duckworth, 2nd edition revised by C. S. C.
Williams, 1954.
Note 40 ....*The Formation Of The New Testament,* by E. J. Good-
speed, Chicago: University of Chicago Press, 1926,
pp. 28-29.
Note 41 ....*Adversus Praxean,* 15.
Note 42 ....*Works,* edited by A. Dyce, London: 1838, vol. 3, pp.
347-361.
Note 43 ....*Introduction To The New Testament,* Zahn, vol. 2,
p. 477.
Note 44 ....*The Infallible Word,* Philadelphia: Presbyterian
Guardian Pub. Co., 1946, p. 162.
Note 45 ....*The Westminster Assembly And Its Work,* by B. B.
Warfield, New York: Oxford University Press, 1931,
p. 239.
Note 46 ....*Criticism Of The New Testament, St. Margaret's Lec-
tures* 1902, by F. G. Kenyon, London: John Murray,
1903, pp. 31-32.

CHAPTER FIVE

Note 1 ...."The Greek New Testament: Its Present and Future

Editions," by Kurt Aland, JBL, vol. 87 (1968).

Note 2 ....*The Text Of The New Testament*, by B. M. Metzger, New York: Oxford University Press, 1964, 2nd edition 1968.

Note 3 ....Aland, JBL, vol. 87 (1968), p. 184.

Note 4 ....Ibid.

Note 5 ....Ibid.

Note 6 ....Ibid.

Note 7 ....Ibid.

Note 8 ....*Introduction* (4th edition), vol. 2, p. 405.

Note 9 ....*New Testament Manuscript Studies*, edited by Parvis and Wikgren, Chicago: University of Chicago Press, 1950, p. 6.

Note 10 ....Ibid.

Note 11 ....NTS, vol. 12, January, 1966, pp. 176-185; vol. 16, January, 1970, pp. 163-177.

Note 12 ....*An Introduction To Theology*, by Cornelius Van Til, 1947.

Note 13 ....*Text Of The New Testament*, Metzger, pp. 72-79.

Note 14 ....*Evangelion Da-Mepharreshe*, by F. C. Burkitt, Cambridge University Press, 1904, vol. 2, p. 5.

Note 15 ....E.g., Metzger, *Text Of The New Testament*, pp. 69-70.

Note 16 ....Idem, pp. 70-71.

Note 17 ....Idem, p. 69.

Note 18 ....Idem, pp. 79-81.

Note 19 ....Idem, pp. 81-84.

Note 20 ....*The Beginnings Of Christianity*, by J. H. Ropes, London: Macmillan, 1926, vol. 3, p. ccxli.

Note 21 ....*The Text And Canon Of The New Testament*, by A. Souter, London: Duckworth, 1912, p. 124.

Note 22 ....*N. T. In The Original Greek*, vol. 2, p. 176.

Note 23 ...."Luke 22:19b-20," by G. D. Kilpatrick, JTS, vol. 47 (1946), p. 54.

Note 24 ...."The Shorter Text of Luke 22:15-20," by Henry Chadwick, HTR, vol. 50 (1957), pp. 249-258.

Note 25 ....*Alterations To The Text Of The Synoptic Gospels And Acts*, by C. S. C. Williams, Oxford: Blackwell, 1951, pp. 47-51.

Note 26 ....*N. T. In The Original Greek*, vol. 2, appendix, p. 73.

Note 27 ....*Introduction To The New Testament*, Zahn, vol. 3, p. 87.

Note 28 ....*Four Gospels*, Streeter, pp. 142-143.

Note 29 ....*Alterations To The Text, etc.*, Williams, pp. 51-53.

Note 30 ...."Neue Neutestamentliche Papyri II," by Kurt Aland, NTS, vol. 12 (1966), pp. 193-210.

Note 31 ...."The Biblical Text of Clement of Alexandria," by P. M. Barnard, TS, vol. v (1899), pp. 1-64.

Note 32 ...."An Early Papyrus Fragment of the Gospel of Matthew in the Michigan Collection," by H. A. Sanders, HTR, vol. 19 (1926) pp. 215-224.

Note 33 ...."A Papyrus Fragment of Acts in the Michigan Collection," by H. A. Sanders, HTR, vol. 20 (1927), pp. 2-19.

Note 34 ....*Four Gospels,* Streeter, p. 57.

Note 35 ...."The Caesarean Text in the Gospel of Mark," by Lake, Blake and New, HTR, vol. 21 (1928), p. 263f.

Note 36 ....*Chester Beatty Biblical Papyri,* by F. G. Kenyon, London: Emery Walker, 1933, Fascic. II, Gospels and Acts, pp. xi-xxi.

Note 37 ....*Text Of The Greek Bible,* Kenyon, pp. 207-210.

Note 38 ....*Codex B And Its Allies,* by H. C. Hoskier, London: Quaritch, 1914, Part I, p. 278.

Note 39 ....*The Gospel According To Luke,* by Alfred Plummer, 4th edition, New York: Scribners', 1901, p. 537.

Note 40 ....*The Gospel According To St. John,* by B. F. Westcott, London: Murray, 1892, p. 159.

Note 41 ....*Codex B And Its Allies,* Hoskier, Part I, p. 7.

Note 42 ....*Text Of The New Testament,* Metzger, p. 42.

Note 43 ...."Whose Name Was Neves," by K. Grobel, NTS, vol. 10 (1964), pp. 381-382.

Note 44 ....*Commentary On The Gospel Of John,* by F. Godet, trans. by Timothy Dwight, New York: Funk & Wagnals, 1886, vol. 2, p. 83.

Note 45 ....*Das Evangelium des Johannes,* R. Bultmann, Goettingen: Vandenhoeck & Ruprecht, 1941, p. 236n.

Note 46 ...."Some Notable Readings of Papyrus Bodmer II," by J. Ramsey Michaels, *The Biblical Translator,* London, vol. 8 (1957), pp. 153-154.

Note 47 ...."Corrections of Papyrus Bodmer II," by G. D. Fee, JBL, vol. 84 (1965), p. 68.

Note 48 ....NTS, vol. 3 (1957), p. 279.

Note 49 ....In a letter to the present writer.

Note 50 ...."Die Evangelienschrift der Chester Beatty Sammlung," ZNTW, xxii, 4, 1933.

Note 51 ....NTS, vol. 10 (1963), p. 74.

Note 52 ....Idem, p. 73.

Note 53 ....*N. T. In The Original Greek,* vol. 2, appendix, p. 67.

Note 54 ....Idem, p. 66.

Note 55 ....*Epiphanius,* Berlin, Erster Band, p. 40.

Note 56 ....*Four Gospels,* Streeter, p. 137.

Note 57 ....*Alterations To The Text, etc.,* Williams, pp. 7-8.

Note 58 ....*Studien zur Geschichte des Neuen Testaments und der Alten Kirche,* von Adolf von Harnack, Berlin: De Gruyter, 1931, pp. 87-88.

Note 59 ....MPG, vol. 7, cols. 957-1088.

Note 60 ....*Tatians Diatessaron,* von Erwin Preuschen, Heidelberg: Winters, 1926, p. 288.

Note 61 ....MPG, vol. 7, col. 936.

Note 62 ....*N. T. In The Original Greek,* vol. 2, Appendix, p. 68.

Note 63 ....NSHE, Article, "Barnabas."

Note 64 ....*Studien zur Geschichte des Neuen Testaments,* pp. 96-98.

Note 65 ....*Four Gospels,* Streeter, p. 138.

Note 66 ....*Alterations To The Text, etc.,* Williams, p. 9.

Note 67 ....*Marcion, Des Evangelium, von Fremden Gott,* von Adolph von Harnack, Leipzig, Hinrichs', 1921, p. 54.

Note 68 ....*The Causes Of The Corruption Of The Traditional Text Of The Holy Gospels,* by J. W. Burgon and E. Miller, London: Bell, 1896, pp. 215-218.

Note 69 ...."The Excerpta ex Theodoto of Clement of Alexandria," edited with translation by R. P. Casey, *Studies And Documents* I, London: Christophers, 1934, p. 45.

Note 70 ....*Rechtglaubigkeit Und Ketzerei Im Altesten Christentum,* von Walter Bauer, Tuebingen: Mohr, 1934, pp. 49, 63.

Note 71 ....*Newly Discovered Gnostic Writings,* by W. C. van Unnik, trans. from Dutch (1958), London: SCM Press, 1960, p. 44.

Note 72 ....*The Gospel According To Thomas,* Guillaumont et al., New York: Harper, 1959, pp. 23, 31, 33, 55.
Evangelium Veritatis, edited by Malinine, Puech, Quispel, Zurich: Rascher Verlag, 1956, p. 106.

Note 73 ....*The Text Of The New Testament,* by K. Lake, 6th edition, London: Rivingtons, 1928, p. 76.

CHAPTER SIX

Note 1 ....*Encyclopaedie der Heilige Godgeleerdheid,* door Dr. A. Kuyper, Amsterdam: Wormser, 1894, Deel Drie, p. 73.

Note 2 ....*Christliche Dogmatik,* von D. Franz Pieper, St. Louis: Concordia, 1924, Erster Band, p. 290.

Note 3 ....*The Revision Revised,* by John W. Burgon, London: Murray, 1883, pp. 334-335.

Note 4 ....*An Account Of The Printed Text Of The New Testament,* by S. P. Tregelles, London: Bagster, 1854, p. 133.

Note 5 ....MPG, vol. 6, col. 712.

Note 6 ....MPG, vol. 7, col. 653.

Note 7 ....*S. Hippolyti Refutationis Omnium Haeresium,* Goettingen, 1859, p. 42.

Note 8 ....*Gospel According To Matthew,* W. C. Allen, ICC Scribners', 1907, p. 208.

Note 9 ....*The Originality of St. Matthew,* B. C. Butler, p. 133.
Note 10 ...."Codex Bezae," TS, vol. 2 (1891), p. 229.
Note 11 ....Valentinus, MPG, vol. 8, col. 1057 (ap. Clem. Alex.).
            Heracleon, Orig., De LaRue, vol. 4, p. 139.
            Ptolemaeus, Berlin, *Epiphanius,* vol. 1, p. 456.
Note 12 ....Berlin, *Origenes Werke,* vol. 10, pp. 385-388.
Note 13 ....*Commentary On The Gospel Of John,* (Eng. trans.),
            Edinburgh, 1871, vol. 1, p. 263.
Note 14 ....*Historisch-Kritische Einleitung,* Leipzig, 1875, p. 782.
Note 15 ....*Theologische Zeitschrift aus der Schweiz,* vol. 4 (1893),
            p. 97.
Note 16 ....MPL, vol. 1, col. 314. Also, Vienna, Pars I, 1890,
            p. 205.
Note 17 ....MPG, vol. 39, cols. 708, 712.
Note 18 ....MPG, vol. 59, col. 204.
Note 19 ....*Tatians Diatessaron,* Preuschen, p. 131.
Note 20 ....*Einleitung,* p. 782.
Note 21 ....*T Z aus der Schweiz,* vol. 4, p. 97.
Note 22 ....MPL, vol. 2, col. 677.
Note 23 ....Used in regard to the Sinaitic Syriac, *Contemporary
            Review,* November, 1894.
Note 24 ....*Evangelium Secundum Matthaeum,* Oxford, 1940.
Note 25 ....*Didascalia et Constitutiones Apostolorum,* F. X. Funk,
            Paderborn, 1905, vol. 1, pp. 213, 410.
Note 26 ....MPG, vol. 51, col. 48; vol. 57-58, cols. 282, 301.
Note 27 ....MPG, vol. 78, col. 1076.
Note 28 ....*Prophezei,* W. Michaelis, Zurich: Zwingli-Verlag, 1948,
            p. 331.
Note 29 ....*N. T. In The Original Greek,* vol. 2, Appendix, p. 9.
Note 30 ....LCL, *Apostolic Fathers,* vol. 1, p. 320.
Note 31 ....*The Greek Liturgies,* London: 1884, pp. 85, 93, 97,
            135, 167, 200, 308-309.
Note 32 ....Vienna, vol. xxxii, pp. 359-360.
Note 33 ....Vienna, vol. xxxi, p. 387.
Note 34 ....*S. S. Patrum* . . . J. B. Cotelerius, Antwerp, 1698,
            vol. i, p. 235.
Note 35 ....MPL, vol. 23, col. 579.
Note 36 ....*Didascalia Apostolorum,* trans. by R. Hugh Connolly,
            Oxford: Clarendon Press, 1929, p. 76.
            Funk, *Didascalia et Constitutiones Apostolorum,* vol.
            1, p. 92.
Note 37 ....Tischendorf, *N. T. Graece,* vol. 1, p. 829.
Note 38 ....*Didascalia Apost.,* p. li.
Note 39 ....LCL, *Ecclesiastical History,* Eusebius, vol. 1, p. 298.
Note 40 ....Idem, vol. 1, p. 296.
Note 41 ....MPL, vol. 13, col. 1077.
Note 42 ....Vienna, vol. iii, p. 638.

Note 43 ....*Einleitung*, p. 782.

Note 44 ....*T Z aus der Schweiz*, vol. 4, p. 98.

Note 45 ...."Codex Bezae," TS, vol. 2 (1891), p. 195.

Note 46 ....*N. T. In The Original Greek*, vol. 2, Appendix, p. 82.

Note 47 ....Idem, p. 86.

Note 48 ...."Codex Bezae," TS, vol. 2 (1891), p. 195.

Note 49 .... *What Is The Best New Testament?* By E. C. Colwell, Chicago, The University of Chicago Press, Copyright 1952 by the University of Chicago, p. 82.

Note 50 ....*Die Schriften des Neuen Testaments*, von Soden, Goettingen: Vandenhoeck & Ruprecht, 1. Teil, 1. Abt., p. 486.

Note 51 ....*Text Of The New Testament*, Metzger, p. 224.

Note 52 ....*Die Schriften des Neuen Testaments*, 1. Teil, 1 Abt., p. 500.

Note 53 ....*The Causes Of The Corruption Of The Traditional Text*, Burgon, p. 250.

Note 54 ....*Text Of The New Testament*, Metzger, p. 223.

Note 55 ....*The Causes Of The Corruption Of The Traditional Text*, p. 257.

Note 56 ....Idem, pp. 259-260.

Note 57 ....*What Is The Best New Testament?*, p. 81.

Note 58 ....*T. Z. aus der Schweiz*, p. 98.

Note 59 ....*The Causes Of The Corruption Of The Traditional Text*, p. 241.

Note 60 ....Idem, pp. 237-238.

Note 61 ....*The Last Twelve Verses Of The Gospel According To S. Mark*, by John W. Burgon, Oxford and London: Parker, 1871. Reprint, The Sovereign Grace Book Club, 1959.

Note 62 ...."The Conclusion of the Gospel According to S. Mark," by J. M. Creed, JTS, vol. 31 (1930), pp. 80-85.

Note 63 ....*The Gospel Message Of S. Mark*, by R. H. Lightfoot, Oxford: Clarendon Press, 1950, pp. 80-85.

Note 64 ....JTS, vol. 31 (1930), p. 180.

Note 65 ....*Galilaea und Jerusalem*, E. Lohmeyer, Goettingen: Vandenhoeck & Ruprecht, 1936, p. 77.

Note 66 ....*Locality And Doctrine In The Gospels*, by R. H. Lightfoot, New York: Harper, 1937, p. 77.

Note 67 ....*The Gospel Of Mark*, by Curtis Beach, New York: Harper, 1959, p. 118.

Note 68 ...."The Ending of St. Mark's Gospel," by W. L. Knox, HTR, vol. 35 (1942), p. 22.

Note 69 ....*The Four Gospels*, Streeter, p. 344.

Note 70 ....G. A. Juelicher, *An Introduction To The New Testament*, trans. by J. P. Ward, New York: Putnam's 1904, p. 328.

Note 71 ....*Alterations To The Text, etc.*, p. 45.

Note 72 ....JTS, vol. 31 (1930), p. 176.
Note 73 ....MPG, vol. 6, col. 397.
Note 74 ....*Tatians Diatessaron*, Preuschen, p. 239.
Note 75 ....MPG, vol. 7, col. 879.
Note 76 ....Funk, *Didascalia*, etc., vol. i, p. 460, vol. ii, p. 72.
Note 77 ....*The Journal Of Religion*, vol. 17 (1937), p. 50.
Note 78 ....JTS, n. s. vol. 2 (1951), p. 57.
Note 79 ....*Last Twelve Verses Of Mark*, Burgon, pp. 44-46, 265-266.   Reprint, pp. 345-346.
Note 80 ....Idem, pp. 239-240; Reprint, 319-320.
Note 81 ....*Text Of The New Testament*, Metzger, p. 227.
Note 82 ....*Account Of The Printed Text*, Tregelles, p. 256.
Note 83 ....*Last Twelve Verses Of Mark*, pp. 142-190.   Reprint, pp. 222-270.
Note 84 ....*N. T. In The Original Greek*, vol. 2, Appendix, p. 51.
Note 85 ....*Four Gospels*, pp. 350-351.
Note 86 ....*Last Twelve Verses Of Mark*, pp. 232-235, Reprint, pp. 312-315.
Note 87 ....Idem, p. 237.   Reprint, p. 317.
Note 88 ....Idem, p. 240. Reprint, 320.
Note 89 ....Idem, p. 227.   Reprint, p. 307.
Note 90 ....Idem, p. 235-236. Reprint, p. 315-316.
Note 91 ....*N. T. In The Original Greek*, vol. 2, Appendix, p. 32.
Note 92 ....*The Apocryphal New Testament*, by M. R. James, Oxford: Clarendon Press, 1926, p. 90.
Note 93 ....Idem, p. 91.
Note 94 ....Idem, p. 92.
Note 95 ....Souter, 1947.
Note 96 ....MPG, vol. 7, Adv. Haer. III, 11, 7.
Note 97 ....Legg, 1940.
Note 98 ....MPL, vol. 23, col. 576, (Dialogus contra Pelagianos).
Note 99 ....Souter, 1947.

CHAPTER SEVEN

Note 1 ....*The Washington Manuscript Of The Four Gospels*, by H. C. Sanders, New York: Macmillan, 1912.
Note 2 ....Idem., p. 41.
Note 3 ....Idem, p. 134.
Note 4 ....Idem, p. 3-4.
Note 5 ....*The Text Of The Epistles*, G. Zuntz, London: Oxford University Press, 1953, p. 55.
Note 6 ....JTS, n.s., vol. 11 (1960), p. 381.
Note 7 ...."Lucian and the Lucianic Recension of the Greek Bible," by B. M. Metzger, NTS, vol. 8, (1962), pp. 202-203.
Note 8 ....*The Traditional Text Of The Holy Gospels*, Burgon and Miller, London: Bell & sons 1896, Appendix II, "Vinegar," pp. 254-255.

Note 9 ....Berlin, *Origenes Werke*, vol. 2, pp. 164-165.
Note 10 ....*Evangelion Da-Mepharreshe*, vol. 2, p. 5.
Note 11 ....*Investigations into the Text of the New Testament used by Rabbula of Edessa*, Pinneberg, 1947.
Researches on the Circulation of the Peshitto in the Middle of the Fifth Century, Pinneberg, 1948.
Neue Angeben Ueber, die Textgeschicht-Zustande in Edessa in den Jahren ca. 326-340, Stockholm, 1951.
Early Versions of the New Testament. Stockholm, 1954.
Note 12 ....*Evangelion Da-Mepharreshe*, vol. 2, p. 225.
Streeter, *Four Gospels*, p. 115.
Note 13 ....*Handbook To The Textual Criticism Of The New Testament*, by F. G. Kenyon, London: Macmillan, 1912, p. 240.
Note 14 ....*N. T. In The Original Greek*, vol 2, pp. 363-376.
Note 15 ....*The Revision Revised*, p. 262, note.
Note 16 ....*Handbook*, p. 302.
Note 17 ....TU, vol. 11 (1894), pp. 97-101.
Note 18 ....*N. T. In The Original Greek*, vol. 2, Appendix, pp. 21-22.
Note 19 ....*An Atlas Of Textual Criticism*, by E. A. Hutton, Cambridge: Cambridge University Press, 1911, p. 58.
Note 20 ....*The Text Of The New Testament*, Metzger, pp. 16-17.
Note 21 ....*N. T. In The Original Greek*, vol. 2, p. 117.
Note 22 ....Idem, pp. 133-134.
Note 23 ....Idem, p. 142.
Note 24 ....Idem, p. 143.
Note 25 ....*Handbook*, p. 302.
Note 26 ...."Chrysostom's Text of the Gospel of Mark," by J. Geerlings and S. New, HTR, vol. 24 (1931), pp. 138-149.
Note 27 ...."The Matthean Text of Chrysostom in his Homilies on Matthew," by C. D. Dicks, JBL, vol. 67 (1948), pp. 365-376.
Note 28 ....JTS, vol. 7 (1956), pp. 42-55, 193-198; vol. 9 (1958), pp. 278-291.
Note 29 ....*Studies In The Lectionary Text*, Chicago: University of Chicago Press; Vol. 1, 1933; Vol. 2, No. 3, 1944; Vol. 2, No. 4, 1958; Vol. 3, No. 1, 1958.
Note 30 ...."The Text of the Gospels in Photius," by J. N. Birdsall, JTS, n.s., vol. 7 (1956), p. 42.
Note 31 ...."The Complex Character of the Late Byzantine Text of the Gospels," by E. C. Colwell, JBL, vol. 54 (1935), p. 212.
Note 32 ....Die Schriften des Neuen Testament, 1. Teil, 2. Abt., pp. 707-893.
Note 33 ....Idem, p. 712.
Note 34 ...."Caesarean Text of the Gospel of Mark," HTR, vol.

21 (1928), pp. 339ff.

Note 35 ....Idem, pp. 341-342.

Note 36 ...."The Byzantine Text of the Gospels," by K. and S. Lake, *Memorial Lagrange*, Paris, Gabaldi, 1940, p. 256.

Note 37 ....HTR, vol. 21 (1928), p. 341.

Note 38 ...."The Significance of the Papyri for Progress in New Testament Research," by Kurt Aland, *The Bible in Modern Scholarship*, Nashville: Abingdon Press, 1965, pp. 342-45.

Note 39 ....JTS, n.s., vol. 7 (1956), p. 43.

Note 40 ....NTS, vol. 10 (1963), pp. 73-74.

Note 41 ....HTR, vol. 21 (1928), pp. 345-346.

Note 42 ....Ibid.

Note 43 ....See Note 29.

Note 44 ....See Note 28.

Note 45 ....See Notes 10 and 11.

Note 46 ....*N. T. In The Original Greek*, vol. 2, p. 152.

Note 47 ....*The Text Of The Greek Bible*, Kenyon, pp. 216-218.

Note 48 ....B. B. Warfield, *Studies In Tertullian And Augustine*, New York: Oxford University Press, 1930.

Note 49 ....M. R. Vincent, *A History of Textual Criticism*, New York: Macmillan, 1899, p. 79.

Note 50 ....A. Souter, *The Text and Canon of the New Testament*, London: Duckworth, 1912, p. 117.

CHAPTER EIGHT

Note 1 ....*Works,* edited by A. Dyce, London: 1838, vol. 3, pp. 347-361.

Note 2 ....De La Rue, vol. 1 p. 16.

Note 3 ....*Erasmus,* T. A. Dorey, London: Kegan Paul, 1970. *Erasmus of Christendom,* by Roland H. Bainton, New York: Scribner's, 1969. *Principles and Problems of Translation,* by W. Schwarz, Cambridge: University Press, 1955, pp. 92-166. *Erasmus,* by Preserved Smith, New York: Harper, 1923. NSHE, Article, "Erasmus," by Ephraim Emerton.

Note 4 ....*Desiderii Erasmi Roterdami Opera Omnia,* Hildesheim: Georg Ohms, 1962, Unveranderter reprographischer Nachdruck der Aufgabe Leiden, 1705.

Note 5 ....NSHE, Article, "Erasmus".

Note 6 ....*Principles and Problems of Translation,* Schwarz, pp. 96-97, 132-39.

Note 7 ....Idem, pp. 163-64.

Note 8 ....Ibid.

Note 9 ....*Erasmus of Christendom,* Bainton, p. 181. *Erasmus,* Smith, p. 180.

Note 10 ....*Erasmus,* Smith, p. 181.

Note 11 ....The first, 2nd, and 4th editions of Erasmus' *New*

Note 12 .... *Testament* are accessible at the University of Chicago. *Plain Introduction,* Scrivener, vol. 2, pp. 182-84.

Note 13 .... *"Principles and Problems of Translation,* Schwarz, p. 139.

Note 14 .... "nisi me consensus orbis alio vocaret, praecipue vero auctoritas Ecclesiae." Note on Rev. 22:20.

Note 15 .... *Works of Martin Luther,* Philadelphia: Muhlenberg Press, 1932, vol. 6, pp. 476-89. (Prefaces to Hebrews, James, Jude and Revelation).

Note 16 .... HTR, vol. 21 (1928), p. 340.

Note 17 .... *The Acts Of The Apostles,* by J. A. Alexander, New York: Scribner, 1967, vol. 1, pp. 349-50.

Note 18 .... *The Beginnings Of Christianity,* London: Macmillan, 1933, vol. 4, p. 101.

Note 19 .... *Concerning The Text Of The Apocalypse,* by H. C. Hoskier, London: Quaritch, 1929, vol. 1, pp. 474-77, vol. 2, pp. 454, 635.

Note 20 .... NSHE, Article, "Stephanus".

Note 21 .... *Text and Canon of the New Testament,* Souter-Williams, pp. 87-88.

Note 22 .... Calvin's Commentaries, Edinburgh: Calvin Translation Society, 1845-55. Reprint, Grand Rapids: Eerdmans, 1948-49.

Note 23 .... "Codex Bezae and the Geneva Version of the Bible," by B. M. Metzger, *New Testament Tools and Studies,* Grand Rapids: Erdman's, 1968, vol. 8, p. 143, note 2.

Note 24 .... See Scrivener, *Plain Introduction,* vol. 2, p. 193, note 1.

Note 25 .... Article, "Elzevir", Encyclopedia Americana.

Note 26 .... *Die Katholischen Briefe,* 3rd. edition, Tuebingen, 1951.

Note 27 .... *Commentary On The Johannine Epistles,* ICC, New York: 1912.

Note 28 .... *The Text Of The New Testament,* pp. 101-102.

Note 29 .... Vienna, vol. iii, p. 215.

Note 30 .... MPL, vol. 67, col. 555.

Note 31 .... A *Plain Introduction, etc.,* Scrivener, Vol. 2, p. 405.

Note 32 .... Vienna, vol. xviii, p. 6.

Note 33 .... MPL, vol. 62, col. 359.

Note 34 .... Vigilius Tapensis, MPL, vol. 62, col. 243. Victor Vitensis, Vienna, vol. vii, p. 60. Fulgentius, MPL, vol. 65, col. 500.

Note 35 .... MPL, vol. 70, col. 1373.

Note 36 .... MPL, vol. 42, col. 796.

Note 37 .... NSHE, Article, "Monarchianism."

Note 38 .... For a convincing defense of the *Johannine Comma* see Bengel's *Gnomon* in loco.

Note 39 .... See Price, Irwin, Wikgren, *The Ancestry Of Our English Bible,* pp. 225-267. Also H. W. Robinson, *The Bible In Its Ancient And English Versions,* Oxford: 1954, pp. 128-195.

Note 40 ....Price, op. cit., pp. 268-277.
H. W. Robinson, op. cit., pp. 196-234.

Note 41 .... *The Authorized Edition of the English Bible,* by F. H. A. Scrivener, Cambridge: University Press, 1884, pp. 296-97.

Note 42 ....Idem, pp. 55-60.

Note 43 ....Idem, p. 117.

Note 44 ....Idem, pp. 302-03.

Note 45 ....Idem, pp. 1-145.

Note 46 ....H. W. Robinson, op. cit., p. 37.

Note 47 ....*Introduction* to the RSV Old Testament, quoted in *Revised Version Or Revised Bible?,* by O. T. Allis, Philadelphia: Pres. & Rfd. Pub. Co., 1953, p. 51.

Note 48 ....Lounsbury, *History Of The English Language,* p. 287, quoted in *Revision Or New Translation?,* by O. T. Allis, Philadelphia: Pres. & Rfd. Pub. Co., 1948, p. 55.

Note 49 ....*The New Testament, An American Translation,* by E. J. Goodspeed, University of Chicago Press, 1923, Preface.

Note 50 ....*Historical Introduction To The New Testament, R.M.* Grant, p. 56.

Note 51 ....*Authorized Edition of the English Bible,* p. 60.

Note 52 ....Idem, pp. 58-59.

Note 53 ....Idem, pp. 56-57.

Note 54 ....See, *The New Testament Octapla,* edited by Luther A. Weigle, New York: Nelson, 1962.

Note 55 ....*Authorized Edition of the English Bible,* pp. 56-60, 242-63.

Note 56 ....*A Full Account and Collation of the Greek Cursive Codex Evangelium 604,* by H. C. Hoskier, London: David Nutt, 1890, Appendices B & C.

Note 57 ....Ibid.

Note 58 ....*The New Testament in Greek According to the Text Followed in the Authorised Version,* Cambridge University Press, 9th Printing, 1949.

Note 59 ....*The New Testament, The Greek Text Underlying the English Authorised Version of 1611,* London: The Trinitarian Bible Society, 1976.

Note 60 ....J. A. Alexander, The Psalms, New York: Scribner, 1860, Vol. 1, p. viii.

Note 61 ....See K. Aland, NTS, vol. 10 (1963), p. 74.

Note 62 ....H. W. Robinson, *The Bible In Its Ancient & English Versions,* pp. 227-234.

Note 63 ....H. W. Robinson, op. cit., pp. 235-274.
Price, *Ancestry Of The English Bible, pp. 278-316.*

Note 64 ...."The New American Revision of the Bible," by F. C. Grant, ZNW, Band 45 (1954), Heft 3-4, pp. 219-220.

CHAPTER NINE

Note 1 ....“Recent Developments In Cosmology,” by Fred Hoyle, *Nature,* vol. 208, Oct. 9, 1965,

Note 2 ....N. Y. Times, Sept. 26, 1961.

INDEX — SCRIPTURE REFERENCES